FOUNDATIONS OF A SUSTAINABLE ECONOMY

This book addresses current practices related to sustainable development, its challenges and the future. People belonging to different genders regardless of their age, social class and education should be equal as citizens and individuals, and identical in their rights and responsibilities.

The business sector, authorities, societies and religious circles have the potential to play a fundamental role in curbing social ills and the degradation of the environment in this modern world. The authors of this book argue that without good governance, the status of a human being is unlikely to improve. They make the case that to achieve sustainability, government, society and the economy must ensure a platform for people to participate in decision-making and benefit from the rights they are accorded. By covering a range of perspectives across economic, social and moral life, the book will shed light on the problems and possible solutions to sustainable development and the triple bottom line, of people, planet and profit, under the umbrella of morals and divine law.

This will be a useful guide for undergraduate and postgraduate students across multiple disciplines, such as economics, religious studies, business studies, political science, anthropology and sociology.

Umar Burki is Associate Professor at USN School of Business, University of South-Eastern Norway, and holds an adjunct position as Associate Professor at Bjorknes University College, Norway.

Toseef Azid is Professor of Economics at the College of Business and Economics, Qassim University, Saudi Arabia and visiting professor at Tazkia Islamic University College, Indonesia.

Robert Francis Dahlstrom is the Joseph C. Seibert Professor of Marketing in the Farmer School of Business at Miami University and Adjunct Professor of Marketing at BI-Norwegian Business School.

FINANCE, GOVERNANCE AND SUSTAINABILITY: CHALLENGES TO THEORY AND PRACTICE SERIES

SERIES EDITOR:

Professor Güler Aras, Yildiz Technical University, Turkey; Georgetown University, Washington, DC, USA

Focusing on the studies of academicians, researchers, entrepreneurs, policy makers and government officers, this international series aims to contribute to the progress in matters of finance, good governance and sustainability. These multidisciplinary books combine strong conceptual analysis with a wide range of empirical data and a wealth of case materials. They will be of interest to those working in a multitude of fields, across finance, governance, corporate behavior, regulations, ethics and sustainability.

Corporate Social Responsibility and Sustainable Development
Social Capital and Corporate Development in Developing Economies
Risa Bhinekawati

Sustainability Accounting and Integrated Reporting
Edited by Charl de Villiers and Warren Maroun

Women on Corporate Boards
An International Perspective
Edited by Maria Aluchna and Güler Aras

Stakeholder Engagement and Sustainability Reporting
Marco Bellucci and Giacomo Manetti

Management Scholarship and Organisational Change
Representing Burns and Stalker
Miriam Green

Ethics, Misconduct and the Financial Services Industry
Towards a Theory of Moral Business
Barbara Fryzel

Foundations of a Sustainable Economy
Moral, Ethical and Religious Perspectives
Edited by Umar Burki, Toseef Azid and Robert Francis Dahlstrom

For more information about this series, please visit www.routledge.com/Finance-Governance-and-Sustainability/book-series/FINGOVSUST
Finance, Governance and Sustainability

FOUNDATIONS OF A SUSTAINABLE ECONOMY

Moral, Ethical and Religious Perspectives

Edited by Umar Burki, Toseef Azid and Robert Francis Dahlstrom

Routledge
Taylor & Francis Group
LONDON AND NEW YORK

First published 2022
by Routledge
2 Park Square, Milton Park, Abingdon, Oxon OX14 4RN

and by Routledge
605 Third Avenue, New York, NY 10158

Routledge is an imprint of the Taylor & Francis Group, an informa business

British Library Cataloguing-in-Publication Data
A catalogue record for this book is available from the British Library

Library of Congress Cataloging-in-Publication Data
Names: Burki, Umar, editor. | Azid, Toseef, editor. |
Dahlstrom, Robert (Robert F.) editor.
Title: Foundations of a sustainable economy: moral,
ethical and religious perspectives / edited by Umar Burki, Toseef Azid and
Robert Francis Dahlstrom. Description: 1 Edition. |
New York: Routledge, 2021. | Series: Finance, governance and
sustainability: challenges to theory and practice |
Includes bibliographical references and index.
Identifiers: LCCN 2021006639 (print) | LCCN 2021006640 (ebook) |
ISBN 9780367818784 (hardback) | ISBN 9781032051888 (paperback) |
ISBN 9781003010579 (ebook)
Subjects: LCSH: Sustainable development. | Social policy. |
Political participation. | Decision making.
Classification: LCC HC79.E5 . F68 2021 (print) |
LCC HC79.E5 (ebook) | DDC 174/.4–dc23
LC record available at https://lccn.loc.gov/2021006639
LC ebook record available at https://lccn.loc.gov/2021006640

ISBN: 978-0-367-81878-4 (hbk)
ISBN: 978-1-032-05188-8 (pbk)
ISBN: 978-1-003-01057-9 (ebk)

Typeset in Times New Roman
by Newgen Publishing UK

CONTENTS

List of illustrations viii
About the editors xi
List of contributors xiii
Preface xxi
Foreword xxvii

1 Sustainability and morality 1
UMAR BURKI, TOSEEF AZID AND ROBERT FRANCIS DAHLSTROM

PART I
Theoretical foundations 19

2 Sustainability principles and triple bottom line performance in supply chains 21
ROBERT FRANCIS DAHLSTROM

3 The circular economy 35
THOMAS BREKKE

4 Environmental policy enforcement 53
GRY TENGMARK ØSTENSTAD

PART II
Religion and sustainability 67

5 Concept of sustainability in Abrahamic religions 69
FAWAD KHALEEL AND ALIJA AVDUKIC

6 A Buddhist approach for a sustainable existence 81
REV. UNAPANA PEMANANDA AND CHAMARA KURUPPU

7 Ontological authority of sustainability in Hindu traditions: the art of planetary maintenance 96
FAWAD KHALEEL AND KULATHAKATTU SHOBA

8 Sustainability and Behavior of Islamic Market 105
TOSEEF AZID, UMAR BURKI AND MUHAMMAD OMER CHAUDHRY

9 Religion and development: an Islamic approach to socio-economic development 121
MOHAMMAD ABDULLAH

10 Accountability and sustainability in Islamic accounting literature 139
MURNIATI MUKHLISIN AND RIFKA MUSTAFIDA

PART III
Empirical evidences 187

11 Financial development and ecological footprint nexus: a comparative analysis 189
MUHAMMAD TARIQ MAJEED

12 Inequality and sustainability 220
JON REIERSEN

13 The socio-economic metabolism of Canada: a case study of energy flows from 1990 to 2011 237
ABDULLAH TOSEEF, UMAR BURKI AND PERVIN EROSY

14 Environmental quality and happiness: a perspective of developed and developing countries 254
MUHAMMAD TARIQ MAJEED

15 Altruism a critical prerequisite for sustainable development: implications for Waqf Institutions in the Islamic Republic of Iran 276
MOHAMMAD SOLEIMANI AND HASAN KIAEE

16 Social enterprise and Waqf: an alternative sustainable vehicle for Islamic social finance 288
NOOR SUHAIDA KASRI AND SITI FARIHA ADILAH ISMAIL

17 Sustainable development and the work of Ibn Khaldun: the case of Indonesia 308
RAHMI EDRIYANTI, ABU UMAR FARUQ AHMAD AND SHAFIQUR RAHMAN

18 People, planet and profitability (3Ps): a gender management perspective 328
ESKIL SØNJU LE BRUYN GOLDENG AND UMAR BURKI

19 Challenges and opportunities 342
TOSEEF AZID, UMAR BURKI AND ROBERT FRANCIS DAHLSTROM

Index 346

ILLUSTRATIONS

Figures

3.1	The three main markets of the economy	37
3.2	The four main markets of the economy: product market, finance market, labour market and the public/common goods market	38
3.3	Linear versus circular economy. As illustrated by the Ellen MacArthur Foundation (2012)	40
3.4	The circular business model. Based on Accenture Five Circular business models	46
3.5	Reklima circular economy model of reuse of bio-degradable waste	47
9.1	Major clusters of Islamic developmental themes	131
11.1	Ecological footprint	200
11.2	Domestic credit to private sector	200
11.3	Domestic credit to private sector by banks	201
11.4	Domestic credit to private sector by financial sector	201
11.5	Ecological footprint trend	201
11.6	Domestic credit to private sector	202
11.7	Domestic credit to private sector by banks	202
11.8	Domestic credit to private sector by financial sector	202
11.A1	Environmental Kuznets curve	219
11.A2	N-shaped Kuznets curve	219
12.1	World digital competitiveness ranking	224
12.2	Organizational change and new technology	225
12.3	Teamwork and decision-making authority within firms	231
13.1	Energy Metabolic Profile for Canada represented in a Sankey diagram for the years 1990, 2000 and 2011	244
14.1	Global happiness	259
14.2	Regional happiness	260
16.1	BRAC's organogram	293

16.2 Larkin Sentral's waqf asset management 295
16.3 Governance structure of Pondok Gontor 297
17.1 Number of poor people in Indonesia (in millions) 317
17.2 Gini ratio in Indonesia (percent) 318
17.3 Net enrollment ratio of elementary schools and junior high schools in Indonesia 320

Tables

10.1 Empirical research of Islamic accounting before AAOIFI (1986–1990) 145
10.2 Empirical research of Islamic accounting after AAOIFI establishment (1993–2001) 146
10.3 Empirical research of Islamic accounting during AAOIFI-IFRS period (2002–2017) 150
11.1 Descriptive statistics 198
11.2 Correlation matrix 199
11.3 Results of pooled OLS for high-income countries 204
11.4 Results of pooled OLS for low-income countries 206
11.5 Results of fixed effects for high-income countries 207
11.6 Results of fixed effects for low-income countries 209
11.7 Results of random effects for high-income countries 210
11.8 Results of random effects for low-income countries 211
11 9 Results of system GMM for high-income countries 212
11.10 Results of system GMM for low-income countries 213
12.1 Dimensions of economic and social performance 222
14.1 Descriptive statistics 258
14.2 Correlation matrix 259
14.3 Pooled OLS regression results 261
14.4 LIML regression results 263
14.5 FE regression results 265
14.6 EE regression results 266
14.7 Driscoll–Kraay standard errors regression results 267
14.8 Regression results of system GMM 268
14.A1 Data and variables description 271
14.A2 Cross-sectional data of developed countries 272
14.A3 Cross-sectional data of developing countries 274
16.1 Economic activities under Kopotren 301
18.1 CEO share of salaries in companies managed by women versus men CEOs 333
18.2 Share of female CEOs in thc top five (5) industries 334
18.3 Share of female CEOs in the bottom five (5) industries 334
18.4 Share of women as IEH contact person 335

18.5 Value creation share of turnover in companies with a female versus male CEO 336
18.6 Return of assets in companies with a female versus male CEO 336

ABOUT THE EDITORS

Umar Burki is an associate professor at USN School of Business, University of South-Eastern Norway, Norway. He holds a PhD in Business Logistics (2009) and has two master's degrees in Industrial Logistics and Economics. He also holds an adjunct position as associate professor at Bjorknes University College, Oslo, Norway. Umar was one of the first farmers to embrace environment friendly IPM (Integrated Pest Management) practices at his family cotton farm, located in Multan (Pakistan). He won a USAID funded scholarship (1992) to participate in Farm and Water Management project at California State University (Chico). He has taught in two Pakistani universities (1991–2010) and several European universities. His research focus is on B2B relationships, green innovations, sustainability issues in supply chains and international marketing, and he has published regularly in international journals. Umar regularly participates in leading international marketing and operations research conferences.

Toseef Azid is a professor of Economics at the College of Business and Economics, Qassim University, Saudi Arabia and vistining professor at at Tazkia Islamic University College, Indonesia. He holds a PhD in Economics from University College of Wales, Aberystwyth, UK (1993). He received Overseas Research Scholarship from the British government, a Fulbright Award Scholar in Residence (2006). He taught in Pakistan, Brunei, UK, USA and Saudi Arabia. His research focuses on technological change, labor economics, Islamic economics and Islamic finance. His five books are published: one book is published in Pakistan (*Some Basic Principles of Islamic Economics*); two are published by Routledge, UK (*Labor in Islamic Setting: Theory and Practice* and *Social Justice and Islamic Economics: Theory, Issues and Practice*); the fourth one is published by Emerald (*Corporate and Shari'ah Governance in the Muslim World: Theory and Practice*) and the fifth one is *Women Empowerment in the Islamic World: Theory and Practice* published by World Scientific Publishers, Singapore.

Robert Francis Dahlstrom is the Joseph C. Seibert Professor of Marketing in the Farmer School of Business at Miami University. He is also an adjunct professor of marketing at BI-Norwegian Business School. He has published articles in *Journal of Marketing Research*, *Journal of Marketing*, *Journal of the Academy of Marketing Science*, *International Journal of Cleaner Production* and elsewhere. His research employs logic from institutional economics and related governance theories to investigate triple bottom line performance. The Chicago Business Press published the thirdedition of his book titled *Sustainable Marketing* in 2021.

CONTRIBUTORS

Mohammad Abdullah is an expert of Islamic Sciences, Islamic Jurisprudence and Islamic finance. Abdullah is a well-trained and highly experienced *Shari'ah* Scholar, providing *Shari'ah* consultancy and advisory services to various Islamic financial institutions in Europe, South America and the UAE. Currently he is working as head of *Shari'ah* at Habib Bank AG Zurich in Dubai. He has produced a number of research papers and book chapters on comparative study of *Waqf* and English trust, *Shari'ah* governance, Islamic finance and development studies. Abdullah holds a Bachelor degree in *Shari'ah* Sciences from Darul Uloom Nadwatul Ulama, Lucknow, India, MA in Islamic Banking, Finance and Management from the Markfield Institute of Higher Education, UK, and PhD from University of Gloucestershire (UK). He is also a Certified *Shari'ah* Advisor and Auditor (CSAA) by the AAOIFI. Abdullah presented papers on Islamic banking and finance in Germany, Norway, Italy, Ireland, Scotland, UK, Trinidad and Tobago, Indonesia, Malaysia, India and Dubai.

Abu Umar Faruq Ahmad is currently an associate professor at Islamic Economic Institute in King Abdulaziz University, Jeddah. He has a significant number of published peer-reviewed refereed journal articles, books, chapters in edited books, conference proceedings, and other intellectual contributions to his credit on *Shari'ah* compliance of Islamic banks' products and structures, Islamic economics, the opportunities and challenges of Islamic finance, case studies of Islamic banks and financial institutions, Islamic insurance and reinsurance, Islamic microfinance, Sukuk, and dispute resolution in Islamic banking and finance, among others. He presented papers at international conferences held in the USA, Ireland, Australia, UAE, Saudi Arabia, Turkey, Brunei, Qatar, Sudan, Nigeria, Malaysia, Indonesia, Bangladesh and Pakistan. His current editorial roles include serving as founding editor, senior editor, editorial advisory board member of a plethora of internationally reputed refereed journals including some of those published by Emerald Group Publishing, UK.

Alija Avdukic is currently working as Associate Professor in Islamic Economics & Finance at Al-Maktoum College of Higher Education, UK. He earned his BA from Al-Azhar University (Egypt) and also BA from Damascus University (Syria); continued for Postgraduate Diploma in Islamic Studies from Al-Fatih Institute (Syria); MA in Islamic Economics, Finance and Management Gloucestershire University (UK) and PhD in Islamic Political Economy and Finance from Durham University (UK). He is Deputy Director of MSc Islamic Finance program at University of Dundee; visiting faculty member for Master's program in Islamic Banking and Finance for the joint program School of Economics, University of Sarajevo (Bosnia and Herzegovina) with University of Bolton (UK). He is also a senior research fellow at Ibn Rushed Centre for Excellence (UK). He is also a visiting research fellow of Durham Centre in Islamic Economics, Banking and Finance (UK).

Toseef Azid is Professor of Economics at College of Business and Economics, Qassim University, Saudi Arabia and International Visiting Scholar, Economics Department, Wayne State University, Detroit, Michigan, USA (2017). He holds PhD in Economics from University College of Wales, Aberystwyth, UK. He received Fulbright Award as Scholar in Residence where he worked on a research project on "Economics of Middle Eastern Countries." His research focuses on technological change, development Economics, labor economics, Islamic economics and Islamic finance. His recent books as co-editor are entitled: "Labour in an Islamic Setting: Theory and Practice" and "Social Justice and Islamic Economics: Theory, Issues and Practice" published by Routledge, UK, "Corporate and *Shari'ah* Governance in the Muslim World: Theory and Practice" published by Emerald, UK and "Economic Empowerment of Women in the Islamic World: Theory and Practice" published by World Scientific Publications, Singapore.

Thomas Brekke is an associate professor at the School of Business, University of South-East Norway (USN). Brekke received his PhD from Norwegian University of Science and Technology (NTNU). His research interests are university–industry interaction and industry transformation. He teaches innovation and entrepreneurship at master and bachelor levels and closely collaborates with regional and local development initiatives to build strong linkages between the university and industry. Brekke has won several national grants from research-leading agencies such as Oslo Fjord Fund and the Research Council of Norway on topics within innovation and entrepreneurship studies. He has authored/co-authored several peer-reviewed articles and attended international conferences.

Eskil Sønju Le Bruyn Goldeng is an associate professor at the US School of Business, University of South-Eastern Norway. He earned his PhD from

Witten/Herdecke University, Norway in 2018. He is doing research on gender diversity, boards, corporate governance and business economics. His work has been published in *Journal of Management Studies, Human Resource Management Journal, Research Methodology in Strategy and Management* and Norwegian journals and international books.

Umar Burki is currently working as an associate professor at USN School of Business, University of South-Eastern Norway. Umar also holds an adjunct position as associate professor at Bjorknes University College, Norway. He holds a PhD in Business Logistics and a master degree in Industrial Logistics from Molde University College, Norway. He has published in several international academic journals, book chapters, and presented conference papers related to B2B relationships, green innovations, supply-chain management and international marketing.

Muhammad Omer Chaudhry is Associate Professor at Bahauddin Zakariya University, Multan, Pakistan and holds PhD in Logistics/Supply Chain Management with specialization in Transport Economics from Molde University College, Norway, MSc in Logistics from the same college, MPhil from BZU, Multan. He published a number of academic papers in national and international journals. He presented many papers at peer-reviewed conferences all over the globe. He also conducted some significant research in religious economics.

Professor Robert Francis Dahlstrom is the Joseph C. Seibert Professor at the Department of Marketing, Farmer School of Business, Miami University. He is also an adjunct faculty of marketing at BI-The Business Norwegian School. Since receiving his PhD in marketing from the University of Cincinnati, he has published articles in *Journal of Marketing Research, Journal of Marketing, Journal of Retailing, Journal of the Academy of Marketing Science* and elsewhere. His research employs logic from institutional economics and related governance theories to investigate triple bottom line performance. The third edition of his book titled "Sustainable Marketing" was published in 2021 by the Chicago Business Press.

Rahmi Edriyanti is graduated student at Islamic State University of North Sumatera (UIN Sumatera Utara), Indonesia, for Master's degree. She also finished her bachelor degree at Institut Tazkia Bogor, West Java, Indonesia in 2013. Her research interest is about Islamic economics, Islamic classical thought and *waqf*. She is ever present in two international conferences on Islamic education and Islamic communication recently. Nowadays, she is preparing for her further research and publication about labor economics and *nazhir waqf* in collaboration with her other colleagues and lecturers in Indonesia.

Pervin Ersoy is working as Assistant Professor, Department of Logistics Management, Yasar University (Izmir), Turkey. She received her PhD from Dokuz Eylül University, Turkey. Her research interests include: green supply-chain management, green logistics, sustainability, retail logistics, disaster and relief logistics. Dr. Ersoy has published her work in *Journal of Cleaner Production*, *Journal of Product and Brand Management*, *Sustainability* and other international peer–reviewed journals.

Siti Fariha Adilah binti Ismail is *Shari'ah* Management Trainee at International *Shari'ah* Research Academy (ISRA). She received her bachelor degree in Islamic Jurisprudence (*Fiqh Wa Usuluh*) from Al al-Bayt University, Jordan. She is currently doing her Master's in Islamic Finance Practice (MIFP) at the International Centre for Education in Islamic Finance (INCEIF). Her recent article as co-writer entitled "Repayment moratorium in Malaysian Islamic banks" was published by Islamic Finance News (IFN) and "Micro-takaful for B40 in Malaysia: Learning from the BIMA Experience" was published by I-Fikr of ISRA.

Noor Suhaida Kasri is the Head of Islamic Capital Market Unit in International *Shari'ah* Research Academy for Islamic Finance (ISRA). She received her Doctor of Philosophy in Islamic Banking Finance and Management from University of Gloucestershire (in collaboration with Markfield Institute of Higher Education), UK. Her Master in Laws was from King's College of London. Her research interest is in law, regulation, social and ethical finance. She has written a number of research papers, articles and textbook chapters and presented in conferences globally.

Fawad Khaleel is working as a lecturer in Accountancy and Finance at Edinburgh Napier University, since 2015. He has a MA in Islamic Banking, Finance and Management and PhD in Islamic Finance from Durham University (UK). His research currently focuses on the philosophy of critical accounting as an ontological authority to explore the epistemology of social, political and economic practices, within societal and institutional context. He is a Victorian explorer of contemporary socioeconomic inefficiencies, with a focus on analytical epistemology.

Hasan Kiaee is Assistant Professor of Economics at Faculty of Islamic Studies and Economics at Imam Sadiq University and specially focused on quantitative area of Islamic economics and finance. He earned his master in 2008 and PhD in 2013 from University of Tehran; his PhD thesis was about using stochastic optimal control theory in modeling the Islamic banking behavior. In addition to contributing in some papers and books in this field, he actively participates in the Islamic banking and finance conferences inside and outside of Iran. Besides this academic background, he has a good practical knowledge in Islamic finance, as he has the experience of working as an advisor for a number of banks and financial institutions in Iran.

Chamara Kuruppu is an associate professor in Management Accounting at the University of South-Eastern Norway. He is also working as an adjunct associate professor at Nord University, Norway and as an adjunct master dissertation supervisory at the Adam Smith Business School, University of Glasgow, United Kingdom. He has received his doctoral degree from Nord University, Norway and his bachelor degree from the University of Ruhuna, Sri Lanka. His research interest includes management control and good governance in the public sector. He has published in international journals and edited books. Chamara is a member of the editorial board of the *Journal of Public Budgeting, Accounting and Financial Management* and one of the guest editors for the *Journal of Accounting in Emerging Economies*. Currently, he is the primary coordinator of the Techno-Economic-Societal Sustainable Development Training Project in Sri Lanka, a project co-funded by the European Commission under the Capacity Building in Higher Education program.

Muhammad Tariq Majeed is Associate Professor of Economics at Quaid-i-Azam University, Islamabad, Pakistan. He did his PhD in Economics from the University of Glasgow, UK in 2012. He has published papers in national and international journals and chapters in research books, and presented papers at various international forums such as Royal Economic Society and Scottish Economic Society. He has supervised 40 plus MPhil theses. His research interests include: Islamic economics, financial development, corruption, inequality, poverty and economic growth. He has also worked as research consultant with International Growth Center, Higher Education Commission, Planning Commission, SDPI and Lead. Moreover, he has delivered various capacity-building trainings related to applied research in social sciences. He has delivered honorary lectures to the executives of Intelligence Bureau, Civil Servants, Member of National Assembly and Senators.

Murniati Mukhlisin earned her bachelor degree in Islamic accounting from International Islamic University, Malaysia and PhD from University of Glasgow, UK. She taught at University of Glasgow and Essex Business School, University of Essex, UK. Mukhlisin works on critical perspective of research in the areas of financial reporting, Islamic accounting, Islamic banking and finance and Islamic financial literacy. Murklisin currently is Rector at Institute Agama Islam Tazkia, Bogor, Indonesia. Murniati co-authored a best seller book "Sakinah Finance" that talks about Islamic family finance.

Rifka Mustafida is a young researcher working in LPPM Tazkia. She is currently studying Master of Islamic Banking and Finance in International

Islamic University Malaysia. Before that, in 2016, she graduated summa cum laude from Tazkia University College of Islamic Economics, Indonesia. She was awarded the best researcher in call for paper of Redenomination held by Bank of Indonesia. She has conducted some researches including Branchless Banking: Towards the Role of Sharia Banking in Reaching Financial Inclusion, Analysis of National Political and Social Readiness in the Application of Redenomination in Indonesia, Contribution of Islamic Microfinance Studies in Achieving SDGs and Implanting Islamic FinTech in GCC Member Countries. Some of her papers already were presented in international forum.

Gry Tengmark Østenstad holds a PhD in Economics from the University of Oslo. Currently, Gry is working as an associate professor at the University of South-Eastern Norway. She teaches International Economics, Mathematics and Statistics. Her research interests include environmental economics, political economy and the economics of migration. She has published research papers on the political economy of migration policies in oil-rich Gulf countries (Oxford Economic Papers) and the role of guest workers in oil-rich countries (Routledge).

Rev Unapana Pemananda is a Buddhist monk scholar and is associated with Oslo Buddhist Vihara, Norway. He holds an MPhil degree in Buddhist Studies and an MSc degree in Human Rights and Multiculturalism. Working as a lecturer at the University of Peradeniya (Sri Lanka), he taught Buddhist Studies. His research interest includes developing effective methods to address cross-cultural conflict, personal and social identity issues, interreligious relations, and effective models of mindfulness practice for well-being. One of his research publications, Buddhist Counseling for Stress Management (මානසිකආතතිය පාලනයට බෞද්ධඋපදේශනය) is a well-referred work in Sri Lanka's university education. In 2018, Rev Unapana presented a research paper on Buddhist Contribution for Sustainable Development in the United Nations Day of Vesak Conference.

Shafiqur Rahman's qualifications include PhD (Macquarie University, Australia), MBA (IBA, Dhaka University) and Marine Engineering. He teaches marketing, management and information systems as well as coordinates those subjects. He has published 19 research papers (including ABDC, ERA and SCOPUS ranked journals), two book chapters and one book. Currently, he teaches at Central Queensland University, Kent Institute Australia and King's Own Institute, Sydney. He acts as a visiting professor for United International University and Northern University of Bangladesh. His industry experiences include serving the American Embassy in Bangladesh as an Economic Specialist and as Vice President for Australian Academy of Business Leadership, Australia. He received many awards for his professional competence as well as research grants for research excellence.

Jon Reiersen is working as an associate professor of economics at the School of Business, University of South-Eastern Norway. He received his doctoral degree in economics from the University of Oslo. Jon's research focuses on labor market institutions in rich and developing countries and the behavioral foundations of economics. He published his work in leading journals such as *Policy and Politics*, *Journal of Agricultural Economics*, *Review of Social Economy*, *International Journal of Social Economics*, *Journal of Business Economics and Management* and in Norwegian journals.

Kulathakattu Shobha has 22 years of experience of teaching, research, administration, training and consultancy. She has authored one book, edited one book and written 65 research papers on banking, rural and economic development issues in various national and international journals of repute. She is on the international editorial advisory boards as a member in international peer-reviewed journals published from Canada, USA and many other countries including India. She has received certificate of excellence for reviewing from Global Journal USA, IJARS, Nigeria, etc. She is a recognized research supervisor to guide MPhil and PhD students in the Departments of Economics. She supervised five PhD and nine MPhil students at Government Arts College, Coimbatore, and currently she is guiding six PhD and two MPhil students.

Mohammad Soleimani joined the Faculty of Islamic Science and Economics, University of Imam Sadiq University in 2014. He is an assistant professor in this faculty. He received his MA degree in Islamic studies and Economics from the University of Imam Sadiq University, Iran, in 2008, and PhD degree in economics from Tarbiat Modares University, Tehran, Iran, in 2013. His PhD thesis is about the effect of social capital on elite's innovations in Iran. His current research interests include financial economics (especially Islamic securitization, financial crisis and derivatives) and development economics. He has some article in the area of social capital, financial crisis, income distributions, and he was the author or supervisor of many policy papers in Islamic Parliament Research Center of Iran in the area of banking system, capital market and central banking.

Abdullah Toseef is an environmental specialist. He earned his Master of Environmental Studies in Sustainability Management from University of Waterloo, Canada in 2018. He is also a supply chain professional with 11 years of experience in packaged goods manufacturing, delivering significant production, supply planning and environmental results. He is formally trained as an engineer, with expertise in supply planning, lean manufacturing, manufacturing sustainability, maintenance, project management and processes. He is experienced in a demand-driven supply chain with achieving deliverable for long-term plus short-term strategy and decision-making. In 2012, he was awarded Unilever Global Hero Award 2012 on Sustainability – Project Recharge to deliver water savings of 38 million liters, among six heroes selected from all over the world. Currently he is working as maintenance manager in Lactalis, Canada.

PREFACE

Under the Paris 2015 agreement, the signatory nations pledged to cut greenhouse gases (GHGs) emissions substantially. Despite high claims, the world's signatory governments and business organizations failed to fulfill their agreed environmental obligations. Business people, corporations, and politicians have either successively circumvented or aborted regulatory measures and plans that ensure a harmonious and sustainable relationship between human activities and the Mother Nature Earth. The natural ecosystems continue to deteriorate and destabilize due to the inexhaustible consumption of natural resources and fossil fuels, and the Earth's temperature continues to rise over successive years. Due to this insatiable depletion of natural resources, we reached the Earth Overshoot Day on 22 August 2020. The Earth Overshoot Day date marks when our Earth can neither renew nor regenerate whatever natural resources we take from our mother planet, Earth. According to the World Economic Forum, COVID-19 decelerated the world's economic activity in 2020, making the Earth Overshoot Day three weeks later than 2019. The empirical data suggest that this tipping point is receding each year, which is likely to raise the global temperature between 2.6°C and 3.9°C. Currently, it will take 1.6 Earths to support human sustainability and its survival. Yet, humans continue to alter the world's land and marine environments, which threatens the survival of more than one million species.

This apocalyptic scenario underscores that if the current human generation fails to alleviate this man-manufactured crisis, our ecological and economic prosperities are doomed. As a rational race, humans need to investigate and integrate abandoned regenerative approaches that guarantee environmental resilience and durable economic and social results. The current delicate situation accentuates the need to formulate a long-term strategy with its foundations in basic human principles. Largely, environment experts disregarded moral and religious values, which are an integral part of human behavior. These values consistently and solidly guide us to one goal – be grateful to God (or the Mother Nature, Earth) for the mortal abundances and respect for diversity, inclusion and equity in reality and practice. Due to a lack of righteous understanding about Judaism, Christianity and Islam (three monolithic Abrahamic religions), climate intellectuals continue to believe in the biased stereotype doubts about the dynamic and amplifying role of moral and religious values in fighting the environmental crises. The absence of moral, ethical and religious values from the current climate research equation demonstrates this denial. Similarly, policy makers assume that cultural and religious embedded moral values have a negligible role in mitigating climate change. Instead, religious and cultural values amplify people's participation at the grassroots levels in achieving global sustainable objectives.

Understanding the modern definition of sustainability owes a lot to John Elkington, the inventor of the triple bottom line (TBL) concept. This concept focuses on achieving synchronized sustainability objectives in three areas, which are referred to as 3Ps, i.e., people, planet and profit. Since its conception, this concept has an exponential role in achieving economic, environmental and social goals. Empirical results show that usually, one or more TBL dimensions underperform, which underlines the need for fresh thinking and a more integrated approach. The COVID-19 pandemic transformed our world and raises questions regarding the validity and resilience of existing economic, environmental and social frameworks. As the new normal has become a routine normal, it offers unprecedented opportunities to change policy measures and extend conceptual notions that can provide proper guidelines. It is a fact that the environmental crises and social development inequalities existing within and between the world nations need a unified solution rather than isolated solutions.

With this standpoint, the current volume argues that moral and religious values play a dynamic role in defying climate change, attaining sustainable development objectives and the necessary outcomes under TBL's social dimension. Moral and ethical foundations drive people's attitudes, which underline the need to integrate moral and religious values in understanding the emerging new normal business context and its contribution towards a more resilient and recovering environment. This imaginative approach allows the cultivation of fresh ideas that help in removing barriers that hinder sustainability objectives.

This volume follows this imaginarium approach and makes a humble effort to integrate this neglected topic but a vital one missing from the current sustainability literature. Business corporations, governments, and climate researchers purposefully ignored this perspective. In truth, this perspective prevailed since the time of Adam and Eve and nurtured over the human generations. This transformative approach represents the close-embeddedness balance between nature and human psychic. We hope our humble endeavor would provide better clarity in developing a deeper understanding of countering climate change.

As a starting point, we follow the assumptions that (1) all religions accentuate that every life has the right to flourish harmoniously on our planet Earth and (2) moral values and mindsets are the foundations of human behavior.

The first assumption fulfills the necessary condition, whereas the second assumption covers the sufficient condition in examining the role of moral and religious values in achieving human welfare objectives (also known as sustainable development goals – SDGs) without destroying the planet. Under these assumptions, this book's primary premise is to bring together scholars from diverse social-cum-religious backgrounds in developing better sustainability and environmental insights and principles.

As editors of this volume, our goal is to provide a desirable platform for starting a discussion regarding moral and religious dimensions in managing the environmental degradation and sustainability goals. We encouraged scholars to present their theoretical views, empirical findings and supporting analysis. The contributors put efforts to discuss the role of religious and moral values in vital issues connected with the environment and sustainability goals, which provides a roadmap for further discussion. Hence, the credit goes to all contributors who identified research gaps in the current sustainability literature and thoroughly discussed them. We avoided either editing or changing the contributing scholars' views, a creditworthy contribution of this modest effort.

In this book, readers from different backgrounds will find something familiar here. We suggest that readers follow the arguments with an open mind regarding moral and religious embedded values in preserving Mother Nature, Earth, and its occupant (including humans). This volume does not cover all the salient areas. Many critical areas, such as blue economy, maritime activities, health and education services, mobilizing socioeconomic factors, etc. are not included.

In our view, achieving sustainable development goals and mitigating environmental crises demands the necessary integration of religious beliefs and moral norms to guide economic actors' economic and social actions. The Earth's future demands that human society and its various stakeholders/actors successfully adopt 3Rs, i.e., responsibility, resilience and regeneration in their daily lives. In this manner, religious and moral values would contribute to achieving sustainable development goals (SGDs) by 2030. Let us strive collectively to achieve 2030 SDGs and mitigate the environmental degradation processes, which guarantee the omission of Earth Overshoot Day in the future.

This volume has three parts. After the introduction section, we discuss theoretical foundations in Part I, the association between religion and sustainability in Part II and Part III provides the state of sustainable development in different countries.

Chapter 2 outlines sustainability-based principles and their role in enhancing TBL performance in marketing supply chains. Dahlstrom argues that raising the global temperature, waning freshwater levels, rising sea levels and declining biodiversity levels are the emerging concerns that prompt the need to incorporate environmental factors into strategic decision-making.

Chapter 3 provides insights into the circular economy (CE) and circular economy business models. In the presence of market failures and system glitches, Brekke argues the need to renew and develop more nuanced policies that stimulate new circular business models and better environment-friendly consumer behavior. Chapter 4 discusses that environmental policy tools only stand valid when polluting agents comply with environmental regulations. Østenstad argues that imperfect enforcement of environmental policy and regulations, and the role of informal control through market agents' ecological concerns affects firms' ecological behavior.

Khaleel and Avdukic, in Chapter 5, explain that leaders of Judaism, Christianity and Islam have publicly advocated action to endogenous sustainable development goals as part of their welfare programs and policies. Within the Abrahamic religions, a robust financial emphasis underscores the necessity of implementing sustainable development goals. Drawing on Buddhist teaching, Pemananda and Kuruppu describe the dominant sustainable development pattern emphasizing economic, societal and environmental issues in Chapter 6. They revisit the definition of sustainable development to identify the pitfalls of this phenomenon and present a natural development approach. Further, the authors identify Buddhist doctrines such as paticcasamuppāda (theory of interdependency) and tilakkhaṇa (three characteristics), which maximize psychological happiness, sustainable consumption level and the perpetuation of humanity towards all living beings on our planet with genuine care and generosity. Khaleel and Shobha elucidate in Chapter 7 that the traditions of Hinduism are interwoven theological constructs, which are complex and rich in meaning. These traditions' narrative focuses on the well-being of the planet by maintaining a harmonious relationship with the environment and sustainable economic development to eliminate poverty. Azid, Burki and Chaudhry attempt to define the Islamic moral economy and Islamic moral market in Chapter 8. They discuss the differences between morals and Islamic morals. The foundations of Islamic epistemology are based on this life as well as on life hereafter. Islamic moral concepts stem from the rules provided by the Qur'an and Sunnah (the practices of Prophet Muhammad). Islam provides firm guidelines to protect the rights and interests of the people, uphold the ecological balance for achieving the human growth targets, i.e., materials and spirituals, such that no human is leaving behind. In Chapter 9, Abdullah discusses conflict vis-à-vis compliments between the Islamic development framework and the modern developmental construct. Finally, the study endeavors to contextualize the Islamic paradigm of development in the contemporary context. The study adopts a qualitative research paradigm and critically reviews the relevant literature to conclude. In Chapter 10, Mukhlisin and Mustafida aim to provide future research direction in Islamic accounting by promoting accountability and sustainability after examining 150 articles published in 38 leading journals. Their research map describes the flow of debates from 1986 to 2017 and identifies the conducted research, analysis levels and research directions.

In Chapter 11, Majeed presents a comparative analysis of financial development and ecological footprint nexus with income levels using a novel index of ecological quality for a large panel of countries from 1971 to 2017. In Chapter 12, Reiersen shows the close link between social and environmental sustainability. By using experiences from a Nordic country, he identifies two learning points. First, implementing a more egalitarian distribution of income is possible without compromising economic efficiency. Under the right institutional circumstances, redistribution can even stimulate economic restructuring, modernization and innovation. Second, the realization of a green transition, reducing fossil-fuel energy consumption and more environment-friendly production methods, involves extensive and demanding restructuring efforts. It will impose considerable short-term restructuring costs on individuals, groups and society. If people experience these costs are equitably distributed, restructuring will be less painful. Besides, innovative forces would be easier to mobilize, and resistance to change diminishes by low-income inequality, high social trust levels, and collective risk-sharing. Abdullah, Burki and Ersoy, in Chapter 13, discuss the role of Canada as one of the world's largest resource-consuming nations. The chapter analyzes the production, consumption and trade flow related to Canada's sustainable energy security and answers three critical questions about Canada's metabolic profile over time, Canada's energy use compared to other nations and Canada's energy sector potentials for a sustainability transition. By employing panel data (1980–2015) of 42 developed and 53 developing economies. Majeed explores the relationship of the environment with happiness in Chapter 14. The environment's quality is measured with total GHGs and principal component analysis of carbon, nitrous and methane emissions. The findings suggest that environmental degradation lowers the happiness level in both developed and developing countries. Comparatively, this effect is more substantial in the context of developed countries. The findings are robust to control of other socioeconomic and demographic indicators. This research implies that maintaining environmental quality is fundamental for happiness in both developed and developing countries. Chapter 15 by Soleimani and Kiaee elucidates the role of *waqf* institution in Islamic countries. Altruistic principles are the foundations of *waqf* institutions. This institution has contributed substantially to achieving development goals in Islamic countries. By using a set of intrinsic motivations, altruism mitigates the problems that arise in a self-interest economy and brings about social optimal and sustainable development goals. Kasri and Ismail describe social finance's role in integrating economic activities with social value in Chapter 16. Social finance is a subset of the universal set of Islamic finance and is the third sector that provides a community with necessities when government and market (being the first and second sectors) fail. Under the Islamic financial system, a number of of institutions perform certain activities which create positive socio-economic impacts, for example, *waqf, zakat, sadaqa,* and many others. In Chapter 17, Edriyanti, Ahmad and Rahman describe the significant contributions of 14th-century North African historian and Islamic philosopher Ibn Khaldun about the concept of sustainable development. They presented a comparative analysis between modern economists' and Ibn Khaldun's sustainable development concepts. The study also discusses the relevance of Ibn Khaldun's thoughts in achieving sustainable developments in Indonesia. In Chapter 18, Eskil and Burki investigate whether the gender of top managers is associated with different indicators related to people, planet and profit. They applied empirical data from one of the gender-neutral societies in Scandinavia (Norway) and found that women tend to work in companies with low salary disparities and have more direct contact with end consumers. Furthermore, women are more occupied than men regarding ethical and environmental issues. Men prefer to be the CEOs of companies with a higher degree of outsourcing and profit margins concerning return on assets.

In the last chapter (Chapter 19), the editors conclude by discussing the opportunities and challenges facing sustainable development vis-à-vis the moral and religious aspects of human life.

FOREWORD

Macromarketing takes a systems view of the interplay between marketing and society (Nason 2006). *The Journal of Macromarketing* celebrated its 40th anniversary in 2020 and has forged a place in marketing scholarship that welcomes a broad view of marketing-related phenomenon. Traditionally, phenomena that connect with one of the following categories of research have much potential for development in macromarketing: (1) quality of life, (2) ethics, (3) the environment, (4) marketing systems, (5) history and (6) developing countries (Peterson 2013, p. 19).

Over the years, macromarketing discourse about sustainability has included recurring critiques of consumption ideology (endorsed by every macromarketer I have ever known), but two differing perspectives on recommended approaches to sustainability challenges for societies (Prothero and McDonagh 2020). Critical scholars in macromarketing tend to favor top–down government-driven approaches, while developmental scholars tend to see markets as sources of solutions to sustainability challenges. As you can imagine, these two schools have brought spirited debate to macromarketing.

While sustainable development that is oriented to intergenerational justice (not consuming following generations' environmental resources) is implied to be important in macromarketing scholarship (because it represents a way markets and society affect each other), so too is globalization (because globalization is a phenomenon related to each of the six major categories of research in **macromarketing**) (Peterson 2013, chapter 9).

In important ways, Foundations of Sustainable Economy: Moral, Ethical and Religious Perspectives can be viewed as resonating with macromarketing. The focus on sustainability and intergenerational justice in the book is strong. The team of authors composing the chapters represents global coverage in their individual histories, but so, too, does the geographic diversity across the content of the chapters – particularly from Muslim and Buddhist cultures. I am very pleased to see authors in the volume willing to explain how religious beliefs and traditions matter in understanding how sustainability can develop in the future. Macromarketing has featured such religious perspectives in the past in explaining market-related phenomena (Jurdi, Batat, and Jafari 2017; Sandıkcı, Peterson, Ekici, and Simkins 2016; Laczniak and Santos 2011).

Perhaps, because of globalization (which has rapidly developed in the 21st century), scholars in business no longer regard religion and social science as unrelated fields of study. This is now true in the realm of public policy research, as well (Johnson *et al.* 2017). I think the illumination scholars receive from having religious concepts included in business research can promote mutual understanding across different cultural groups of the world. This is a valuable outcome of such research. Even state-run or secularly oriented schools of business can teach about religion in marketing and management courses, while not teaching religion (Peterson and Minton 2018). In this way, students will be better equipped to succeed in cross-cultural and global business contexts.

Foundations of Sustainable Economy: Moral, Ethical and Religious Perspectives offers readers valuable views of sustainability scholarship from around the world. Together, these studies and cases offer readers the elements of a mosaic that readers can use to form their own interpretation of what is happening on planet Earth today regarding sustainability.

Mark Peterson
Editor, Journal of Macromarketing (2016–2019)
Professor of Marketing
University of Wyoming

References

El Jurdi, H.A., Batat, W., & Jafari, A. (2017). Harnessing the power of religion: Broadening sustainability research and practice in the advancement of ecology. *Journal of Macromarketing*, *37*(1), 7–24.

Johnson, K.A., Liu, R.L., Minton, E.A., Bartholomew, D.E., Peterson, M., Cohen, A.B., & Kees, J. (2017). US citizens' representations of God and support for sustainability policies. *Journal of Public Policy & Marketing*, *36*(2), 362–378.

Laczniak, G.R. & Santos, N.J. (2011). The integrative justice model for marketing to the poor: An extension of SD logic to distributive justice and macromarketing. *Journal of Macromarketing*, *31*(2), 135–147.

Nason, R.W. (2006). The macromarketing mosaic. *Journal of Macromarketing*, *26*(2), 219–223.

Peterson, M. (2013). Sustainable enterprise: A macromarketing approach. Newbury Park, CA: Sage.

Peterson, M. & Minton, E.A. (2018). Teaching belief systems in marketing classes. *Journal of International Education in Business, 11*(1), 43–66.

Prothero, A. & McDonagh, P. (2020). Ambiguity of purpose and the politics of failure: Sustainability as macromarketing's compelling political calling. *Journal of Macromarketing*, *41*(1), 166–171.

Sandıkcı, Ö., Peterson, M., Ekici, A., & Simkins, T. (2016). Development and quality of life in Turkey: How globalization, religion, and economic growth influence individual well-being. *Journal of Macromarketing*, 36(3), 304–320.

1

SUSTAINABILITY AND MORALITY

Umar Burki, Toseef Azid and Robert Francis Dahlstrom

The world is experiencing a successful and indispensable paradigm shift at all levels to save the earth's environment from the climate change. One hundred and ninety-five (195) countries signed the ambitious Paris Agreement to combat and strengthen the global response to the possible precarious outcomes of climate change. A majority of the signatory countries are developing countries and extremely vulnerable to climate change. This scenario underscore that a large majority of the participating countries need to improve their national institutional and other necessary capacity-building frameworks to achieve the ambitious goals of the Paris Agreement.

Correspondingly, the United Nations (UN) program, "Transforming our world: The 2030 Agenda for Sustainable Development," focuses on eradicating poverty through meaningful sustainable development action connected with 3Ps (people, planet and prosperity). Restoring our planet health is an indispensable condition to liberate and free the human race from the cruelty of poverty. The program outlines 17 Sustainable Development Goals (SDGs)[1] and pledges that "no one will be left behind." Among others, SDGs primarily focus on the realization of universal human rights, gender equality, women empowerment, etc. Concisely, SDGs are a set of indivisible goals targeted to achieve sustainable development simultaneously at three vital tiers, i.e., at the economic, social and environmental levels. To achieve the agenda's targets, the program underscore that it is important to share common morals, apply diverse religious values, and follow 5Ps (people, planet, prosperity, peace and partnership) to protect human life and the environment.

Hence, the Paris Agreement and the 2030 Agenda for Sustainable Development guide us to redefine our political, economic and social systems, and transform socioeconomic activities in achieving a carbon-neutral sustainable world. In addition to new technologies and green innovations, national governments are gradually realizing the significant role of moral values and religious paradigms in achieving SDGs, eradicating poverty and mitigating the negative effects of climate change. Developed, emerging and developing economies need to make substantial structural transformations to achieve sustainability targets at national and international levels.

The flagrancy of climate change is inspiring young individuals to speak against it and support the sustainability cause. This generation also recognizes the possible negative consequences if the world fails to achieve SDGs. Young activists comprehend that their future is at stake and their generations must participate in the crucial fight to save the planet earth. India's Licypriya Kangujam is the world's youngest climate activist, who is urging the world leaders to "*act now against climate change.*" Greta Thunberg,[2] a celebrated young Swedish climate activist refutes "*the children should not worry*" mantra and ascertains the actions of world leaders as empty words and promises. This chapter classifies crucial sustainability issues that are vital for the survival of humans on the earth.

1.1 Sustainability issues and sustainable development

In accordance with the United Nations, the following issue will play a crucial role in protecting the environment, achieving the SDGs and safeguarding the planet earth.

1.1.1 Greenhouse gases emission and costs

Under the Paris Agreement, the central focus is on taking measures that keep the global temperature considerably below 2 degrees Celsius, which is above the pre-industrialized level. The agreement decided to reduce greenhouse gases (GHG) emission by 50% in 2030. However, the majority (75%) of the signatory countries, partially or totally are unable to reduce the targeted GHG emissions by 2030. Out of the 184 countries, only 12% are capable of reducing GHG emissions sufficiently, 6% have incomplete sufficient capabilities, 4% have partly insufficient capabilities and the remaining 70% have insufficient capabilities to achieve the GHG emissions target by 2030.

China, USA, EU and India are the major (56%) producers of GHG emissions. Under the Paris Agreement, these contributors committed to reduce GHG emissions significantly by 2030. For example, China committed to reduce GHG by 60–65% from the 2005 level by 2030. USA committed to cut its GHG emission by 26–28% from the 2005 level by 2025. (The Trump government withdrew the USA from the agreement.) The European Union (28 member countries) committed to reduce GHG emission by 40% from the 1990 level by 2030 and India committed to reduce GHG emission by 30–35% from the 2015 level by 2030. So far, the Russian Federation, the fifth largest GHG emitter, has not submitted its emission reduction plan.

Coal-fired power plants are one of the main contributors of GHG emissions as well as providers of cheap energy. Despite their high GHG emissions, 2,400 new coal-fired power plants are in the planning phases globally. This is a blunt divergence to the actions needed to keep the global temperature rise below 2 degrees Celsius limit. Research suggests that if the household sector used the efficient, environment-friendly energy sources, then CO_2 could be reduced by 40% by 2040, which can save $500 billion (Watson *et al.* 2019). However, a number of political, economic, social and technological reasons limit the signatory countries to achieve this global target. Therefore, 130 countries including the four largest emitter are unable to meet the GHG emission reduction target, which is likely to cause an economic loss of $2 billion per day by 2030.

There is a sizeable social cost associated with GHG emissions and global warming. For instance, GHG emissions will significantly decrease the agriculture sector's productivity, increase global wildfires, raise sea levels and increase flooding, upsurge extreme temperatures, and raise the frequency of severe weather storms (Bhatt 2019). The International Monetary Fund (IMF) proposed that by imposing a tax of US$75 on the per-ton production of CO_2, we are in a position to achieve the GHG emission target agreed under the Paris Agreement. Moreover, this cost is less expensive than the cost of producing nuclear energy (Bhatt 2019).

Consequently, it is an appropriate call of the hour to reduce the global GHG emission levels by reducing dependence on fossil fuels and increasing technological innovations. The world should focus on low-cost greenhouse gas mitigation and low carbon innovation (Gillingham 2019). Although adopting green technologies is expensive, yet it is vital to adopt green and clean technologies even though the initial results may show an insignificant impact on the climate. Nevertheless, the cumulative continuous benefits outweigh the initial setup costs. Suitable technological innovations that help in reducing CO_2 emissions will generate positive externalities for an economy. For example, the semiconductor industry illustrates the capability to raise good externalities and lower per-unit costs (Irwin and Klenow 1994).

1.1.2 Carbon-based pricing strategy

Public consumption of economic goods is associated with economic growth and defines the living standards of a society. On the other hand, it has a significant impact on the environment because of its production–consumption link. The extraordinary increase in greenhouse gases reflects market failures and free-rider behavior regarding the consumption of public goods. In the presence of positive externalities, policy makers and people face no negative consequences. When consumption of public goods results in negative externalities, policy makers have to intervene through fiscal policy instruments. For instance, imposing carbon taxes will lead to a decrease in GHG emissions, increase governmental revenues, and help in cleaning the local environment. Similarly, the pricing policy tools are effective domestic instruments to fulfill climate change commitments and reduce carbon dioxide levels.

Such fiscal measures are quite easy to implement without any administrative problems (Parry 2019; Costanza *et al.* 1997). Parry (2019) writes, "Carbon pricing is in China and India's interests because of the benefits from reduced air pollution mortality are considered; a US$35 a ton carbon tax in 2030 would save an estimated 300,000 premature deaths a year in China and an estimated 170,000 in India. This fiscal action will decrease the GHG emissions and will protect the future generations. Bhatt (2019) commented, "Ian Parry estimates that aggressive carbon taxes would help individual nations meet their emission-reduction goals and scale up action globally. Mark Carney and others show how harnessing finance can open enormous opportunities – from transforming energy to reinventing protein."

Instead of mitigating environmental issues, a number of global megaprojects increase environmental problems, which leads to higher levels of GHG emissions. For example, GHG emissions increased by 80% in China between 2005 and 2018, and expected to increase in the near future (Watson *et al.* 2019). In other parts of the world, especially in Europe, GHG emission environmental risk and economic opportunities are moving in a parallel manner (European Environment Agency 2019). Different environmental challenges burden economic and social agents. Governments and civil societies have equal responsibility towards achieving the SDGs. Hence, there is a need to redefine economic priorities, restructure current policies, reorganize infrastructures and change the behavior of the producers and consumers.

1.1.3 Circular economy

The concept of circular economy promotes sustainability and sustainable development by utilizing waste as a resource. A circular economy is a regenerative approach to production and consumption, in which products and materials are redesigned, recovered and reused to reduce environmental impacts (Ghisellini *et al.* 2016; Gregon and Crang 2015). The objective of circular economy is to change the present perception of the production sector, based on the linear economic model, i.e., take–make–dispose (from raw material to wastage). Under the circular economy approach, economies should shift themselves from "cradle to grave" to "cradle to cradle"[3] to achieve the sustainable development (Despeisse *et al.* 2017; Ghisellini *et al.* 2016; Gregon and Crang 2015). The concept has a number of practical limitations such as industrial interdependence, longer shelf life of consumable products and recycling. Globally, recycling is considered as "dirty and illegal trade." Recycling is a way towards moral economy as we can find solutions regarding ecological modernization, environmental justice and resource (in) security (Gregon and Crang 2015). The European Environment Agency (2019) reports that the circular economy model will increase the efficiency of resources utilization, lower waste generation, and the generated wastes will become useable resources. In this manner, the concept reduces the levels of environmental pollution, thereby creating a new path for the low carbon emissions, renewable energy innovations and simultaneously solving raw material availability.

Several organizations are working on the economic logic of circular economy by developing required networks. For example, organizations such as Ellen MacArthur Foundation and McKinsey[4] published a series of reports in 2012, 2013 and 2014 arguing that through circular economy, we can increase the resources, lower costs, minimize the wastage, decrease the degree of degradation of environment and simultaneously it enables us to achieve the targets of economic growth. Furthermore, the reports argued economic system should be based on renewables and recycling, which has two dimensions, namely (a) first is the industrial ecology and (b) second is the extended life of the product (Gregon and Crang 2015; Georgescu-Roegen 1971). Through them, economies should move from linear to circular model (Frosch and Gallopoulos 1989). In the production–consumption equation, the extended product life minimizes the waste and shifts the economy towards the sustainable development (Cooper 2005, 2010). Further, in the circular model, one can calculate the cost of externalities through various methods. For example, life-cycle analysis, materials flow analysis and triple bottom line accounting are some of the useful methods (Alexander and Reno 2012). Nevertheless, the world is far away from becoming a circular economy as it is still using more resources, creating more wastes and unable to recycle it. Hence, the earth should move towards closed-loop recycling cycle (Olugbenga *et al.* 2019).

Extraction and processing of natural and man-made resources for the production of consumer goods are the main sources of GHG emissions. According to reasonable estimates, around 62% GHG emissions come from extraction and production processes. During the past 50 years, the use of natural resources has tripled. If this trend continues, the use of natural resources will double by 2050. Currently, the world reused only 9% of the waste material. It is an alarming state. To save the planet earth, it is vital to reuse the available scarce resources. The solution lies in adopting models of circular economy. World Economic Forum reports that a transition towards a circular economy could generate $4.5 trillion in additional economic output by 2030.[5]

1.1.4 Shifting from green to blue economy

Green economy focuses on reducing the environmental risk in a given consumption–production link, that is, achieving sustainable development that improves as well as maintains the environment. The emergence of ecology scarcity of land resources is forcing the world economies to explore and exploit maritime resources without destroying their environmental sustainability[6] and demonstrate the shift from green economy to the blue economy.[7] Blue economy's prime objective is also to increase economic growth, standard of living and social inclusion without disturbing the environmental balance.

Like green economy, blue economy has the same objective, i.e., reducing CO_2 from the atmosphere, reduce the global temperature and develop the new technologies, which are helpful in the environmental sustainability. For instance, marine biologists discovered that the great whales capture a significant amount of CO_2 in their bodies from the atmosphere (Roman *et al.* 2014). Chami *et al.* (2019) described this process as follows:

> The carbon capture potential of whales is truly startling. Whales accumulate carbon in their bodies during their long lives. When they die, they sink to the bottom of the ocean; each great whale sequesters 33 tons of CO_2 on average, taking that carbon out of the atmosphere for centuries. A tree, meanwhile, absorbs only up to 48 pounds of CO_2 a year.

They further explained about the ocean's smallest creature known as phytoplankton. Phytoplankton are present in areas where whales are present because the waste (nitrogen and iron) produced by whales is used by phytoplankton to grow. Phytoplankton contribute towards oxygen formation in the atmosphere (at least 50%). They capture 37 billion metric tons of CO_2 (an estimated 40% of all CO_2 produced), which is equivalent to CO_2 capturing capacity of 1.70 trillion trees. The phenomena known as a "whale pump" and "the great whale conveyor belt," increases the phytoplankton productivity, ultimately capturing hundreds of millions of tons of CO_2 per year, which is equivalent to billion mature trees. Ironically, no one is interested to pay for this public good, produced by whales and their activities, a highly significant positive externality (Chami *et al.* 2019). Furthermore, governments and international organizations should support and develop a mindset that supports a transition towards blue economy.

1.1.5 The climate change and human health

Burning of fossil fuels drastically increased the world's air pollution levels. Likewise, excessive use of fossil-fuel energy has increased the quantity of CO_2 in the earth's atmosphere. Health studies (e.g., Kampa and Castanas 2007) suggest that air pollution has very bad impact on the health of human being and deteriorates functions of human body organs, reduces the life expectancy and increases the pre-mature mortality rates. Kampa and Castanas (2007, p. 362) also quote,

> Air pollution has both acute and chronic effects on human health, affecting a number of different systems and organs. It ranges from minor upper respiratory irritation to chronic respiratory and heart disease, lung cancer, acute respiratory infections in children and

> chronic bronchitis in adults, aggravating pre-existing heart and lung disease, or asthmatic attacks.

Furthermore, they state,

> Air pollutants, such as carbon monoxide (CO), sulphur dioxide (SO2), nitrogen oxides (NOx), volatile organic compounds (VOCs), ozone (O_3), heavy metals, and respirable particulate matter (PM2.5 and PM10), differ in their chemical composition, reaction properties, emission, time of disintegration and ability to diffuse in long or short distances.

Research published in *New England Journal of Medicine*[8] report that car exhausts has respirable particulate matter PM_{10}, which penetrates lungs, and $PM_{2.5}$, which enter the blood, and causes respiratory and cardiovascular problems and increases the death rate (seven million deaths a year worldwide). "These respirable particulate matters also cause fatigue, headaches and anxiety, irritation of the eyes, nose and throat, damage to reproductive organs, harm to the liver, spleen and blood, and nervous system damage."[9]

1.1.6 Food transformation: food, health and environment

Transformation in the world's food habits raises a number of questions, ranging from what we eat, how we produce food and what is the impact of our food consumption on the environment. Researchers are focusing on the consumption–production–environment link (Batini 2019; Willett *et al.* 2019).

Professor Willett (2019) MD[10] summarizes in the EAT-Lancet Commission Report (EAT Lancet Commission 2019, p. 3) as follows: "Transformation to healthy diets by 2050 will require substantial dietary shifts. Global consumption of fruits, vegetables, nuts and legumes will have to double, and consumption of foods such as red meat and sugar will have to be reduced by more than 50%. A diet rich in plant-based foods and with fewer animal source foods confers both improved health and environmental benefits."

According to the estimates of European Environment Agency (2019), Europe's five risk factors for premature death (high blood pressure, cholesterol and body mass index) are associated with poor food intake and alcohol abuse. Trichopoulou (2009) stated that consuming food from outside has tremendously increased, whereas the time spent in the kitchen has reduced. Similarly, food and drink on the go increases the quantity of litter, and is becoming an environmental concern (EC 2018).

Presently, the agro-food sector contributes one-fourth in the human production of GHG emissions, which is expected to increase by 50% in 2050. Moreover, 8% of GHG emissions is from non-food agro and deforestation activities (IPCC 2019 Special Report on Climate Change and EAT-Lancet Commission 2019). Livestock (e.g., cow and sheep) emit methane gas, which contributes 51% annually to the world GHG emissions (FAO estimations). These emissions are equivalent to all types of transportation emission at world level.

Batini (2019) expressed, "Beyond its direct impact on climate change, the agri-food sector uses a lot of the planet's resources, including about half the world's ice- and desert-free land and three-quarters of its fresh water." Moreover, the excessive use of chemicals and synthetics in the agricultural sector is increasing the globe pollution rate. According to UN's Intergovernmental Science-Policy Platform on Biodiversity and Ecosystem Services (2019), the agricultural sector is the most active actor that has a destructive effect on the earth. According to FAO reports, around 650 million people fall under the obese category, whereas 2 billion people are overweight because of the wrong food habits. According to Batini (2019), the EAT-Lancet Commission (2019) and IPCC suggested the following three policy measures:

1. Reduce the consumption of red meat and dairy products by 50% and substitute by the proteins of plants.
2. Shifting on large-scale basis from "monoculture agriculture" to that system which should support biodiversity ("organic and mixed crop-livestock farming").
3. Increasing the number of plants in the forests and simultaneously strictly reducing deforestation.

Batini (2019) stated that we should remember and follow "no animal products for breakfast or lunch" rule. Further, he added that a shift from meat to plant-based diet supports the planet and the people because it reduces the risk of cancer, cardiovascular diseases, type 2 diabetes and obesity. Batini summarizes this discussion in this way,

> Critical progress would be made in eradicating world hunger, income inequality, and social immobility, averting mass migration due to climate change. Climate health is land and seas' health, 'whereas consequently', it is human health and economies' health. If we can muster the will before it is too late, we can have our nutritious food, thriving economies, and a habitable planet too.

1.1.7 Financial sector and sustainable development

Financial institutions evaluate business projects on factors such as risk, liquidity, interest rate, credit, market and operational risks. They are normally least concerned about evaluating the impact of a project on the climate. According to Chenet (2019) words, "Move along, nothing to see."

However, in 2000, environmental NGOs and activists pressurizing the financial institutions to examine that how the projects which they are financing are risky for the environment.

After the Paris Agreement, the financial sector took some significant steps in adopting sustainability approach. Financial regulators, supervisors and other related departments realize the close risk that the financial sector faces due to the climate change. Chenet (2019) presented them in a chronological order. Financial portfolio's first carbon foot prints (2005), green bonds (World Bank 2015), low-carbon stock indices (2008–2009), Financial "carbon bubble and unburn able carbon" buzz (2011–2012), Green credit guidelines (China 2012), fossil fuels divestment campaigns, shareholder resolutions on carbon bubble and climate risk (2014), UNEP Inquiry platform (2014), Investors pledges and high-level pre-COP21 policy push at theclimate risks for the financial system Article 173 of the Energy Transition Act, on financial institutions' disclosure of climate risks (France 2015), adoption of the Paris Agreement (esp. Art. 2.1(c) on finance flows Climate Finance Bill), International Network of Central Banks and Supervisors for Greening the Financial System and published the EU Action Plan "Financing Sustainable Growth" (EU 2018). These aforementioned actions and measures show the financial sector's long-term attempts to deal with the climate change.

1.1.8 Morality and religion

Economics assumes that man is "homo economicus." Accomplishing SDGs shifted this paradigm because in addition to economic rationality, a man's moral action and ethical values also motivate his behavior with fellow human beings and the environment, the planet earth. All monolithic and earthly religions follow similar moral values, whose primary focus include enhancing people's welfare and prosperity, protecting the planet we live in, maintaining peace and increasing the partnership among people (5Ps). Singh and Clark (2016) discuss different religions under these five Ps. Studies (Kinsley 1995) identify a significant link between ecosystem and moral values. Hence, it is difficult to ignore the importance of religion in development projects, development practices and in formulating development policies (Rakodi 2012).

Following the Brundtland definition, the religious organizations started the discussion on how to integrate religious and moral values with sustainable development. In 2003, a special issue of *Development* journal on religion and development provided the needed credibility to this notion. Today, academicians regularly deliberate the link between religion and sustainability and sustainable development. A regular stream of academic literature is published. For example, *Development* journal published again a special issue on religion and development in 2012. Several books (i.e., Clarke 2011; Deneulin and Bano 2009; Giri *et al.* 2004; Eric Kauffman 2010) were published on this emerging topic. Interestingly, the national and international donors fund faith-based organizations (FBO) to carry out development projects (Tomalin 2012). In this perspective, Narayanan (2013) raised two questions about religion and sustainable development. First, why is it important that a religion should appreciate or more to the point, enabled to have a role in sustainable development discourse and practice? Why is sustainable development alone not enough? Second, what sorts of role religion may play in sustainable development?

The main objective of the 2030 agenda of sustainable development is to improve humans' living standards without destroying the environment, i.e., respecting the limits of our planet (Singh and Clark 2016). Such approach requires a complete alliance of minds and hearts. Religion plays a significant role in changing the minds and hearts of people. It is also observed that fundamentally, people's minds and hearts follow their religion. Historical data and events identify that when communities needed social and economic support, religious institutions provide the desirable help and support. For example, religious institutions such as *Waqf* have a solid significance in Islamic history. Similarly, the philanthropic role of church, *Satrams* in Hinduism, institution of Tzedakah in Judaism and Dharma Drum Mountain in Buddhism underline the vital role of religious foundations in human behavior.

If we want to achieve the 2030 SDGs, the role of religious institutions becomes imperative. Philosophically, five Ps are also constituting an integral part of every religion, and form the nucleus of 2030 agenda (Singh and Clark 2016). Religious values guide us in maintaining the needed balance between the material and spiritual worlds. Every religion disproves extravagant behavior and careful thoughtfulness about the needs of future generations. Religion teaches us about the purpose of our lives and provide fundamental guidance about issues related to our social life, poverty, injustice, pollution, dishonesty, vice, etc. Every religion endorses the concept of partnership. In 1993, the Parliament of World Religions declared, "Every individual has the right to be treated humanely" and "we must treat others as we wish others to treat us." Singh and Clark (2016) quoted the statement of German theologian Hans Küng, "No peace among the nations without peace among the religions. No peace among the religions without dialogue between the religions."

Similarly, Narayanan's (2013) accentuates that we should engage religion in the process of sustainable development on a fair basis instead of treating religion 100% "relevant" or "irrelevant." Synod of Western Australia (2001, p. 4, para. 2) gave the following moral call to its followers:

> We affirm our belief that the natural world is God's creation; good in God's eyes, good in itself, and good in sustaining human life. Recognising the vulnerability of the life and resources of creation, we will work to promote the responsible management, use and occupation of the earth by human societies. We will seek to identify and

> challenge all structures and attitudes, which perpetuate and compound the destruction of creation.
>
> (cited in Narayanan 2013, p. 133)

Narayanan (2013) quoted from The Book of Genesis, "serve the garden in which we have been placed" (Genesis 2:15). Hence, all religions provide the necessary moral support for achieving the SGDs (Singh and Clark 2016; Narayanan 2013). In short, science teaches us how we can achieve SDGs, whereas morals and religious values guide us why we need it. A combination of both is a necessary condition for achieving SDGs. Sfeir-Younis (2001) reasoned the necessary need of religion and spirituality in planning economic development. In his view, people are dissatisfied with the adverse effect of current economic policies. Economies cannot survive if they follow selfish behavior and economic policies are devoid of religious, ethical and moral values. All societies have groups and organizations that serve people. The world economy is global and therefore demands a collective approach to economic problems. Finding a global solution is only possible when scientific principle and ethics, moral and religious virtues are applied collectively. Practically, sustainability and sustainable development requires both religious and moral values.

1.1.9 Inclusiveness – leaving no one behind

Under the UN sustainable development 2030 agenda, all the member states pledged to guarantee, "no one is left behind." The statement underscores that no human should face discrimination based on their place of residence, socio-economic position, governance and weakness to stand unanticipated shocks. In this manner, every individual can get identical opportunities and dignity levels. The first beneficiaries are those people who lack basic life criterions due to the presence of discriminate inequality among people and the world nations (UN Sustainable Development Report 2016).

A recent ILO (International Labour Organization 2020) on Global Employment Trends for Youth 2020 (p. 13) states the employment condition of youth,

> The continuing decline in young people's engagement in the labour market reflects not only the increasing enrolment in education but also the persistence of the youth NEET (not in employment, education or training) challenge, especially among young women … Young people across the world are worried that new technologies – particularly robotics and artificial intelligence – may take away their jobs.

Furthermore, at the world level, youth unemployment is 13.6%, which is three times more than adults' unemployment rate.

There is no comparison between the access of health facilities available to the rich and poor segments of the world. Similarly, poor households have a higher number of dependent children than rich households. Eighty percent (80%) inhabitants of urban regions have the facility of piped water whereas more than 33% from rural areas have not this facility. Malnourishment is a norm in the developing countries, especially those belonging to Western Asia and African regions (UN Sustainable Development Report 2016). Further, socioeconomic inequalities discriminate exploitation and criminal activities increase the degree of vulnerability in the poor households' segment. For example, 43% of the victims are between the age of 10 and 29 years among 200,000 homicides cases. Child trafficking is another dark side of human underdevelopment. The United Nation's report on the Sustainable Development Goals (2016) concludes,

> In every developing region, the poorest women are the least likely to have a skilled attendant during delivery ... People in rural areas are disadvantaged when it comes to many health-related services ... People in the least developed countries are twice as likely to be undernourished as those in developing regions as a whole.

1.1.10 The COVID-19 pandemic and the need for sustainable development

The COVID-19 pandemic is affecting all humans' aspects. The world's economy is facing bottomless crises and all economies are in downturn. Nevertheless, the strict lockdowns has lowered economic activities, which is having a significant positive effect on the earth's environment. We experience a substantial reduction in GHG emissions, revival in animals' ecology and reduction in the use of natural resources. Dynamic experiences learned during the COVID-19 period provide valuable guidelines about finding a rational balance between the environment and the drive towards economic prosperity. The crisis period demonstrates that our current preference order is invalid and substantially self-centred. With a borderless reach, the pandemic underline the need to develop a global approach that contains similar situations through partnerships and strong public health systems.

In rich and poor nations, the health system collapsed. This failure demonstrates that out of the 17 SDGs, SDG 3 (Good Health and Well-Being) failed. To quantify in economic terms, the pandemic severely reduced the global trade transactions, tourism industry, investment opportunities, education sector and people's mobility, especially, the airline industry. Sachs *et al.* (2020) suggest that it is important to restructure and realign our short-term and long-term priorities, where short-term priorities focus on controlling current and future pandemic-like situations, and long-term priorities address to develop strong health systems. The only possible way to overcome the current pandemic situation is to develop an effective public health system (van Dorn *et al.* 2020).

The world societies are experiencing strict regressive lockdowns because of the COVID-19 pandemic. Lockdowns are survivable for the rich segments of the world population. For the have-not's segments of the world populations, it is a question of surviving hunger, poverty and maintaining basic economic viability. This is extremely important for those developing countries that import food and other basic nutrition diet items (FAO 2020; IFPRI 2020).

On the economic front, the world is experiencing high inflation rates, depreciating currencies, and fluctuating exchange rates, which are going to create an even bigger debt crisis than 2007 (Adrian and Natalucci 2020). Sachs *et al.* (2020) warns the world as: "Beyond the most direct impacts on poverty (SDG 1), food security (SDG 2), health (SDG 3), the economy (SDG 8), and multilateralism (SDG 17), the Covid-19 pandemic will impact other SDG impacts that are less widely discussed." Furthermore, as the world's inequalities rise under the COVID-19, it will be difficult to achieve SDG 10 (reduced inequalities) and SDG 5 (gender equality). In addition, the impact on SDG 16 (political and legislative systems and the rule of law), and on the environment is still not clear (SDG 12–15). The COVID-19 resulted in lowering the traffic accidents and traffic accidents (SDG 3.6) related deaths (Kopf 2020). Sachs *et al.* (2019) suggested six major societal transformations for achieving the 17 SDGs. These are (1) education and skills, (2) health and well-being, (3) clean energy and industry, (4) sustainable land use, (5) sustainable cities and (6) digital technologies.

All the discussion around the COVID-19 pandemic fails to mention moral training at the world (Sachs *et al.* 2020). It is important to transform our societies and develop immunity from vices greediness, dishonesty and fraud. In our opinion, SDGs should integrate moral and religious values to enhance partnership among the world communities.

Notes

1 The list of SDGs is as follows: 1: No poverty, 2: Zero hunger, 3: Good health and well-being, 4: Quality education, 5: Gender equality, Goal 6: Clean water and sanitation, 1 7: Affordable and clean energy, 8: Decent work and economic growth, 9: Industry, innovation and infrastructure, 10: Reduced inequalities, 11: Sustainable cities and communities, 12: Responsible consumption and production, 13: Climate action, 14: Life below water, 15: Life on land, 16: Peace, justice and strong institutions, 17: Partnerships for the Goals (UN Sustainable Development Goals 2016).

2 Swedish teenage climate activist Greta Thunberg, whose lone school strike has morphed into a global movement holding world leader to account, has been named Time Person of the Year for 2019. The US magazine, which wrote a lengthy profile of Thunberg, praised her for succeeding in "creating a global attitudinal shift,

transforming millions of vague, middle-of-the-night anxieties into a worldwide movement calling for urgent change". (www.euronews.com/2019/12/11/greta-thunberg-named-time-magazine-s-person-of-the-year-2019, retrieved on 23 July 2020)

3 "reconditioning, remanufacturing and recycling" (Gregon and Crang, 2015)

4 See also McKinsey & Company, 2018.

5 www.weforum.org/projects/circular-economy, retrieved on 01 January 2021.

6 The "blue economy" concept seeks to promote economic growth, social inclusion, and the preservation or improvement of livelihoods while at the same time ensuring environmental sustainability of the oceans and coastal areas. (World Bank Group and United Nations 2017; Gillsater 2018)

7 Manikarachchim, I (2014) Stepping up from green revolution to blue economy: a new paradigm for poverty eradication and sustainable development in South Asia, World Maritime University Dissertations. 473, Malmö, Sweden (Unpublished).

8 www.activesustainability.com/environment/effects-air-pollution-human-health/, retrieved on 23 July 2020.

9 www.activesustainability.com/environment/effects-air-pollution-human-health/ retrieved on 23 July 2020.

10 Harvard T.H. Chan School of Public Health.

References

Adrian, T. and Natalucci, F.. (2020). COVID-19 Worsens Pre-Existing Financial Vulnerabilities. IMF Blog (blog), https://blogs.imf.org/2020/05/22/covid-19-worsens-pre-existing-financial-vulnerabilities/.

Akinade, O.O. and Oyedele, L.O. (2019). Integrating construction supply chains within a circular economy: An ANFIS-based waste analytics system (A-WAS). *Journal of Cleaner Production*, 229, 863–873.

Alexander, C. & Reno, J. (Eds.) (2012). Economies of Recycling: The Global Transformation of Materials, Values and Social Relations. London: Zed Books.

Batini, N. (2019). Reaping what we sow: Smart changes to how we farm and eat can have a huge impact on our planet. *Finance and Development* (December), 30–33.

Bhatt, G. (2019). A new climate economy (Editor's letter). *Finance and Development* (December), IMF, 2.

Chami, R., Cosimano, T., Fullenkamp, C., and Oztosun, S. (2019). Nature's solution to climate change: A strategy to protect whales can limit greenhouse gases and global warming. *Finance and Development*, IMF.

Chenet, H. (2019). Climate Change and Financial Risk, ENS/X/ENSAE Working Paper. London: University College London (UCL).

Clarke, M. (2011). Development and Religion: Theology and Practice. Cheltenham: Elgar.

Cooper, T. (2005). Slower consumption: Reflections on product life spans and the "throwaway society". *Journal of Industrial Ecology* 9 (1–2): 51–67. doi: 10.1162/1088198054084671

Cooper, T. (Ed.) (2010). Longer Lasting Products: Alternatives to the Throwaway Society. London: Gower.

Costanza, R., d'Arge, R., de Groot, R., Farberk, S., Grasso, M., Hannon, B., Limburg, K., Naeem, S., O'Neill, R.V., Paruelo, J., Raskin, R.G., Suttonkk, P., & van den Belt, M. (1997). The value of the world's ecosystem services and natural capital. *Nature* 387, 253–260.

Deneulin, S. and Bano, M. (2009). Religion in Development: Rewriting the Secular Script. London: Zed Books.

Despeisse, M., Baumers, M., Brown, P., Charnley, F., Ford, S.J., Garmulewicz, A., Knowles, S., Minshall, T.H.W., Mortara, L., Reed-Tsochas, F.P., and Rowley, J. (2017). Unlocking value for a circular economy through 3D printing: A research agenda. *Technological Forecasting and Social Change* 115, 75e84. https://doi.org/10.1016/J.TECHFORE.2016.09.021.

Dorn, F., Fuest, C., Göttert, M., Krolage, C., Lautenbacher, S., Link, S., Peichl, A., Reif, M., Sauer, S., Stöckli, M., Wohlrabe, K., and Wollmershäuser, T. (2020). Die volkswirtschaftlichen Kosten des Corona-Shutdown für Deutschland: Eine Szenarienrechnung. *ifo Schnelldienst* 73(04), 29–35.

EAT-Lancet Commission (2019). Food, Health, Planet: Healthy Diets from Sustainable Food Systems. Stockholm: EAT. https://eatforum.org/content/uploads/2019/07/EAT-Lancet_Commission_Summary_Report.pdf, retrieved on 24 July 2020.

European Environment Agency (2019). The European Environment State and Outlook: Knowledge for Transition to a Sustainable Europe. Luxemburg: European Union.

EC (2018). Commission Staff Working Document accompanying the document Communication from the Commission to the European Parliament, the Council, the European Economic and Social Committee and the Committee of the Regions — A European strategy for plastics in a circular economy (SWD (2018) 16 final).

FAO (2020). Prevalence of Undernourishment (% of Population). Rome: Food and Agriculture Organization. http://data.worldbank.org/indicator/SN.ITK.DEFC.ZS

Frosch, R. & Gallopoulos, N. (1989). Strategies for manufacturing. *Scientific American* 261(3), 94–102.

Ghisellini, P., Cialani, C., and Ulgiati, S. (2016). A review on circular economy: The expected transition to a balanced interplay of environmental and economic systems. *Journal of Cleaner Production* 114, 11e32. https://doi.org/10.1016/J.JCLEPRO.2015.09.007.

Gillsater, B. (2018). The potential of the blue economy, https://blogs.worldbank.org/voices/potential-blue-economy#:~:text=The%20blue%20economy%20provides%20food,trillion%20to%20the%20world%20economy.

Gillingham, K. (2019). Carbon calculus: For deep greenhouse gas emission reductions, a long-term perspective on costs is essential. *Finance and Development,* December 2019.

Giri, A.K., van Harskamp, A., and Salemink, O. (eds) (2004). The Development of Religion, the Religion of Development. Delft: Eburon.

Gregon, N. and Crang, M. (2015). Interrogating the circular economy: The moral economy of resource recovery in the EU. *Economy and Society* 44(2).

Georgescu-Roegen, N. (1971). The Entropy Law and the Economic Process. Cambridge, MA: Harvard University Press.

IFPRI (2020). Preventing Global Food Security Crisis Under COVID-19 Emergency. Washington, DC: International Food Policy Research Institute.

Intergovernmental Panel of Climate Change (2019). Special Report on Climate Change, www.ipcc.ch/site/assets/uploads/2019/08/Fullreport-1.pdf, retrieved on 24 July 2020.

Intergovernmental Science-Policy Platform on Biodiversity and Ecosystem Services (IPBES) (2019). Global Assessment Report on Biodiversity and Ecosystem Services, IPBES Bonn, Germany.

International Labour Organization (2020). Global Employment Trends for Youth 2020: Technology and the Future of Jobs. Geneva: International Labour Office.

Irwin, D. and Klenow, P. (1994). Learning-by-doing spillovers in the semiconductor industry. *Journal of Political Economy* 102(6), 1200–1227.

Kampa, M. and Castanas, E. (2007). Human health effects of air pollution. *Environmental Pollution*, 151(2), 362–367.

Kauffman, E. (2010). Shall the Religious Inherit the Earth? Demography and Politics in the Twenty-First Century. London: Profile.

Kinsley, D. (1995), *Ecology and Religion: Ecological Spirituality in Cross-Cultural Perspective*. Prentice Hall, Englewood Cliffs, NJ.

Kopf, D. (2020). Traffic collisions are plummeting in several US cities. Quartz, 24 March 2020. https://qz.com/1822492/trafficaccidents- are-plummeting-because-of-the-pandemic/.

McKinsey & Company (2018). Decarbonization of industrial sectors: The next frontier, Amsterdam (www.mckinsey.com/business-functions/sustainability/our-insights/howindustry-can-move-toward-a-low-carbon-future), accessed 22 November 2018.

Narayanan, Y. (2013). Religion and sustainable development: Analysing the connections. *Sustainable Development* 21, 131–139.

Parry, I. (2019). Putting a Price on Pollution: Carbon-Pricing Strategies Could Hold the Key to Meeting the World's Climate Stabilization Goals. Washington, DC: Finance and Development, IMF.

Rakodi, C. (2012). A framework for analysing the links between religion and development. *Development in Practice* 22(5/6), 634–650.

Roman, J., Estes, J., Morissette, L., Smith, C., Costa, D., McCarthy, J., Nation, J.B., Nicol, S., Pershing, A., and Smetacek, V. (2014). Whales as marine ecosystem engineers. *Frontiers in Ecology and the Environment* 12(7), 377–385.

Sachs, J., Schmidt-Traub, G., Mazzucato, M., Messner, D., Nakicenovic, N., and Rockström, J. (2019). Six transformations to achieve the sustainable development goals. *Nature Sustainability* 2(9), 805–814. https://doi.org/10.1038/s41893-019-0352-9

Sachs, J., Schmidt-Traub, G., Kroll, C., Lafortune, G., Fuller, G., and Woelm, F. (2020). The Sustainable Development Goals and COVID-19. Sustainable Development Report 2020. Cambridge: Cambridge University Press.

Sfeir-Younis, A. (2001). The Spiritual Imperatives of This Millennium: Healing Humanity. www.worldpeacecongress.net/en/2004/speakers/alfredo.html [accessed 25 July 2012].

Singh, K. and Clark, J.S. (2016). Voices from Religions on Sustainable Development, German Federal Ministry for Economic Cooperation and Development (BMZ), Division 111: Churches; political foundations; social structural programmes; religion and development, Bonn, Germany.

Synod of Western Australia (2001, p. 4, para. 2). Social Justice Commission: Draft Synod Proposal on Environmental Issues. www.sustainability.dpc.wa.gov.au/docs/BGPpapers/Ethics%20papers/UnitingChurch2.pdf [accessed 12 March 2012].
Tomalin, E. (2012). Thinking about faith-based organisations in development: Where have we got to and what next? *Development in Practice* 22(5/6), 689–703.
Trichopoulou, A. (2009) Hector — Healthy Eating Out. Eating Out: Habits, Determinants, and Recommendations for Consumers and the Catering Sector. Final Report to the European Commission, National and Kapodistrian University of Athens, Greece.
UN (2016). The Sustainable Development Goals Report 2016
van Dorn, A., Cooney, R.E., and Sabin, M.L. (2020). COVID-19 exacerbating inequalities in the US. *Lancet*, 395 (10232), 1243–1244.
Watson, S.R., McCarthy, J. J., Canziani, P., Nakicenovic, N., and Hisas, L. (2019). The Truth Behind the Climate Pledges. Buenos Aires, Argentina, The Universal Ecological Fund.
Willett, W., Rockström, J., Loken, B., and others. (2019). Food in the Anthropocene: The EAT-Lancet Commission on healthy diets from sustainable food systems. *Lancet* 393(10170), 447–492.
World Bank (2015). What are Green Bonds? Washington, DC : The World Bank, NW.
World Bank Group and United Nations (2017). The Potential of the Blue Economy, Increasing Long-term Benefits of the Sustainable Use of Marine Resources for Small Island Developing States and Coastal Least Developed Countries. Washington, DC: International Bank for Reconstruction and Development.
World Economic Forum, From the Margins to the Mainstream Assessment of the Impact Investment Sector and Opportunities to Engage Mainstream Investors (A report by the World Economic Forum Investors Industries Prepared in collaboration with Deloitte Touche Tohmatsu). Geneva, Switzerland: World Economic Forum.

Part I

THEORETICAL FOUNDATIONS

2

SUSTAINABILITY PRINCIPLES AND TRIPLE BOTTOM LINE PERFORMANCE IN SUPPLY CHAINS

Robert Francis Dahlstrom

A supply chain refers to the set of organizations linked directly to the flow of products from a source to the consumer. At each step in the chain, marketers attend to the economic, social and ecological constraints. Standards for achieving economic and social returns are well established in marketing (Stern and Reve 1980), yet the role of the physical environment has historically received less attention in research.

Political-economy approaches to supply-chain management provide the basis for theoretical developments (Arndt 1983). Many enhancements to the knowledge of distribution channels – including perspectives on long-term buyer–seller relationships (Dwyer, Schurr, and Oh 1987; Palamatier, Dant, and Grewal 2007), interfirm governance (Heide 1994), market orientation (Gebhardt, Carpenter, and Sherry 2006), environmental orientation (Banerjee, Iyer, and Kashyap 2003), and the institutional environment (Grewal *et al.* 2018; Gundlach 1994) – draw from the political economy paradigm.

Prior research recognizes the importance of the marketing context (Achrol, Reve and Stern 1983), yet it does not consider macro-environmental conditions that influence dynamism, opportunism and organizational outcomes. Market dynamism clearly influences organizational productivity, yet the dynamics of the physical environment increasingly influence organizational outcomes. Similarly, volatility in the availability of scarce physical resources (e.g., oil) influences the level of interfirm monitoring. Large channel participants such as Walmart have increased the level of monitoring of their suppliers (Jiang 2009). Field studies increasingly encounter ecological issues that influence the flow of products to consumers, yet extant distribution theory does not sufficiently address these environmental concerns. Socio-political and economic activity operate as a subset of the ecosystem (Robèrt *et al.* 1997), yet influences of exchange activity on the ecosystem have received limited attention (Mendleson and Polonsky 1995).

Clos, Speier, and Meacham (2011) examine external forces that shape the environment and provide rich insight into the interaction between strategy and the firm's physical context (Connelly, Ketchen, and Slater 2011). This line of research recognizes that political and economic factors influence a firm's orientation to the environment, but ecological theory is not central to these studies. Hult (2011a) similarly recognizes that a firm achieves market-based sustainability by aligning itself with stakeholders concerned about economic, social and environmental conditions. Prior research recognizes the role of the environment, but treatment of ecological concerns focuses on organizational (e.g., Pfeffer and Salancik 1978), economic (e.g., Williamson 1985) and social (Jones, Hesterly, and Borgatti 1997) theory. Ecologically oriented research (Vitousek 1994) provides insight into channel strategy, but ecology (e.g., Kassarjian 1971) has rarely been incorporated into analyses of channel decision-making.

In this chapter, we outline guiding principles designed to enhance interaction with the physical environment (Robèrt 1997). These principles incorporate triple bottom line logic (Elkington 1997) associated with relational, economic and ecological dimensions of exchange. We briefly review environmental issues associated with climate change and outline some implications for distribution systems. We examine the pursuit of sustainability and provide a number of principles relevant to the pursuit of sustainably oriented practice.

2.1 Environmental issues

Climate change refers to a change in the state of the climate identifiable by changes in the mean or the variability of its properties that persists for an extended period (Intergovernmental Panel on Climate Change 2017). Climate change yields critical consequences for distribution channels.

Higher temperatures and increased risk. The climate takes time to respond to greenhouse gas emissions, and the actual period of time can take decades. The result of these effects is higher temperatures for long periods after stabilization of greenhouse gases.

Rising temperatures complicate multiple aspects of supply chains. Modifications in the seasonal patterns make it more difficult to predict crop yields and maturity dates (Hoogenboom 2000), and they also constrain habitat for humans and other living things. For example, increases in sea surface temperature contribute to destruction of coral reefs that provide habitat for fish important to the food supply (Hoegh-Guldberg *et al.* 2007).

Decline in the quantity and quality of freshwater. Population growth, migration to urban areas, rising wealth and resource consumption and climate change influence the quantity and quality of freshwater (Vörösmarty *et al.* 2000). One-sixth of the world's population do not have access to clean drinking water whereas two-fifths of the world population lack access to adequate sanitation services (Brundtland and Bellamy 2000). Thirty-six US states face water supply problems and global temperature is threatening to reduce the California water supply by 25% (Rogers and Leal 2010).

Decline in freshwater availability has a number of influences on the distribution channels. The cost of water necessarily increases and scrutiny over the use of freshwater simultaneously increases. For example, Pepsi and Coca-Cola have encountered criticism in India concerning the amount of water and consumption methods associated with beverage processing (Brady 2007). Habitat for freshwater fish is also imperiled by declines in freshwater. Oxygen solubility decreases with rising temperatures, yet fish metabolic rates simultaneously increase. Heightened demand and reduced availability of oxygen shift geographic regions for fish and contribute to extirpation of local species. Changes in habitat limit the availability of an inexpensive source of protein and a revenue source in emerging economies. In industrialized countries, changes in freshwater habitat limit recreational opportunities and the associated revenue and employment they generate (Ficke, Myrick, and Hansen 2005). Freshwater declines also limit the feasibility of a body of water to support transportation and maritime employment.

Increased health risk. The World Health Organization estimates that anthropogenic climate change claims over 150,000 lives annually (Patz *et al.* 2005). Many prevalent human diseases – including cardiovascular mortality, respiratory illnesses, infectious diseases and malnutrition – are linked to climate fluctuations. Heightened levels of disease demand distribution systems that enable humans to respond to stress. For example, malnutrition levels can be reduced via channels that enhance the physical and economic access to food (El-Ansary 1986).

Rising sea levels. Climate change associated with higher temperatures is resulting in higher sea levels. Evidence indicates that changes in the Antarctic and Greenland ice sheets are contributing to rising sea levels (Etteman *et al.* 2009; Zwally *et al.* 2005). Meteorological research indicates that the global average sea level will continue to rise throughout the 21st century (Church *et al.* 2011). Rising sea levels influence substantial populations given that 20 of 30 global mega-cities are threatened by rising sea levels (Nicholls 1995).

Rising sea levels require investments at multiple levels of distribution channels (Church *et al.* 2008). Building codes and infrastructure policies should be revised to ensure that structures and roadways to cope with erosion and flooding.

Threats to biodiversity. Biodiversity refers to the animal and plant life within an ecosystem. Increases in average temperatures are associated with increasing levels of species extinction such that 20–30% of species face an increased risk of extinction (Thomas *et al.* 2004). This trend is attributed to shifts in vegetation zones, shifts in ranges of individual species, interaction between climate change and habitat fragmentation, and changes in ecosystem functioning (Kappelle, Van Vuuren, and Baas 1998). Increased species extinction is likely across regions on the planet.

Reductions in biodiversity have significant implications for distribution because plant and animal species provide provisional, regulatory and supportive, and cultural services to an ecosystem. Provisional services refer to the supply of food, fuel or fiber made available for consumption in an ecosystem. For example, the first sale value of the 2008 world fish catch exceeded $93 billion (Food and Agriculture Organization of the United Nations 2010). Regulatory services control interaction between factors in an ecosystem. For example, wild bee pollination of US agricultural products is a regulatory service whose value is estimated at over $3 billion annually (Losey and Vaughan 2006). Supporting services maintain the conditions for life on Earth and include soil formation, soil protection, nutrient cycling and water cycling. Cultural services refer to the spiritual, recreational and aesthetic benefits afforded to an ecosystem through biodiversity. For instance, coral reefs provide fisheries and tourism value estimated at $30 billion (United Nations Environment Programme 2006).

Each of these consequences of climate change complicates efforts to ease the flow of goods and services to consumers. Exposure to climate change is greatest among the poor and those with limited resources to invest in mitigating and preventing effects of climate change. In addition, the effects of climate change are realized most noticeably in Arctic and tropical settings. Changes in climate have potential to force departures from the Arctic climates due to lack of biodiversity and habitat degradation. Simultaneously, climate change may force departures from tropical areas where inhabitants live just above sea level. These trends lead to increased displacement and higher numbers of refugees (Esty and Winston 2006).

Climate change also has several direct influences on distribution channels. Manager must be cognizant of the effects on transportation, petroleum, agriculture and insurance (Esty and Winston 2006). As climate change increases, governments are more actively seeking to control greenhouse gas emissions (Stavins 2003, 2008). Industries that have heavy transportation needs (e.g., retailing) consequently face higher costs of operations, and industries that use petroleum-related raw materials (e.g., plastics production) face greater operating costs (Barboza 2008). Rising and volatile weather patterns adversely affect the agricultural sector and complicate efforts to speculate on future values of agricultural-based commodities (e.g., frozen orange juice) (Trostle 2008). Climate-related volatility also complicates the insurance industry. As the costs associated with underwriting policies become more difficult to assess, costs increase and the number of providers decreases (Botzen and Van Den Bergh 2008).

Despite these critical changes in business operations, climate change presents enormous opportunities for entrepreneurs that develop technologies, services and products. Consumer demand for products that reduce energy costs or eliminate the need to rely on carbon-based fuels will receive greater attention. Moreover, organizations are inclined to make investments that raise prospects for environmental as well as economic returns.

2.2 Sustainably oriented principles

In 1987, the United Nations published research on the development and the environment that characterized sustainable development as efforts to meet the needs of the present without compromising the ability of future generations to meet their needs (Brundtland 1987). Importantly, this edict recognizes that there are at any time limits on the ability of the biosphere to absorb human activity. This definition provides tremendous breadth for interpretation but does not offer specific guidelines by which to enhance sustainability (Hult 2011a). The recognition of the environmental realities previously outlined has led researchers operating in physical sciences, medicine and social sciences to work together towards developing a sustainable society. *The Natural Step* (TNS) is one notable eclectic perspective developed initially by oncologist Karl-Henrik Robèrt (1997) and colleagues in Sweden. This approach seeks to offer a proactive approach to the environment. The goal of the project is to develop a society in which the resources are not consumed faster that they can be replaced.

The guiding principles of TNS are grounded in scientific principles in the laws of thermodynamics and fundamental conservation laws. Based on these scientific principles, TNS offers four guiding principles required for sustainability and action designed to enhance sustainability. Since observation of the need for sustainability emerges from recognition of unsustainability, the guiding principles are cast as channel conditions that must be avoided. Consider four guiding principles in turn:

> System Condition 1: Substances extracted from the Earth's crust by a supply chain must not systematically increase in the biosphere.

The first system condition addresses the mining and extraction of fossil fuels, minerals and metals. To the extent that the extraction of these materials is greater than the re-disposition and reintegration, the concentration of these materials increases in the atmosphere and ecosphere. Since nature cannot sustain systematic increases of any substance, every molecule extracted from the Earth's crust must end up somewhere (Robèrt 2002). For example, cadmium is a metal used in rechargeable batteries and metal plating. Research provides evidence of a causal link between this metal and bone disease and kidney dysfunction (Hood 2002). As the concentration of cadmium increases, the threat to humans and animals increases.

This first guiding principle has upstream and downstream implications for distribution channels. The upstream challenge is to reduce the use of fossil fuels, mined materials and other elements accumulating in the ecosphere (Robèrt *et al.* 1997). By reducing the need for an element, the long-term accumulation of the element should decrease. For example, researchers in the aerospace industry have developed aluminum–molybdenum-based platings that offer non-toxic alternatives to cadmium (Bielawski 2004). Manufacturers, retailer, consumers and all other members of the channel should examine whether they can reduce their reliance on elements extracted from the lithosphere. Importantly, the development of alternative means to achieve the same ends should attempt to limit overall levels of element extraction rather than the mere replacement of one substance for another. Thus, solutions to energy needs should focus on net reductions of resources employed and their adverse effects on the environment.

Reductions in the amount of fossil fuels and mined materials should be accompanied by efforts to consider the utility of products that no longer offer value to consumers. For example, recycling centers enable users to recycle cadmium rather than dispose of it through incineration or placement in a landfill. Increased recycling reduces the seepage of this hazardous chemical from landfills and reduces the harmful airborne components released during incineration (Plachy 2003). In addition, recycling also saves energy associated with processing of new materials. Metallurgists have reported that recycling of batteries is about 50% more energy efficient. Since less fuel is consumed in the production process, the environment benefits from lower levels of air pollution (Plachy 2003).

System Condition 2: Substances produced by a supply chain must not systematically increase in the biosphere.

Human-produced substances abound in society, but their production and dispersion should not exceed the pace at which they decay and are integrated back into natural cycles or the Earth's crust. When substances developed in society reach critical thresholds, they can have dramatic influences on the ecosphere. Benzene, for example, is an organic compound formed from natural processes and human activity (Turton *et al.* 1998). Benzene is used in the lubricant, insecticide and paint remover industries (Wallace 1996), and heavy exposure results in anemia, leukemia, bone marrow degeneration and dysfunction of the immune system (Yardley-Jones, Anderson, and Parker 1991; Ghittori *et al.* 1995). Benzene not only produces adverse effects via its distribution, but it also contributes to particulate pollution via soot generation (Zhang *et al.* 2009). The benzene example underscores the need for managers to assess the upstream effects of the production and the downstream effects throughout the supply chain. Organization must assess the extent to which they are economically dependent on these substances. Benzene, for instance, is critical to the production of pharmaceuticals and plastics. Organizations reliant on these products need to consider the costs and merits of benzene relative to alternative chemicals.

System Condition 3: The biodiversity and productivity on the Earth must not be physically deteriorated by the activities of a supply chain.

System Condition 3 recognizes that natural resources have finite limits, and ecosystems should not be manipulated in ways that deteriorate productive capacity and diversity. Numerous flora and fauna species have been declining and recent analyses indicate continuing declines for vertebrates, forest-based plant life, mangroves, seagrass beds and coral reefs (Butchart 2011). Human health and prosperity rely on nature to restructure waste and re-concentrate resources to valued levels. For example, inadequate access to safe freshwater results in habitat loss (Bond, Lake, and Arthington 2008), and contributes to malnutrition, poverty, waterborne disease, economic and political instability, and conflict within and between countries (Levy and Sidel 2011). Action undertaken that limits the productivity of the environment ultimately leads to limited productivity for humans. When the ability of nature to renew resources is compromised, it leads to less stability in the ecosphere and the markets that operate within it.

The implication of this principle is the need for conservation of resources. The productivity of fertile areas, the quality of soil and the availability of freshwater should be monitored. For example, soft-drink producers facing scrutiny over water usage must address complaints about the drying up of some wells, the contamination of other wells and increases in calcium and magnesium associated with operations (Ghoshray 2006-2007). The fertileness of the ecosphere also relies on maintaining levels of biodiversity and therefore warrants consideration of the potential for deterioration associated with overharvesting, mismanagement or displacement. For example, many species of plants and animals in the rainforests of Borneo have been threatened by logging and land conversion (Curran *et al.* 2004). Preservation of the ecological integrity of endangered areas requires that managers assess the extent to which their operations rely upon provisional, regulatory and supportive, and cultural services.

System Condition 4: The needs of humans must be met with efficient and fair use of energy and other resources within a supply chain.

System Conditions 1–3 underscore the need to use resources efficiently and preserve biodiversity. By contrast, System Condition 4 emphasizes that the basic needs of humans must be met. This task is considerable given the current shortfalls with respect to hunger, water, healthcare and energy consumption. In each of these areas, changes in distribution practices can enhance human living conditions. The Food and Agriculture Organization of the United Nations (2011) reports that 850 million people (roughly 13% of the world population) are undernourished. The Food and Agriculture Organization of the United Nations estimates that 1.3 billion tons of food are lost or wasted globally each year, and most of this waste is in developing countries. Distribution systems with improved methods of post-harvest management and enhanced logistical systems increase the amount of food available in these markets.

The lack of access to clean water and sanitary services is also problematic. Water deficiencies result in more than two million deaths per year, yet investments in distribution systems that regulate provision and reclamation raise the availability of water (Rogers and Leal 2010). In the agricultural sector – the largest user of water – investments in center pivot irrigation systems provide water efficiently and flexibly to thousands of acres of farmland (Kincaid 2005). The recycling of wastewater yields clean water to communities at relatively low economic cost and reduced pollution of oceans, lakes and rivers. Similarly, condominial-based sewage systems provide sanitary services with lower excavation and maintenance costs relative to conventional systems (Melo 2005). These systems have great potential to increase access to sanitary facilities in emerging markets. Removal of fats, oils and greases from water systems can eliminate up to 47% of sewer system blockages in the United States, yielding fewer sewer overflows, improved operations and better customer service (U.S. Environmental Protection Agency 2007).

World Health Organization data on child mortality illustrate the opportunities to enhance distribution systems to enhance living conditions. In 2009, the global number of deaths of children under 5 years old was 8.1 million (World Health Organization 2011). Pneumonia and diarrhea are two of the biggest killers of children, accounting for 18% and 15% of all deaths, respectively, in 2008. Enhanced distribution systems that increase access to oral hydration therapy and zinc enable physicians to treat diarrhea, and distribution systems that increase access to antibiotics enable doctors to treat pneumonia. The World Health Organization (2011) estimates that most child deaths due to pneumonia could be avoided if interventions were implemented on a broad scale to the most vulnerable populations.

Current data on energy consumption indicate significant disparities among countries (Hertwich and Peters 2009). At the extremes, Malawi, Bangladesh, Mozambique and Uganda have average per-capita carbon footprints of 1.1 ton per year or less whereas carbon footprints in Hong Kong, USA and Luxembourg exceed 28 tons per capita per year. Distribution can directly influence greenhouse gas emissions associated with households and transportation which account for nearly 21% and 25% of emissions, respectively (International Energy Agency 2008). Supply chains that trace raw materials from farmers to food manufacturing provide a basis for ensuring environmental performance (Hamprecht *et al.* 2005). Similarly, managers of distribution systems can influence personal transportation costs via retail location analyses (Huff 1968).

2.3 Implications for research

Organizational theory provides another approach to analysis of the channel design and the natural environment. Zucker (1986), for instance, distinguishes between characteristic-based trust tied to the person and institutional-based trust tied to formal societal structures. As the challenges associated with assessing desirable outcomes becomes more appreciable, monitoring costs become more formidable (Ouchi 1980). An efficient alternative to monitoring is an investment in developing characteristic-based trust (Moorman, Zaltman, and Deshpandé 1992). Firms that recognize appreciable challenges associated with the supervision of sustainability efforts may forego these efforts and elect to nurture personal trust with partners in the distribution channel.

In contrast to characteristic-based trust, institutional trust focuses on the social structures that safeguard transactions. Law, regulation and professional credentials exemplify some ways to establish institutional-based trust (Zucker 1987). In the sustainability context, institutional trust is manifest through certification and standardization. The company can indicate sustainability via ISO 14001 (health, environment, safety regulations), ISO 14020-14025 (certifications and declarations), ISO 14040 (lifecycle analyzes), ISO 14067 (standards of carbon footprint) and ISO 14045 (water) standards. Zucker's (1986) perspective on the development of trust indicates that various forms of trust can serve as substitutes for one another (Dahlstrom and Nygaard 1995). Organizations that invest in institutional mechanisms to ensure sustainability require lower investments in internal governance structures.

2.4 Conclusions

The goal of this chapter has been to outline sustainability-based principles and their potential to enhance triple bottom line performance in marketing supply chains. Logic from the natural step (Robèrt 1997) provides the basis for a triple bottom line perspective that augments traditional approaches with consideration of the natural environment. Increasing temperatures, waning freshwater levels, rising sea levels and declining biodiversity levels are emerging concerns that prompt the need to incorporate environmental factors into strategic decision-making.

References

Achrol, R.S., Reve, T., & Stern, L.W. (1983). The environment of marketing channel dyads: A framework for comparative analysis. *Journal of Marketing* 47, 55–67.

Arndt, J. (1983). The political economy paradigm: Foundation for theory building in marketing. *Journal of Marketing* 47, 44–54.

Banerjee, S.B., Iyer, E.S., and Kashyap, R.K. (2003). Corporate environmentalism: Antecedents and influence of industry type. *Journal of Marketing* 67, 106–122.

Barboza, D. (2008). China's inflation hits American price tags. *The New York Times* (February 1).

Bielawski, M. (2004). Development of unbalanced magnetron sputtered Al–Mo coatings for cadmium replacement. *Surface and Coatings Technology* 179, 10–17.

Bond, N.R., Lake, P.S., & Arthington, A.H. (2008). The impacts of drought on freshwater ecosystems: An Australian perspective. *Hydrobiologia* 600, 1–3.

Botzen, W.J.W. & Van Den Bergh, J.C.J.M. (2008). Insurance against climate change and flooding in the Netherlands: Present, future, and comparison with other countries. *Risk Analysis* 28, 413–426.

Brady, D. (2007). Pepsi: Repairing a poisoned reputation in India. *Business Week* (June 11), 46.

Brundtland, G. (1987). Our Common Future: The World Commission on Environment and Development. New York: Oxford University Press.

Brundtland, G. & Bellamy, C. (2001). Global Water Supply and Sanitation Assessment Report 2000. Retrieved 20 October 2011 from www.who.int/water_sanitation_health/monitoring/jmp2000.pdf.

Butchart, S.H.M., Walpole, M., Collen, B., van Strien, A., Scharlemann, J.P.W., Almond, R.E.A., Baillie, J.E.M., Bomhard, B., Brown, C., Bruno, J., Carpenter, K.E., M. Carr, G.M., Chanson, J., Chenery, A.M. Csirke, J., Davidson, N.C., Dentener, F., Foster, M., Galli, A., Galloway, J.N., Genovesi, P., Gregory, R.D., Hockings, M., Kapos, V., Lamarque, J.F., Leverington, F., Loh, J., McGeoch, M.A., McRae, L., Minasyan, M., Morcillo, M.H., Oldfield, T.E.E., Pauly, D., Suhel Quader, S., Revenga, C., Sauer, J.R., Skolnik, B., Spear, D., Stanwell-Smith, D., Stuart, S.N., Symes, A., Tierney, M., Tyrrell, T.D., Vié, J.C., & Watson, R. (2011). Global biodiversity: Indicators of recent decline. *Science* 328, 1164–1168.

Church, J.A., White, N.J., Aarup, A., Wilson, W.S., Woodworth, P.L., Domingues, C.M., Hunter, J.R., & Lambeck, K. (2008). Understanding global sea levels: Past, present and future. *Sustainable Science* 3, 9–22.

Church, J., Gregory, J.M., White, N., Platten, S.M., & Jerry Mitrovica, J. (2011). Understanding and projecting sea level change. *Oceanography* 24, 130–143.

Closs, D., Speier, C., & Meacham, N. (2011). Sustainability to support end-to-end value chains: the role of supply chain management. *Journal of the Academy of Marketing Science* 39(1), 101–116.

Connelly, B., Ketchen, D., & Slater, S. (2011). Toward a "theoretical toolbox" for sustainability research in marketing. *Journal of the Academy of Marketing Science* 39(1), 86–100.

Curran, L.M.,Trigg, S.N., McD onald, A.K., Astiani, D., Hardiono, Y.M., Siregar, P., Caniago, I., & Kasischke, E. (2004). Lowland forest loss in protected areas of Indonesian Borneo. *Science* 303, 1000–1003.

Dahlstrom, R. & Nygaard, A. (1995). An exploratory investigation of interpersonal trust in new and mature market economies. *Journal of Retailing* 71, 339–361.

Dwyer, F.R., Schurr, P.H., & Oh, S. (1987). Developing buyer-seller relationships. *Journal of Marketing* 51, 11–28.

El-Ansary, A.I. (1986). How better systems could feed the world. *International Marketing Review* 3, 39–49.

Elkington, J. (1997). Cannibals with Forks, Gabriella Island, BC: New Society Publishers.

Esty, D. C.&Winston, A. W. (2006). Green to Gold. New Haven, CT: Yale University Press.

Ettema, J., van den Broeke, M.R.,van Meijgaard, E., van de Berg, W.J., Bamber, J.L., Box, J.E., & Bales, R.C. (2009). Higher surface mass balance of the Greenland ice sheet revealed by high-resolution climate modeling. *Geophysical Research Letters* 36, L12501.

Ficke, A.A., Myrick, C.A. & Hansen, L. (2005). Potential Impacts of Global Climate Change on Freshwater Fisheries. Gland, Switzerland: WWF-World Wide Fund for Nature.

Food & Agriculture Organization of the United Nations (2010). The State of the World's Fisheries and Aquaculture. Rome, Italy: Food and Agriculture Organization of the United Nations.

Food and Agriculture Organization of the United Nations (2011). The State of Food Insecurity in the World. Retrieved 21 October 2011 from www.fao.org/docrep/014/i2330e/i2330e.pdf.

Gebhardt, G.F., Carpenter, G.S., and Sherry, Jr., J.F. (2006). Creating a market orientation: A longitudinal, multifirm, grounded analysis of cultural transformation. *Journal of Marketing* 70, 37–55.

Ghittori, S., Maestri, L., Fiorentino, M.L., & Imbriani, M. (1995). Evaluation of occupational exposure to benzene by urinalysis. *International Archives of Occupational and Environmental Health* 67, 195–200.

Ghoshray, S. (2006-2007). Searching for human rights to water amidst corporate privatization in India: Hindustan Coca-Cola Pvt. Ltd. v. Perumatty Grama Panchayat. *Georgetown International Environmental Law Review* 19, 643–672.

Grewal, R., Saini, A., Kumar, A., Dwyer, F.R., and Dahlstrom, R. (2018). Marketing channel management in foreign markets: Integrative framework for multinational corporations. *Journal of Marketing* 82 (4), 49–69.

Gundlach, G.T. (1994). Exchange governance: The role of legal and nonlegal approaches across the exchange process. *Journal of Public Policy and Marketing* 13, 246–258.

Hamprecht, J., Corsten, D., Noll, M., & Meier, E. (2005). Controlling the sustainability of food supply chains. *Supply Chain Management* 10, 7–10.

Heide, J.B. (1994). Interorganizational governance in marketing channels. *Journal of Marketing* 58, 71–85.

Heide, J.B., Wathne, K.H., & Rokkan, A.I. (1999). Interfirm Monitoring, social contracts, and relationship outcomes. *Journal of Marketing Research* 54, 425–433.

Hoegh-Guldberg, O., Mumby, P.J., Hooten, A.J., Steneck, R.S., Greenfield, P., Gomez, E., Harvell, C.D., Sale, P.F., Edwards, A.J., Caldeira, K., Knowlton, N., Eakin, C.M., Iglesias-Prieto, R., Muthiga, N., Bradbury, R.H., Dubi, A., & Hatziolos, M.E. (2007). Coral reefs under rapid climate change and ocean acidification. *Science* 318, 1737–1742.

Hertwich, E.G. and Peters, G.P. (2009). Carbon footprint of nations: A global, trade-linked analysis. *Analysis Environmental Science and Technology* 43, 6414–6420.

Hood, E. (2002). A causal connection. *Environmental Health Perspectives* 110, A413.

Hoogenboom, G. (2000). Contribution of agrometeorology to the simulation of crop production and its applications. *Agricultural and Forest Meteorology* 103, 137–157.

Huff, D.L. (1968). A programmed solution for approximating an optimum retail location. *Land Economics* 42, 293–303.

Hult, G.T.M. (2011). Market-focused sustainability: Market orientation plus! *Journal of the Academy of Marketing Science* 39, 1–6.

Intergovernmental Panel on Climate Change (2007). *Climate change 2007: Synthesis report. Contribution of working groups I, II and III to the fourth assessment report of the intergovernmental panel on climate change* [Core Writing Team, Pachauri, R.K. & Reisinger, A. (eds.)]. Geneva, Switzerland: IPCC.

International Energy Agency (2008). Worldwide Trends in Energy Use and Efficiency. Paris: International Energy Agency.

Jiang, B. (2009). The effects of interorganizational governance on supplier's compliance with SCC: An empirical examination of compliant and non-compliant suppliers. *Journal of Operations Management* 27, 267–280.

Jones, C., Hesterly, W.S., and Borgatti, S.P. (1997). A general theory of network governance: Exchange conditions and social mechanisms. *Academy of Management Review* 22(4), 911–945.

Kappelle, M.,Van Vuuren, M.M.I., and Baas, P. (1998). Effects of climate change on biodiversity: A review and identification of key research issues. *Biodiversity and Conservation* 8, 1383–1397.

Kassarjian, H.H. (1971). Incorporating ecology into marketing strategy: The case of air pollution. *Journal of Marketing* 35(3), 61–65.

Kincaid, D. C. (2005). Application rates from center pivot irrigation with current sprinkler types. *Applied Engineering in Agriculture* 21, 605−610.

Levy, B.S. and Sidel, V.W. (2011). Water rights and water fights: Preventing and resolving conflicts before they boil over. *American Journal of Public Health* 101, 778–780.

Losey, J.E. & Vaughan, M. (2006). The economic value of ecological services provided by insects. *BioScience* 56, 311–323.

Melo, J.C. (2005). The Experience of Condominial Water and Sewerage Systems in Brazil. Retrieved 25 October 2011 from www.wsp.org/wsp/sites/wsp.org/files/publications/BrasilFinal2.pdf.

Mendleson, N. & Polonsky, M.J. (1995). Using strategic alliances to develop credible green marketing. *Journal of Consumer Marketing* 12, 4–18.

Moorman, C., Zaltman, G., & Deshpandé, R. (1992). Relationships between providers and users of market research: The dynamics of trust within and between organizations. *Journal of Marketing Research* 29, 314–329.

Nicholls, R.J. (1995). Coastal megacities and climate change. *GeoJournal* 37, 369–379.

Ouchi, W.G. (1080). Markets, bureaucracies, and clans. *Administrative Science Quarterly* 25, 129–141.

Palmatier, R.W., Dant, R.P., & Grewal, D. (2007). A comparative longitudinal analysis of theoretical perspectives of interorganizational relationship performance. *Journal of Marketing* 71, 172–194.

Patz, J.A., Campbell-Lendrum, D., Holloway, T., & Foley, J.A. (2005). Impact of regional climate change on human health. *Nature* 438, 310–317.

Pfeffer, J., & Salancik, G. (1978). The External Control of Organizations. New York: Harper & Row.

Plachy, J. (2000). Cadmium Recycling in the United States in 2000. U.S. Geological Survey Circular1196–O. Reston: U.S. Geological Survey.

Robèrt, K.H. (1997). The Natural Step: A Framework for Achieving Sustainability in Our Organizations. Cambridge, MA: Pegasus Communication.

Robèrt, K.H. (2002). The Natural Step Story: Seeding a Quiet Revolution. Gabriola Island, BC: New Catalyst Books.

Robèrt, K-H., Daly, H., Hawken, P., & Holmberg, J. (1997). A compass for sustainable development. *International Journal of Sustainable Development and World Ecology* 4, 79–92.

Rogers, P. & Leal, S. (2010). Running Out of Water. New York: Palgrave Macmillan.

Stavins, R. N. (2003). Experience with market-based environmental policy instruments. In Maler, K.-G. & Vincent, J. (eds.), Handbook of Environmental Economics, vol. I. Elsevier Science: Amsterdam, pp. 355–435.

Stavins, R.N. (2008). Addressing climate change with a comprehensive US cap-and-trade system. *Oxford Review of Economic Policy* 24, 298–321.

Stern, L.W. & Reve, T. (1980). Distribution channels as political economies: A framework for comparative analysis. *Journal of Marketing* 44, 52–64.

Thomas, C.D., Cameron, A., Green, R.E., Bakkenes, M., Beaumont, L.J., Collingham, Y.C., Erasmus, B.F.N., Ferreira de Siqueira, M., Grainger, A., Hannah, L., Hughes, L., Brian Huntley, B., van Jaarsveld, A.S., Midgley, G. F., Miles, L., Ortega-Huerta, M.A., Peterson, A.T., Phillips, O.L. & Williams, S.E. (2004). Extinction risk from climate change. *Nature* 427, 145–148.

Trostle, R. (2008). Global Agricultural Supply and Demand: Factors Contributing to Recent Increases in Food Commodity Prices. Retrieved 2 November 2011 from www.ers.usda.gov/Publications/WRS0801/.

Turton, R., Bailie, R.C., Whiting, W.B., & Shaeiwitz, J.A. (1998). Analysis, Synthesis, and Design of Chemical Processes. Old Tappan, NJ: Prentice Hall.

United Nations Environmental Programme (2011). IEA Training Manual - Module 5. Retrieved 2 November 2011 from www.unep.org/IEACP/iea/training/manual/module5/1212.aspx.

United States Environmental Protection Agency (2007). Controlling Fats, Oils, and Grease Discharges from Food Service Establishments. Retrieved 25 October 2018 from www.epa.gov/npdes/pubs/pretreatment_foodservice_fs.pdf.

Vitousek, P.M. (1994). Beyond global warming: Ecology and climate change. *Ecology* 75, 1861–1876.

Vörösmary, C.J., Green, G., Salisbury, J., & Lammers, R. (2000). Global water resources: Vulnerability from climate change and population growth. *Science* 289, 284–288.

Wallace, L. (1996). Environmental exposure to benzene: An update. *Environmental Health Perspectives* 104, 1129–1136.

Williamson, O.E. (1985). The Economic Institutions of Capitalism. New York: Free Press.

World Health Organization (2003). The Health Impacts of 2003 Summer Heatwaves. Briefing Note for the 53rd Session of the World Health Organization Regional Committee for Europe.

World Health Organization (2011). World Health Statistics 2011. Retrieved 25 October 2018 from www.who.int/gho/publications/world_health_statistics/EN_WHS2011_Full.pdf.

Yardley-Jones, A., Anderson, D., & Parker, D.V. (1991). The toxicity of benzene and its metabolism and molecular pathology in human risk assessment. *British Journal of Industrial Medicine* 48, 437–444.

Zhang, H.R., Eddings, E.G., Sarofim, A.F., & Westbrook, C.K. (2009). Fuel dependence of benzene pathways. Proceedings *of the Combustion Institute* 32, 377–338.

Zucker, L.G. (1986). Production of trust: Institutional sources of economic structure, 1840-1920. *Research in Organizational Behavior* 8, 53–111.

Zucker, L.G. (1987). Institutional theories of organization. *Annual Review of Sociology* 13, 443–464.

Zwally, H.J., Giovinetto, M.B., Li, J., Cornejo, H.G., Beckley, M.A., Brenner, A.C., Saba, J.L., & Yi, J. (2005). Mass changes of the Greenland and Antarctic ice sheets and shelves and contributions to sea-level rise: 1992–2002. *Journal of Glaciology* 51, 509–524.

3

THE CIRCULAR ECONOMY

Thomas Brekke

The economy of the future might be called the "spaceman economy" in which the earth has become a single spaceship, without unlimited reservoirs of anything.

(Kenneth E. Boulding 1966)

3.1 Introduction

The famous words by Kenneth E. Boulding from 1966 (Boulding 2013) have nailed some of the key problems of today's economic model which is characterized as a linear economic model or "end-of-life" model that have led the world into an enormous cycle of waste production. In the last decade an alternative economic model, the circular economy (CE) model, emerged as a way of solving climate changes, reducing human negative footprint on the earth, preventing the deterioration of the environment and using limited resources. The CE is defined as "an economic system that is based on business models which replace the 'end-of-life' concept with reducing, alternatively reusing, recycling and recover materials in production/distribution and consumption processes" (Kirchherr, Reike, and Hekkert 2017). The CE approach emphasizes that values of products, materials and resources are maintained in the economy for as long as possible, and the generation of waste minimized.

Within the Paris Climate Change Agreement, the United Nations called for 17 Sustainable Development Goals (SDGs) and the Organisation for Economic Co-operation and Development (OECD) called for greener production, increased social justice, a fairer distribution of welfare, sustainability in consumption patterns and new ways of producing economic growth (OECD). Progressive countries/political parties/institutions are acting on the Paris Agreement and the SDGs by making plans and acting to promote rapid transition to sustainability by taking a CE approach to meet these climate challenges. The CE concept is not only about material reduction of limited resources, inherited in the CE concept, but there is also a strong economic growth argument. The European Commission recently estimated that this type of CE transition can create 600 billion euros of annual economic gains for the EU manufacturing sector alone. A report by World Economic Forum (2014) estimated that the global economy would benefit to the tune of 1 trillion US dollars annually from new sustainable business, which goes from ownership to more performance-based payments models aimed to reuse resources, integrating them into attractive value propositions.

The narrative of CE may seem reasonable enough at first glance, but there are good reasons to think twice about challenges in achieving sustainability via CE which warrant our attention as countries and companies transform into a "green growth" economy. One (1) of the key factors in adopting and implementing sustainability is the extent of complexity of system changes needed to reach the SDGs. We know from decades of research from social and technology innovation policies that new technological solutions often have a negative impact side, on the environment and in relation to social life, which is seldom considered when new innovation policies are formed or when new technology is taken into use (Schot and Steinmueller 2018a). Another issue concerns the increased demand for (2) extraction of physical resources such as metals and rare-earth minerals used for producing new energy solutions, with real ecological and social costs. And, finally, (3) new promising circular business models are highlighted as key enablers for successful sustainability transitions, both at the system level as well as organizational and individual levels.

This chapter investigates the theoretical foundation for CE and sustainability challenges. The chapter has two research objectives. The first objective is motivated by the fact that the scientific research content of the currently popularized business community originated CE concept remains superficial and lacks critical analysis. Second, we will construct the concept of CE from the perspective of interdisciplinary studies of socio-technical-systems (evolutionary economic) and sustainability studies. The chapter is organized in five main subchapters. The first subchapter is the above-presented (1) introduction section that frames the CE. In the second subchapter we will present the (2) theoretical foundation of the CE. In the third subchapter the (3) circular business model characteristics will be described. (4) Policies for sustainability transition and CE will be presented in the fourth subchapter. Then, at the end of the chapter (5) a conclusion will be presented which will address potential research themes and objects for scholars interested in making progressive studies in sustainable development.

3.2 Understanding the theoretical foundation of the circular economy

In this section, we will clarify the theoretical foundation by describing three main interwoven trends that drive the development of new sustainable business models within CE; the (1) sustainability problem that moves the society from material waste and energy use towards a more sustainable development, which asks for a new understanding of how an economy works when CE is to be achieved – the logic of the economy, (2) CE as complex evolutionary systems change, and (3) changing consumer behaviour and lifestyle.

3.2.1 The logic of the economy!

In an ideal economy, the equilibrium stage happens when the three markets of product, finance and labour are in balance, where households offer labour and pay for product and services. On the other hand, companies pay for workforce and services and then get paid. Money flows between the markets of the economy. This ideal model of the economy is described in Figure 3.1, the three main markets.

Wages are paid, goods are produced and income is received. In addition, government takes taxes and pay money out, banks are securing that savings are productable in the economy as investment. If everything is running well the economy is in equilibrium and the market provides the best outcome.

However, it is well acknowledged among scholars that the market is never in equilibrium, which means that imperfect markets lead to sub-optimal outcomes and new (circular) business models emerge. A relevant example of a market failure is the use of public goods, something that everybody can use as much as they want without paying for it, such as carbon dioxide being released into the air without any consequences for those who pollute. Another example of market failure is common goods where users withdraw resources to secure short-term gains without regard for the long-term consequences. One example of a common goods problem is the free use of a sea area for

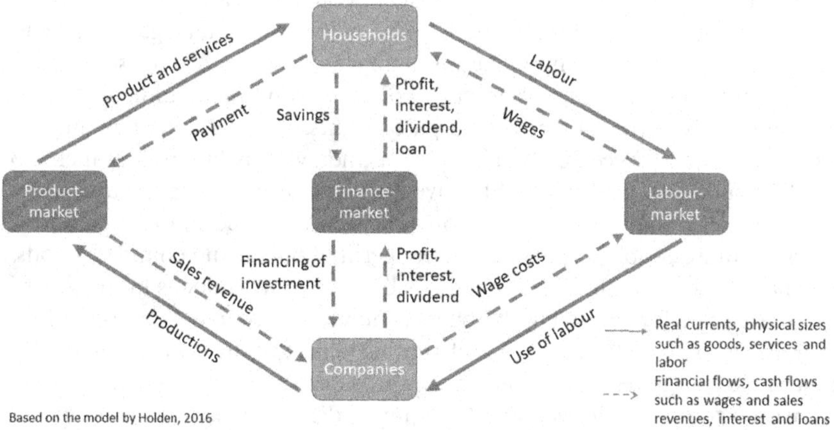

Figure 3.1 The three main markets of the economy.

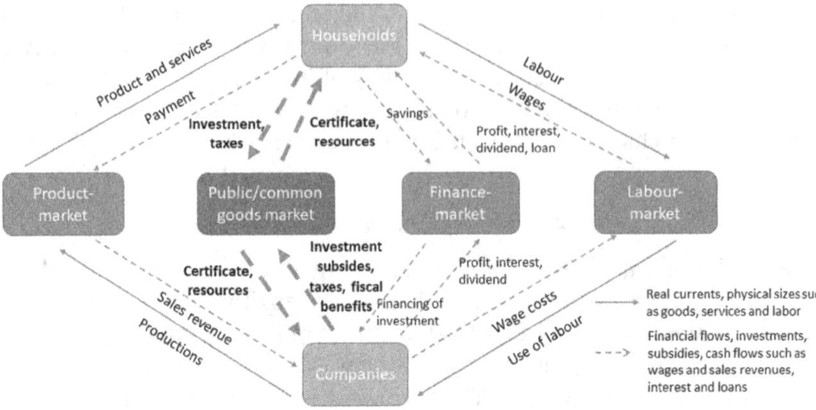

Figure 3.2 The four main markets of the economy: product market, finance market, labour market and the public/common goods market.

fish farming, which has significant negative consequences for the local maritime environment in the form of escaped fish, pollution of water bodies and the seabed. The market failure arguments can also be used to understand why sub-systems fails to support or enhance larger system changes, such as sustainability transitions to renewal energy resources. As sub-systems might work in a counterproductive way, such as how the legislative or regulatory system maintains and protects existing product market solutions. Solving the problem of market failure concerning use of scarce resources will mostly lead to new and more sustainable circular business models that include the cost of use of public and common goods (Figure 3.2).

The discussions make it apparent that market failures are partly a function of the ability (or lack thereof) of entrepreneurs to create new business models using the resources available to them such as use of scarce resources or use of free public and common goods. The problem is quite general. When value delivery involves employing intangible assets (such as releasing carbon dioxide into the atmosphere), pricing and value capture are difficult because of the non-existence of perfect property rights, which means that markets can't work well (Teece 2010). The market and systems failure arguments of public goods and property rights have also been used to explain and justify why state interventions and new policy tools are needed in order to correct market failure problems particularly concerning public and common goods.

Another challenging issue, which has become more in focus in the years is global demand for new renewable energy sources, aimed to replace use of fossil fuel. British scientists[1] claims that if the world isn't careful, searching for new renewable energy resources could become as destructive as fossil fuels, as the transition to renewables is going to require a dramatic increase in the extraction of metals and rare-earth minerals, with real ecological and social costs.

Researchers argue that further growth of energy use, even by clean energy, at the existing rate is not sustainable in the long run. These British scientists calculate that if we are going to end the sales and use of combustion engines, it is going to require an explosive increase in mining of valuable minerals. According to some estimations made by this group of scientists, mining of copper will need to more than double, and cobalt will need to increase by four times today's extraction. As demands for use of materials and energy for sustainability transition increases, material extraction for renewables will become more aggressive and, the higher the growth rates, it will get. If we don't do something about the way we perceive economic growth from a more deep and complex system perspective, we may end up triggering new waves of destruction.

Several scholars argue that the role of the state need to become much more proactive in order to shape and create new markets and correct systems failures, rather than just fixing them (Schot and Steinmueller 2018a; Fagerberg 2018). Ostrom (2010), Mazzucato (2018) and Schot and Steinmueller (2018a) argue that policies with a clear purpose (reducing waste, keeping resources in circular flow and solving property problems of public goods) needs to involve participatory network of public and private actors which can act partly independent of each other but at the same time cooperate constructively, in the solution of system changes that adds to their short-term costs because they do see a long-term benefit for themselves and others (Mazzucato 2018, Ostrom 2010). As argued by Schot and Steinmueller (2018b), mission-oriented policies need to be directed towards transformation and be implemented in an open and tentative way, when such policies need to target outcome rather than the policy itself. This type or form for mission-oriented policies are what Ostrom holds as a "polycentric" approach and are highly relevant for dealing with climate change, which needs system changes to happen on different system levels by use of more environmentally friendly business models that consider public and common goods as a cost factor. That is circular economy (CE).

3.2.2 Circular economy – the need for complex system changes

According to the Ellen MacArthur Foundation (2012), sustainable development was originally defined as a development that meets the needs of the present without compromising the ability of future generations to meet their own needs. However, despite the rapid growth of peer-reviewed articles and consultancy reports on CE approach in the last decade, the approach is not a well-defined concept. Rather there exists various possibilities for defining. The circular economic approach sees flow of biological as well as physical materials and renewable energy as a cyclical flow where materials become low-grade raw material to be reused, recirculated, remanufactured and refurbished into the human economy (Korhonen, Honkasalo, and Seppälä 2018) (Figure 3.3).

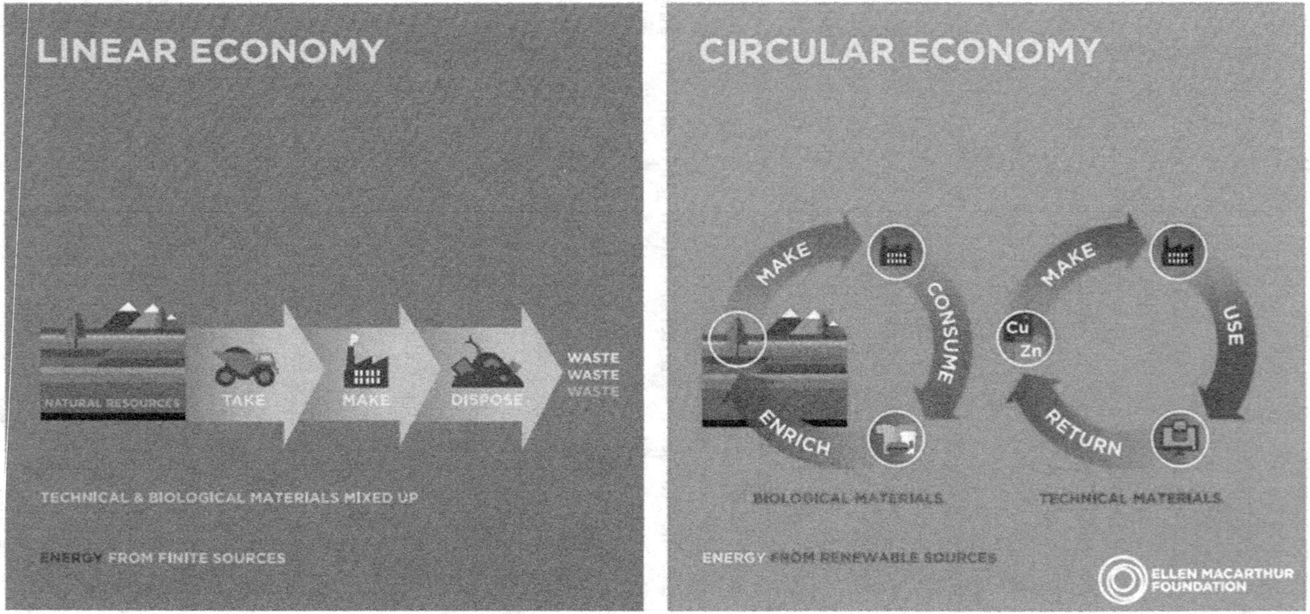

Figure 3.3 Linear versus circular economy. As illustrated by the Ellen MacArthur Foundation (2012).

Based on a peer-review literature study of the concept of CE, Kirchherr, Reike, and Hekkert (2017, 224) identified more than 114 different definitions which they have condensed into a unifying definition; that is:

> *the circular economy as an economic system that is based on business models which replace the "end-of-life" concept with reducing, alternatively reusing, recycling and recovery materials in production/distribution and consumption processes, thus operating at the micro level (products, companies, consumers) meso level (eco-industrial path) and macro level (city, region, nation and beyond), with the aim to accomplish sustainable development, which implies creating environmental quality, economic prosperity and social equity, to the benefit of current and future generations.*

This definition sees CE from an evolutionary system (Baycan, Nijkamp, and Stough 2017; Kogler 2015; Nelson and Winter 1982; Nill and Kemp 2009; Sunley 2008) approach where new business models emerge on the core principles of cyclical flow of resources through reuse, recycle and recovery, which creates new roles for producers and consumers. The evolutionary system perspective emphasizes transformative changes in many system levels that go behind the change of production, distribution and consumption. It includes all actors and processes in the economy and society on a much deeper level.

A CE transition is assumed to create a radical shift of our society, which in a Schumpeterian understanding means qualitative changes in the composition of output, the organization of economic activities and the structure of the economy, that is, innovation. The work by Schumpeter provides us with a theory of innovation as "new combination" where existing and new resources can be recombined into new use. Innovation is not only about qualitative changes of physical material or energy, it also includes the way these resources are organized, the skills and knowledge and the institutional mindset of what sustainability transition is about (Schumpeter 1934). Such transition and subsequent innovation do not occur in isolation. Contemporary sustainability transition is influenced by past events and innovations, just as today's sustainability transition, with its innovation activities, contribute to shape future path development (Fagerberg 2018). The Schumpeterian way of thinking of change, as innovation, gives us a much more nuanced analytical tools for understanding systems changes a deeper layer of those mechanisms that impact human activities, technological changes, and the way the human economy is working. These types of transitions include adjustment of the socio-technical systems where formation of new types of relationship between the state, the market and civil society occur in a participatory way (Schot and Steinmueller 2018b).

A successful CE transition needs to involve a broader and a more fundamental social change process that includes changes in infrastructure, markets, regulations, user practices, productions and cultural values in addition to resources such as skills, knowledge and finance that need to be mobilized in order to create system changes. If not, the transition might become as destructive as today's linear model of flow of materials and energy by trashing ecosystems, lobbying against environmental regulations and pursuing short-term interest (Schot and Steinmueller 2018b).

3.2.3 Consumer preferences and lifestyle behaviour

A CE is best explained as an evolutionary system that strives to be regenerative and restorative while reducing the speed of waste generation. The CE framework sees economic growth in a way that reduces environmental impacts and the use of finite resource consumption by improving the quality and maintaining the value of materials, resources and products or reusing them over and over again (Oghazi and Mostaghel 2018). The main assumption is that economic development can also be realized in conjunction with environmental sustainability, which the most cited CE definition by the Ellen MacArthur Foundation (2012, 7) argues:

> industrial system that is restorative or regenerative by intention and design. It replaces the "end-of-life" concept with restoration, shifts towards the use of renewable energy, eliminates the use of toxic chemicals, which impair reuse, and aims for elimination of waste through the superior design of materials, products, systems, and, within this, business models.

The Ellen MacArthur Foundation's definition highlights the impotency of "design out waste and pollution (1), keep product and material in use (2), regenerate natural systems (3)" and through the entrance of new sustainable business models (4) as enabling mechanisms for system changes to occur. It is commonly assumed that CE models are more sustainable in the long run than existing linear business models as CE business models keep resources to be used for new purposes (e.g., innovation), and they are more adaptable and responsive towards new society or policy demands.

However, there are several concerns with the definition by the Ellen MacArthur Foundation as the definition does not pay much attention to the role of the consumer or the entrance of new circular business models as driver for change. Kirchherr, Reike, and Hekkert (2017) provide a much more nuanced definition in their study of some vital aspects or principles for the implementation of CE. Environmental impact happens through a hierarchy of reduce, reuse, recycle and recover of waste that create economic benefits through the redesign of products, supply chains and choice of materials. System changes need to be implemented at all levels (meso and macro level) that aim to redesign the use of materials, as well as reuse and recycle. While the macro-system perspective highlights the need to adjust industrial composition and structure of the entire economy, the meso-system perspective focuses on eco-industrial parks or the regional level, and the micro-system perspective considers products, and companies and their needs to make changes in order to increase their circularity as well as consumers. Implementation of CE requires all system-level actors to be aligned and active. The entire cycle degenerates if even one system-level actor behaves not sustainably. Novel circular business models are required as enablers for sustainability transition and economic growth. As such, circular business models are the "driving force" in the shift towards a CE and the way that the private sector is supposed to lead the transitions that includes new roles for the consumer to become more responsible for consumer behaviour, and value-chain logistics need to become more aware of the consumption process. As mentioned, changed consumer behaviour is also recognized to have a significant impact on the flow of resources, not only through their "consumer demand," but as consumers who become producers or prosumers of new value offerings by sharing their resources with other consumers (Jørgensen 2018). In particular, growth of new services based on a service-dominant logic (Lusch and Vargo 2014) combined with digital-platform providers (Parker, Van Alstyne, and Choudary 2016) that enable effective sharing of resources are also assumed to drive the transition of new circular business models that have less environmental impact than linear business models (Parida, Sjödin, and Reim 2019). Radical business models, such as Airbnb and UBER, have inspired business models in other part of the economy. These models are based on digital platforms that connect actors who own a resource to actors who would prefer to rent a resource for a limited time.

3.3 Circular business models

Circular business models aims to modify the pattern of the flow of products and materials through the economy. By doing so, circular business models offer solutions towards achieving zero waste, improving environmental impacts through reuse, reduce, recycle and recover, and by that increase economic profit. Teece (2010) describes that business model is the articulation of the logic by which companies create and deliver value to customers, entice customers to pay for value (value creation) and converts payments to profit. The value-creation dimension describes what is offered to the customer which refers to the type of products and services offered by the company. How these values are delivered is explained by how a company's activities and processes are employed to deliver the promised values. This includes specific delivery resources, capabilities and routines that are needed. The third component of value capture concerns the revenue model and its financial viability, with particular attention to potential revenue streams and the cost structure. Current linear business models, described as "take-make-waste" approach, use physical flow of materials and energy flow in a linear input and output style where material resources are "running" down the system in which it is in operation. There are four main problems with linear business models (Lacy and Rutqvist 2015). These are: loss of resources, loss of values, loss of capacities and loss of life cycles. Loss of resources is connected to resources which can only be used once, such as fossil resources and some minerals. The second problem of loss of values happens when resources become waste and are not put into use. Some resources are loss of capacities, such as cars or other equipments, which mostly are not in use during much of their living time. The last problem of loss of life cycles happens when a product is replaced or has a shorter life expectancy than expected. All of these value problems represent opportunities and challenges for entrepreneurs to disrupt linear business models by introducing circular business models that strive to work to preserve materials, components and products as long as possible in the economy.

A circular business model is the rationale of how an organization creates, delivers and captures value with and within closed material loops and by utilizing economic value retained in products after use in the production of new offerings. In its simplistic sense it means "the rationale of how an organisation creates, delivers, and captures value with slowing, closing, or narrowing flows of the resource loops" (Oghazi and Mostaghel 2018). By that, circular business models operate and innovate in different parts of the value chain by changing how organizations collaborate for the benefit of the environment. Circular business models have the following sustainable value characteristics (Oghazi and Mostaghel 2018):

- Value proposition. Provide products and services that decrease environmental impacts, increase social and economic impacts. Better alignment with customers is required.
- Value creation. Significant changes may be applied to value chain and production design for reuse, reduce, recycle, recover.
- Value capture. New offering may have new cost structure and revenue models that focus on keeping resources in a long lifespan.
- Value delivery. New value delivery that needs to become more aware of the consumption process and its environmental impact.

Circular business models can reduce the adverse environmental side effects resulting from the extraction, use and eventual disposal of natural resources and materials. This results not only from facility-level improvements in material productivity, but also from more fundamental changes in production and consumption patterns which leads to five basic headline types of circular business models for a more CE (OECD 2019, Lacy and Rutqvist 2015):

1. Circular supply-chain models, by replacing traditional material inputs derived from virgin resources with bio-based, renewable or recovered

materials, reduce demand for virgin resource extraction in the long run and increase predictability and control.

2. Resource recovery and recycling models recycle waste into secondary raw materials, thereby diverting waste from final disposal while also displacing the extraction and processing of virgin natural resources into new use.
3. Product life-extension models extend the use period of existing products, slow the flow of constituent materials through the economy, and reduce the rate of resource extraction and waste generation.
4. Sharing platforms that facilitate the sharing of under-utilized products, and can therefore reduce demand for new products and their embedded raw materials.
5. Product as a service, where services rather than products are marketed, incentives for green product design and more efficient product use, thereby promoting a more sparing use of natural resources (Figure 3.4).

These typologies of circular business models do not emerge or operate in isolation. Circular business models are characterized by strong alliances, partnership and joint venture with other companies who either are part of the same value chain or operate within different industrial sectors and public organizations (Jørgensen 2018). Several examples of partnership or alliance circular business models are found in the care manufacturing industry. According to Jørgensen (2018), Renault is one example who have managed to build strong alliances and partnership with other companies that recycle steel and waste. There are promising circular business model cases that offer new solutions to solve complex sustainability challenges (soil, water, CO_2 and energy) by combining some circular business model concept.

One such company is the Norwegian company Reklima. Reklima offers new solutions based on reuse of bio-waste. The company was founded by public and private actors who all work within waste solutions. Reklima's ambition is to develop new recycling solutions that aim to contribute to reach the SDG climate goal reduction of carbon dioxide. The company offers farmers higher productivity and increased profitability, while helping to solve the world's environmental and climate problems. Their solutions aim to reuse biodegradable waste, produce renewable energy and reduce CO_2 levels in the atmosphere. The company ambition is to produce carbon-negative food and energy on a large scale based on food waste from 1.2 million households, and animal manure from farms which is recycled for climate-friendly biogas and valuable bio fertilizer. The biogas consists of methane gas, which is used for local public transport that produces green CO_2. The fertilizer and the green CO_2 are used in a big pilot greenhouse (Figure 3.5). Inside the pilot greenhouse, plants grow in earthworm-based garden waste compost. Here the sweetest and most crisp cherry tomatoes grow, capturing carbon. The greenhouse is based on unique bubble-technology. Between double-walls soap bubbles are used to cool, insulate and create shade for the plants as needed. Energy consumption

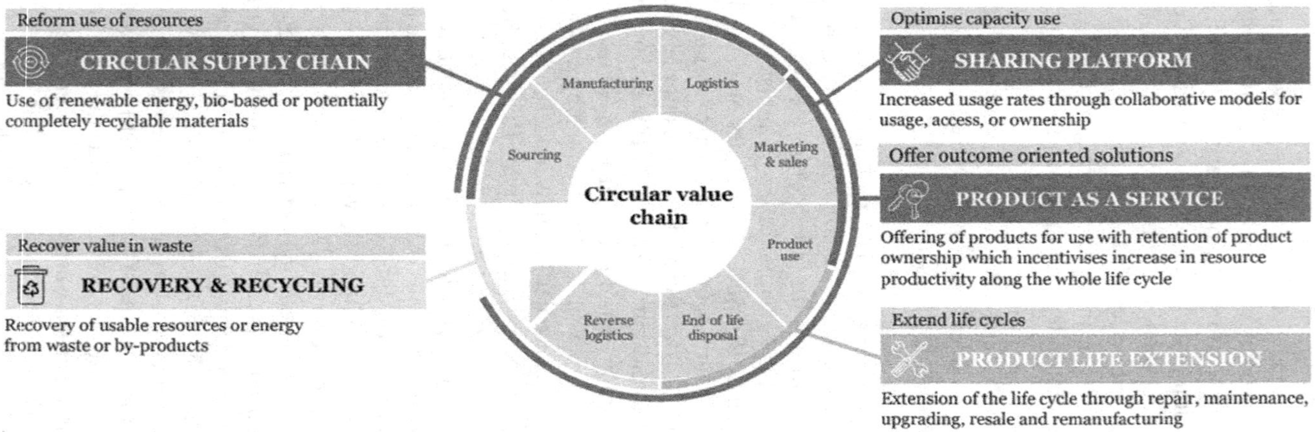

Figure 3.4 The circular business model. Based on Accenture Five Circular business models.

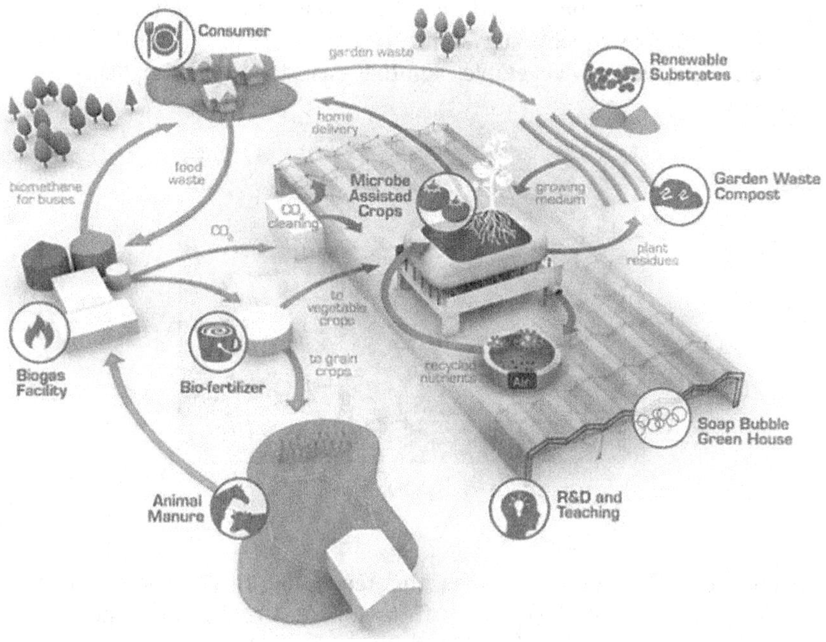

Figure 3.5 Reklima circular economy model of reuse of bio-degradable waste.
Source: Reklima.

is reduced with over 80%, and water consumption by up to 75%. When adding green CO_2 from the biogas production into the greenhouse, plant photosynthesis contributes to the capture of CO_2 in the tomatoes.

The company is targeting four sustainability areas with new innovative value offerings:

Figure 3.6

The first value offering is **binding CO_2**. Unlike fossil production, which increases CO_2 levels in the atmosphere, Reklima captures and binds CO_2 from biogas production through photosynthesis. The unique company technology binds more CO_2 than they add to the cycle when we grow vegetables. On that basis they achieve a "carbon negative effect."

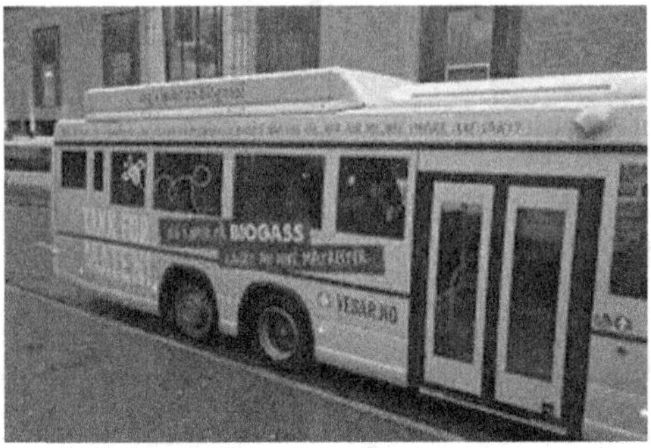

Figure 3.7

The second value offering is the **renewable energy sector**. The bioenergy they produce comes from source-sorted food waste and organic waste from agriculture. Energy consumption is 80% lower than in conventional plant production. During cultivation they use energy from the sun, as well as some clean electricity.

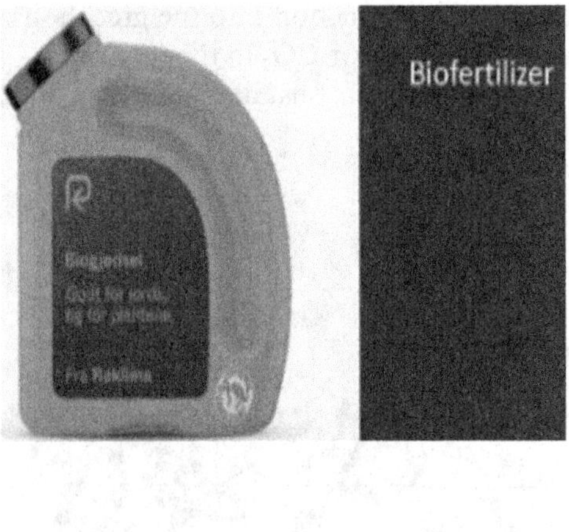

Figure 3.8

The third value offering is **local food production**. The closer the food is grown to where it is eaten, the less energy is wasted on the transport of fertilizer and finished food. Value creation takes place locally, the quality becomes higher.

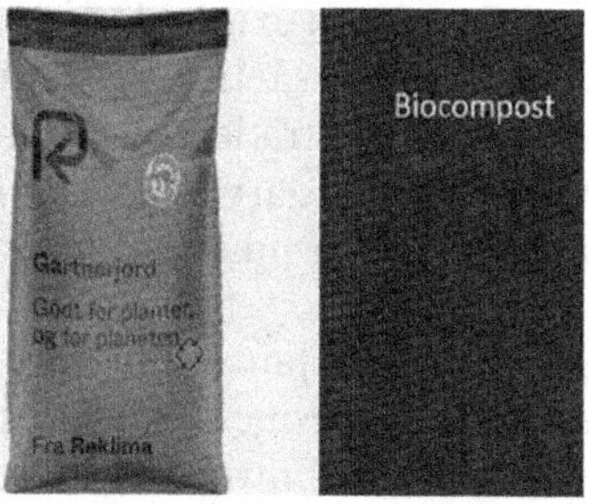

Figure 3.9

And finally, **restoring food soil**. Bio-fertilizers nourish the plants, but also the microorganisms that bind the soil. This in turn has significance for both taste and nutritional content in plants.

The case of Reklima illustrates how sustainability transition challenges (SDGs) create entrepreneurial opportunities for new circular business models to enter the market (Figure 3.2). The illustrated circular business case shows how new value offerings (propositions, creation, delivery and capturing) emerge from complex system challenges (industry and waste sectors) and where new consumer behaviours by recycling household to be used for food and energy production keep valuable resources to be maintained in the economy. The case also shows how resource recovery and recycling models recycle waste, thereby diverting waste from final disposal while also displacing the extraction and processing of virgin natural resources into new use. Waste is normally seen as a downgrade of resources. In this case, the opposite happens where bio-waste as resource increases in value in the form of higher returns for the end user such as farmers, households and energy users (public transport actors).

3.4 Policies for sustainability transition and circular economy

The implementation of CE is assumed to take the form of a top–down approach through policies and legislation or from the bottom up through entrance of new entrepreneurial circular business models. Public policy might play an important role in order to leverage on circular business models if policies on many system levels manage to recognize the need for coherent approaches. In order to address the potential of transboundary and intergenerational policy effects for domestic and international action, policies need to ensure that "no one is left behind" and policy silos need to become more coherent in order to realize the benefit of synergistic actions (Schot and Steinmueller 2018a; OECD 2018a). There are many examples, but these are some of the widely cited barriers that need to be solved within a coherent policy framework; the mispricing of natural resources and public goods that results from under-priced externalities and the provision of subsidies for extractive sectors; the transaction costs that hinder collaboration within and across value chains; the trade policies that restrict cross-border flows of used products and secondary material feedstock; and, finally, the status quo biases that are often inherent in investment and consumer behaviour.

All of these features of the sustainability transition of the economy and the entrance of new circular business models discussed in this chapter challenge the prevailing agendas of control and short-run accountability policies which characterize much of today's consensus-based policy approach. Several scholars (Matti, Consoli, and Uyarra 2017, Schot and Steinmueller 2018a, Fagerberg 2018) call for more nuanced multilevel and dynamic policies that coordinate different system-level policies (international commitment, national and regional level), balancing policies for changed (social) consumer behaviour, and market regulation by means of regulation of technological standards and public-common goods. These multilevel policies need to be aligned with numerous and complex interaction between sectors such as water, land, energy and agriculture (such as the Reklima case). Any policy implication in one of these sectors at different system levels can have significant impact on sustainability development and entrepreneurial behaviour of new circular business models. Such sustainability transition policies should reflect that all technological and social changes have directionality embedded (positive and negative outcome) within them, that actors need to become aware of this, and there is a need to engage more actors on all system levels to be involved in sustainability transition.

3.5 Conclusions

This chapter has sought to provide insight into the current challenges of CE and CE business models. The chapter identifies opportunities (and challenges) for CE and circular business innovation to prosper and solve some of the fundamental problems with the linear "make-waste" flow of resources. The primary challenge concerns the multiplexity of different definitions of CE operating within this field which makes it hard to define measurement tools and key enabling mechanisms that drive the sustainability transition towards a better environment. New circular business models are entering the market by disrupting different parts of the linear value chain by recombining and offering new sustainable value offerings which put more emphasis on new user behaviour. However, in order to solve the market-failure and system-failure problems there is a present need to renew and develop more targeted nuanced policies that aim to stimulate new circular business models as well as more environmental consumer behaviour.

Note

1 A letter authored by Natural History Museum Head of Earth Sciences Prof Richard Herrington and fellow expert members of SoS MinErals (an interdisciplinary programme of NERC-EPSRC-Newton-FAPESP funded research) has delivered a letter to the UK Committee on Climate Change on 5th of June 2019. www.nhm.ac.uk/press-office/press-releases/leading-scientists-set-out-resource-challenge-of-meeting-net-zer.html

References

Baycan, T., Nijkamp, P., & Stough, R. (2017). Spatial spillovers revisited: Innovation, human capital and local dynamics. *International Journal of Urban and Regional Research* 41 (6):962–975. doi: 10.1111/1468-2427.12557.

Boulding, K.E. (2013). "The Consumption Concept in Economic Theory," *American Economic Review*, 35:2 (May 1945), pp. 1–14; and "Income or Welfare?," *Review of Economic Studies*, 17 (1949–50), pp. 77–86.

Fagerberg, J. (2018). Mobilizing innovation for sustainability transitions: A comment on transformative innovation policy. *Research Policy 47(9)*, 1568–76. DOI: 10.1016/j.respol.2018.08

Foundation, E.M. (2012). Towards the Circular Economy. Economic and Business Rationale for an Accelerated Transition.

Jørgensen, S. (2018). RESTART Sustainable Business Model Innovation (Palgrave Studies in Sustainable Business in Association with Future Earth Series). Cham: Palgrave Macmillan.

Kirchherr, J., Reike, D., & Hekkert, M. (2017). Conceptualizing the circular economy: An analysis of 114 definitions. *Resources, Conservation & Recycling* 127:221–232. doi: 10.1016/j.resconrec.2017.09.005.

Kogler, D.F. (2015). Editorial: Evolutionary economic geography – theoretical and empirical progress. *Regional Studies* 49(5), 705–711. doi: 10.1080/00343404.2015.1033178.

Korhonen, J., Honkasalo, A., & Seppälä, J. (2018). Circular economy: The concept and its limitations. *Ecological Economics* 143, 37–46. doi: 10.1016/j.ecolecon.2017.06.041.

Lacy, P. & Rutqvist, J. (2015). Waste to Wealth: The Circular Economy Advantage. Basingstoke: Palgrave Macmillan.

Lusch, R.F. & Vargo, S.L. (2014). Service-Dominant Logic: Premises, Perspectives, Possibilities. Cambridge: Cambridge University Press.

Matti, C., Consoli, D., & Uyarra, E. (2017). Multi level policy mixes and industry emergence: The case of wind energy in Spain. *Environment and Planning C: Politics and Space* 35(4), 661–683. doi: 10.1177/0263774X16663933.

Mazzucato, M. (2018). Mission-oriented innovation policies: Challenges and opportunities. *Industrial and Corporate Change* 27, 803–815. doi: 10.1093/icc/dty034.

Nelson, R.R. & Winter, S.G. (1982). An Evolutionary Theory of Economic Change. Cambridge, MA: Belknap Press.

Nill, J. & Kemp, R. (2009). Evolutionary approaches for sustainable innovation policies: From niche to paradigm? *Research Policy* 38(4), 668–680. doi: http://dx.doi.org/10.1016/j.respol.2009.01.011.

OECD. (2018). Policy Coherence for Sustainable Development 2018.

OECD. (2019). Business Models for the Ciruclar Economy. Opportunities and Challenges from a Policy Perspective. OECD Publishing, Paris, https://doi.org/10.1787/g2g9dd62-en.

Oghazi, P. & Mostaghel, R. (2018). Circular business model challenges and lessons learned—an industrial perspective. *Sustainability* 10(3), 739.

Ostrom, E. (2010). Polycentric systems for coping with collective action and global environmental change. *Global Environmental Change* 20(4), 550–557. doi: https://doi.org/10.1016/j.gloenvcha.2010.07.004.

Parida, V., Sjödin, D., & Reim, W. (2019). Reviewing literature on digitalization, business model innovation, and sustainable industry: Past achievements and future promises. *Sustainability* 11(2). doi: 10.3390/su11020391.

Parker, G.G., Van Alstyne, M.W., & Choudary, S.P. (2016). Platform Revolution: How Networked Markets are Transforming the Economy and How to Make Them Work for You. New York: Norton.

Schot, J. & Steinmueller, W.E. (2018a). Three frames for innovation policy: R&D, systems of innovation and transformative change. *Research Policy* 47(9), 1554–1567. doi: 10.1016/j.respol.2018.08.011.

Schot, J. & Steinmueller, W.E. (2018b). New directions for innovation studies: Missions and transformations. *Research Policy* 47(9), 1583–1584. doi: 10.1016/j.respol.2018.08.014.

Schumpeter, J.A. (1934). The Theory of Economic Development an Inquiry into Profits, Capital, Credit, Interest, and the Business Cycle (Harvard Economic Studies). Cambridge, MA: Harvard University Press.

Sunley, P. (2008). Relational economic geography: A partial understanding or a new paradigm? *Economic Geography* 84(1), 1–26. doi: 10.1111/j.1944-8287.2008.tb00389.x.

Teece, D.J. (2010). Business models, business strategy and innovation. *Long Range Planning* 43(2), 172–194. doi: 10.1016/j.lrp.2009.07.003.

World Economic Forum (2014). Towards the Circular Economy: Accelerating the scale-up across global supply chains. Prepared in collaboration with the Ellen MacArthur Foundation and McKinsey & Company

4

ENVIRONMENTAL POLICY ENFORCEMENT

Gry Tengmark Østenstad

4.1 Introduction

This chapter discusses enforcement issues in environmental regulation and possible mechanisms that can compel firms to comply with regulation. The chapter is organized as follows: Section 4.2 offers a brief introduction to the basic theory of environmental regulation and the policy tools to control pollution. Section 4.3 reviews the classic economic theory of law enforcement and the essential elements of environmental policy enforcement. Section 4.4 discusses the problem of non-compliance with environmental policy and firms' investments in concealment activities that lower the probability of being detected and sanctioned. Section 4.5 considers forms of informal regulation through market forces, such as consumers' purchasing decisions, stock market reactions to environmental news, community pressure, and workers' choice of employers. Finally, Section 4.6 offers a concluding discussion.

4.2 Environmental regulation

Pollution is a negative externality, meaning that it is an unintended by-product of production and consumption, which harms third parties. In a market with no anti-pollution restrictions, producers and consumers can emit freely at no cost, causing great external harm. We call this a public goods problem. The private market fails to consider all costs incurred in production, resulting in socially excessive levels of pollution. In order to achieve socially optimal equilibrium, regulating authorities must put in place measures to constrain private agents' polluting activities and increase abatement.

4.2.1 The instruments of environmental policy

We can divide the instruments of environmental policy into two broad groups: command-and-control (CAC) regulation and market-based regulation.[1] CAC regulation sets restrictions on the level of emissions or requires that specific abatement technologies are used. By setting an emission standard, regulating authorities can directly restrict the level of emissions to the socially optimal level. Requirements on specific abatement technologies set constraints on *how* firms obtain the emission level target. For example, regulating authorities can require that a particular end-of-pipe cleaning product or equipment is installed and in use. Other examples include mandated installation of catalytic converters in vehicle exhaust systems and limits on the maximum permitted lead content in engine fuels.

Market-based regulation includes policy instruments such as emission taxes and marketable permits. A marketable permit scheme is a program under which regulatory authorities issue permits allowing a specific quantity of emissions. Firms can buy and sell permits freely. Thus, the firms that find it the least expensive to cut emissions will cut the most. Note that the regulatory authority sets the level of aggregate emissions, while firms choose how much to invest in abatement versus permits.

An emission tax is charged per unit of a firm's emissions. Thus, the firm is given an incentive to figure out cost-reducing ways to cut emissions. The regulatory authority cannot control the level of aggregate emissions directly, but it can target the desired level by noting that profit-maximizing firms will set the marginal cost of abatement equal to the pollution tax.

Market-based policy tools create incentives to reduce emissions while leaving firms flexible to adjust according to profit maximization. This means that, assuming perfect compliance, market-based policy tools can achieve any desired reduction in pollution at a lower cost than CAC regulation. However, compliance with environmental regulations requires enforcement, and, as Heyes (2000) puts it: "the most carefully crafted set of regulations is only as good as the enforcement program put in place to implement it."

4.3 Enforcement of environmental policy

The basic elements of any enforcement strategy are monitoring and sanctions. When environmental regulation is directed at emissions, ideal monitoring would rely on a direct measure of each firm's emissions. While direct measures of emissions are feasible for certain pollutants, more often regulations rely on estimated emissions. Environmental regulation that is not directed at emissions requires different monitoring strategies. For example, technology standards may specify particular abatement and production equipment requirements, like an end-of-pipe cleaning product or equipment. Enforcement of such standards involves an initial check of the required equipment, and possibly continuing controls to confirm that the technology is operating properly (Stranlund 2013).

The sanctions imposed on firms that do not follow environmental regulation vary greatly and range from warnings to criminal sanctions. For minor violations, a common procedure is to send the firm a simple warning letter, and no further sanction is carried out if the firm adhere to the instructions in the letter (Nyborg and Telle 2006). Violations that are more substantial, and repeated violations, are sanctioned with financial penalties or even prison terms (Stranlund 2017).

4.4 The classic economic theory of rational crime

The economic literature on law enforcement started with Becker's (1968) classic theory of rational crime. In Becker's model, potential criminals are rational agents. They make a binary decision to comply or violate the law, basing their decision on a comparison of the expected costs and benefits of each option. The expected benefits of violation are the expected savings in compliance costs, while the expected costs of violation are determined by the probability of detection times the sanctions' magnitude. For example, a rational car thief would weigh the potential benefits of stealing a car versus the expected costs. The expected benefits would be immediate advantage of possessing the car, while the expected costs consist of the prison term he would face if caught, discounted by the probability of arrest. In a similar vein, we can imagine how a firm can rationally consider whether to discharge toxic wastewater directly into the nearby river at the risk of facing the associated penalty, by weighing expected costs and benefits.

Likewise, the optimal enforcement strategy balances the expected social benefits of monitoring and detection against their costs. The optimal sanction equals the damage caused by the crime, divided by the probability of detection. Faced by the optimal sanction, agents violate regulation if and only if the individual gain exceeds the social harm of violation, i.e., securing an "efficient" level of crime.

The probability of detection is determined by enforcement effort. Enforcement of environmental policy is costly for the public in terms of financing monitoring officials and the administration of sanctions. To economize public enforcement costs, Becker suggests that fines should be as high as possible, and the probability of detection should be correspondingly low. If the fine were not maximal, society could save enforcement costs by simultaneously raising the fine and lowering the probability without affecting the level of deterrence.

Downing and Watson (1974) and Harford (1978) applied Becker's theory of rational crime to environmental regulation analysis. Downing and Watson (1974) investigated how firms' cost of complying with environmental regulation and the social cost of enforcement affect the optimal level of pollution control. They showed that the incorporation of enforcement costs into the analysis of environmental policy suggests that the optimal level of pollution control will be less than the level after ignoring such costs. Harford (1978) considered a pollution tax and found that the evasion of the tax increases in its level. He thus challenged the standard pollution tax that equates marginal damages to marginal costs of treatment or prevention. Rather, marginal damages should equal marginal costs of treatment or prevention plus the marginal costs of enforcement.

4.5 Noncompliance with environmental regulation

4.5.1 Empirical evidence of non-compliance

Extensive and mostly theoretical literature on non-compliance with environmental regulation followed Becker's (1968) theory of rational crime. However, the empirical evidence of firms' non-compliance did not seem to fit the classic theory. For example, Harrington (1988) revealed an empirical puzzle: US firms seemed to comply with environmental regulations even though expected sanctions were usually low. The observation appeared to be at odds with the standard theory of rational crime and was later termed the "Harrington Paradox" (Heyes and Rickman 1999).

The Harrington Paradox has been referred to as a "stylized fact" by, among other, Cohen (1999, p. 4) and Heyes (2000, p. 116). However, Nyborg and Telle (2006) challenged the validity of the result. They studied enforcement data from Norway, which revealed a less paradoxical pattern. Minor violations that were subjected to lax penalties flourished. In fact, as much as 80% of all inspections in the period 1997–2001 revealed violations. The Norwegian Pollution Control Act classified most of these violations as minor. Meanwhile, more severe violations, subjected to credible threats of harsh punishment, were less common. They concluded that the data "seems quite consistent with the theory of rational crime" (p. 3).

Telle (2013) studied a natural field experiment conducted by the Norwegian Environmental Protection Agency. He found that "in on-site audits, 54% of the firms had at least one violation, while the corresponding figure for self-audits is 24 percentage points lower" (Telle 2013, p. 28), and concludes that there is clear evidence of evasive behavior.

Many violations of environmental regulation may not be deliberate, but rather a result of accidents such as pollution leaks. When there is a risk of accidents, the regulatory authorities should incentivize firms to take appropriate precautionary actions (see, e.g., Shavell 1984; Beard 1990). In a similar vein, violations of environmental regulation may be a result of the firm being ignorant of reporting requirements. Brehm and Hamilton (1996) hypothesized that "failure to comply with regulations mandating information provision is as much due to ignorance of reporting requirements as to willful evasion," and tested their hypothesis using various sources of data on manufacturing firms in Minnesota. While they found considerable support for "ignorance" as an explanation for non-compliance, they also found evidence of evasive behavior.

There are several examples of international pollution scandals that have revealed firms' engagement in deliberate non-compliance with environmental regulations. For example, Shapira and Zingales (2017) investigated the pollution scandal by the international chemical company DuPont. Their study reveals that the decision to emit highly toxic waste knowingly was shareholder-value-maximizing and rational from the firm's point of view.

The Volkswagen emissions scandal, also known as Dieselgate, is another clear example of deliberate cheating. In 2015, the United States Environmental Protection Agency discovered that Volkswagen had intentionally installed software, which activated the emissions controls only during laboratory emissions testing. The technology was designed to mislead monitoring agents and was later discovered in vehicles from a wide range of carmakers, including Fiat, Renault, Mercedes-Benz and Audi.

Reynaert and Sallee (2021) studied European data on cars' actual fuel usage, and found that car producers actively manipulate the fuel efficiency rating at a fixed cost. Moreover, the gap between actual and reported fuel usage increased after a policy stringency in 2007, suggesting that tougher standards might lead to more cheating.

There is also empirical evidence of deliberate cheating at the consumer level. For example, Oliva (2015) studied the prevalence of cheating by car owners on emission tests in Mexico City. The most common way to cheat is for smog check centers to find a "donor" car with lower emissions and record the donor's emission reading under the cheater's registration information. She found that 63 out of 80 centers in the study used such donor cars. Simulations of individual decisions showed that about 9% of car owners cheated on the emission tests.

4.5.2 Investments to evade enforcement

Evasive behavior of firms may include activities that lower the probability of being detected and sanctioned. For example, firms may falsify reports, tamper with monitoring equipment or install emission control equipment on a temporary basis in order to meet the requirements of a prearranged onsite inspection (Linder and McBride 1984; Cohen 1999).

In some cases, environmental inspectors are limited to conducting inspections from outside the firm's fence, due to legally established rights to privacy. Often, the accuracy of inspectors' remote-sensing devices decreases with distance. This means that firms can invest in uninspectability simply by "buying more land – putting greater distance between the source of the pollutant in question and the nearest point from which surveillance can legally be conducted" (Heyes 1994a, p. 481).

The above are examples of *ex ante* investments to reduce the probability of detection. The firm can also engage in activities to erode the penalty *ex post*, that is, after detection has taken place. For example, the firm can invest in good lawyers to contest sanctions in court and reduce penalties (Kambhu 1989). Both *ex ante* and *ex post* concealment activities serve to lower the expected penalty of non-compliance.

Investments to evade enforcement are socially costly, as they deter resources from productive uses. Depending on the magnitude of the violation to be concealed, the concealment costs may be substantial. Moreover, evasive behavior by the firm increases enforcement costs, as discovery, verification and prosecution of violations become more difficult and expensive for the regulator.

4.5.3 Firms' evasive behavior undermines environmental policy

Firms' investments to conceal evasive behavior challenge Becker's basic optimal penalty result and complicate environmental regulation. When firms invest in concealment activities, higher penalties do not necessarily increase compliance and more stringent policy instruments do not reduce emissions unambiguously.

Lee (1984) developed a model of pollution control that explicitly considered that firms can invest in evading the payment of emission taxes. In the model, raising the emission tax might actually harm the environment as firms find it more profitable to expend resources to evade taxation than to reduce emissions. When avoidance is significant, the policy prescription is to lower the emission tax and increase enforcement efforts. Oh (1995) found a similar result: raising the emission tax might have the unintended consequence of raising emissions. The result occurs as firms invest in policy evasion when compliance becomes more expensive. He concluded that a higher emission tax must be backed up with a high detection probability in order to be effective.

Kambhu (1989) investigated the consequences of firms' engagement in activities to erode the severity of the penalty of non-compliance with environmental policy. He found that raising regulatory standards can cause compliance to fall, as firms influence the size of the expected penalty through deception and litigation expenditures. Similarly, Kadambe and Segerson (1998) investigated the effect of raising the fine of non-compliance, when firms can challenge the enforcer's actions. They found that the direct effect of raising penalties is for firms to increase compliance. However, there is also an indirect effect: a higher penalty increases the incentives to engage in activities to challenge enforcement. If the indirect effect is positive and large, an increase in the penalty can reduce firms' compliance.

Heyes (1994b) developed a model where the regulator is unable to fully enforce the tax on all firms. A firm might be located outside the regulator's formal jurisdiction, e.g., in a neighbouring state or province. Alternatively, and more relevant for our discussion, a firm may have technological or other characteristics that enables it to conceal the pollution that it emits to the extent that the enforcement agency is prevented from determining or demonstrating the firm's liability to pay the tax. In this sense, the firm falls outside of the regulator's *de facto* jurisdiction. Heyes called such firms "outsiders."

Modeling a duopoly, where one of the firms is an outsider, he showed that an environmental tax can cause aggregate emissions to increase. The reason is that a pollution tax gives the outsider a competitive advantage, such that the firm's share of the industry output increases. He concluded that if the firm that can evade is the dirtiest, the effects of an environmental tax can be detrimental.

Hjort and Oestenstad (2020) analysed a similar problem in a richer framework of monopolistic competition and heterogeneous firms. As in Heyes (1994b), cheating firms completely conceal non-compliance. In contrast to Heyes (1994b), the decision to cheat or comply is not an exogenous choice, but an endogenous one. Profit maximization leads to a decision to cheat or comply depending on the firm's productivity. In the model of Hjort and Oestenstad (2020), there is a continuum of firms that all have different productivity levels. The firms face a trade-off in the decision to cheat or comply with environmental regulation. Both alternatives involve a fixed and a variable cost. The fixed cost of compliance reflects investments in abatement technology, machines and equipment, while the variable cost reflects that abatement effort increases with output. The fixed cost of cheating captures the cost of developing a cheating technology, such as the device installed in Volkswagen cars initiating Dieselgate (di Rattalma 2017; Siano *et al.* 2017). The variable cost of cheating reflects that necessary concealment efforts increase with the amount of emissions.

A more stringent environmental standard, associated with higher fixed or variable abatement costs, will have an ambiguous effect on aggregate emissions. Hjort and Oestenstad (2020) pointed to two effects that cause the ambiguity: the direct effect of a policy stringency is that compliant firms reduce emissions. The indirect effect is that cheating firms obtain a competitive advantage. More firms will decide to cheat and cheating firms expand production and thus also emissions. The indirect effect will dominate for a sufficiently high fixed or variable cost of abatement, such that aggregate emissions will start to increase.

The relative cost structure of the two alternatives, cheat or comply, will determine the selection of firms into the two categories following profit maximization. When the fixed cost of abatement is high compared to the fixed cost of non-compliance, a selection of low-productivity firms will choose to violate the environmental regulation, while high-productivity firms will choose to abate. When the fixed cost of abatement is low compared to the fixed cost of non-compliance, a selection of high-productivity firms will choose to violate the environmental regulation, while low-productivity firms will choose to abate.

Hjort and Oestenstad (2020) concluded that the optimal policy is to specify an abatement standard that requires either high fixed abatement costs while the variable cost is held down, or a high variable cost of abatement while the fixed cost is held down. The optimal policy combination induced complying firms to apply the most effective abatement technology, while restricting cheating firms' competitive advantage.

Other studies have also discussed alternative policies to reduce emissions in the presence of non-compliance. Oliva (2015) discussed policies for reducing vehicular emissions when car owners cheat on emission tests. She proposed that technological standards, such as a requirement to use catalytic converters and a tightening of fuel economy standards, are easier to enforce and possibly preferable to other policy tools. Using a comprehensive dataset of pollution in India, Greenstone and Hanna (2014) found that this type of a technological standard was one of the few policies that successfully reduced air pollution.

4.6 Informal regulation: the role of market agents' environmental concerns

In the preceding section, we have seen examples of how enforcement of environmental regulation can fail its target of reducing environmental emissions. However, firms' environmental performance is not solely determined by formal regulation. Mechanisms in the private market can operate as a form of informal regulation. For example, consumers can influence firms' environmental performance with their purchasing decisions, investors can punish firms that exhibit poor environmental performance, neighboring communities can exert pressure to change the environmental behavior of firms, and morally motivated workers may self-select into employment associated with better environmental performance. In order for such informal sanctions to be effective, reliable information about firms' environmental performance must be available.

4.6.1 Public disclosure programs

Several countries have introduced public disclosure programs to provide stakeholders with information about firms' environmental performance. In the United States, the Environmental Protection Agency (EPA) passed the Emergency Planning and Community Right to Know Act (EPCRA) in 1986 in response to the Bhopal tragedy.[2] The EPCRA mandated disclosure of toxic releases by US industrial facilities, which resulted in the creation of the Toxics Release Inventory (TRI) (Arora and Gangopadhyay 1995). The yearly TRI announcement attains considerable attention by environmental groups and the media (Pargal *et al.* 1997). The success of the TRI program has inspired similar initiatives in other countries, including the Pollution Inventory (PI) in the United Kingdom, the Program for Pollution Control, Evaluation and Rating (PROPER) in Indonesia, and EcoWatch in the Philippines (World Bank 2000).

4.6.2 Consumers' influence on firms' environmental performance

The aim of public disclosure programs is amongst other things to equip consumers with the necessary information to exercise their preferences for products that are produced in an environmentally friendly manner. Arora and Gangopadhyay (1995) argued that firms respond to consumers' preferences by voluntarily overmeeting environmental standards in situations where consumers' awareness is strong enough to affect their buying habits.

An example of firms' overmeeting environmental standards is participation in EPA's 33/50 program, which invites firms to reduce releases of a given set of toxic chemicals voluntarily. Arora and Cason (1996) provided empirical evidence that participation rates in the program are higher in industries that are closer to final consumers, which indicates that public recognition is key to influencing firms' environmental performance.

Consumers can also punish firms that exhibit bad environmental performance by buying less or boycotting their products. For example, consumers started a boycott of BP p.l.c gas stations in response to the Deepwater Horizon oil spill in the Gulf of Mexico in 2010. In the legal aftermath, the judge ruled that BP would be "subject to enhanced civil penalties" due to its "gross negligence" and "willful misconduct." In 2012, BP accepted liability for the disaster and paid a fine of $4.5 billion to the US government (BBC 2014). However, it is not clear what role the boycott has played. While gas station and convenience store owners lost from reduced sales, the top management responsible for the spill may not have been affected to the same extent (Ho 2010). Generally, there is mixed evidence of the effect of consumers' boycotts on firms' sales revenue (McDonnell and King 2013).

4.6.3 Community pressure

Communities in the neighborhood of a polluting plant can initiate a negotiation to reduce pollution in line with the Coase theorem (Coase 1960). Cribb (1990) provided an illustrative example of Coasian bargaining between a cement factory on the outskirts of Jakarta and the neighboring community. The factory's emissions coated the nearby regions with a layer of dust. While denying liability for the dust, the factory management compensated neighboring communities with a monthly cash payment of Rp. 5,000 and a can of evaporated milk.

Such pressure from neighboring communities can be particularly important in developing countries where formal regulation is weak or absent. However, empirical studies reveal that the effectiveness of community pressure varies greatly between communities. Pargal *et al.* (1997) and Pargal and Wheeler (1996) explored the effects of community characteristics on neighboring plants' pollution in Indonesia and the United States. They found that lower-income communities with lower levels of education tend to neighbor more polluting plants, and concluded that income affects both preferences for environmental quality and the ability to pressure polluting plants.

4.6.4 Stock market reactions

The financial community also responds to new information about firms' environmental performance. Badrinath and Bolster (1996) examined stock market reactions to environmental enforcement actions by EPA. They found that there was a significant drop in the market value of firms that have been judged to be in violation of environmental regulation. Similarly, Hamilton (1995) provided empirical evidence that the first TRI reports had significant effects on publicly traded firms' market returns. Konar and Cohen (1997) took the analysis one step further to determine the firms' responses to the stock price reductions after the TRI disclosures on firm behavior. They found that the firms with the largest stock price reactions responded with the largest reductions in future pollution levels. The results indicate that firms respond to investor actions by changing their environmental performance for the better.

Stock market reactions to news about firms' environmental performance have also been explored in developing countries. Dasgupta *et al.* (1998) studied the impact of environmental news on stock prices in Argentina, Chile, Mexico and Philippines. They found that stock prices responded positively to news of good environmental performance and negatively to news about citizens' complaints. The stock market responses are in fact substantially larger than those found in studies of US firms. Dasgupta *et al.* (1998) did not address the effect of stock price movements on firms' environmental behavior. However, they cited an example of anecdotal evidence:

> after Chilgener (Chile) had released a cloud of toxic air pollution over Santiago and suffered a loss of 5% of its market value in April 1992, it announced on September 25 1992, an investment of 115 million dollars to control air pollution.
>
> (p. 25)

4.6.5 Morally motivated workers

Morally motivated workers can influence firms' environmental behavior. Brekke and Nyborg (2008) developed a theoretical model which shows that it can be in the private interest of firms to act in a socially responsible way. The reason for this is that workers with high moral motivation will self-select into the socially responsible firms. Morally motivated workers will presumably derive satisfaction not only from contributing to a greener society, but also from doing a good job and contributing to productivity. Hence, socially responsible firms can survive in the market, even when workers' willingness to trade higher pay for green employment is very modest.

Hedblom *et al.* (2019) found similar results in a natural field experiment. In order to study workers' responses to firms' corporate social responsibility (CSR) performance they created their own firm and hired actual workers. They found strong evidence that advertising the firm's CSR efforts attracted employees that were more productive and produced higher-quality work. In particular, CSR advertising increased the number of applicants by 25%, which is tantamount to the effect of increasing wages by 36%.

4.7 Concluding remarks

In this chapter, I have discussed how non-compliance undermines environmental policy. When firms are able to conceal non-compliant behavior, a more stringent environmental policy can have detrimental effects as non-compliance becomes more tempting. The result can be higher rather than lower aggregate emissions.

As noted by Heyes (1994a, p. 278), "it is generally taken for granted by environmentalists and others that imposing and enforcing a pollution tax on a subset of polluters on whom it can be imposed and enforced would constitute a 'step in the right direction'." In this chapter, we have seen that this conclusion is questionable. Not only does non-compliance reduce the efficacy of environmental policy, but if a stringency of environmental policy increases incentives to engage in evasive activities, the policy can cause more environmental harm than good.

A common response to non-compliance is to set higher penalties. In fact, Becker (1968) concluded that optimal law enforcement involved setting penalties as high as possible and investing minimal effort on costly monitoring. This makes sense as long as the size of the penalty and the probability of detection are perfect substitutes. Taking into account that firms engage in evasive activities, however, it is no longer true. Consequently, studies that considered firms' concealment efforts came to a different conclusion: when monitoring is imperfect, a higher penalty might have the detrimental effect of increasing non-compliance.

The presence of non-compliance also complicates the choice of appropriate tools of environmental policy. The standard prescription is that market-based policy instruments (taxes and permit systems) are preferable to command-and-control instruments as they are more cost effective. Considering non-compliance could turn this conclusion on its head. Command-and-control instruments, like a technology standard, may be easier to enforce than market-based policy instruments, such as an emission tax that requires continual monitoring of emissions.

Informal regulation can also play an important role in stimulating better environmental performance. Market agents that are concerned with environmental sustainability can influence polluting firms through their consumption, investment and employment decisions. Formal regulators still play an important part, but it is no longer confined to traditional enforcement of environmental regulation. In addition, formal regulators have a key role in providing communities and markets with accurate information and the institutional framework to enforce legal agreements.

In summary, we have seen that the presence of non-compliance complicates environmental policy design. Events such as Dieselgate and the DuPont scandal remind us that firms do not simply follow the regulations of environmental protection agencies. Rather, firms challenge environmental enforcement in a variety of ways. Environmental policies that fail to consider firms' non-compliant behavior can have detrimental outcomes. Thus, it is pertinent to obtain a proper understanding of firms' responses to various forms of environmental regulation. Only by including such considerations into the design of environmental policy, can we build a proper foundation of environmental sustainability.

Notes

1 The dividing line between CAC and market-based regulation is not always so clear. See Cropper and Oates (1992, p. 699) for a discussion of this.

2 The Bhopal tragedy was a toxic gas leak incident in 1984 at the Union Carbide India Limited (UCIL) pesticide plant in Bhopal, Madhya Pradesh, India, which exposed more than 500,000 people to toxic chemicals and killed more than 5,000 people (Mandavilli 2018).

References

Arora, S. & Cason, T.N. (1996). Why do firms volunteer to exceed environmental regulations? Understanding participation in EPA's 33/50 program. *Land Economics*, 72(4), 413–432.

Arora, S. & Gangopadhyay, S. (1995). Toward a theoretical model of voluntary overcompliance. *Journal of Economic Behavior & Organization 28*(3), 289–309.

Badrinath, S.G. & Bolster, P.J. (1996). The role of market forces in EPA enforcement activity. *Journal of Regulatory Economics 10*(2), 165–181.

BBC (2014). BP Found 'Grossly Negligent' in 2010 Gulf Oil Spill. Retrieved 4 December 2019 from www.bbc.com/news/business-29069184

Beard, T.R. (1990). Bankruptcy and care choice. *The RAND Journal of Economics* 21(4), 626–634.

Becker, G. S. (1968). Crime and punishment: An economic approach. *Journal of Political Economy* 76(2), 169–217.

Brehm, J. & Hamilton, J.T. (1996). Noncompliance in environmental reporting: Are violators ignorant, or evasive, of the law? *American Journal of Political Science* 40(2), 444–477.

Brekke, K.A. & Nyborg, K. (2008). Attracting responsible employees: Green production as labor market screening. *Resource and Energy Economics 30*(4), 509–526.

Coase, R.H. (1960). The problem of social cost. *The Journal of Law and Economics 3*, 1–44.

Cohen, M.A. (1999). Monitoring and enforcement of environmental policy. In Folmer, H. & Tietenberg, T. (eds.), International Yearbook of Environmental and Resource Economics, Vol. 3. Cheltenham: Edward Elgar Publishing Limited.

Cribb, R. (1990). The politics of pollution control in Indonesia. *Asian Survey 30*(12), 1123–1135.

Cropper, M.L. & Oates, W.E. (1992). Environmental economics: A survey. *Journal of Economic Literature 30*(2), 675–740.

di Rattalma, M.F. (Ed.) (2017). The Dieselgate: A Legal Perspective. Cham: Springer International Publishing.

Dasgupta, S., Laplanta, B. & Mamingi, N. (1998). Capital Market Responses to Environmental Performance in Developing Countries (Vol. 1909). Washington, DC: World Bank Publications.

Downing, P.B. & Watson Jr, W.D. (1974). The economics of enforcing air pollution controls. *Journal of Environmental Economics and Management 1*(3), 219–236.

Greenstone, M. & Hanna, R. (2014). Environmental regulations, air and water pollution, and infant mortality in India. *American Economic Review 104*(10), 3038–3072.

Hamilton, J.T. (1995). Pollution as news: Media and stock market reactions to the toxics release inventory data. *Journal of Environmental Economics and Management 28*(1), 98–113.

Harford, J.D. (1978). Firm behavior under imperfectly enforceable pollution standards and taxes. *Journal of Environmental Economics and Management 5*(1), 26–43.

Harrington, W. (1988). Enforcement leverage when penalties are restricted. *Journal of Public Economics* 37(1), 29–53

Hedblom, D., Hickman, B.R., & List, J.A. (2019). Toward an Understanding of Corporate Social Responsibility: Theory and Field Experimental Evidence (No. w26222). Cambridge: National Bureau of Economic Research.

Heyes, A.G. (1994a). Environmental enforcement when 'inspectability' is endogenous: A model with overshooting properties. *Environmental and Resource Economics 4*(5), 479–494.

Heyes, A.G. (1994b). Discharge taxes when regulatory jurisdiction is incomplete: A simple application of the theory of the second best. *Scottish Journal of Political Economy 41*(3), 278–285.

Heyes, A. & Rickman, N. (1999). Regulatory dealing–revisiting the Harrington paradox. *Journal of Public Economics 72*(3), 361–378.

Heyes, A. (2000). Implementing environmental regulation: Enforcement and compliance. *Journal of Regulatory Economics* 17(2), 107.

Hjort, I. & Oestenstad, G. T. (2020). Environmental policy under imperfect compliance. Unpublished working paper.

Ho, D. (2010). BP boycotts hurt local stations; gas giant offers help. CNN. Retrieved 13 December 2019 from http://edition.cnn.com/2010/US/06/12/bp.protest.atlanta/index.html

Kadambe, S. & Segerson, K. (1998). On the role of fines as an environmental enforcement tool. *Journal of Environmental Planning and Management, 41(2),* 217–226.

Kambhu, J. (1989). Regulatory standards, noncompliance and enforcement. *Journal of Regulatory Economics* 1, 103–114.

Konar, S. & Cohen, M.A. (1997). Information as regulation: The effect of community right to know laws on toxic emissions. *Journal of environmental Economics and Management 32*(1), 109–124.

Lee, D.R. (1984). The economics of enforcing pollution taxation. *Journal of Environmental Economics and Management* 11, 147–160.

Linder, S.H. & McBride, M.E. (1984). Enforcement costs and regulatory reform: The agency and firm response. *Journal of Environmental Economics and Management* 11(4), 327–346.

Mandavilli, A. (2018). The World's Worst Industrial Disaster Is Still Unfolding. *The Atlantic*. Retrieved 4 December 2019 from www.theatlantic.com/science/archive/2018/07/the-worlds-worst-industrial-disaster-is-still-unfolding/560726/

McDonnell, M.H. & King, B. (2013). Keeping up appearances: Reputational threat and impression management after social movement boycotts. *Administrative Science Quarterly 58*(3), 387–419.

Nyborg, K. &Telle, K. (2006). Firms' compliance to environmental regulation: Is there really a paradox? *Environmental and Resource Economics 35*(1), 1–18.

Oh,Y. (1995). Surveillance or punishment? A second-best theory of pollution regulation. *International Economic Journal* 9(3), 89–101.

Oliva, P. (2015). Environmental regulations and corruption: Automobile emissions in Mexico City. *Journal of Political Economy 123*(3), 686–724.

Pargal, S. & Wheeler, D. (1996). Informal regulation of industrial pollution in developing countries: Evidence from Indonesia. *Journal of Political Economy 104*(6), 1314–1327.

Pargal, S., Hettige, H., Singh, M., & Wheeler, D. (1997). Formal and informal regulation of industrial pollution: Comparative evidence from Indonesia and the United States. *The World Bank Economic Review 11*(3), 433–450.

Reynaert, M., & Sallee, J.M. (2021). Who benefits when firms game corrective policies? *American Economic Journal: Economic Policy, 13*(1), 372–412.

Shapira, R., & Zingales, L. (2017). Is pollution value-maximizing? The DuPont case (No. w23866). Cambridge: National Bureau of Economic Research.

Shavell, S. (1984). A model of the optimal use of liability and safety regulation. *The Rand Journal of Economics 15*(2), 271–280.

Siano, A., Vollero, A., Conte, F., & Amabile, S. (2017). "More than words": Expanding the taxonomy of greenwashing after the Volkswagen scandal. *Journal of Business Research 71*, 27–37.

Stranlund, J. (2013). Enforcement. *Encyclopedia of Energy, Natural Resource, and Environmental Economics 3,* 150–154.

Stranlund, J. (2017). The economics of enforcing emissions markets. *Review of Environmental Economics and Policy 11*(2), 227–246.

Telle, K. (2013). Monitoring and enforcement of environmental regulations: Lessons from a natural field experiment in Norway. *Journal of Public Economics 99*, 24–34.

World Bank (2000). Greening industry: New roles for communities, markets, and governments. Washington, DC: World Bank and Oxford University Press.

Part II

RELIGION AND SUSTAINABILITY

5

CONCEPT OF SUSTAINABILITY IN ABRAHAMIC RELIGIONS

Fawad Khaleel and Alija Avdukic

Since ancient times civilisations are exposed to demographic transformations, urbanisations, climate changes, commodity cycles, technological disruptions, fragility and violence and the constant shift of economic centres and power. Impact resulting from these phenomena is constant, and across history, civilisations, movements, governments and religions have attempted different solutions, by seeking answers to these ongoing problems. Humans are vulnerable to extremes and are dominated by the need to survive amid the harshness of nature, as a primary goal in life. People's knowledge based on their ontologies suggests solutions which are explored here via the religious narratives of the Abrahamic religions.

A new focus for research bodies centres on sustainable development and its implementation in economic, environmental, social and governance domains. Despite huge efforts from a diversity of institutions to provide meaningful insights into sustainable development, it seems that the world has largely ignored the contributions of religious narratives and welfare programmes as possible solutions to resolve the accumulative problems of humanity. Hence, it is essential to revitalise the beliefs, ethics, knowledge, research, guidelines, codes and recommendations of Abrahamic religions to promote a value-based understanding of sustainability which people can comprehend, believe in and accept.

As a result of inherited misconceptions and superstition, many people believe that humanity's current problems lack relevance to the historical context of past religious scriptures. However, in both ancient and modern times, people tended to consider issues of poverty, environmental disasters, social problems and leadership as intrinsic to the nature of human life. Sole reliance on science to adequately protect people has been proved ineffective as it ignores a range of workable solutions which have operated more effectively than modern solutions provided by scientific models. Explored within this paper are solutions derived from the sources of the Abrahamic religions, offering models for tackling human disadvantage resulting from ongoing phenomena.

Today, the constant focus on scientific approaches and tools to solve humanity's misfortunes ignores the solutions, contributions, efforts and welfare programmes offered within religious communities. It is a new approach which aims to create a value-free society as a spin-off resulting from globalisation seeking to introduce universal values and solutions for humanity.

Within an articulation of sustainability that acknowledges the importance of science, research, technology and common sense, it is also vital to review the previous contributions of religious scholarship appealing to human nature and belief systems to adopt traditional strategies within a new framework and context. As part of postmodernist studies, a society cannot survive without a belief system which determines its God-given divine knowledge, trust and wisdom.

While the multidimensional meanings of the holy books were considered, the authors of this paper were determined to show that religious teaching can be adapted to the principle of sustainable development and that benefit derived from religious teaching can create a stronger incentive and will for sustainable development goals. Based on the authors' understanding of Islam, the concepts introduced can be related to other monotheistic faiths who share belief in one God. The discussion retains relevance to other aspects of our lives and is not limited to sustainability, as there are important objectives of human life shared across Abrahamic religions. A future objective is to strengthen this project via the input of experts derived from all religions in order to provide a value-based platform for a sustainable development agenda.

5.1 Judaism and sustainability

Research in developmentalism has stressed the positive effects of religion on economic development, related to discussions surrounding sustainable development. Many inherited issues which sustainable development goals (SDGs) are trying to resolve have been documented by monotheistic religions.

In relation to demographic transitions, Judaism acknowledges and promotes the "oneness" of God and imposes lower barriers to entry in the Jewish religious market, whereas there are substantially lower entry blockages when there are many gods. As a consequence, Judaism introduces a monopoly of power and elements of inclusiveness for its religious members.

Taken together, the One God/One Faith duality inherent in Judaism monotheism made it exclusive vis-à-vis other faiths. That exclusivity, in turn, enabled the monotheistic faith of Judaism to become more likely to emerge as a socially dominant or even the national state religion, once it gained traction within a society. A monotheistic state religion, then, can make it fairly difficult for other faiths to surmount entry barriers, precisely due to the mutual exclusivity inherent in its creed, and its association with, and endorsement of, state political authorities (Mayoral and Esteban 2019).

In analysis of *dina de-malkhuta dina*, R. Yosef Eliyahu Henkin (New York, 1881–1973) argues that the disappearance of the self-governing Jewish community makes for a compelling case to follow R. Isserles' view in contemporary society. In the Middle Ages, secular governments granted Jews autonomy in matters of civil law. Under that license, Jews established a communal organisation, called *kehillah*, and enacted legislation (*takkanot ha-kahal*, lit., ordinances of the community) and imposed penalties for violations of law. In former times, the legal import of *dina de-malkhuta dina* was no more than to establish a duty to conduct oneself as a good citizen vis-à-vis civil laws and regulations of the government. Currently, however, in the absence of the *kehillah* organisation, *dina de-malkhuta* may assume the legal character of *takkanot ha-kahal* themselves. Specifically, in democracies where various governmental entities either legislate or have regulatory authority, Jews, who have a say in these matters, effectively cede their *takkanot ha-kahal* function to those governmental bodies. When civil law assumes the status of *takkanot ha-kahal*, civil law prevails, according to R. Henkin, even when the statute involved varies from Jewish law's position on the matter at hand. Accordingly, as the venue of initial jurisdiction for disputes between Jews, the Jewish court (*Beit Din*) must consider the relevant civil law before rendering its decisions (Levine 2015).

Adopting R. Isserles' guidepost for the parameters of *dina de-malkhuta dina* entitles a resident of a neighbourhood zoned as a residential area to protest the operation of a manufacturing enterprise in that area. In the absence of a successful application for a variance clause, the objection should be valid even when the manufacturing enterprise does not generate noise or additional traffic. Thus, in contemporary society, the *halakhic* rights of a manufacturer to conduct a noise-generating enterprise in his home would give way to the zoning codes.

Focusing now on other related concerns, societies are constantly facing the issue of climate change and loss of resources which traditional societies tried to explain using religious narratives. The concept of God's will or expressions of His wrath are religious explanations of such phenomena. Therefore, a sustainable development approach based on risk mitigation provides a new way of dealing with an old issue. Modernist scholars of Judaism emphasise the importance of science, research, technology and common sense to save precious human lives and resources, but only where believers stop attributing negligence and bad deeds to God's wrath. It is necessary to clarify misconceptions of fundamental precepts in Judaism, such as those relating to fatalism and God's will regarding whether individuals will be saved or sacrificed to disaster, and holy places are immune to damage (Ghafory-Ashtiany 2015).

In relation to commodity cycles, modern financial currencies have maintained a connection in Judaism by using a physical commodity base, such as gold, or by tracking a basket of real goods. However, the ability of the financial system to create debt – obligations for the future – is completely detached from the ability of the environment to generate the growth or supply the real resources needed to meet those obligations. Financial market liberalisation and deregulation during the latter half of the 20th century has enabled an unprecedented explosion of debt. Overall debt levels have been rising much faster than the growth of real assets. Indeed, there is no longer any necessary link between the monetary economy and the real *oikonomia*. There is in other words a systemic disconnection between the modern economic order and the environment on which it ultimately depends (Levine 2010).

While the recent economic emphasis within religious literature has put socio-economic inequality across religious groups back to the centre of debate in economics, and social sciences more generally, the literature in its attempt to estimate the causal effect of religious beliefs on socio-economic outcomes has largely overlooked another (equally) plausible explanation of the phenomenon: that of sorting or self-selection on socio-economic status (henceforth, SES) into religions. This hypothesis was first put forward by Weber himself when he noted that conversions to Christianity and Islam in India were more concentrated among the lower Hindu castes (Weber, Collins and Parsons 1996). Another example of the self-selection hypothesis is the study by Botticini and Eckstein (2005), who argued that Rabbinic Judaism with its emphasis on literacy in order to be able to read the Torah and the Talmud drove Rabbinic Jews who placed less emphasis on education, out of Judaism, leading the remaining Jews to shrink into a better-off minority. Their thesis seems to combine the two hypotheses. On the one hand, there is self-selection on socio-economic status into religion, since less educated (likely poorer) Jews systematically converted out of Judaism. On the other hand, there is a causal impact of religious beliefs on the accumulation of human capital, since investment in a child's human capital is driven here by belief in Judaism, and this higher preference for human capital is in turn the primary cause of the positive selection on education of the remaining (non-convert) Jews.

There is also an idea of price control to achieve sustainable consumption. The theological narrative argues that all prices today, with the exception of those under government control, are inherently unstable and should therefore not be considered well defined. The *yatza ha-sha'ar* mechanism does not work to free the short sale from the *se'ah be-se'ah* prohibition, the *yesh lo* mechanism, discussed earlier, accomplishes this objective. What is needed to free the short sale from *avak ribbit* is for the short seller to be in possession of some small number of shares of stock of the company he wants to sell short before executing his trade. Given that the "small portion" criterion is met even if the portion is acquired from the very person who will be making the commodity loan, this condition can easily be satisfied in the organised financial markets today.

In addition, to satisfy the requirements of *yesh lo*, ideally both the short seller and the shareholder that is lending the short seller the stock should be aware that the short seller is in possession of some number of shares of the company and that this factor legitimises the short sale. As discussed earlier, however, this condition is not indispensable.

5.2 Christianity and sustainability

Christianity like all religions has many strands and sects. We concentrate specifically on Catholicism due to its ethical emphasis. While it would be unfair to argue that Catholicism provides an overarching understanding of Christianity, however, at most it provides a point of orientation to examine the principles of the religion in relation to SDGs.

Pope Francis during the UN's Sustainable Development Summit in 2015 endorsed the SDGs. Placing a focus on sustainability is not entirely a new narrative (broadly speaking) within the archives of Catholicism; however, endorsing SDGs maybe also considered as pious fiction. Catholicism has a rich tradition of ethics and values, while the goal of these moral judgements is not earthly and theological, as the value goodness embedded within them is not final, but instrumental. However, the ethical policies and conceptual framework within the teachings of Catholicism has contained a dimension of sustainability for centuries. Such sustainability is engrained within the notions of shared and public values that are considered common principles and maintained by religiously guided social processes (Kenter *et al.* 2015). Christie *et al.* (2019) argues that these shared values historically provided the "source of sense-making narratives, and codes of conduct." The historical role of these shared values is interesting as it allowed human civilisation to prosper during times where a majority of resources were scarce. Prior to the industrial revolution economic resources were extremely scarce across the world, so sustainability was dependent on sharing resources. The idea of shared values synchronises with the notion of Common Good within Catholicism. The concept of a Common Good first appears in the Epistle of Barnabas (70–132 CE), which was then later codified by St Augustine (Christie *et al.* 2019). This idea then paved the idea of a "Cosmic Common Good" (Scheid 2016), which is inclusive of "all people of good will" (Pope Francis 2015).

Catholicism has embedded the notion of "common good" within the framework of justice and morality, by categorically focusing on it as a virtue instead of a righteous norm and underpinning it with altruism and social cooperation. Catholicism's overarching focus is balanced between economic progress while maintaining a minimum standard based on the concept of human dignity.

Catholicism's social policies focus on collectivism, while its economic emphasis is on individualism, by arguing that the "the economy exists for the person, not the person for the economy" (National Conference of Catholic Bishops 1996). The two-tiered policies are entwined with the key concepts of human dignity and common good, which sets the sustainable approach that is theologically constructed and spiritually rationalised. Moreover, the anti-materialistic notion of virtue discourages urbanisation, while the prominence of working with the God's grace and God's creation generates the boundaries of environmental protection. The overall ethical and spiritual structure creates a worldview that values preservation, rather than change. Wealth is viewed largely through the lens of consumption's function, which creates a moral restriction on consumption. From today's perspective, this creates a narrative that encourages recycling and waste reduction.

Christianity's notion of sustainability contains an underlying view of human development, which is construed as development that works with nature (God's creation) and the environment and causes least disruption to the natural order. Overall, Christianity creates a moral value judgement that inspires sustainable development; however, the theological understanding of sustainability remains slightly different from that defined by the UN sustainability goals. The recent literature on Catholic social teaching has a societal focus with an embedded environmental value, nonetheless, there has always been an implicit, unrecognised tone of sustainability within the Catholic ethical framework, which has fuelled many socio-economic projects aimed at supporting what already exists and resisting change. The current literature has refocused the narrative and made the implicit focus on sustainability into an explicit objective.

A contemporary focus on sustainability and moral concerns within Catholicism has fused with a narrative of identity, especially within the Americas. The emergence of Catholic sustainable ethics has produced a correlation between the significance of being a Catholic and being environmentally friendly (Warner 2008). The moral concern for the environment is now incorporated within the teachings of the Catholic Church. The impact of this narrative is visible through the operations of Christian faith-based organisations like the Christian Association of Nigeria (Ogbonnaya 2012). Consequences emerging from this are apparent in transnational activism on sustainability and the increasing engagement of religiously motivated aid workers during environmental disasters (DeTemple 2006).

5.3 Islam and sustainability

While Islamic sustainable thought has circulated for centuries through institutions and practices in the Muslim world, the concept of sustainable development in Islamic scriptures is relatively new. It is generally acknowledged that efforts to conceptualise the modern Islamic system dates back to the recent history of developmentalism in the Muslim world which compromised expectations of Islamic economics: incorporating social justice, the environment, concepts of equality and spirituality. As the Muslim world saw the rise of modernity and its negative impact on traditional communities, a desire arose for bringing the postmodernist agenda of sustainability through an Islamic moral economy, which necessitated the formulation of viable models of community building of which economics constituted a major part (Zaman 2008).

Islamic economics as a developmental economic theory essentialises the sustainability agenda and furthers the goal of introducing radical change to the existing political and economic order. It is not surprising that one of the most appealing aspects of a proposed Islamic economic system was its difference from the dominant systems of the day, capitalism and before its collapse, communism. It provided an escape route away from a Eurocentric hegemonic dominant view of economic social reality that individuals behave rationally regardless of their environment, different cultural backgrounds and values.

The vast majority of Muslims around the world live in economically underdeveloped countries, with high rates of unemployment and demographic transmission, technological disruptions, inflation, illiteracy, violence, low rates of economic growth and low life expectancy (Alatas 2006). These are the problems which sustainable development aims to solve. Poor national health services, inadequate nutritional status, alongside undeveloped health and safety regulations have serious implication on citizens' lives. Such factor is compounded by endemic corruption which results in an unjust environment and low educational standards. This is a fair description of the Muslim world during the 1930s, 1940s, 1950s and 1960s, when the attention of Western economists and socialists started to focus on the pains of the Third World. It was a period when development theory and uncritical imitation of external ideas and techniques were applied and adopted in a wholesale manner throughout the Third World (Alatas 2006, p. 588). That was a general alienation from the main issues of local society, and unquestioning imitation of the Occident.

The founding fathers of Islamic economics, due to the failure of forms of sustainable development in the post-independent states of Asia and Africa in the 1960s and 1970s considered flawed capitalist economic development strategies, which ignored the importance and centrality of human beings and their well-being (Asutay 2007, p. 5). Neoclassical economic theories view economic development as an end in itself, whereas Islam considers economic activity as a means to an end, and not an end in itself (Zaman 2008, p. 16), thereby relating to the sustainability of individuals and community by responding to old as well as modern challenges. From this, Islamic scripture across history essentialises building an economic system as a part of the order of an Islamic worldview (El-Ghazali as quoted in Asutay 2007, p. 5) which aims to provide harmony between individuals, society and the environment. Profit itself as part of a utilitarian theory cannot be the principal driving factor for humanity (Khaleel and Avdukic 2020).

The founders of Islamic economics Mohammad Baqir Al-Sadr and Sayid Abul A'la Maududi emphasised the universal validity of Islamic sustainable developmentalism based on the assertion that the Islamic tradition demands building society through the application of justice (*adl*) and benevolence (*ihsan*) which does detrimentally impact anyone in the process (Asutay 2007). The authenticity of Islamic notations is derived from the anthology of Islam and the Sunnah (Mergaliyev *et al.* 2019). It provides a systemic way of solving human problems by producing a theoretical policy base to counter the underdevelopment of Muslim societies through the norms, values and principles of Islamic ontology with the objective of creating a human-centred sustainable development process (Asutay 2007).

Unpacking the Islamic notation of sustainability provides universality along with the holistic approach of Islamic economics, based on the distinctiveness of homogeny embedded within Muslim societies, thereby targeting the observed reality of the Muslim world. The theoretical development of Islamic developmentalism started by discussing and relating historical and contemporary civil organisations and institutions found in or derived from ontological sources in Islam such as *zakah* and *waqf* (Zaman 2008, p. 19). For Alatas, it was a call to revamp theoretical perspectives and create visions of a new Islamic order of sustainable development along social, economic and political lines (Asutay 2007, p. 5).

Islamic traditional sources, according to Volibeigi, aim to transform Muslim communities based on a dependent economy into an economically sustainable society (1993, p. 794) citing dissatisfaction with hegemonic capitalist models of development in the 1950s, and rejection of the ideology of "caching up" with the West (Chapra 1992). The failure of developmentalism in the Muslim world was always related to different reasons such as: urban biases, external biases, a backward sloping supply curve, management inefficiency, while the application of a Eurocentric theory to develop the Islamic world while attempted can be deemed inappropriate (Ozey 2002, p. 97; Carvalho, J.Iyer and Rubin, 2019). The conventional Western notation of value-free and objective economics for all people regardless of their philosophical and ideological endorsements undermines the reality that the conventional capitalist economics itself is socially constructed, and hence is merely the "expression of ethical and political commitments of a particular society (Zaman 2008, p. 14). A so-called universal capitalist theory, according to Ahmad is a product of certain religio-moral and politico-economic contexts of Western-European societies in a particular episode (2003, p. 182); therefore, it is not in conformity with the one inspired by Islam, and cannot advance human welfare in regards to handling economic affairs in Muslim states.

The newly emerged Islamic concept of sustainability has a different stance on life and the nature of social change which implies a unique set of policy options for the solution of development issues. Islamic economists have attempted to articulate an alternative concept of sustainable development, refusing to evaluate the backwardness and progress of Muslim societies in terms of Western theoretical perspectives and values. In this way, Islamic economics is post-modernist in tone and can be added to other critiques of development (Alatas 2006, p. 592). It refuses the modernist projection of universal values, in the everyday life of an ordinary individual.

The most notable distinction of postmodernist literature on sustainable development is underestimation of the value elements and ethics that have directly or indirectly shaped production, distribution, consumption, price and so on. The founding fathers of Islamic economics explain that religion, ideology or any strong set of values, ideals and morals have an impact and influence in forming the normative base of an Islamic developmentalism, which has to be taken into consideration. Therefore, Asutay rightly says: "the rationale behind a distinct sustainable model as articulated in [the] religion of Islam, is obvious since the values, axioms and foundational principles" (2007, p. 5), and the imperatives are different (Zaman 2008, p. 18).

When Islamic economists discuss inherited problems intrinsic to both modern and traditional societies, such as, demographic transitions, urbanisation, climate and resources, commodity cycles, technological disruptions, fragility and violence, shifts in the global economy and globalisation, they do so in terms of ethical statements and prescriptions and not in terms of analyses and empirical theory (Alatas 2006, p. 592). As Asutay explains: "no human endeavour is value-free, which implies that reality including economic reality is socially constructed" (2007, p. 5).

Taken from the discussion outlined above, the foundational base of Islamic sustainable developmentalism can be summarised as:

(i) The explicit acceptance of Divine Revelation as a source of knowledge and certain detailed pivotal institutions that are explicitly ordered or deduced from Islamic sources. These institutions are the prohibition of *Riba* (interest), *Ghrara* (uncertainty), *haram* (prohibitive products and services), the private–public mix of property/ownership, the spiritual–material mix of success, *Zakah*, *Awqaf*, *etcetera*. Following on from these, Islamic sustainable developmentalism prevailed within the pre-modern societies of Islamic civilisation which implies that the sustainable agenda is embedded in Islamic ontology and epistemology (Kahf 2012, p. 4).

(ii) The acceptance of the moral characteristics induced via Divine Revelation was formed on both the levels of principle and those enshrined within practical rules and regulations. The morally assigned codex delineates a boundary demarcating the accessible set of actions/decisions/behaviours intrinsic to sustainable development. The system is equipped with an ability to judge possible courses of action on moral grounds, just like any other system, although an Islamic system differs by adding additional external screening apparatus manifest in a set of morally based prescriptive rulings derived from Shari'ah law. Therefore, since Islamic morality originates from Divine Resources it includes items not conventionally considered as part of a sustainable agenda, such as, spiritual development in addition to material progress (Kahf 2015).

A great consensus prevails on these foundational bases shared between the major monotheistic faiths of Judaism, Christianity and Islam. According to Islam such commonalities arise due to the continuity and similarity of the value systems of these revealed religions. Therefore, if modernist theories had continued to develop in the image of a Judeo-Christianity worldview as fashioned before the Enlightenment Movement of the 17th and 18th centuries, there is a probability that the subsequent creation of a secular, value-neutral, materialist and social Darwinist worldview of developmentalism may not have emerged (Chapra 2010, p. 4), established upon modernist ideological reasoning (Hashim and Rossidy 2000) and, consequently, a Western vision of reality and rejection of revealed Truth, which has never deviated from a sustainable agenda. Muslim economists "with reference to God as being [the] origin (of knowledge), is the arrival in the soul of the meaning of a thing or an object of knowledge; and with reference to the soul as being its interpreter, knowledge is the arrival of the soul at the meaning of thing or an object of knowledge" (Al-Attas as quoted in Hashim and Rossidy: 2000, p. 5).

5.4 Conclusion

The implicit focus on sustainability is embedded within the ethical framework of almost all religions, although the role of the three monotheistic Abrahamic faiths in promoting sustainable development is outlined in this discussion. The theological nature of religious moral argument creates a need for appreciating what exists as it is seen as part of God's grace upon humanity. The human-initiated development is approached within the shadow of this understanding. Nature – and indirectly the environment – are approached as unconditionally good. The human-initiated development is approached as a conditional good, where the condition of goodness can change. The moral value assigned by religions to nature as a whole has always created an underling tone for its preservation and safety within a religious discourse. This makes such a religious discourse one of the earliest narratives created on sustainability by humans.

The purpose of this article is to briefly survey relevant themes within the religious traditions of Islam, Christianity and Judaism to demonstrate that the theologically constructed narrations within these religions are the pioneer texts within the broader generator of sustainability. While this article argues for the primacy of religious thoughts in general, as the Abrahamic religions produced the first narratives on sustainability. It is also acknowledged that these narratives were never developed nor contextualised within prevailing socio-economic conditions, and the significance of sustainable development remained implicit within their narratives. Consequently, we can trace the need for sustainable development within the religious discourse and we can highlight the traces of such narratives within the social institutions and programmes constructed on religious narratives. However, we also acknowledge that the emphasis on sustainable development was lost within the moral contextualisation of theological beliefs. This is consistent with the discussions on the origin of moral judgements across cultures and traditions within the Moral Foundations Theory (Graham *et al.* 2013).

Sustainable development requires the promotion of values while narratives within the Abrahamic religions can help promote sustainable development practices within religious communities around the world. However, there is also a need for reconciling the concept of sustainable development within the Abrahamic faith traditions to reflect notions of sustainability expressed within the United Nation's sustainable development goals.

References

Alatas, F. (2006). The Idea of Autonomous Sociology: Reflections on the State of the Discipline. London: Sage.

Asutay, M. (January 01,2007). A political economy approach to Islamic economics: Systemic understanding for an alternative economic system. *Kyoto Bulletin* 1(2), 3–18.

Botticini M. & Eckstein, Z. (2005). From Farmers to Merchants, Voluntary Conversions and Diaspora: A Human Capital Interpretation of Jewish Economic History. Tel-Aviv: Tel Aviv University, the Eitan Berglas School of Economics.

Carvalho, J.-P., Iyer, S., & Rubin, J. (2019). Advances in the Economics of Religion. Cham: Palgrave Macmillan.

Chapra, M. U. (1992). *Islam and the economic challenge* (No. 17). International Institute of Islamic Thought (IIIT), USA.

Chapra, M. U. (2010). Muslim Civilization: The Causes of Decline and the Need for Reform. Leicester: The Islamic Foundation.

Christie, I., Gunton, R.M., & Hejnowicz, A.P. (2019). Sustainability and the common good: Catholic social teaching and 'integral ecology' as contributions to a framework of social values for sustainability transitions. *Sustainability Science 14*(5), 1343–1354.

Christie, I., Gunton, R.M., & Hejnowicz, A.P. (2019). Sustainability and the common good: Catholic social teaching and 'integral ecology' as contributions to a framework of social values for sustainability transitions. *Sustainability Science*, 1–12.

DeTemple, J. (2006). "Haiti appeared at my church": Faith-based organizations, transnational activism, and tourism in sustainable development", *Urban Anthropology and Studies of Cultural Systems and World Economic Development*, 1, 155–181.

Ghafory-Ashtiany, M. (2015). View of Abrahamic religions on natural disaster risk reduction. In *Hazards, risks and disasters in society* (pp. 373–390). Academic Press.

Graham, J., Haidt, J., Koleva, S., Motyl, M., Iyer, R., Wojcik, S.P., & Ditto, P.H. (2013). Moral foundations theory: The pragmatic validity of moral pluralism. In Advances in Experimental Social Psychology, Vol. 47. Cambridge, MA: Academic Press, pp. 55–130.

Hashim, R. & Rossidy, I. (2000). Islamization of Knowledge: A Comparative Analysis of the Conceptions of AI-Attas and AI- Fārūqī. Intellectual Discourse *8*(1).

Kahf, M. (2012). Islamic Economic, What Went Wrong? Islamic Development Bank Roundtable on Islamic Economics: Current State of Knowledge and Development of the Discipline, Jeddah May, 26–27, Westminster.

Kahf, M. (2015). Islamic Economic Development, Policy & Public Finance & Sustainable Development. CreateSpace Independent Publishing Platform; 1st edition; California, USA.

Kenter, J.O., Kenter, J.O., Bryce, R., Davies, A., Jobstvogt, N., O'Brien, L., Hockley, N., ... Williams, S. (March 01, 2015). What are shared and social values of ecosystems? *Ecological Economics*, 111, 86–99.

Kenter, J.O., O'Brien, L., Hockley, N., Ravenscroft, N., Fazey, I., Irvine, K.N., Reed, M.S., Christie, M., Brady, E., Bryce, R., Church, A., Cooper, N., Davies, A., Evely, A., Everard, M., Fish, R., Fisher, J.A., Jobstvogt, N., Molloy, C., Orchard-Webb, J., Ranger. S., Ryan, M., Watson, V., & Williams, S. (2015). What are shared and social values of ecosystems? *Ecological Economics* 111, 86–99.

Khaleel, F., & Avdukić, A. (2020). History of Economic Thought Hidden Within the Archives of Abrahamic Religions. In *Islamic Finance Practices* (pp. 1–21). Cham : Palgrave Macmillan.

Levine, A. (2010). The Oxford Handbook of Judaism and Economics. New York: Oxford University Press.

Levine, A. (2015). Economic Morality and Jewish Law. Oxford: Oxford University Press.

Mayoral, L. & Esteban, J. (2019). Religiosity and Economic Performance: The Role of Personal Liberties. In *Advances in the Economics of Religion*, pp. 405–422. Cham: Palgrave Macmillan.

Mergaliyev, A., Asutay, M., Avdukic, A., & Karbhari, Y. (January 01, 2019). Higher ethical objective (Maqasid al-Shari'ah) augmented framework for Islamic banks: Assessing ethical performance and exploring its determinants. *Journal of Business Ethics* 19, 1–38.

National Conference of Catholic Bishops (1996). A Catholic Framework for Economic Life. Washington, DC: United States Catholic.

Ogbonnaya, J. (2012). Religion and sustainable development in Africa: The case of Nigeria. *International Journal of African Catholicism* 3(2), 17–25.

Pope Francis (2015). Encyclical letter Laudato Si' of the Holy Father Francis on care for our common home. http://w2.vatican.va/conte nt/francesco/en/encyclicals/documents/papa-francesco_20150 524_enciclica-laudato-si.html

Scheid, D. (2016). The Cosmic Common Good: Religious Grounds for Ecological Ethics. Oxford: Oxford University Press.

Warner, K.D. (2008). The greening of American Catholicism: Identity, conversion, and continuity. *Religion and American Culture* 18(1), 113–142.

Weber, M., Collins, R., & Parsons, T. (1996). The Protestant Ethic and the Spirit of Capitalism. Los Angeles, CA: Roxbury.

Zaman, A. (2008). Islamic economics: A survey of the literature. University of Birmingham: Religions and Development Research Programme, Working Paper, (22).

6

A BUDDHIST APPROACH FOR A SUSTAINABLE EXISTENCE

Rev. Unapana Pemananda and Chamara Kuruppu

The United Nations (UN) as a supranational organisation focuses its attention particularly on sustainable development and has presented sustainable development goals (SDGs). Said organisation's expectations are considered by various stakeholders, whilst pursuing economic benefits (Jamali *et al.* 2017). Most of the countries cooperate with national and international not-for-profit organisations, various civil organisations and individual activists to attain the UN's SDGs. In addition, a bottom–up approach is also promoted to garner contribution from a broad range of stakeholders. For centuries, such an approach has been promoted by Buddhism, which could contribute to accomplishing SDGs.

SDGs, well recognised for the sustainable survival of the world, is in line with Buddhist thinking on sustainability. Yet, in contrast to Buddhism, the UN's perspective on sustainability is mainly concerned with the economic aspect of development. However, economic growth-centred sustainability can be a trajectory of unsustainable practices. Such a trend has critically been examined in the philosophical discourse of sustainable development and alternative paradigms have been pinpointed by scholarly research and philosophical thinkers.[1] Based on such efforts, this chapter aims to conceptualise the concept of sustainable development through a Buddhist point of view. In addition, the paper explores how Buddhist teaching specifically focuses its attention on the maximisation of psychological well-being, perpetuation of humanity towards all living beings, a sustainable level of consumption, and genuine care and generosity. Overall, our study aims at demonstrating how Buddhist teachings could contribute to the manifestation of sustainable living.

The reminder of the chapter is structured as follows. The next section delineates a Buddhist perspective on sustainability and is divided into three subsections. The first subsection defines sustainable development on the basis of Buddhist doctrinal foundation, whereas the second subsection elaborates how the four noble truths could nurture sustainable living. The third subsection sheds light on the relationship between mindfulness and sustainability. Finally, the third section underscores the need to re-specify the boundary of sustainable development based on a broad range of religious perspectives for our common future.

6.1 A Buddhist perspective on sustainability

Buddhist and non-Buddhist scholars have discussed Buddhist perspectives on sustainable development in theory and practice. For example, the UN's Day of Vesak (UNDV), the most venerable annual Buddhist celebration, has focused its attention on sustainable development as a key theme in its annual research symposium. In 2018, the symposium contributed to the publishing of more than 100 research papers under five categories on sustainable development; (1) Buddhist Approach to Mindful Leadership for Sustainable Peace; (2) Buddhist Approach to Harmonious Families Healthcare and Sustainable Societies; (3) Buddhist Approach to Global Educations in Ethics; (4) Buddhist Approach to Responsible Consumption and Sustainable Development and (5) Buddhism and the Fourth Industrial Revolution. Researchers have also focused their attention on SDGs, millennium goals and practical Buddhist approaches towards sustainable development. The existing literature proves that Buddhist teaching consists of profound perspectives on sustainability and addresses a broader range of issues than the UN's scope of sustainable development.

Buddhism can also contribute to both top–down and bottom–up sustainable development efforts by providing theoretical foundation, conceptual models and methods. Buddhism can be understood as a human nature-based philosophy which envisages the fact that sustainability requires us to critically analyse the true nature of our existence. Similarly, we are urged to consider the true nature of life, and the reality of our existence and the world, whilst pursuing development. Whilst efforts for sustainable development are individual or collaborative, our understanding about the reality of our existence on the earth cannot be neglected. It is therefore crucial to comprehend how Buddhism views the existence of the world and humanity to redefine sustainable development.

6.2 Interdependency and sustainable development

The Buddha pinpointed that everything is interrelated and interdependent. The existence of the world and beings can be conceived through the theory of causality (*paticcasamuppāda*). The universal law of interdependency in Buddhism does not allow us to construct an independent and everlasting existence. Early Buddhist texts theoretically formulate the *paticcasamuppada* principle as follows:

> If this exists, that exists; if this ceases to exist, that also ceases to exist[2]
> (MN.9 2013)

In terms of human beings, Buddhism does not argue for the persistence of being over time. Human existence is nothing other than this specific conditionality (*idappaccayatā*). The world where living beings live can also be conceived through this conditionality. Constructing a human-centred world cannot be accepted when all conditioned things are explained from the theory of interdependency (*paticcasamuppāda*). Based on Buddhist teaching, conditioned phenomenon along with all sentient beings are subject to three characteristics, namely, impermanence (*anicca*), suffering (*dukkha*) and non-self (*anatta*).

The term *anicca* denotes that all conditioned things (i.e., divine or human, animate or inanimate, organic or inorganic) are impermanent, transient and dynamic. In Buddhist scriptures, it is clearly explained in the frequently appearing phrase:

> "Sabbe sankharā aniccā ti" – All conditioned things are impermanent.
> (MN 1995, p. 322; SN.II_utf8)

The *Samyutta Nikaya* analyses impermanence in relation to the distinction between internal and external. Internal (*ajjhattam*) means subjective experience, whereas external (*bhāhiram*) refers to the corresponding objective world.

The second characteristic of conditioned things is suffering (*dukkha*). The Buddhist doctrine strongly elaborates that life and the world accompany *dukkha*. The Pali word *dukkha* is one of the most difficult terms to translate into any other language due to the sphere of reality it comprehends through its usage in the Pali Canon. Many translations of the word have been used such as suffering, unsatisfactoriness or incapable of satisfying, stress, lamentation, grief and pain. However, *dukkha* signifies the key universal characteristic of our existence, very simply called unsatisfactoriness. When we analyse a person's life, it is obvious that dukkha covers mainly physical and psychological aspects of life and all experiences from birth to death (see DN 1995, p. 344).

The stated above first and second characteristics envisage the basic Buddhist teaching of non-self or non-substantiality (*anatta*). In the doctrine of *anatta*, the Buddha teaches that whatever is non-self, that is not of me, that I am not, that is not myself. This characteristic is discussed in relation to the five groups constituting individuality (the physical form, feelings and sensations, perception and cognitions, mental processes and reflexes, and the individual's consciousness itself). In fact, analysis of *anicca* and *dukkha* in a way promotes non-self to comprehend interdependency of every phenomenon.

When everything is an interdependent dynamic process what we conventionally call an individual person, a woman, a man, I or self are merely such a collection of processes. Therefore, our understanding of impermanence is the key to relinquish the egoistic idea of self. In his seminal work, namely, Bodhicaryāvatara (Guide to the Bodhisattva's way of life), Shāntideva, the Mahāyāna philosopher states:

> *Even the parts can be broken down into atoms, and the atoms into directions. Being without parts, the directions are space. Therefore, the atom has no [ultimate] existence. Who, upon reflection, would take delight in this dream-like form? And since the body does not [ultimately] exist, what is "woman", what is "man"?*
>
> (Shantideva, n.d., pp. 428/86, 87-7 ; Todd 2013, p. 194)

His view, however, should not be understood as a nihilistic view on existence. Buddhism holds the theory of dependent co-origination as the middle path which avoids two theories of eternalism (*sassata-diṭṭhi*) and annihilationism (*uccheda-diṭṭhi*). Going beyond the views on existence and non-existence, the middle path of the Buddha leads to the deconstruction of egoistic selfishness and sees interdependency of every phenomenon. Further, Buddhism accepts conventional truth, which helps us communicate our understanding of complex concepts concerned with reality and existence.[3]

The theory of interdependency, as the foundation of Buddhism, and the concept of the three characteristics, as the cornerstones of the whole edifice of Buddhism shed light on how Buddhism can contribute to our conventional knowledge. Based on this Buddhist doctrinal foundation, *sustainable development can be defined as a human nature development that is accomplished, whilst protecting the interdependency of all living beings and environment.* Instead of economic development, this point of view urges adoption of human nature development and happiness becomes its ultimate goal.

As mentioned earlier, *dukkha* is the intrinsic nature of human life – this should be understood as the interconnected thread of human family on this planet. This means that the apprehension of intrinsic human nature unveils the interconnectedness of human family regardless of their constructed identities, which could be based on nation, ethnicity, religion, gender or any other form. If sustainable development is measured in terms of happiness, it is essential to treat all human beings on this planet as the intrinsic nation.

Paticcasamuppāda[4] (MN 1995, pp. 355–356) envisages how the entire mass of dukkha or the saṃsāric experience of being conditionally existent, and how it can be reversed. The Buddhist view concerning individuals is intended to result in the affirmation of fundamental equality of all sentient beings. Buddhism promotes this cardinal quality as *boundless openness*, which is the central aspect of *mettā* or noble friendliness. Based on this universal principle, making oneself in the place of another (*attānam upamam katvā*), all forms of well-being can be maintained. Overall, Buddhism prescribes *metta* practice towards every living being with boundless openness. As analysed by Shāntideva:

> One should first earnestly meditate on the equality of oneself and others in this way: All equally experience suffering and happiness, and I must protect them as I do myself.
>
> (Kelley 2015, p. 123; Shantideva n.d., p. 355)

For the causal continuity of an impermanent process, this is fundamentally the same for every living being. Whereas the relative identities differ from each other, absolute identities are equal as explained in the common predicament. This aspect of the Buddhist approach therefore emphasises harmonious co-existence of living beings as the most essential aspect of sustainable development.

Happiness is a key element in the foregoing discussion. It can be viewed as the development of human nature. As a philosophy of living, Buddhism aspires to eliminate suffering of human beings, whilst discouraging unsustainable development. In other words, Buddhism seeks to avoid both spiritual and material unsustainability. Unsustainable development as a consequence of unskilful thoughts and practices is challenging to the existence of living beings and nature. According to the definition by WCED (1987), sustainable development focuses its attention on the balance between economic development and environmental protection to ensure intragenerational and intergenerational equity. As emphasised by the Buddhist teaching, the balance between spiritual and material development should be considered as the development of human nature. The Buddha teaches that the greatest wealth is contentment (*santutthi paramaṃ dhanaṃ*). Similarly, Buddhism underscores the importance of refraining from accumulating material wealth, whilst admiring less wants as a virtue. In other words, Buddhism takes happiness into account in terms of spiritual sense rather than in terms of material sense.

SDGs are primarily concerned with a material form of sustainable development. Max-Neef (1991) has presented a theoretical framework, namely, Human Scale Development (HSD) for the analysis of sustainable development process, as dominant social and economic theories, leading the process of development, are incomplete and inadequate. Accordingly, a framework consisting of three pillars (i.e., promotion of self-reliance, balanced relationship among people, institutions and dimensions, and satisfaction of fundamental human needs) was pinpointed. Whilst acknowledging its positive contribution to sustainable development, the following section exhibits how the four noble truths of Buddhism guide to attain sustainable living.

6.3 The four noble truths for sustainable living

The teaching of the Buddha demonstrates the middle path or *majjhimāpatipadā* as the path leading to happiness and to end suffering of human beings. Basically, the middle path guides us to abandon two main views, namely, self-mortification (*attakilamātanuyoga*) and self-indulgence (*kamasukallikānuyoga*). Nevertheless, Buddhism does not propagate extreme implementation or adoption of its teaching. The Buddha has elaborated the Four Noble Truths to live as per the middle path, which could direct to attain the ultimate happiness. The Four Noble Truths could be depicted as a formula for sustainable living. As explained in the Buddhist discourses, they are as follows:

> The first truth is *Dukkha,* which means suffering (in general) should be understood;
>
> The second truth is *Dukkhasamudaya,* which means cause of suffering should be relinquished;
>
> The third truth is *Dukkhanirodha,* which means cessation of suffering should be realized;
>
> The fourth truth is *Dukkhanirodhagāminī Patipadā,* which means the path leading to the cessation of suffering should be practiced
>
> (SN.56.11 2013; Tan 2012, pp. 3–4)

As envisaged by the above-stated discourses, the Buddha endeavours to heal the world like a physician, who prescribes treatments for the suffering of human beings. When focusing our attention on the Four Noble Truths, the first truth describes the condition or mass of predicaments in life and the world. Whereas the second truth as the cause or diagnosis uncovers craving or attachment as the cause to such predicaments, the third truth can be identified as the prognosis and holds the solution for the state of ultimate happiness in the abolition of dukkha. The fourth truth is the treatment. In doing so, Buddhism suggests the formula of Four Noble Truths to address issues, which challenge our existence and the depletion of resources and their sources. Interestingly, the Four Noble Truths can be accommodated in achieving the UN's SDG also.

The fourth truth is concerned with eight limbs (*ariyo aṭṭhṅgiko maggo*), contributing to yielding the middle path that would lead to happiness. The eight limbs are Right View (*sammā diṭṭhi*), Right Intention (*sammā saṁkappa*), Right Speech (*sammā vācā*), Right Action (*sammā kammanta*), Right Livelihood (*sammāājiva*), Right Effort (*sammā vāyāma*), Right Mindfulness (*sammā sati*) and Right Concentration (*sammā sāmādhi*). These eight limbs are grouped into three basic disciplines, namely, moral virtues (*sīla sikkhā*), concentration (*samādhi sikkhā*) and wisdom (*paññā sikkhā*).

The *moral virtue* consists of three divisions: right speech, right action and right livelihood. It refers to the development of moral or ethical behaviour. As deliberated by Bodhi (2010, p. 65), such behaviour leads to harmony at several levels – social, psychological, karmic and contemplative. The *concentration* includes right effort, right mindfulness and right focus. This discipline helps train the mind by releasing unwholesome states and habitual patterns, whilst encouraging the development of wholesome. The *wisdom* as a discipline includes right view and right intention, presented as the accurate knowledge or insight that is essential to understand why this discipline should be followed. In terms of development, these three disciplines or eight limbs lead to the maximum level of happiness, including the development of personality and the creation of ethically and cognitively well-established human existence.

As elaborated upon, unskilful thoughts and practices cause unsustainable patterns of development. Buddhism identifies such development as an internal and external unsustainable way of living. Based on Buddhist teaching, an unwholesome course of human actions (*akusala-kamma-patha*) could particularly be distinguished into three types of main actions that are not beneficial either to one who performs them, to stakeholders affected by them or to both parties. They can be labelled as physical, verbal and mental unwholesome actions.

Physical actions: killing, stealing and unlawful sexual intercourse or sexual misconduct
Verbal actions: lying, slandering, rude speech and foolish babble
Mental actions: covetousness, ill will and evil views (MN.9 2013)

Greed, hatred and delusion are considered to be the root cause of unwholesome. Whatever it is unwholesome should be eradicated. In other words, an individual should practice non-greed, non-hatred and non-delusional actions that are the root cause of wholesome. Buddhism seeks to develop wholesome by means of internal and external sustainability (*kusala-kamma-patha*). As underscored by Venerable Sāriputta, a noble disciple of Buddha:

> When a noble disciple has understood the unwholesome, the root of unwholesome, wholesome and the root of the wholesome, he entirely abandons the underlying tendency to lust, he abolishes the underlying tendency to aversion, he extirpates the underlying tendency to view and conceit "I am," and by abandoning ignorance and arousing true knowledge he here and now makes an end of suffering.
>
> (MN.1.1.9 2005)

The above-stated quotation explicitly reveals how the wholesome leads to avoidance of suffering, whilst contributing to augmenting sustainable living. In comparison to Max-Neef's HSD (1991), Buddhism is firmly compatible with the pillars of human needs development. In addition, Buddhism emphasises the importance of acknowledging the interdependence of existence, including behaviour-centred sustainability.

6.4 Application of mindfulness for sustainability

The UN and various organisations adopt a range of strategies and approaches to attain SDGs that are particularly concerned with economic prosperity and human well-being. Buddhist philosophy-based teaching and approaches could be a driving force in the process of reaching most of the SDGs. As delineated by Buddhist teaching, because of intrinsic human nature, people are pleasure seekers (*sukha-kāmā*), who are keen to avoid pain and discomfort (*dukkha-patikkūlā*). Based on such nature and behaviour, Buddhism demonstrates the four greatest achievements in life:

ārogyaparamā lābhā	- Health is the greatest gift
santuṭṭhiparamaṃ dhanaṃ	- Contentment is the greatest wealth
vissāsaparamāñātī	- A trusted friend is the best relative
nibbāṇaparamaṃ sukhaṃ	- Nibbana or the liberation from suffering is the greatest bliss
	(Dhp_utf8, 204)

The above-stated accomplishments contribute to fostering health and well-being. As defined by the World Health Organization (WHO), "Health is a state of complete physical, mental and social well-being and not merely the absence of disease or infirmity" (WHO 2014). Researchers have unveiled that mindfulness effectively supports well-being. At present, mindfulness practice can be identified as one of the most popular spiritual aspects in many religious and secular settings around the world. Practice of mindfulness meditation can be traced as far back as to the ancient Buddhist traditions.

Mindfulness receives significant attention within the scope of Buddhist teaching. Buddhism discusses qualities, which are conductive to enlightenment or awakening (*bodhipakkhiyādhammā*). The purpose of mindfulness is to release a person from illusionary thinking and increase realistic views of mental and physical experience (*yathā bhūta ñanadassna*) (Bodhi 2011). The English term mindfulness is derived from *sati* (Pāli) or *smṛti* (Sanskrit). Nevertheless, alternative terms such as awareness, attention, bare attention, mindful attention, recollecting mindfulness, recollection, self-recollection, inspection and retention are also used as synonyms.

Satipatthana Sutta demonstrates four objects of practicing mindfulness, namely, observing of body, feelings, status of mind and mental qualities. This Sutta (discourse) distinguishes introspective techniques and composed guidance for the practical application. In the Buddhist approach to mindfulness, moral conduct and right view that exhibit the reality of being and nature become the foundation, and thereby it is applied to realise "self" and "other." In addition, the mindfulness practice requires the awareness of three characteristics (*tilakkhaṇa*) of all conditioned things, namely, impermanent (*anicca*), unsatisfactoriness (*dukkha*) and non-self or empty nature of reality (*anatta*). Such awareness fosters potential for the full awakening.

In the second half of last century, mindfulness emerged within the western psychological foundation. Theories, models and techniques on mindfulness, manifested in the West, integrate psychological and meditative elements. According to Goleman and Davidson (2017), scholars have published at least 6,838 manuscripts in English between the 1970s and 2016. The early Buddhist thought of mindfulness is incorporated to gain a vast range of benefits relating to health and well-being. In her social psychological approach, Langer (2014) pinpoints several benefits of mindfulness practice and its prevalence in daily life. Amongst them, mindfulness and its potential benefits for mental and physical health, ageing, behavioural regulation, interpersonal relationships and creativity are noteworthy. For example, Henrietta H. Fore – UNICEF Executive Director – urged people to use meditation and mindfulness apps, whilst staying inside during the Covid-19 pandemic.

Kabat-Zinn (2003, 2011) has taken a clinical approach to mindfulness integrating mindfulness into medical techniques through which individuals could perceive how the mind functioned. In addition, individuals gained knowledge of being aware of thinking, feeling and responding to stimuli. Mental health-related outcomes of mindfulness practice assert a significant place in the studies on well-being. Benson and Klipper, the authors of *The Relaxation Response* (1975) and Richard Davidson (2017) have uncovered how mindfulness effects negative psychological reactions associated with stress. They have used a group of mindfulness meditators and modern techniques of neuroscience in this respect.

Several studies concerning mindfulness practice and mental health demonstrate the relationship between mindfulness and cognition, the effect of mindfulness for self-regulation and well-being (Scott, Schultz, and Ryan 2014), attitudes and persuasion (Luttrell, Briñol, and Petty 2014), mental energy (Herbert 2014), cognitive functioning and creativity (Carson 2014) and social integration (Niedderer 2014). Brewer (2019) reveals how mindfulness could help relinquish addictions such as smoking and food craving. Similarly, mindfulness intervention in conjunction with physical health identification can be used for pain management (i.e., clinical colds, psoriasis, irritable bowel syndrome, post-traumatic stress disorder, diabetes, HIV) (Creswell and Dutcher 2018; Creswell *et al.* 2019). Lippold *et al.* (2021) argue that mindfulness-based childbirth and parenting positively impacts on pregnant women, children, adolescents and families for their mental health and well-being. Whilst theories, models and scales are introduced for the study of mindfulness, *Handbook of Mindfulness: Theory, Research, and Practice* (2015) sheds light on how researchers have adopted Buddhist foundations of mindfulness to develop such theories, models and scales.

Mindfulness is also adopted to propagate sustainable peace education. In Sri Lanka, a mindfulness training programme under the rubric of Sati Pasala has been implemented in schools, universities and other relevant institutions to introduce and share in a non-sectarian and non-religious manner since 2017. Having endured a 30-year conflict until 2009, the country now promotes mindfulness, which is free of ethnic, religious and political dimensions as a common platform for unity and harmony amongst all ethnic communities. A team of volunteers, representing mindfulness practitioners of Sati Pasala, main religions and ethnic communities in Sri Lanka, conduct mindfulness training to enhance mental health, well-being, self-understanding, emotional resilience, tolerance and empathy amongst children and youth. This programme is acknowledged by the country's education department as a fruitful approach to promote peace and harmony among mistrusted communities.

Mindfulness could play a role in nurturing righteous livelihood (*sammāājiva*). Right living must be acquired by righteous means without immoral and exploitative methods. Individuals' endeavours for the accumulation of wealth must be in accordance with right livelihood. The programmes for sustainable development sometimes contradict with Buddhism when policy makers disregard moral values of societies. For instance, promotion of economic activities, harmful to our existence, undermines basic values of a society and could generate disastrous consequences. According to Buddhist principles, a balanced stance towards fundamental needs implies a sustainable level of consumption. The Buddha explains four necessities of life – clothing, food, shelter and medicine. These requisites must be fulfilled with a good awareness of sustainable living. Such a way of living encourages preservation and reuse of resources and also shares resources with others. A number of discourses in the *Sutta Pitaka*, and the *Kandhakas* of the *Vinaya Pitaka* provide reflective evidence for meeting needs and sharing generously without compromising the ability of future generations to meet their needs.

6.5 Concluding remarks

The phenomenon of sustainable development has immerged due to the consideration of our common future. Our essay aims at contributing to the sustainable development literature and attempts to conceptualise sustainable development on the basis of Buddhist doctrines such as the theory of interdependency (*paticcasamuppāda*) and three characteristics (*tilakkhaṇa*). The central thesis of this perspective is the necessity of accomplishing human nature development in line with the interdependency of all living beings and the environment. The theory of interdependency and the three characteristics envisage our interdependent existence on this planet, and thereby promotes harmonious co-existence of humanity. We therefore consider Buddhist conceptualisation of sustainable development is the uniqueness of this manuscript. Moreover, it is propagated as an alternative to the UN's perspective on sustainability which is mainly concerned with the economic aspect of development. In doing so, we urge the UN and policy makers to revisit their development strategies, whilst articulating new development policies to preserve our common future.

In addition, the paper emphasises the importance of acknowledging the fact that identifying *dukkha* (unsatisfactoriness) as the common predicament of our existence. It underscores the importance of maintaining balance between spiritual development and material development. Similarly, the Four Noble Truths are pinpointed as an alternative formula for the achievement of SDGs. This formula is absolutely paramount as it is far beyond a religious dimension. As noted in our discussion, the Four Noble Truths reach diagnosis by analysing the problem that is to be resolved. Thereby, it endeavours to guide sustainable development discussion in a new direction, which would be the healthiest and safest for both humanity and the environment.

Amongst the SDGs, mental health and well-being has also been discussed from the Buddhist perspective of sustainability. Abundant application of mindfulness practices underscores the relevance of health and well-being for sustainable living. This manuscript reveals the potential of practicing mindfulness by means of righteous livelihood, reducing inequalities, responsible consumption and production, sustainable peace education and harmonious co-existence, which are in line with a number of SDGs.

Drawing on the core values of Buddhist teaching, we demonstrate the necessity of revisiting the phenomenon of sustainable development. Nevertheless, it is meaningless to redefine this concept on the basis of no religious dimension. Therefore, we urge world religions to rally around this discussion to redefine the boundary of sustainable development for the betterment of our common future. In doing so, the paper invites diverse religions in the world to make strides in nurturing our knowledge paradigms on sustainable development in line with ethical and cognitive foundations of religious scriptures. Such a move would strengthen the debate on sustainable development, whilst preserving our sustainable survival.

Abbreviations

Dhp - The Dhammapada
DN - MN – Digha Nikaya (The Long Discourses of the Buddha)
HSD - Human Scale Development
MN - Majjhima Nikaya (The Middle Length Discourses of the Buddha)
SD - Sustainable Development
SDGs - Sustainable Development Goals
SN - The Samyutta Nikaya (The Connected Discourses of the Buddha)
UN - The United Nations
UNCED - Rio Declaration on Environment and Development (1992)
UNDV - United Nation's Day of Vesak
WCED - World Commission on Environment and Development (1987)
WHO - World Health Organization

Glossary

- ajjhattam – internal world / subjective experience
- akusala-kamma-patha – unwholesome course of actions
- ariyo aṭṭhṅgiko maggo – The Noble Eightfold Paths
  1. right view (sammā diṭṭhi)
  2. right intention (sammā saṁkappa)
  3. right speech (sammā vācā)
  4. right action (sammā kammanta)
  5. right livelihood (sammāājiva)
  6. right effort (sammā vāyāma)
  7. right mindfulness (sammā sati)
  8. right concentration (samm sāmādhi)
- attakilamātanuyoga – self-mortification
- bhāhiram – external world / objective experience
- bodhipakkhiyādhammā – qualities which are conductive to enlightenment or awakening
- cattāri ariyasaccāni – The Four Noble Truths
  1. dukkha (suffering - in general)
  2. dukkhasamudaya (cause of suffering)
  3. dukkhanirodha (cessation of suffering)
  4. dukkhanirodhagāminī Patipadā (the path leading to the cessation of suffering)
- dukkha – suffering / unsatisfaction / unsatisfactoriness or incapableof satisfying / stress / pain / lamentation / grief / or despair
- idappaccayatā – conditionality
- kamasukallikānuyoga – self-indulgence
- kusala-kamma-patha – wholesome course of actions
- mettā – noble friendliness
- paññā sikkhā – the discipline of wisdom
- paticcasamuppāda – the theory of causality / the theory of interdependency
- samādhi sikkhā – the discipline of concentration
- sammā-diṭṭhi – right view
- sassata-diṭṭhi – view of eternalism
- sati – mindfulness
- sīla sikkhā – the discipline of moral virtues
- tilakkhaṇa – the three characteristics
  1. anicca (impermanence)
  2. dukkha (unsatisfactoriness)
  3. anatta (non-self or empty nature of reality)
- uccheda-diṭṭhi – view of annihilationism

Notes

1 Arne Jernelov for instance states that the principle of sustainable development requires to define philosophically. *"The term sustainable development has not actually been defined. It is a philosophical principle which has been described only as a development which makes it possible for today's generation of mankind to satisfy its needs without making it more difficult for future generations to satisfy theirs. This is a politically attractive description, but it provides little foundation for decision as to whether one form of technology or economic programme is compatible with the objectives or not (Jernelov, 1994, p. 10)."*

2 "*imasmim sati idam hoti – imassa uppādā idaṃ uppajjati imasmiṃ asati idaṃ na hoti – imassa nirodhā idaṃ nirujjhati*" (SN.II_utf8)

3 Theravāda Buddhist commentaries and Mahāyāna Buddhist schools emphasize that the Buddha teaches only two truths: conventional truth and ultimate truth (Pali: sammuti sacca and paramattha sacca, Sanskrit: Smvrti satya and paramārtha satya). "The teaching of the doctrine of the Buddhas is based upon two truths: truth relating to worldly convention and truth in terms of ultimate fruit" (Nāgārjuna 2004, p. 331).

4 Ignorance is the condition for (the arising of) the *formations*
The *formations* is the condition for (the arising of) consciousness
Consciousness is the condition for (the arising of) *mentality and materiality*
Mentality and materiality are the condition for (the arising of) the six senses
The six senses are the condition for (the arising of) contact
Contact is the condition for (the arising of) feeling
Feeling is the condition for (the arising of) craving
Craving is the condition for (the arising of) clinging
Clinging is the condition for (the arising of) becoming
Becoming is the condition for (the arising of) birth
Birth is the condition for (the arising of) aging, death, sorrow, lamentation, pain, grief and despair
Such is the whole mass of dukkha ("D.N.," 1995, Mahanidana Sutta)
(avijjāpaccayā saṅkhārā, saṅkhārapaccayā viññāṇaṃ, viññāṇapaccayā nāmarūpaṃ, nāmarūpapaccayā saḷāyatanaṃ, saḷāyatanapaccayā phasso, phassapaccayā vedanā, vedanāpaccayā taṇhā, taṇhāpaccayā upādānaṃ, upādānapaccayā bhavo, bhavapaccayā jāti, jātipaccayā jarāmaraṇaṃ sokaparidevadukkhadomanassupāyāsā sambhavanti. Evametassa kevalassa dukkhakkhandhassa samudayo hoti.)

References

Benson, H. & Klipper, M.Z. (1975). The Relaxation Response. New York: Harper Collins.

Bodhi, B. (2010). The Noble Eightfold Path: Way to the End of Suffering. Kandy: Buddhist Publication Society.

Bodhi, B. (2011). What does mindfulness really mean? A canonical perspective. *Contemporary Buddhism* 12(1), 19–39.

Brewer, J. (2019). Mindfulness training for addictions: Has neuroscience revealed a brain hack by which awareness subverts the addictive process? *Current Opinion in*

Psychology 28, 198–203. Retrieved from www.sciencedirect.com/science/article/pii/S2352250X18301714?via%3Dihub

Brown, K.W., Creswell, J.D., & Ryan, R.M. (2015). Handbook of Mindfulness: Theory, Research, and Practice. New York, NY: The Guilford Press.

Carson, S. (2014). The impact of mindfulness on creativity research and creativity enhancement. In The Wiley Blackwell Handbook of Mindfulness (Vol. II). New York: John Wiley. pp. 328–344.

Creswell, D.J., Lindsay, E.K., Villalba, D.K., & Chin, B. (2019). Mindfulness training and physical health: Mechanisms and outcomes. *Psychosomatic Medicine* 81, 224–232.

Creswell, J.D. & Dutcher, J.M. (2018). The role of brain reward pathways in stress resilience and health. *Neuroscience and Biobehavioral Reviews* 95, 559–567.

Davidson, R.J. (2017). Altered Traits: Science Reveals How Meditation Changes Your Mind, Brain, and Body. New York: Avery.

DN (1995). Digha Nikaya: The Long Discourses of the Buddha (M. Walshe, Trans.). Boston: Wisdom Publication.

Goleman, D. & Davidson, R.J. (2017). Altered Traits: Science Reveals How Meditation Changes Your Mind, Brain, and Body. New York: Avery.

Herbert, W. (2014). Mindfulness and Heuristics. In The Wiley Blackwell Handbook of Mindfulness (Vol. II) New York: John Wiley. pp. 279–289.

Jamali, D., Karam, C., Yin, J., & Soundarajan, V. (2017). CSR logics in developing countries: Translation, adaptation and stalled development. *Journal of World Business* 52, 343–359.

Jernelov, A. (1994). On the General Principles of Environment Protection: A Report from the Swedish Environmental Advisory Council. Retrieved from https://data.kb.se/datasets/2015/02/sou/1994/1994_69%28librisid_17210109%29.pdf

Kabat-Zin, J. (2003). Mindfulness-based interventions in context: Past, present, and future. *Clinical Psychology: Science and Practice* 10(02), 144–156. Retrieved from https://greatergood.berkeley.edu/images/uploads/Kabat-Zinn-Mindfuless_History_and_Review.pdf

Kabat-Zinn, J. (2011). Some reflections on the origins of MBSR, skillful means, and the trouble with maps. *Contemporary Buddhism* 12(1), 281–306. doi:10.1080/14639947.2011.564844

Kelley, D.C. (2015). Toward a Buddhist Philosophy and Practice of Human Rights. PhD Thesis, Columbia University. Retrieved from https://academiccommons.columbia.edu/.../ac.../Kelley_columbia_0054D_12597.pdf

Langer, E.J. (2014). Mindfulness forward and back. In The Wiley Blackwell Handbook of Mindfulness (Vol. I), New York: John Wiley. pp. 7–20.

Lippold, M.A., Jensen, T.M., Duncan, L.G., Nix, R.L., Coatsworth, J.D., & Greenberg, M.T. (2021). Mindful parenting, parenting cognitions, and parent-youth communication: Bidirectional linkages and mediational processes. *Mindfulness* 12, 381–391. doi:10.1007/s12671-019-01119-5

Luttrell, A., Briñol, P., & Petty, R.E. (2014). Mindful versus mindless thinking and persuasion. In The Wiley Blackwell Handbook of Mindfulness (Vol. II), New York: John Wiley. pp. 258–278.

Max-Neef, M.A. (1991). Human Scale Development: Conception, Application and Further Reflections. New York: The Apex Press.

MN (1995). Majjhima Nikhaya (Bhikku Bodhi. & Bhikkhu Nanamoli., Trans.). In Teaching of the Buddha: The Middle Length Discourses of the Buddha Majjhima Nikhaya (1st ed.). Kandy, Sri Lanka: Buddhist Publication Society.

MN.9 (2013). Sammaditthi Sutta: Right View. Majjhima Nikaya. Retrieved from www.accesstoinsight.org/tipitaka/mn/mn.009.than.html

Nāgārjuna (2004). Mūlamadhyamakakārikā of Nāgārjuna: The Philosophy of Middle Way. In Kalupahana, D.J. (Ed.). Delhi: Motilal Benarsidass Publishers.

Niedderer, K. (2014). Mediating mindful social interactions through design. In The Wiley Blackwell Handbook of Mindfulness (Vol. II). New York: John Wiley. pp. 345–366.

Scott, R.C., Schultz, P.P., & Ryan, J.D. (2014). Mindfulness, interest-taking, and self-regulation: A self-determination theory perspective on the role of awareness in optimal functioning. In The Wiley Blackwell Handbook of Mindfulness (Vol. II). New York: John Wiley. pp. 216–235.

Shantideva (n.d.). Bodhicaryavatara. In Zopa, G.T. (Ed.), Shantideva's Guide to the Bodhisattva's Way of Life. Malaysia: Losang Dragpa Buddhist Society.

SN.56.11 (2013). Dhammacakkappavattana Sutta: Setting the Wheel of Dhamma in Motion. Retrieved from www.accesstoinsight.org/tipitaka/sn/sn56/sn56.011.than.html

SN.II_utf8. Assutavantusuttaṃ Access to Insight. Retrieved from www.accesstoinsight.org/tipitaka/sltp/SN_II_utf8.html#pts.094

Tan, P. (2012). The Notion of Diṭṭhi: The Nature of Doubt, Views and Right View in Early Buddhism. Retrieved from http://dharmafarer.org/wordpress/wp-content/uploads/2013/04/40a.1-Notion-of-Ditthi-piya.pdf

Todd, W.L.T. (2013). The Ethics of Śāntideva and Śaṅkara: A Selfless Response to an Illusory World. London and New York: Routledge.

UN (2007). The Millennium Development Goals Report. Retrieved from www.un.org/millenniumgoals/pdf/mdg2007.pdf

UN (2015). Transforming Our World: The 2030 Agenda for Sustainable Development. Retrieved from sustainabledevelopment.un.org/post2015/transformingourworld

UNCED (1992). Rio Declaration on Environment and Development. Retrieved from https://sustainabledevelopment.un.org/outcomedocuments/agenda21

WHO (2014). "Mental Health." from www.who.int/features/factfiles/mental_health/en/.

WCED (1987). Our Common Future: Report of the World Commission on Environment and Development. Retrieved from http://netzwerk-n.org/wp-content/uploads/2017/04/0_Brundtland_Report-1987-Our_Common_Future.pdf

7

ONTOLOGICAL AUTHORITY OF SUSTAINABILITY IN HINDU TRADITIONS

The art of planetary maintenance

Fawad Khaleel and Kulathakattu Shobha

There is consensus among the ethical theorists that most of the practices and beliefs are common in most religions. The moral foundation theory discusses the universally accepted virtues and vices among them (Graham *et al.* 2013). Such universal values are visible to the ethical approaches of Hinduism. Hinduism has four primary goals of life, known as Artha (wealth), Kama (pleasure), Dharma (absolute reality) and Moksha (freedom). B.G. Tilak[1] elaborated these goals as: "The acceptance of the Vedas with reverence; recognition of the fact that the means or ways to salvation are diverse; and the realization of the truth that the number of gods to be worshipped is large, that indeed is the distinguishing feature of the Hindu religion" (Bhat *et al.* 2010).

Rautela (2015) explained Hinduism as: "Hinduism has a collection of sacred texts, as a whole known as *Sanatan Dharma*, i.e., the eternal teaching. Hinduism firmly believes in Karma's theory, the universal law of cause and effect, and fundamentally holds that one's actions (including one's thoughts) directly determine one's life, both one's current life and one's future lives. It has four major sects: *Shaiva* (devotees of the god *Shiva*), *Vaishnava* (devotees of the god *Vishnu*), *Shakta* (devotees of the goddess) and *Smarta* (those who understand the ultimate form of the divine to be abstract and all-encompassing, *Brahman*)." It is essential to know that local customs and traditions significantly impact practices and rituals. Noy (2009) opines that we can find a different worldview about the same religion in other parts of the world. Such a view is essential in understanding religious practices in local contexts and the same as Hinduism.

The global view of Hinduism is complex and dynamic. Our chapter describes that the Hinduism foundation relies on two beliefs, i.e., the planet and people. The Hindusim narratives broadly revolve around the themes of the earth and people. Prosperity and profit are attached to people and the world. Theoretically, Lakshmi (wealth) is a goddess and worshipped by the followers of Hinduism as they worship trees. It is worth noting that Mother Nature is preferable over human-made structures, which makes the ecological approach a part of Brahman.

Following this religious logic, our chapter explains different Hinduism themes regarding people and the planet to support sustainability within the religion-ethical framework of Hinduism. The following sections explore the conceptualization of these two themes concerning sustainable development. This remaining chapter is organized in the following way. Section 7.1 discussed the planet and the views of Hinduism about it and sustainable development. Next, Section 7.2 discussed the people, prosperity and their relationship with sustainable development. In the end, the conclusion is presented.

7.1 Planet

7.1.1 Dharti Mata *(Earth as mother)*

Essentially, Hinduism is related to the planet and particular to earth. Hinduism is promoting the relationship between nature and human beings. Singh and Clark (2016, p. 74) quote, "The Bhagavadgītā condemns and describes as thieves those who selfishly exploit the planet's resources without regard for its sustainability. It recommends a life of moderation in consumption and mutuality in receiving and giving." Furthermore, the notion in Atharva Veda (12.1.12) explains this relationship, which says, "*Mata Bhumih Putroham Prithivyah*," the Earth is my mother, and I am her child. Rautela (2015, p. 16) quoted as: "The Prithvi Sukta in Atharva veda states "Mata Bhumih Putroham Prithivyah" My Mother is Earth, and I am her Son. This notion reflects ancient wisdom as Rautela (2015) quotes, "Our ancient seers knew and appreciated that living beings are made of five elements; water (jal), air (vaayu), earth (prithvi), sky (Akash), and fire (Agni), and the approach of our ancient seers was to keep the five elements pure." By following this attitude, Hindus protect the essential ingredients of the environment.

Rautela (2015) further explains that *dharma* exists for the welfare of all beings, and by which the welfare of all beings is sustained, that for sure is dharma" (Mahābhārata 109.101; Singh and Clark 2016, p. 73). The sacred religious text of Vedas has four Vedas: Rigveda, Yajurveda, Samveda and Atharvaveda, and each of them starts the narrative with the worship of gods of nature, which emphasizes the preservation of the environment with the theological construct. One can observe from the following religious rituals, prayers as mentioned by Rautela (2015), Singh, and Clark (2016).

Rautela (2015, p. 15) explained, "The value system of Hinduism is full of love for nature. Earth is respected as a mother goddess; lessons for the purity of the five elements- space, air, fire, water, and earth, to take care of mother goddess is 'dharma' as a key element of value system." Whereas Singh and Clark (2016, p. 77) mentioned a Hindu prayer from the oral tradition,

"Lokāh. samastāh. sukhino bhavantu" "May the world be happy." It appears from the above quotations that Hinduism wants to see everyone happy in this world, i.e., human beings and nature.

Hinduism observes the focus on collectiveness, rather than individuality. The homeland is considered *dharti mata*, which focuses on the earth's role as a mother that sustains life and living things and therefore qualifies a treatment and care as one's mother. From here, one can conclude that protecting the earth and environment is the religious duty of Hinduism's followers.

7.1.2 Peace and nature

In Hinduism's ancient literature, one can find several prayers that are seeking peace from God about everything in this world. As we discussed earlier, human beings and nature are entirely aligned and connected. Every prayer has two dimensions, i.e., nature (environment) and human beings, both contextualized within the idea of universal peace. For instance, an ancient prayer mentioned in Yajur Veda (36:17) argues that there is no peace without universal peace as quoted in Singh and Clark (2016, p. 78), "Aum dyauh śāntirantariksam śāntih, prthivīśāntirāpah śāntirosadhayah śāntih, vanaspatayah śāntirviśvedevāh śāntirbrahma śāntih, sarvam śāntih śāntireva śāntih, sā māśāntiredhi Aum śāntih, śāntih, śāntih (May there be peace in the skies and on earth, May there be peace in the waters, plants and in the forests, May there be peace in the divine beings. May there be peace everywhere, and may that peace be ours)." Practically, peace in the world promotes and protects the environment. Otherwise, the reverse happens for nature and human beings. Conflicts accelerate the production of weapons armaments, disturb the ecological balance of life, deplete and abuse natural resources, and increase carbon dioxide concentration in the environment.

7.1.3 Protection of environment

Hinduism implants the metaphysical concepts and examines them within the behavior of its followers. "Here is a hymn from Isha Upanishad-Everything in the universe belongs to the Supreme God. Therefore, one should take what you need that is set aside for you. Do not take anything else, for you know to whom it belongs," as quoted by Rautela (2015, p. 15). This hymn suggests that wastage of resources and extravagance behavior is not appreciated. *Vastu shastra* (*vāstu śāstra* – the science of architecture) is a traditional Indian architecture system that originated in ancient India. According to this philosophy, building's design should not impact the surrounding environment and local ecology. The religious songs of the *Atharava Veda* also have the rhythmic words for the ecological and environmental values of Earth (*Bhumi-Sukta*).

Similarly, it is a sacred duty to protect the forests and the animals because they do not give any disadvantages to human development. Rautela (2015, p. 16) quoted from *Varah Purana*, "One who plants one *peepal* (Ficus religiosa), one *neem* (Azadirachta indica), one bar, ten flowering plants or creepers, two pomegranates, two oranges, and five mangos, does not go to hell." Likewise, *Charak Samhita* mentions that there is a positive correlation between the development of forests and states. So this is Hindus' duty to protect the forests if they want to develop their land and must consider it as their sacred duty. Similarly, the protection of animals is a religious duty of the followers of Hinduism. In Hinduism, some particular trees' worship is allowed, such as *tulsi* (*Ocimum tenuiflorum*), *peepal, aamla* (*Phyllanthus emblica*), and considered a source of nature's blessing and planted in almost every Hindu's homes. According to *Padma Purana*, "A person who is engaged in killing creatures, polluting ponds, wells, and tanks and destroying gardens certainly goes to hell" (Rautela 2015, p. 17). Scientific evidence verifies that planting trees is the cheapest and most natural way to reduce carbon dioxide from the atmosphere.[2] The trees mentioned above are beneficial in the upgradation of the environment, especially the tree of neem. Overall, Hinduism tries to create a sense of harmony between human beings and their surrounding environment. This idea of progress and development is the narrative of sustainability. The aspiration towards universal well-being and an end to economic deprivation within the Hinduism theology brings it closer to the delivery of the fundamental sustainable development goals (SDGs).

Rāmāyana, the life story of Rama, conceptualizes a vision of utopia, where human development is complementary to the natural world, and there is no suffering of conscious material beings (living things) and the unconscious material world. Similarly, *Raksha Sukra Movement* started in Uttarakhand, India. Under *Rakhsha Bandan*,[3] women consider trees are their brothers and tie a holy thread on a selected tree. Women protect the chosen tree as their brothers and consider it as a sacred duty for them. "*Ahimsa*[4]" is the religious belief of Hinduism, which reflects avoiding violence. Under this belief, a majority of Hindus are vegetarians and do not kill animals. Rautela (2015, p. 17) debates the *Ahimsa* claims that raising animals for food generating more greenhouse gases than all the trucks and cars in the whole world, one of the key areas mentioned in the UN Global Sustainable Development Report (2016).

The Bishnoi movement in the 15th century is the best example of protecting the environment and animals.[5] This tradition is derived from the Vedic era. Another Hinduism concept is Vasudhaiva Kutumbakam, a Sanskrit phrase found in Hindu texts such as the Maha Upanishad. The word means the world is one family.[6]

Singh and Clark (2016) summed up the whole discussion as: "In his popular version of the *Rāmāyana,* which tells the life story of *Rama,* the great 16th century religious poet Sant Tulsidas writes of an ideal community in which "there is no premature death or suffering of any kind; everyone enjoys beauty and health. No one is poor, sorrowful, or in want; no one is ignorant." There are no violence and nature flourishes. As Tulsidas narrates, "The trees in the forests bloom and bear fruit throughout the year; the elephant and lion live together as friends; birds and beasts of every kind are no longer hostile and live in harmony with one another." This metaphoric communal paradise of the Hindu vision makes the overcoming of suffering as its ideal. The aspiration towards universal literacy and healthcare and an end to poverty articulates the SDGs' fundamental aims. All Hindus can commit to these goals and to working with our fellow human beings for their attainment" (pp. 81–82).

7.2 People

7.2.1 Religious pillars and welfare

Hinduism gives a central stage to all human beings by saying that "God exists in the heart of all beings" (Bhagavadgītā 18:61). Clark and Singh (2016, p. 74) quote, "The equal presence of God in all beings is the source of the inherent dignity and equal worth of every human being. It is the Hindu spiritual antidote to any effort to deny the personhood, value, and dignity of another."

Hinduism's four primary goals follow the discourse within Bhagavadgītā, which formulates the four pillars of religious narrative. *Artha* is wealth and the first goal of life; this aligns Hinduism with the economic comprehension of economic beings. This goal lays the structure for religious life and provides a practically viable perspective for living a life. Economic development emphasis supported by the religious narrative encourages entrepreneurial activities and fight against voluntary poverty. Within Hinduism, the accumulation of wealth is not a pointless endeavor. Instead, it is a part of the second goal of *Kama* (pleasure). Wealth through fair means is for enjoying the necessities of lives. The above two goals lead the third goal of life is *Dharma*, i.e., serving the community, where excess wealth is utilized. Therefore, Hinduism takes a pragmatic approach and argues that it is a religious duty first to sustain oneself financially and then help others. *Dharma* (serving the community) focuses on building social capital within the community and applying this social capital for development. *Daan* (voluntary giving) plays a significant role in the life of Hindus. The concept of *daan* focuses on community cohesion.

The final pillar is *Moksha* (liberation, freedom from rebirth), which concentrates on the life of spirituality. This can be achieved through a lot of efforts, continuous worship and serving the community. According to Hinduism, this will lead to the cycle of rebirth. A Hindu can understand what before he was not able to know and then overcome the *avidyā* (ignorance), follow the relationship between *Brahman* (absolute reality) and human self (*ātman*). At this stage, the worshiper will be free from the greed, and the person becomes generous with others and shares the joy and sorrow of the other members of the community (Singh and Clark 2016). Besides, they added that the Hindu teaching about *karma* is connected to the belief in a cycle of birth, death and rebirth, called *sam˙sāra*. Our choices in the present are shaping our futures and our future lives. These choices are essential to avoid suffering and should be guided by the values of non-injury, compassion, truth, generosity and self-control.

The fundamental notion within these pillars is expressed within a traditional prayer. "May all be happy; May all be without disease; May all have well-being; May none have the misery of any sort" – *Brihadaaranyaka* Upanishad (1.4.14). Singh and Clark (2016, p. 77) discuss this theological construct and argue that: "Hinduism recognizes the need of every human being for access to those material necessities, such as food, healthcare, shelter, and clothing, that make life possible and that enable human beings to live with dignity." Narayanan (2013) mentioned, "The Hindu notion of the *purusharthas* re-conceptualizes sustainable consumption by acknowledging the human tendency to want and directing ways for material and sensuous consumption to be under the rules of *dharma* or duty (Narayanan (2010). The dharma stage, where the most productive partnerships between the Hindu religion and sustainable development may be realized" (p. 136).

7.2.2 Sacred or secular

It is worth noting that in Hinduism, some activities are sacred, which are considered secular in other religions, for example, worshiping Lakshami or worshiping trees, etc. One of the Hindu tradition's essential insights is its critique of greed and the culture of consumerism but explained differently. Narayanan (2013, p. 136) elaborates and quotes, "The notion of *dharmic* sustainability should rely on the complementary strengths of science and religion. Seen this way, if dharma is the value, then sustainability becomes the strategy by which to live and realize the value." However, Ilaiah (1996) criticizes self-realization and argues that the relationships between Hinduism and the environment promote materialism. Jug Suraiya (2007) says that this leads to more consumption, which harms society's poor and middle-income groups. Moreover, some authors, like Ilaiah (1996) criticized various practices in India, i.e., suppression through the caste system, which is unlawful and morally wrong. According to the teaching of Hinduism, there is no difference among human beings. The Upaniṣad prayer "*Saha vīryam karavāvahi*" says, "May we work together, energetically." The Hindu tradition does not make a sharp distinction between the sacred and the secular (Singh and Clark 2016, p. 80). They further wrote, "Asserting our rights is only possible and meaningful in a context were equal, if not greater, recognition is given to our duties and obligations. In Hindu mythology, the symbol of *dharma* is the bull, whose four feet are truth, purity, compassion and generosity" (p. 81).

Similarly, Agrawal (2000) criticizes self-realization, and in his opinion, it harms the relationship between the Hindu self and the environment and promotes materialism. In contrast, Jug Suraiya (2007) says that this leads to more consumption, which harms society's poor and middle-income groups. Narayanan (2013, p. 134) cited, "Central to the worship of Lakshmi in Hinduism, for instance, is the emphasis on enlightened spending and experience of materialism in a manner that assists self-realization, which is consistent with sustainable consumption Narayanan (2010)." Mahatma Gandhi placed a question, "Does economic progress clash with real progress?" (Iyer 1990, p. 94). "If economic development means the accumulation of wealth and profit without limit, then, Gandhi believed, 'economic progress … is antagonistic to real progress" (Iyer 1990, p. 97).

Narrating the dignity of the human being, even as a child, Singh and Clark (2016, p. 77) quote, "The Yajur Veda speaks of the womb as the birthplace of the divine. Children have the same dignity and value as adults since the divine exists equally in the child. Dignity is not dependent on biological age, or emotional and intellectual maturity. Children's value does not lie in fulfilling economic or adult needs. In honoring the child, we honor God."

The preceding discussion underscores that Hindusim's main objective is to keep the peace in the earth and increase the human being's welfare, which are the essential ingredients of sustainable development and guides how to achieve the SDGs.

7.3 Conclusion

The traditions of Hinduism are interwoven theological constructs, which are complex but carry rich meanings. The key themes that emerge within the Hinduism narrative are the well-being of the planet by maintaining a harmonious relationship with the environment and eliminating poverty through sustainable economic development. Worshiping Lakshmi demonstrates that wealth is a crucial requirement in Hinduism as poverty is not allowed. If people are poor, then *Daan* is the solution. Hence, religious worship, people and prosperity are complementary to each other. Worshiping *Tulsi*, *Peepal* and *Neem* indicates this phenomenon. The World Economic Forum suggests that tree plantation is the cheapest way to reduce carbon dioxide. Through this sacred religious duty, the followers of Hinduism can upgrade the environment. All of the rituals of Hinduism follow sustainable development objectives and complement economic and environmental research work such as *Limits to Growth* (1972), *Brundtland Report* (1977) and *The Kyoto Protocol* (1987). If a person is a true believer and follower of Hinduism, he will become the dedicated representative of the United Nations' SDGs.

Notes

1 Tilak was the first leader of the Indian Independence Movement.
2 www.weforum.org/agenda/2019/12/climate-change-carbon-capture-conditions/
3 "*Raksha Bandhan* (or *Raksha Bandhana, or Rakhi*) is a Hindu festival that celebrates the relationship between brothers and sisters, and families, on the full moon of the Hindu month of *Shravana (Shravan Poornima*), or around July and August. This day is also called Brother and Sister Day". (www.timeanddate.com/holidays/india/raksha-bandhan)
4 (in the Hindu, Buddhist and Jainist tradition) respect for all living things and avoidance of violence towards others. (https://en.wikipedia.org/wiki/Ahi%E1%B9%83s%C4%81).
5 "Bishnoi faith is a religious offshoot of Hinduism founded on 29 principles, most of which promote environmental stewardship. Bishnois strictly forbid the harming of trees and animals" (Rautela 2015, p.18).
6 https://en.wikipedia.org/wiki/Vasudhaiva_Kutumbakam

References

Agarwal, A. (2000). Can Hindu beliefs and values help India meet its ecological crisis? In Chapple, C. & Tucker, M.E. (Ed.), Hinduism and Ecology: The Intersection of Earth, Sky and Water. Cambridge, MA: Harvard University Press, pp. 165–182.

Bhat, P.I., Gopalan, S., & Dongre, Y. (2010). Philanthropy and religion, Hinduism. In Anheier, H.K. & Toepler, S. (Eds.), International Encyclopedia of Civil Society. New York: Springer.

Graham, J., Haidt, J., Koleva, S., Motyl, M., Iyer, R., Wojcik, S.P., & Ditto, P.H. (2013). Moral foundations theory: The pragmatic validity of moral pluralism. *Advances in Experimental Social Psychology* (Vol. 47). Cambridge, MA: Academic Press, pp. 55–130.

Ilaiah, K. (1996). Why I Am Not a Hindu: A Sudra Critique of Hindutva Philosophy, Culture and Political Economy. Calcutta: Samya.

Iyer, R. (1990). The Essential Writings of Mahatma Gandhi. New Delhi: Oxford University Press.

Suraiya, J. (2007). Why Diwali Is Such a Gilt Trip. *The Times of India*. http://timesofindia.indiatimes.com/Opinion/Sunday_Specials/Why_Diwali_is_such_a_gilt_trip/articleshow/2515779.cms [4 November 2011].

Narayanan, Y. (2013). Religion and sustainable development: Analysing the connections. *Sustainable Development 21*(2), 131–139.

Narayanan, Y. (2010). Sustainable consumption as a means to self-realization: A Hindu perspective on when enough is enough. *Sustainable Development 18*(5), 252–259.

Noy, D. (2009). Material and spiritual conceptions of development: A framework of ideal types. *Journal of Developing Societies 25*(23), 275–307.

Rautela, R. (2015). Role of Hinduism in maintaining sustainable. *International Journal of Socio-Legal Analysis and Rural Development* 2(1), 15–18.

Singh, K & Clark, J.S. (2016). Voices from Religions on Sustainable Development, German Federal Ministry for Economic Cooperation and Development (BMZ),

Division 111: Churches; political foundations; social structural programmes; religion and development, Germany.

United Nations (2016). Global Sustainable Development Report 2016. New York: Department of Economic and Social Affairs.

Zinnbauer, B.J., Pargament, K.I., Cole, B., Rye, M.S., Butter, E.M., Belavich, T.G., Hipp, K.M., Scott, A.B., & Kadar, J.L. (1997). Religion and spirituality: Unfuzzying the fuzzy. *Journal for the Scientific Study of Religion* 36(4), 549–564.

8

SUSTAINABILITY AND BEHAVIOR OF ISLAMIC MARKET

Toseef Azid, Umar Burki and Muhammad Omer Chaudhry

As global communities struggle with the consequences of the COVID-19 pandemic, it is becoming increasingly important to debate the moral and ethical decisions that are being taken. Prior research (e.g., McArthur and Rasmussen 2018) claims that the majority of the world's nations, including underdeveloped economies, have improved their health and education systems in recent years. However, the evident unpreparedness of both developed and developing economies for the current crisis has led to the widespread collapse of health systems that have been exposed as being extremely fragile. National governments and multilateral organizations such as the World Health Organization (WHO) are struggling to understand the virus and provide a clear plan on how to deal with the COVID-19 pandemic. The enormity of the crisis has left governments and international organizations alike unable to steer a clear path for the future.

Prior research (e.g., Kharas 2017; Desai and Kharas 2017) examines the role of qualitative economic variables such as per-capita income in achieving the sustainable development goals (SDGs) without integrating vital socio-economic variables from the health sector. Research studies (Schmidt-Traub 2018; Nnadi *et al.* 2017; McArthur and Rasmussen 2016) report that amongst 123 countries aspiring to reach the targets, only seven are on track to meet all four relevant SDG targets, namely, access to clean water, access to sanitation, undernourishment and primary school completion rates. Current literature (Gertz and Kharas 2018) found that the majority of countries are seriously off track in their attempts to achieve the SDGs because they ignore the health-related life-sustaining variables that are essential in fighting the global pandemic.

The global pandemic threat accentuates the essential need for training in the moral aspects that play a vital role in confronting the prevalent global socio-economic and ethical inequalities and are integral to achieving the SDGs.

Hence, policy makers, economic analysts, health experts and academics are frequently raising questions related to the SDGs; for example: What do we need to change in our current world? What actions are needed in order to make these changes? How can we organize the necessary transformation? What measures are needed to eradicate social injustice and prejudice from our world?

The United Nations Environment Program (UNEP) report (2017) underlined that the world's climate is continuing to heat up at a faster pace even after the signing of the Paris Climate Agreement. Desai *et al.* (2018) argue that the world can achieve some of the SDGs such as undernourishment, malnutrition, increased smallholder productivity, sustainable agriculture and biodiversity through the application of the right technologies, suitable access to finance, proper (rather than perverse) incentives and cross-border cooperation mechanisms. However, a majority of studies (Hayek 1976; Rothbard 1993; Kirzner 1989) fail to discuss the role of non-market variables that play a prominent role in the deterioration of ordinary people's lifestyles, health and daily economic opportunities.

It is therefore crucial to question the role of moral and ethical values in achieving the SDGs. We argue that without addressing this moral deficit, it will be extremely challenging to meet the targets of the SDGs. Religious norms provide the needed moral foundations that have a significant positive effect on protecting both people and the environment and thereby can help in realising the aims of the SDGs, consequently increasing the welfare of society.

Religion and moral philosophies are becoming an integral part of economics. The literature (Boettke 1995; Langrill and Storr 2012; Storr 2009; Ratnapala 2006) outlines various efforts to critically assess different theories of conventional economics through the lenses of religion and moral values. Among these, Islamic economics is now becoming very popular. The supporters of Islamic economics follow the teaching of the Holy *Qur'an* and the traditions of the Holy Prophet, Muhammad (PBUH), known as *the Sunnah*. Islamic economists argue that Islam is a universal religion and promotes a value-based economy. The foundation of Islamic economics is its all-inclusive approach that increases the welfare of all the individuals in a society and, indeed, the whole universe. Under Islamic economics, religious injunctions support the well-being of the entire human race and the environment through the tenets of peace and justice. Material comfort and social welfare are equally essential in Islamic economics. Preference wise, the first priority is all human life, followed by the environment and lastly economic benefits.

Under a traditional economic system, worldly accomplishments show the success of an individual or market. Supporters of a market economy argue that individuals, even when they act opportunistically, make an overall contribution to the welfare of the economy and its society. The presence of self-interest does not limit the benefits to society. Accordingly, an increase in the number of exchanged goods will deliver higher welfare levels, which provide benefits that are more substantial to society. In this manner, material prosperity enhances the welfare of society. As a result, higher economic transactions increase social, psychological and human capital, which eventually helps both the growth of an economy and the well-being of society.

On the other hand, value-based societies focus on building an exchange environment that creates trust, love, hope, faith, courage, temperance and justice. Conventional economics sidesteps such issues and fails to emphasize the role of religious and moral dimensions in economic transactions and the critical role of the moral economy. There is a consensus among the supporters of the moral economy that religion is the primary source of moral values (Qutub 1980; Novak 1993; Islahi 2007). A value-based economy increases the level of cooperation among the members of its society. In such a moral economy, most economic exchanges, whether with strangers or known individuals, rely on value-based characteristics such as honesty, trust, reliability, generosity, brotherhood, justice and fairness. Even in moderately regulated markets, the presence of moral behavior (e.g., trust) is a necessary condition for all kinds of economic exchanges.

Islamic economics postulates that human beings are more valuable than worldly assets because moral values play a more significant role in the evolution of the welfare of society. Orthodox economics focuses primarily on market concepts such as value, price and economic exchanges. Such a contrast between the philosophy behind conventional and Islamic economics raises several vital questions. Does traditional economics miss essential elements in analyzing market functions? How is it possible for an individual to become better off and, at the same time, make others better off during the exchange process? Is the price mechanism, one of the necessary foundations of orthodox economics compatible with the Islamic *Shariah*?

This chapter attempts to develop an understanding of societal welfare by applying the principles of Islamic economics. Section 8.1 discusses traditional economic perspectives on the free market and the moral values of a market economy/society. Section 8.2 discusses the Islamic market economy and how guiding moral principles promote virtuousness. The chapter concludes with a discussion of the issues raised and suggestions for future research directions.

8.1 Is the free market desirable?

The economic literature provides contrasting arguments both for and against the free market. Several philosophers, academics and intellectuals (e.g., McCloskey 2006; Hayek 1976; Kirzner 1989; Rothbard 1993) support the idea of a free market and claim that it encourages virtuousness. In contrast, a large number of critics (e.g., Gray 1998; Sacks 2002; Polanyi 1944) argue against how the free market functions and consider it a cause of socio-economic strife.

On balance, the literature favors the free market. Some have argued that the free market teaches its participants to behave morally by demonstrating that virtuous actions have a positive impact on the functioning of their firms. However, others believe that the free market is more likely to create vice rather than virtuousness.

8.1.1 What the free market can do

McCloskey (2006) claimed that market forces improve the moral and ethical behaviors of market participants. The Nobel laureate Hayek (1976)[1] was a passionate supporter of free market economics and believed it to be the only institution that can increase societal welfare and equitably distribute resources. In his opinion, a free market has a neutral moral environment, i.e., a market itself is not moral or immoral. Instead, it is the behavior of the market participants that determines the moral or immoral aspects of their actions. Based on these arguments, Hayek considers the free market as an institution that allows the whole of humanity to participate. Kirzner (1989) and Hayek (1976) believed that the market itself is not a just or unjust exchange entity, and it would be unfair if the fruits of the endeavors of its participants were redistributed under the umbrella of any regulatory body. Rothbard (1993) argued that a market allows strangers to conduct economic transactions without any knowledge of each other to satisfy their needs and potentially, the needs of others. Storr (2009) claims that the market is a moral space for virtuous actors as it provides an opportunity to be virtuous by satisfying the needs of the community and creating an environment of trust and tolerance.

A number of researchers (Weber 1998; Ger and Belk 1996; McCloskey 2006; Langrill and Storr 2012; Mueller 1999) argue that markets can only grow in an environment of freedom. Storr (2009, p. 291) underscores that: "The market, of course, is no panacea. However, if they are given a chance to flourish, we will grow wealthier, healthier, better connected with far-flung relatives and friends, better educated, better behaved, more generous, more compassionate, more tolerant, more trusting, and more just. The market will deliver cures for cancer and new, post-crude oil, energy sources. If allowed to flourish, the market will also make us better connected and more virtuous."

8.1.2 What the free market cannot do

Conversely, several leading economic researchers (Gray 1998; Sacks 2002; Polanyi 1944) reason that a market creates an environment of greed, escalates immorality, promotes materialism, accelerates a sense of selfishness, boosts dishonesty, makes people corrupt and leaves no space for virtuousness.

Whenever a market expands, it erodes the sense of mutuality in a society/community and then slowly demolishes its moral and ethical principles (Storr 2009). Langrill and Storr (2012) affirmed that it is a proven fact that markets make people act in a selfish, greedy and dishonest manner. Many have argued (Gray 1998; Sacks 2002; Polanyi 1944) that if there is no space for love, fairness, generosity, justice, prudence, tolerance and temperance in the free market then we do not need it, and we should attempt to reduce its size and influence.

Gray (1998) asserted that because of the influence of markets, societies and communities are losing their human bonds and ties, reducing their moral beliefs and seeing trust among individuals, groups and institutions weakened. He further added that a typical free market is unable to improve the overall condition of a society as it lacks infrastructural support necessary to develop the material, social, psychological, cultural, spiritual and religious aspects of a community. Sacks (2002) argued that societal income inequality is one of the by-products of a free market. He explained that markets give first preference to individual desires and can't deliver the needed spiritual and community goods that are needed to cultivate a firm moral bond between social agents. A free market's prime focus is on the provision of material products and thus demonstrates a lack of concern in producing social and spiritual goods (Sacks 2002).

Other leading researchers (Gudeman 2001; Marx 1994; Lefebvre 1991; Harvey 2001; MacIntyre 1979) also argue that there is a continuous decline in the communal space available for society as markets transform every activity of social and economic agents into a commercialized action. Hence, human bonds develop around individual needs and necessities and elements such as benevolence (altruism) and kindness are ignored. Polanyi (1944, 2001) discussed the concept of double movement and said that marketization creates an environment of self-interest, greediness, stinginess and lacks a sense of generosity. In contrast, an economy based on society and community establishes an atmosphere of mutuality, generosity, fairness, justice and kindness. In his opinion, markets and communities function in totally different directions.

8.1.2.1 Does the free market help in responding to pandemic

The COVID-19 pandemic has proved that poorly regulated markets cannot effectively support sustainable development. It has been proved that some products which are highly profitable but a cause of decreasing the human immunity and dangerous for human health. For example, the production and consumption of intoxicating goods such as alcohol generate considerable profits, but harm human health as they reduce the effectiveness of the immune system (Burke 1988; Cook and Moore 2002).[2] Similarly, many products produced by multinational food corporations produce harmful effects on the human body, such as obesity, that result in comorbidities. Likewise, the global armament industry is having a hazardous impact on the peace and security of our world (United Nations 1977). Arms manufacturing firms reap phenomenal economic benefits at the cost of human lives. Global military expenditure has increased by 75% in the last 20 years. In the year 2018 alone, China and the USA spent 14% and 36%, respectively, of their GDP on military expenditures, which were 5.8% and 45.3% of GDP, respectively, a decade earlier.[3] Instead of this, countries can spend this amount for the development of the health sector.

In contrast, the annual World Health Organization report (2019)[4] states that global health expenditure grew in real terms by only 3.9% (p. ix). Hence, it is hard to believe that the current value-neutral market approach can play any decisive role in achieving the SDGs. The current order of preferences established in the global market places economic profit as the priority, followed by the environment and finally by the people. Such market preferences completely ignore the socio-moral dimensions that are essential for achieving the triple bottom line objectives of people, planet and profit (Elkington 1999).

8.2 Islamic moral market economics and sustainable development

In this section, our focus is on the economics of the Islamic moral market and how it supports sustainable development. Islamic teachings integrate the worldly human life and the life hereafter under the faith and stipulate that worship and worldly affairs have a singular objective: to please Allah (SWT). A society needs love, mercy, help, cooperation, brotherhood, equity and reasonable equality among human beings. Fairness, justice and honesty are the necessary norms to achieve this singular objective. In the eyes of Allah (SWT), everyone is equal, and exploiting others for individual gain is forbidden.

8.2.1 The Islamic moral market: a different paradigm

The *Qur'an* and *Sunnah* (practices and sayings of Prophet Muhammad) are the primary sources of all Islamic norms. Islam provides specific training to its followers, especially for those who drive businesses and are involved in economic activities.

8.2.1.1 The fundamental assumptions of the Islamic model

a. Allah (SWT) created everyone with good nature.[5] When individuals are following the right path, they become the best people (*Momin*).[6] Allah (SWT) has given dignity to every human being, but every person is accountable for his actions in this and the life hereafter.
b. Islam considers endeavoring for a livelihood as a holy war[7] and allows a reasonable or just profit. After achieving the target of just profit, a Muslim entrepreneur must take care of his family, neighbors and marginalized people in society,[8] and at the same time, protect the environment.

c. These Islamic principles negate self-interest and allow all economic and social agents to seek personal benefits as well as work for the welfare of the general public and the environment.
d. Honoring business and social contracts is a mandatory divine duty for a Muslim, and anybody who breaches his contractual obligations is not a Muslim (Azid *et al.* 2007). Furthermore, accomplishing one's contracts symbolizes the degree of religiosity in an Islamic society.
e. Trust has a paramount position among the members of the Islamic community. A Muslim entrepreneur can use all available options to function in the way permitted under the *Shari'ah* (Islamic jurisprudence). Furthermore, the entrepreneur must ensure that all entrepreneurial activities promote benevolence and virtuousness, which support and protect the general public and the environment.

8.2.1.2 A way towards the Islamic moral market

Moral hazards and adverse selection are absent in an Islamic moral market. Voluntary disclosure is an essential part of the market, which allows complete information symmetry to all the market stakeholders. Credit in the money markets is commodity-based, and no financial institution can issue a loan that is beyond its capacity.

Financial institutions act as the trustees of the depositors' money. Similarly, goods and labor markets follow the equity standard for distributing income and resources. A person who has more than he requires must distribute the excess among the needy members of society. Islam appreciates equity in place of equality in the market, i.e., prices and wages should be just. The equity standard ensures that if someone has bountiful resources, others should not become destitute. That is why Islamic injunctions support the distribution of wealth and resources through *sadaqah* (charity), *usher*, *zakat*,[9] an interest-free economy and the law of inheritance. There is a consensus among Muslim jurists that without the proper distribution of resources, a market can't function properly or be called a moral market.

8.2.1.3 The holy Quranic injunction and the Islamic moral market

The Holy *Qur'an* explicitly mentions the market in two places in the *Surrah Al Furqan*.[10] Explicitly, The Holy *Qur'an* underscores the Islamic position about the market in a transparent manner, i.e., a market has no negative connotation in Islam. In the *Surah*, *Al Maida* (verse 100, Chapter 5), the Holy *Qur'an* explicitly outlines how the production of goods and services should take place.

> *Say, "Not equal are the evil and the good, although the abundance of evil might impress you." So fear Allah, O you of understanding, that you may be successful* (5:100) .

Under the Islamic framework, a market has two sub-categories: market A and market B. Market A is for worldly transactions and market B for divine transactions, i.e., with Allah (SWT) as stated consistently in The Holy *Qur'an*. For instance, some of the verses and commandments from Allah (SWT) are:

> *These are people who bartered true guidance for waywardness. Their commerce did not profit them, nor are they rightly guided* (2:16).[11]

The above verse underscores that it is crucial to understand that when the preferences are not right, Allah (SWT) will punish the buyer (humans/human being). Hence, making the wrong preference order is punishable.

It is clear from the following verse that when the preference order is correct, Allah (SWT) will become the purchaser, and accordingly, man will receive the reward from Allah (SWT). Contrary to the verse (2:286), (9:111) narrates that Allah (SWT) is the buyer, and he will give the reward.

> *God has purchased from the believers their souls and their wealth and, in exchange, the Garden shall be theirs. They fight in the cause of God; they kill and are killed—a true promise from Him in the Torah, the Evangel, and the Qur'an. Who is more truthful to his promise than God? So be of good cheer regarding that business deal you transact. That is the greatest of triumphs* (9:111).

Islam instructs the believers that when they perform transactions in "Market A," they should concurrently prepare themselves for the transactions of "Market B." Therefore, transactions in "Market A" should be conducted by following the guidance provided in the *Qur'an* and the *Sunnah*. For this reason, believers should make their rational preferences (choices) wisely, i.e., preference of life hereafter over the present life, reward over punishment, right over wrong, virtuousness over vice, etc. These preferences require good deeds, submission to oneself, paying in the way of Allah (SWT) generosity, honesty and sacrifice. To get a reward in "Market B," some specific types of dealings are required.

> *A commerce that will save you from a painful torment. [t]hat you believe in God and His Messenger; that you exert yourselves with your wealth and persons* (61:10).[12]

It is apparent that "Market B" also deals in a unique way with financial transactions. These transactions follow the concept of Islamic philanthropy, which is different from the conventional definition. Under the Islamic epistemology, these transactions are between the creator and his creations.

> *Who shall be the one who offers up to Allah a handsome loan, which Allah shall multiply for him many times over? It is Allah Who holds back or gives in abundance, and to Him you shall return* (2:245).[13]

In the *Surrah Al-Baqarah* (chapter 2), Allah (SWT) states that the reward for spending in the way of Allah (SWT) and performing other good deeds is:

> *Those who spend their wealth in the cause of Allah, and do not follow up their gifts with reminders of their generosity or with injury, their reward is with their Lord. On them shall be no fear, nor shall they grieve* (2; 262).[14]

Omer Ibn Khattab (*the Second Caliph*) formulated a market committee and appointed a woman as chief, whose duty was to monitor the daily functions of the market. The committee observed market prices, the quality of the goods and services, and dealt severely with matters related to market exploitation and the adulteration of items offered for sale.

8.2.1.4 The price mechanism

The Holy Prophet (SAW) referred to price fixation as: "it is Allah (SWT) who pushes prices up or down, [and] I do not want to face Him with a burden of injustice" (Reda 2013, p. 446). He also emphasized that all Muslims are one body; all are brothers and if one Muslim is in an adverse situation, then all others must feel it. In a similar vein, the Prophet (SAW) said: "The faithful are like a unique body in cooperation and in showing mercy to each other. When an organ falls ill, other parts of the body also accompany it" (quoted by Reda 2013, p. 447). Another saying is, "All of you are shepherds and responsible for those whom you have under your control" (quoted by Reda 2013, p. 447). These statements reflect that in Islam there should be an authority that will look after the interests of all stakeholders.

Old Muslim jurists like Yahya bin Umar al-Kinani, Ibn Taimiyah, Ibn Qayyam, Ibn Khaldun and Al-Ghazali were not in favor of price fixation, but also opposed price wars and aggressive cutthroat competition that encourages malpractice and compromises social justice (cited in Islahi 2007).

In the opinion of Ibn Taimiyah (1976), price should only be fixed if there are some imperfections due to the malpractice of market agents. Al-Ghazali is in favor of pricing determined by market forces, but he also emphasized that prices should be in line with mutual benevolence. Ibn Tulun (1998) and Ibn Iyas (1960) have a different opinion with regard to the price of necessities. They are in favor of fixing the prices of necessities for the welfare of the common citizen. They supported the role of the *hisbah* (an institution which looks after the functioning of the market and other offices) to supervise the activities of market agents (Islahi 2007, p. 4; Islahi 1985).

During the period of the Ottoman Empire it was the duty of *muhtasib* (Judge of the Court) to fix prices in consultation with stakeholders on the basis of cost-plus financing whereby profit should not be more than 12% of the cost (Islahi 2007, p. 4). Al-Baji (1332 AH) and Ibn Khaldun (1967) were also in favor of cost-plus financing. However, Ibn Qudamah (1972) was not in favor of price fixing. In his opinion, price fixation has a negative effect on production, consumption and the import of goods and services. Al Baji (1332 AH) is of the opinion that low price levels lead to low profit margins and are ultimately the cause of hoarding and corruption. Abu Yusuf (1979) asserted that price fluctuations are not only due to market forces but also other variables. In his opinion, the changes in prices are through Allah's order. Ibn Khaldun (1967) said that low profits decrease trade, moderate profits increase trade, but high profits discourage the demand for a product. Al-Ghazali (2009) insisted that sellers should seek the profit from the ultimate market, i.e., "Market B," instead of the temporal one, i.e., "Market A" (Islahi 2007).

8.2.1.5 Negating exploitation

Al-Ghazali (2009) emphasized that although believers should involve themselves in market activities and fulfill their social and economic needs, this should not be their ultimate goal. They are accountable to Allah (SWT) for all of their actions. They should therefore follow Islamic moral and ethical norms. Al Dimishiqi (1977) and Ibn Iskandar appreciated the necessity of self-interest but stated that these dealings should be virtuous, i.e., based on honesty, charity, generosity, etc. Al Dimishiqi and Ibn Iskandar (cited in Hosseine 2003) are in favor of just profits, which cannot be made as a result of the exploitation of the community. According to them, excessive profit taking will deter customers from the market. According to Al Dimishqi (1977), a competitive market is the best strategy, though this competition is not like a conventional economic market, but follows the moral teachings of the *Qur'an* and *Sunnah*. He was a strong advocate for a transparent process of exchange and said that all market agents should have a complete knowledge of the market; transactions should not be polluted and preference given to humans over profit.

Reda (2013, p. 448) summarizes the behavior of market actors in this way: "The prophet also invokes the bee metaphor in the following hadith: 'The faithful resemble a bee. It eats only what is clean and with clear products. When it settles on a thin plant it does not break it. The faithful believer is defined as one who strives in this world for God and arranges his life according to what God has ordered. Like a bee on a plant, the believer in this world seeks moderation by only taking what is necessary, thereby making use of nature but without breaking it; he also stays clean by not falling into the rash temptations of a fleeting world.'"

8.2.1.6 Negating exploitation caused by the use of monopolies

Muslim jurists support market competition and refuse to accept the establishment of monopolies. As we have mentioned above, in the Islamic environment there is no room for moral hazards and adverse selection, which ultimately reduces the negative impact of market imperfections. Al-Jaziri (n.d.) condemned the involvement of the ruling class in business and trading activities. He emphasized that if the ruling class is running a business, it will in effect be a monopoly, making it difficult for an ordinary person to run a business on an equal footing. He criticized trading by the Sultan and his monopolization of certain trades. He stressed that if rulers began trading, the general populace would not survive as they would be unable to compete (Islahi 2007, p. 3). Qadi Abd al-Jabbar (1965) appreciated and acknowledged market forces but in believed that as Allah (SWT) ultimately controlled everything all fluctuations in the market come from the order of Allah (SWT). He did however argue that the state has to intervene whenever there are malpractices in the market.

It is worthwhile to note that one aspect that distinguishes the conventional moral market from the Islamic moral market is the guidance which is provided to the latter by Allah (SWT) through the *Qur'an* and the practices of his messenger, Prophet Muhammad (SAW). In the conventional moral market, the focus is on "Market A." There is no "Market B." All trade that takes place is solely for this world whereas the exchanges that take place in the Islamic moral market also take into account the rewards that traders expect to receive from Allah (SWT) in the life hereafter.

8.3 Islamic injunctions and the "Triple Bottom Line"

The world faces major challenges with the rapid advance of climate change and the overall degradation of the environment. The main contributors to these ecological hazards are the activities of humans in propagating a system of unsustainable production and consumption. Rising greenhouse gas emissions have a proven negative impact on the environment. Islam forbids such disturbances to the ecological balance. In chapter 55 (al Rahman) of al Qur'an (Allah (SWT) says: "so weigh all things fairly and do not disturb the (God-ordained) balance" (55:7). In chapter 57 (al Hadedd) of al Qur'an, Allah (SWT) states: "We have already sent Our messengers with clear evidences and sent down with them the Scripture and the balance that the people may maintain [their affairs] in justice (57: 25). The word *mizan* is used for balance, which means a perfect equilibrium. According to the teaching of Islam, this system is disturbed when there is human corruption, referred to as *fasad.* Allah (SWT) made human beings the vicegerent (*khalifa*) of this earth. As a result, humans are invested with a great deal of responsibility in acting as the custodians of the trust placed in them by Allah (SWT). It is the duty of humans to protect the environment, to look after the interests of the present as well as future generations when using the resources of the earth. As we discussed in the above sections, Islam does not support any kind of exploitation in its societies, frowns on extravagance and forbids the misuse of the earth's resources. Islamic injunctions are therefore aligned with the triple bottom line: people, planet and profit (Elkington 1999). The first priority is given to human beings (people), the second to the earth and its resources (planet) and the third to economic benefits (profit). Al-Ghazali (2009) explained that the objective of *shari'ah* (Islamic jurisprudence) is to protect faith, life, intellect, posterity and wealth, in a way that is aligned with the triple bottom line.

8.4 Conclusion

Initially starting as a global health crisis, the COVID-19 pandemic has now fundamentally become a global economic crisis, which has negatively affected every human life and business activity in our world. Businesses, whether large or small, domestic or international, struggle to cope with the exponential complexities generated by the spread of the virus. The USA, the world's largest and most powerful economy, has reported more than 40 million unemployed. The COVID-19 pandemic has completely transformed the dynamics of our societies, especially the socio-economic and moral dimensions. From the above discussion, we can conclude that authorities would be well advised to focus on moral training for all sectors of their socio-economic systems. Governments should concentrate more on the welfare of all people without considering nationality, race, religion or language. Simultaneously, entrepreneurs should turn their attention to the production of products that have a positive impact on people and the environment.

The teachings and guidance of Islam support the rights and interests of people, protect the environment and still enable the achievement of growth targets, i.e., in material as well as spiritual terms, which mean that no individual remains overlooked.

Notes

1 Hayek won the Nobel Prize in 1974 and died in 1992.

2 "Chronic heavy drinking causes organ damage that results in disability and early death. Other possible consequences include cognitive impairment, addiction, reduced productivity, neglect of family responsibilities and birth defects. The acute effects of alcohol abuse are still more costly: traumatic injury and property damage from accidents, criminal victimization, domestic violence, unwanted sexual encounters and venereal diseases, and hangovers. In sum, alcohol is not just another commodity" (Cook and Moore 2002, p. 120).

3 https://ec.europa.eu/knowledge4policy/foresight/topic/changing-security-paradigm/world-military-expenditure_en
4 World Health Oorganization. (2019). *Global Spending on Health: A World in Transition*. Geneva: WHO.
5 We have certainly created man in the best of stature (95:4).
6 Except for those who believe and do righteous deeds, for they will have a reward uninterrupted (95:6).
7 The Holy Prophet (PBUH) said: "the worship consists of seventy parts and earning Halal income is the best of all. The good deeds for those who earn a life for their families with difficulty and austerity, equals those who are involved in a struggle in the Holy War in the way of Allah." And "some of the sins will be forgiven only in an attempt to earn honorable income".
8 The Holy Prophet (PBUH) said: "one who seeks the Halal income in order to develop his life and enriches his wife and children to be independent from others and intends to help neighbors and the poor will meet God in a bright face".
9 *Usher* (10% tax on the harvests of irrigated land and 10% tax on harvest from rain-watered land and 5% on land dependent on well water and *Zakat* (every Muslim has to pay annually 2.5% on his savings) are religious duties.
10 "This is but falsehood which he contrived, and other people have helped him with it. They have committed iniquity and perjury" (25:4). They say: "What is it with this Messenger who eats food and wanders in the marketplace? If only an angel were sent down to be alongside him as a warner! Or if only a treasure were dropped down upon him or he had an orchard from which he could eat!" The wicked say: "You are merely following a man bewitched" (25:7–8). Behold how they draw parables for you and how they go astray, and cannot find the right way (25:9). We sent not before you any messengers but they ate food and wandered in the marketplace. Some of you. We appointed as a temptation to others. Will you bear this in patience? Your Lord is All-Seeing (25:20).
11 Approximately the same command was given in different verses of chapter 2, chapter 3 and chapter 6 of the *Qur'an* (i.e., 2:86; 2:90; 3:77; 61:10; 35:29–30).
12 The same commands are given in chapter 35 from verse 29 to 30 of *Al Qur'an*.
13 Verses 11 and 18 in chapter 64 of Qur'an are teaching the same.
14 This is related to warnings about hubristic or niggardly behavior, mentioned in chapter 2, verses 264 and 263.

References

Al-Ghazali, A.H. (2009). *Ihya Ulum al-Din*, Vol. 2. Beirut: Dar Al-Hilal.

Azid, T., Asutey, M., & Burki, U. (2007). Theory of the firm, management and stakeholders: An Islamic perspective. *Islamic Economic Studies 15*(1), 1–30.

Boettke, P. (1995). Morality as cooperation. *Religion & Liberty 5*(3), 6–9.

Burke, T.R. (1988). The economic impact of alcohol abuse and alcoholism. *Public Health Report 103*(6): 564–568.

Cook, P.J. & Moore, M.J. (2002). The economics of alcohol abuse and alcohol-control policies. *Health Affairs 21*(2), 120–133.

Desai, R.M. & Kharas, H. (July 2017). Is a growing middle class good for the poor? Social policy in a time of globalization. *Brookings Global Economy and Development Working Paper 105.*

Desai, R.M., Koto, H., Kharas, H., & McArthur, J.W. (2018). The need for innovations to implement the sustainable development goals. In Desai, R.M., Koto, H., Kharas, H., & McArthur, J.W. (2018), Innovations in Implementing the Sustainable Development Goals: From Summit to Solutions. Washington, DC: The Brookings Institution.

Elkington, J. (1999). Cannibals with Forks: The Triple Bottom Line of 21st Century Business. Oxford: Capstone.

Ger, G. & Belk, R.W. (1996). Cross-cultural differences in materialism. *Journal of Economic Psychology 17*(1), 55–77.

Gray, J. (1998). *False Dawn: The Delusions of Global Capitalism.* New York, NY: New Press.

Gertz, G. & Kharas, H. (February 2018). Leave no county behind: Ending poverty in the toughest places. *Brookings Global Economy and Development Working Paper 110.*

Gudeman, S. (2001). The Anthropology of Economy. Malden, MA: Blackwell.

Harvey, D. (2001). Spaces of Capital: Towards a Critical Geography. New York, NY: Routledge.

Hayek, F.A. (1976). Law, Legislation and Liberty, Vol. 2: The Mirage of Social Justice. Chicago, IL: University of Chicago Press.

Hosseini, H. (2003). Understanding the market mechanism before Adam Smith: Economic thought in medieval Islam. In Ghazanfar, S.M. (Ed.), Medieval Islamic Economic Thought: Filling the "Great Gap" in European Economics. London: Routledge.

Khaldun, I. (1967). Muqaddimah of Ibn Khaldun (An Introduction to History), Rosenthal, F.P. (Trans.). Princeton, NJ: Princeton University Press.

Islahi, A.A. (2007). Perception of Market and Pricing Among the Sixteenth Century Muslim Scholars. KAAU, Jeddah, KSA: Islamic Economics Research Center. Also available at http://mpra.ub.uni-muenchen.de/18281/ MPRA Paper No. 18281, posted 4 November 2009.

Islahi, A.A. (1985). Ibn Taimiyah's concept of market mechanism. *Journal of Research in Islamic Economics 2*(2), 51–60.

Kharas, H. (February 2017). The unprecedented expansion of the global middle class. *Brookings Global Economy and Development Working Paper 100.*

Kirzner, I. (1989). Discovery, Capitalism, and Distributive Justice. New York, NY: Blackwell.

Langrill, R. & Storr, V.H. (2012). The moral meanings of markets. *Journal of Markets & Morality 15*(2), 347–362.

Lefebvre, H. (1991). The Production of Space. Malden, MA: Blackwell.

MacIntyre, A. (1979). Corporate modernity and moral judgment: Are they mutually exclusive? In Goodpaster, K.E. & Sayre, K.M. (eds), Ethics and Problems of the 21st Century Notre Dame: University of Notre Dame Press, pp.122–133.

Marx, K. (1994). On the Jewish question. In Simon, L. (Ed.), Karl Marx: Selected Writings. Indianapolis, IN: Hackett.

McArthur, J.W. & Rasmussen. K. (November 2016). How Close to Zero? Assessing the World's Extreme Poverty-Related Trajectories for 2030. Brookings Global Views, No. 6. Brookings Institution. Washington, D.C., United States

McArthur, J.W. & Rasmussen. K. (2018). Change of pace: Accelerations and advances during the millennium development goal era. *World Development 105*(May), 132–143.

McCloskey, D. (2006). The Bourgeois Virtues: Ethics for an Age of Commerce. Chicago, IL: University of Chicago Press.

Mueller, J. (1999). Capitalism, Democracy, and Ralph's Pretty Good Grocery. Princeton, NJ: Princeton University Press.

Novak, M. (1993). The Catholic Ethic and the Spirit of Capitalism. New York, NY: Free Press.

Nnadi, C., Etsano, A., Uba, B., Ohuabunwo, C., Melton, M., Wa Nganda, G., Esapa, L., Bolu, O., Mahoney, F., Vertefeuille, J., Wiesen, E., & Durry, E. (2017). Approaches to Vaccination Among Populations in Areas of Conflict. *The Journal of Infectious Diseases 216*(suppl 1), S368–S372.

Polanyi, K. ([1944] 2001). The Great Transformation: The Political and Economic Origins of Our Time, 2nd ed. Boston, MA: Beacon Press.

Qutub, S. (1980). The Nature of Social Justice in Islam. New York, NY: Octagon Books.

Ratnapala, S. (2006). Moral capital and commercial society. In Higgs, R. & Close, C.P. (Eds.), The Challenge of Liberty: Classical Liberalism Today. Oakland, CA: Independent Institute.

Reda, A. (2013). Trading with Allah: An examination of Islamic scripture in relation to markets. *Journal of Markets & Morality 16* (2), 441–462.

Rothbard, M.N. (1993). Man, Economy and State: A Treatise on Economic Principles. Auburn, AL: Ludwig von Mises Institute.

Sacks, J. (2002). The Dignity of Difference: How to Avoid the Clash of Civilizations. New York, NY: Continuum.

Schmidt-Traub, G. (2018). The role of the technical review panel of the global fund to fight HIV/AIDS, tuberculosis and malaria: An analysis of grant recommendations. *Health Policy and Planning 33*(1), 335–344.

Storr, V.H. (2009). Why the market? Markets as social and moral spaces. *Journal of Markets & Morality 12*(2), 277–296.

United Nations (1977). Economic and Social Consequences of the Armaments Race and its Extremely Harmful Effects of World Peace and Security. Report of the Secretary-General to the UN General Assembly. New York, NY: UN.

United Nations (2015). Transforming Our World: The 2030 Agenda for Sustainable Development. Resolution adopted by the General Assembly A/RES/70/1. September 25. Published October 21. Available at: www.un.org/ga/search/view_doc.asp?symbol=A/RES/70/1&Lang=E).

United Nations Environment Program (UNEP) (2017). The Emissions Gap Report 2017. Nairobi: UNEP.

Weber, M. (1998). The Protestant Ethic and the Spirit of Capitalism. Los Angeles, CA: Roxbury.

World Health Organization. (2019). Global Spending on Health: A World in Transition. Geneva: World Health Organization.

Arabic References

Abd al-Jabbar, Qadi. (1965). al-Mughni fi 'Ajai'b al-Tawhid wa'l-'Adl. Edited by Najjar, M.Ali & Najjar, Halim, al-Muassash al-Misriyyah al-Ammah li'l-Talif, Cairo.
Abu Yusuf (1979). Kitab al Khairaj, Dar al Ma'rifah, Beirut.
al-Baji, Abu'l-Walid (1332 A.H.). al-Muntaqa Sharh al-Muwatta, Dar al-Kitab al-Arabi, Beirut.
al-Dimashqi, Abu'l-Fadl Ja'far (1977). al-Isharah ila Mahasin al-Tijarah, edited by al-Shorabji, Maktabah al-Kulliyyat al-Azhariyyah, Cairo.
al-Jaziri, Abd al-Qadir b. Muhammad (n.d.). al-Durar al-Fara'id al-Munazzamah fi Akhbar al-Hajj wa Tariq Makkat al-Mu'azzamah, Dar al-Yamamah, Riyadh.
Ibn Iyas, Muhammad b. Ahmad (1960). Bada'i' al-Zuhur fi Waqa'i' al-Duhur, Lajnat al-Talif wa'l-Tarjamah, Cairo.
Ibn, Taimiyah (1976). Al Hisbah fi'l Islam, edited by Azzam, S., Dar al Sha'b, Cairo.
Ibn Tulun, Muhammad b. Ali (1998). Mufakahat al-Khullan fi Hawadith al-Zaman, Dar al Kutub al-Ilmiyah, Beirut.
Ibn Qudamah (1972). al-Mughni, Dar al-Kitab al-Arabi, Beirut.

9

RELIGION AND DEVELOPMENT

An Islamic approach to socio-economic development

Mohammad Abdullah

Development is a multidimensional phenomenon. To achieve an inclusive development across the board, it requires coordination among many key players from different areas and disciplines (Abdullah 2020a; Sen 1999). Between the process of drawing up the conceptual framework of developmental policies and their implementation, various individual and institutional actors are closely involved (Abdullah 2018). In recent years, in the realm of development, the factor of religion and religious debates has attracted the attention of international policy makers (Haar and Ellis 2006). The nexus between development and religion is both complex as well as complimentary (Haynes 2007). The complexity of this relationship between religion and development is inherent in the differing premises on which the philosophy of religion vis-à-vis modern development framework lies (Jones and Petersen 2011). Comparatively, religion is complimentary to the developmental causes so far as the schema of development is accommodative to religious values and is not in an explicit conflict with the religious worldview (Deneulin and Rakodi 2011).

A conciliatory approach between development and religion can be crucial in mobilising support from religious authorities, which is vital for translating the developmental agenda into practice (Lunn 2009). This is particularly the case in regions where religion wields considerable influence (Haar and Ellis 2006). In contrast, a value-neutral approach to developmental schemes runs the risk of being greeted with confrontation in extreme situations, or at least being deprived of potential support from those who are associated with a particular religion (Tyndale 2003).

In the context of religion and development, Islam and its approach towards development has been on the forefront of academic discussion. The available literature on this issue delineates both the supportive and conflicting aspects of Islamic traditions towards modern schema of development (Clarke and Tittensor 2016). Divergent views on gender equality, family planning and female leadership, for example, are some of the pertinent issues in this discussion. Similarly, the contention that certain Islamic values, practices, prohibitions and injunctions may conflict with the modern developmental roadmap has drawn significant attention (Deneulin and Bano 2013).

Notwithstanding this, several aspects and dimensions of Islam offer support to developmental causes, which may pave the way for a complimentary role of the religion in development initiatives (Mirakhor and Hamid 2009). A convergent path between Islam and developmental scheme is drawable by locating and embedding such complimentary dimensions in the development plan. To materialise this, an investigation into Islamic approach of development is warranted. Once the concept of development and its framework is located within the ambit of Islamic teachings, the points of convergence and divergence between Islamic vis-à-vis modern developmental approaches can be mapped and reconciled wherever possible.

Islam as a comprehensive religion governs almost all dimensions of life (Hasan 2017). Its guidelines cover, inter alia, spiritual, financial and social spheres of life among others (Kamali 2010). On social front, it engrains the merits of service-orientation and model behavioural attributes in its followers (Abdullah 2015). Volunteerism, community service, selfless initiatives, welfare-friendly approach, kindness, sympathy and philanthropic behaviour as infused by Islam into its followers can be instrumental towards developmental causes (Abdullah 2020c). In the classical as well as contemporary literature, Islamic scholars have made strong plea on maintaining equilibrium between the spiritual as well as socio-economic aspects of development (Mirakhor and Askari 2010; Sadeq 1987). However, in practice, often the focus of religious injunctions is shifted to the development of moral and spiritual aspects with the exclusion of its socio-economic dimensions (Mirakhor and Askari 2010; Tahir 1995). This phenomenon stimulates questions on how the framework of development is understood by the contemporary religious leaders, and how the existing inconsistencies, if any, can be remedied.

This chapter aims to delineate the significance of religion, particularly Islam, in achieving developmental goals, and it attempts to find out how a greater reconciliation can be achieved between the Islamic and modern framework of development. The chapter analyses the determinants of compatibilities and incompatibilities between Islamic approach to development and the modern framework of development. Finally, the chapter aims to dissect the Islamic framework of development by delving into the key constituents of Islamic approach towards development. The study employs a qualitative research paradigm. An intensive review of relevant literature is conducted to understand how the phenomenon of religion has emerged to intersect with the modern developmental policies. The discussion of the study would help understand whether there are some inconsistencies in the perspective of the religious thoughts and developmental policies. If any inconsistencies exist, then the factors underlying them would be examined and dissected further to generate policy implications.

The chapter is divided into four sections including the introduction and conclusion of the chapter. Section 9.2 discusses the concept, mechanism and significance of development in the modern context. The relationship between religion and modern developmental framework is examined in this section. Section 9.3 delves into the premises and building blocks of Islamic framework of development. This section underlines the foundations of Islamic paradigm of development in comparison to the modern development approach. The summary, conclusion and recommendations of the study are presented in the last section of the chapter.

9.1 Development and religion: the concept and framework

Over the last few decades, academic discussion on the term 'development' has gained a noted traction across the globe (Madrueño and Vázquez 2018). Though there is hardly any unanimously agreed upon definition of 'development', the contours of the term find some agreement in the literature. Development as a concept is a subjective term, as it may imply transition from one stage to another, growth, improvement and enhancement depending on the underlying context and the subject matter (Kenneth 2012; Clarke and Islam 2004).

In socio-economic terms, broadly, development may refer to a phenomenon of enabling the human society to avail and enjoy the essential resources in a dignified manner (Abdullah 2018; Allen and Thomas 2000). The conceptual definitions aside; in practice, the state of development can be defined as being free from deprivation of basic necessities while progressing towards enhancement and advancement of living standard of a society as a whole (Madrueño and Vázquez 2018; Kenneth 2012). The cause of development has ignited a global response, albeit, in different capacities. There is no dispute of opinion among the policy makers and other stakeholders on the need and significance of global development. An emphasis on global action plan for development has been repeatedly underlined by international agencies in various forms (Kates, Parris, and Leiserowitz 2005). International programmes such as Millennium Development Goals (MGDs) and Sustainable Development Goals (SDGs) are some of the typical examples of developmental initiatives on a global scale (Abdullah 2018; Sach 2012).

It is widely believed that the modern developmental schema is based on secular principles. The framework of international development is value-neutral, and it does not incorporate the factor and dimensions of religion and religious values within the development plan (Selinger 2004). In this context, the roadmap and strategy of modern development is often shaped without taking into consideration any particular religion and its teachings in the process of policy formulation (Haar and Ellis 2006). The justification for the religion aversion can be that the religious principles and values may pose limitations on how the developmental policies are shaped and what initiatives and objectives can be adopted (Haynes 2007). This is in view of the fact that there are certain value-based limitations that almost each religion, in general, puts for those believing in it. Once embraced and applied in practice, such restrictive ethos and values may come into a direct clash with certain developmental policies as promoted by the national and international development programmes.

Issues such as gender equality, family planning, patriarchy, feminism, unnatural sexual orientation, family values, ethics and morality, rights and obligations of individuals, property rights of women, education, marriage system and liberal ideas have often been points of clash between religion and development (Madrueño and Vázquez 2018; Jones and Petersen 2011). In addition, for being premised on an agnostic and atheistic paradigm, the schema of development, at occasions, runs counter to religious belief system (Deneulin and Bano 2013). Similarly, in the context of theological issues, religion may appear to stipulate certain restrictions on the extent of rationality, leading to qualification of what could be debated and disputed and what could not be. In contrast, the value-free developmental programmes which promote open and free debates without any restriction may collude with such restrictive policies of religion. For these reasons, for a long period of time, religion and religious injunctions have been purportedly at odds with the modern development framework (Lunn 2009). Perhaps, the practice of overlooking the religious considerations in the development discussion is attributable to this phenomenon.

However, of late, there has been a general realisation among the stakeholders of development that bypassing religion is not an effective mechanism of achieving fruitful results on ground. Rather, this practice may fuel scepticism among the followers of different religions on the religious-acceptability and compliance of such schemes (Haar and Ellis 2006). As, for not being taken into confidence, the local religious leadership may end up resisting such programmes which in turn inhibits the scope of their implementation at ground level. Practically, by ignoring the religious factor and its different dimensions, the developmental programmes are often deprived of potentially great complimentary roles of closely knitted and fervently loyal religious workforce.

In view of this lacuna, there is a growing body of recent literature advocating for creation of bridge between religion and development. To this end, there has been postulations that engagement with religion, rather than estrangement, is beneficial towards smooth and efficient implementation of developmental initiatives (Deneulin and Rakodi 2011). Religion wields loyalty of its followers, and generally it governs their behaviour and actions. It controls a ready workforce of volunteers, and plays an instrumental role in motivating or discouraging them to engage or disengage in certain activities (James 2011). Among the variety of benefits that collaboration with religion may ensue for developmental initiatives are availability of scope for leveraging the local support from religious leadership and gaining easy penetration among the masses through them (Jones and Petersen 2011). By coalescing development programmes with religious endorsement, the effect of such initiatives can be efficiently magnified. Collaboration with religion is also critical to benefit from the community-based social network and in attracting volunteers to participate in delivery of the benefits within the community at comparatively much lesser costs (Tomalin 2018).

Engaging religion in development initiatives is vital to build trust and win commitment. Religiously inspired communities are also critical in developing self-help groups and in running free educational and community-based vocational training programmes which is complimentary to developmental programmes (DFID 2012). The imprints of charity and charitable activities are more commonly visible among the religiously oriented communities (James 2016). Through various religiously motivated redistributive mechanisms, an easy transmission of resources from the privileged to underprivileged can be a common practice. Religion is also crucial in shaping good characters and motivating the followers to imbibe many universal moral and ethical values. The values of honesty, integrity, patience, perseverance, sympathy and kindness, etc. are among the fundamental teachings of religion. Thus, being characterised by these values, the religious people are envisaged to be away from fraud, deceit, embezzlement, bribery, selfishness, greed and other immoral behavioural traits.

To sum up, involving religion in developmental programmes may be critical from different angles. For instance, in order to secure acceptability and garnering local support from the religious groups in implementing developmental programmes, engaging the religious leadership is imperative (Tomalin 2012). Islam, which is the second largest religion of the world, cannot be simply ignored in this discussion. For being a comprehensive and practice-oriented religion, Islam commands relatively greater magnitude of influence over the convictions, actions and behaviour of its followers (Iqbal and Mirakhor 2010). Islamic lays a broader set of religious guidelines in all spheres of life for its followers (Kamali 2012. The subsequent part of this chapter analyses the Islamic vision and framework of development with an objective of identifying the potential points of collaboration between Islam and modern principles of development. The discussion in the next section also covers the junctures of possible clash between the Islamic and modern developmental frameworks followed by pinpointing the areas in which there are possibilities of compromise and reconciliation and the areas which apparently defies reconciliation.

9.2 Islamic approach and framework of development

The Islamic approach to development is premised on *Shariah*-based principles and philosophies. The *Shariah*-prescribed world view and injunctions play a vital role in shaping the Islamic approach of development (Kamali 2012 Kahf 2002). *Shariah* represents a blend of Islamic rules, principles,, beliefs, ethics, norms, values and dealings (Abdullah, 2018; Mirakhor and Hamid 2009). The primary sources of *Shariah* are Quran and the traditions of the Prophet (PBUH) known as *Hadith*. Since the origin of *Shariah* is believed to be Divine in nature, for Muslims the principles and values of *Shariah* command a supremacy over other man-made principles (Ahmad 1994). Thus, *Shariah* compliments the developmental initiatives so far as such initiatives are not in a direct conflict with its ethos and fundamental principles. For Muslims, in a scenario of a direct clash between the secular developmental policies and the principles of *Shariah*, the principles of *Shariah* would receive precedence over secular propositions (Kamali 2012).

The conceptual underpinnings of development from an Islamic perspective is informed and shaped from the unique world view which Islam presents to its followers (Ahsan 2015). The Islamic world view informs the believers on two phases of human life, comprising this world's temporal and eventually the Hereafter's permanent life (Abdul Muthaliff 2019). The true success and salvation in both the two phases of life, from an Islamic viewpoint, is dependent on complying with the divinely inspired rules and principles of *Shariah*. Within the Islamic paradigm, obedience to the *Shariah*-based values is key to achieve a divinely desired developmental outcome (Chapra 2008). Any discussion on development, within the Islamic context, is tightly connected with its belief system. The belief system of Islam commences from believing in oneness of God and extends to having firm conviction in the eventual returning of all human being to Him (Abdul Muthaliff 2019). The process, in between is a prototype of test, which is in place to examine the loyalties and truthfulness of believers to the Creator in all their activities and practices (al-Qaradawi 2010). The point of reference for this test of loyalty is Quranic injunctions and the Prophetic traditions. The test is conducted by scrutinising the extent of abidance by Muslims to these two references (Gunthen and Lawson 2017).

The implications of the Islamic belief system unfold in several ways. For example, with the belief in oneness of God emerges the conviction in unity of all human, without distinction of faith, caste and creed, in terms of being creation of one Creator (al-Quran, 49/13[1]). This belief in oneness of the Creator sets the stage for the Islamic philosophical stance on equal treatment of all, while negating any superiority of one over another merely by virtue of his/her worldly belonging or socio-economic standing (Saeed 2018). The implication of this philosophical position manifests in affording the analogous rights, claims and entitlements to all on the natural resources without discrimination. The moral obligation imposed on believers to respect the dignity, integrity and propriety of all is informed from this Islamic approach of equal treatment. Similar to this, the imperative of being impartial and just to all is another Quranic injunction substantiating the premises of this philosophy (al-Quran, 4/31[2]).

Within the Islamic belief system falls the role of man as the custodian of the planet earth (al-Quran, 2/30). The *Shariah* directive to the believers to assume the responsibility of custodianship and to behave like a trustee of this planet is instructive of its vision on why believers need to be responsible and kind to the well-being of all (Dien 2000). This approach is also critical in underlining the need and significance of being considerate to others and being desirous of an inclusive model of development. Since the role of stewardship and trusteeship can be duly played only by treating the planet with delicacy and being considerate to its sustainability, believers are exhorted to be careful of what they do on this planet (Abdullah 2018).

Other than the belief system, *Shariah*-injunctions encompass several other aspects of life. These include a set of commandments pertaining to prayers, charity, social and commercial dealings, transactions, family system, governance and behavioural ethics (al-Qaradawi 2010). A developmental policy designed in consideration to these prescriptions so as to either compliment these or to avoid any direct collusion with their underlying principles is bound to successfully culminate from an Islamic perspective. Arguably, for believers, the spiritual aspect of development is equally or even more important than the material or temporal aspect of development. Thus, development of one aspect with the neglect of another is neither desired nor validated in *Shariah*. In case there arises a necessity of compromise between the two, it is preferred to compromise on the temporal rather than the spiritual aspect, except in dire circumstances (Chapra 2008). Within the prism of *Shariah* values, temporal development is a means rather than an end which enables the believers to continue in their spiritual pursuit. To this end, the objective of material development is lost if it is secured by compromising on or at the cost of spiritual development.

In this context, arguably, if a roadmap to development is drawn in a way that it does not respect or make allowances for the belief in monotheism, which is the foundation of Islamic belief system, it is set to be resisted. Similarly, since the prayer system of Islam is considered a typical mechanism of expressing one's loyalty to Allah, establishing the system and institution of worship in line with the *Shariah* tenets is an integral pillar of Islamic development (Ahsan 2015; Kahf 2002). Thus, a developmental framework, which curtails the scope of Mosque (place of worship) establishment in its roadmap, entails a high likelihood of rejection by the community. In addition, in the name of development, if the sanctity of *Shariah* rules pertaining to marriage and family life is endangered, such plan of development is clearly exposed to receiving vigorous opposition at the ground (Kamali 2012). Similarly, for being against the basic tenets and ethos of Shariah, promotion of concepts such as live-in relationship, having mistress or extra marital affairs is completely indefensible and is destined to face vigorous disapproval (al-Quran, 17/32[3]). In the same vein, a development scheme which eventually ends up promoting body exposure, nudity, vulgarity, obscenity or whatever is deemed as immorality in Islam (al-Quran, 7/33[4]) is bound to invite harsh criticism at the ground, be it in the name of art, skills or talent development.

Other than these, since Shariah strictly prohibits dealing in interest, usury, gambling and certain other Shariah non-compliant financial activities and commercial dealings, a scheme of development with interest-based loan-offerings or gambling-oriented reward mechanism is set to be meted out with disapproval (AAOIFI 2015). Though, there may be evidences of Muslims being involved in similar *Shariah*-prohibited activities at an individual level, securing acceptance for promoting such programmes at an institutional level is a non-viable endeavour.

Islamic approach to development combines between the temporal and spiritual aspects (al-Quran, 2/201[5]). Material development with the exclusion of or at the cost of spiritual development is not feasible within the Islamic world view (al-Quran, 2/200). The validity of a development policy is intact so long as it is amenable to the Islamic principles of inclusiveness between both the two aspects. *Shariah* does not condone promotion of such developmental schemes and activities which may be secular in nature and tend to drive away the believers from their attachment to the religion and its principles (al-Quran, 2/132-33[6]). To strike a high success rate, ideally, whatever developmental plan is drawn shall be drawn in view of these basic criteria. As meeting this condition is vital in order to be accommodative and acceptable from an Islamic viewpoint.

The Islamic framework of development covers a multi-layered set of guidance on the means, mechanism, methods and objectives of development. Within the Islamic guidelines, while the belief system is envisaged to infuse faith and confidence in an Omni-present Creator who determines fate and capabilities, the mechanism of prayers is meant to support this (al-Quran, 2/153[7]). The ultimate aim of these two is to create a link between the economic agent's mundane endeavours and his/her spiritual well-being. A combination of the two is instrumental in keeping the believers mindful of the objective of life (al-Quran, 5/48[8]; 2/155[9]). Ideally, a balance between the material as well as spiritual orientation of believers serves to bring about behavioural moderation in them. This phenomenon also helps put a check on extreme reactions in cases of either intense grief or delight. Within the Islamic philosophy of human behaviour, the concept of neither all doom and gloom nor such euphoria and ecstasy exist which may render a believer forgetful of his/her faith and religious duties (al-Quran, 12/87[10]; 57/22-23[11]). There is also a system of spiritual consolation and solace for the one who may have suffered a financial, material, physical or emotional shock or loss, which plays a vital role in helping the believers to recover from the state of depression and dejection. There are a number of prophetic *Hadith* which promise a spiritual reward for the one who has been patient during any such loss or setback (al-Bukhari 1999[12]).

The Islamic vision of development unlocks with the *Shariah* emphasis on achieving self-dependence in socio-economic terms at an individual level, progressing to assuming the responsibilities of one's dependents at a family level (Abdullah 2018). The manifestations of self as well as dependent's development are ideally reflected through the requirement of arranging means of sustenance, education and socio-economic empowerment for the self and one's dependence (al-Quran, 2/233[13]; al-Bukhari 1999[14]). This requirement also extends to the responsibility of inculcating religious-discipline and spiritual orientation among the family members (Tirmidzi 1999[15]). In practice, to smoothly entertain these requisites, physical, mental and financial efforts have to be exerted. In this context, the Quranic concept of *Ihsan* (excellence) ushers in (al-Quran, 2/195). To translate the conceptual underpinnings of *Ihsan* in practice, there is a repeated *Shariah* emphasis on an optimal utilisation of all human faculties in acquiring the resources and their efficient deployment (al-Quran, 53/39[16]). To encourage the embodiment of this phenomenon, *Shariah* instructs that by adopting and applying *Ihsan* in life one can simulate the method of none other than God Himself (Abdullah 2015a).

The *Shariah* ethos indicate the desirability of an inclusive development at community and then at society level. For this, *Shariah* envisions the responsibility of development of the community being shouldered by the community itself. For this, the pitch for an atmosphere of shared responsibility is created by commanding that each one of you is responsible for other (al-Muslim 1999[17]). Be it in a material or spiritual term, the affluent and enlightened group of the community is envisaged to share and redistribute a portion of their resources among the deprived ones. Adoption of such sharing mechanism ensures that the privileged is considerate to impoverished and the developed is concerned about underdeveloped. This, in turn, entails an atmosphere of harmony and cohesiveness, bringing about a shared prosperity which eventually benefits all.

Creation of an atmosphere which is conducive to ease, peace and mutual considerations is at the heart of *Shariah* paradigm of development. *Shariah* desires a society which is readily geared up towards sharing rather than shifting the onus of mutual well-being and thus reinforcing the thread of interdependence rather than breaking the knots of mutuality (Abdullah 2015). *Shariah* motivates its followers to fulfill their responsibilities towards the community and render services in a selfless manner with the ultimate objective of attaining piety and spiritual reward in the sight of Allah (Abdullah 2020b). Infusing the sense of volunteerism, charitable behaviour and responsible engagement through its injunctions, *Shariah* provides a fertile pitch for mutuality, cooperation and collaboration in shaping the ground for mutual development and delivering it in the society (Abdullah 2020a). This helps to shape a society where every member enjoys the bliss of contentment rather than being inundated with the sense of dejection or feeling of deprivation.

For being inspired by religious motivational mechanism, ideally the believers are not envisaged to weigh their charitable activities in material terms. The concept of opportunity cost, time value of money and efficiency are not always the only factors determining the decision and choices of spiritually charged believers. They are supposed to do a trade-off for spiritual rewards and ultimate salvation over the mundane utility and enjoyment of the resources. Through this mechanism, the scope of redistribution of resources is moulded and encouraged over the concept of amassing and accumulating. As a result, a smooth and cost-effective dispensation of monetary and non-monetary resources are channelized from the haves to haves-not, which may play a pivotal role in the developmental arena (Abdullah 2020a).

Broadly, the salient features and key pillars of developmental programme within the Islamic framework of development can be classified in a few major clusters. These clusters comprise four major themes of development consisting of belief system along with individual discipline, physical efforts, social responsibility and the wider role of custodianship. The ingredients of these 4 clusters are further sub-divided into 6 each and thus making cumulatively 24 sub-themes. These major themes along with their sub-themes are illustrated in Figure 9.1.

The cluster one with the major theme of Islamic world view and belief system is central to the developmental progress of Muslim community. The belief that there is only one Creator, guides the believers towards treating all creatures as the members of one family. It helps unite the community with the reminder of an invisible bonding which ties together them all. The following six sub-themes in this cluster are essentially connected with the spiritual ingredients which help develop a God-conscious individual. These sub-themes in one way hold the believers from taking life too seriously to be forgetful of their main objectives and the final abode. The second cluster is made up of *Shariah* prescriptions for individual efforts and maintaining moderation in life. The sub-themes of this cluster are mainly focused on instructing the merit of excellence, self-discipline, hard work, proper planning and fulfillment of responsibilities towards sustaining oneself and the dependents. The next cluster determines the framework of social responsibility and its sub-themes contain the attributes of being socially active and charitable in order to enable the community to progress. Finally, the theme and sub-themes of cluster four constitutes the role of custodianship to the planet and the means of practically acknowledging this.

All these themes combined together represent the model attributes and behaviour of a devout Muslim. Once adopted and personified by the believers, these clusters along with their sub-themes are believed to give rise to an imitable society for being made up of the members who are spiritually enlightened, economically developed, emotionally balanced and practically pragmatic. The implications of such developmental journey of a society can be self-evident for all, impressing the allies and adversaries equally, something

Unique Worldview-Belief System
Urge for Nearness to Allah
Belief in Spiritual Reward
Focus on Ultimate Salvation
Conviction in Temporality of World
Worldly Priviledges are Means and not an End
Conviction in Pre-determined Destiny
Aim at Excellence (*Ihsan*)
Proper Planning and Strategy
Balance between Material and Spiritual Aspects
Optimum Utilisation of Mental and Physical Capacities
Maximum Efforts and Endevour
Moderation in Living Standard
Priority to Self and Dependents' Need fulfilment
Social Responsibility
Community Engagement and Mutuality
Volunteerism and Social Service
Charity and Selfless-ness
Patience and Consideration of Others
Discipline and Honesty in Dealings
Awareness and Activism
Role of Custodianship
Maqasid-based Orientation of Life
Efforts to Make World a Better Place to Live
Continuous Improvement in Living Conditions
Enhancement of Resources and their Proper Utilisation
Careful Usage of Natural Resources
Consideration to the Future Generation

Figure 9.1 Major clusters of Islamic developmental themes.

Source: developed by author.

categorically prescribed and highly desired by *Shariah* as part of its *Dawah* (calling people to the righteous path) mechanism.

Besides the Islamic approach of development as described earlier, the standing issues of conflict with modern developmental schemes such as gender equality, women rights and rights of those having an unnatural sex orientation, etc. can be delineated within the broader *Shariah* framework of policy design. While points of conflict on issues such as gender equality and women empowerment can be simply resolved by putting the Islamic position into a right perspective, the issue of unnatural sex orientation represents an uncompromising situation for *Shariah*. In other words, the rift between the two paradigms on women and their right-related issues is more artificial than being based on a genuine ground (Golnaz and Albert 2013; Jawad 2010; Afkhami 1997). Whereas *Shariah* emphasises on securing and maintaining the dignity and honour of women and prescribes certain rulings to ensure this, the secular approach of development targets on achieving equality and impartiality for them at an equal footing. If understood properly, a middle path for the two approaches can be struck. However, a real clash between *Shariah* underpinnings and the modern approach arises in the case of unnatural sexual orientation. Though, in the modern context, there may be scope of being tolerant to this issue, *Shariah* can neither provide an acceptability to this phenomenon nor can it engage in endorsing or promoting this simply due to the fact that this falls under the category of a direct clash with the fundamentals of *Shariah*.

9.3 Summary, conclusion and recommendations

In recent years, the phenomenon of development has effectively unified the interests of different actors and stakeholders across the board. In the context of development, religion and its role has emerged as a significant factor to be reckoned with. In geographies where religion commands a significant hold over the public, endorsement and support of religion and its forces can be crucial for smooth implementation of developmental schemes. The terms of relationship between religion and development play an instrumental role in defining the fate of developmental schemes in such areas. Whether religion compliments a developmental plan or complicates it is dependent on the extent of convergence or divergence of views between religious vis-à-vis developmental programmes. In scenarios where the ethos and values of religion synchronise with the developmental plan or vice versa, the scope of collaboration between the two surfaces. However, religion may turn out to be the most vigorous opponent where it perceives a direct challenge to or conflict with its fundamentals.

Though often the contemporary literature tends to imply that the notion of modern development has its roots in a value-free secularism-oriented philosophy, there is a growing call and gradual recognition of religious factor in developmental initiatives. In several geographies, it is considerably hard to introduce and implement certain developmental policies without taking the local religious leadership into confidence. Thus, developing a bridge between religious leadership and other stakeholders of development may entail a positive impact and help securing local support.

This study set out to analyse the role of Islam in the context of development. The objective of the study was to examine the potential points of convergence and divergence between Islam and the modern schema of development. The study analysed the premises and the philosophical underpinnings of development from an Islamic perspective.

This study finds that by accommodating fundamental Islamic values and honouring its limitations, rather than deliberately subverting, ignoring or bypassing the same, an integrated pitch of collaboration can be developed between the Islamic and modern paradigms of development. A collaborative rather than colliding approach between the two paradigms is vital to achieve the desired results at the ground. In comparison, overlooking the religion and its considerations may be inimical to the cause of development as the approach of neglect and dereliction towards key religious principles is bound to invite ground-level opposition. In addition, the study contends that a deliberate or otherwise attempt to ravage religious values or distort their original moulds in the name of development may cause an unwarranted scepticism towards not only the underlying disputed initiatives, but to the overall programme of development. Any such misadventure may ensue undue hindering in the process of development. Thus, a scheme which is apparently contrary to the set ethos and values of religion shall be thoroughly discussed and deliberated with the religious stakeholders. With some concerted efforts and engagement with the stakeholders, many disputed territories can be avoided, amended or aligned with the established principles of the religion. At occasions, the religious authorities may be helpful in tweaking the initiative in line with the Islamic framework of development.

The study noted that the Islamic approach of development is premised on *Shariah*-based principles and philosophy. The conceptual underpinnings of development from an Islamic perspective are shaped from the unique world view which Islam presents to its followers. The Islamic world view informs the believers on two phases of human life, comprising this world's temporal and eventually the Hereafter's permanent life. The true success and salvation in both the two phases of life, from an Islamic viewpoint, is dependent on complying with the divinely inspired rules and principles of *Shariah*. The Islamic paradigm of development combines between the temporal and spiritual aspects. Material development with the exclusion of or at the cost of spiritual development is not feasible within the Islamic world view.

The study argued that Islamic vision of development unlocks with the *Shariah* emphasis on securing self-dependence in socio-economic terms at an individual level, progressing to assume the responsibilities of one's dependents at a family level. The manifestations of self as well as dependent's development are ideally reflected through the requirement of arranging means of sustenance, education and socio-economic empowerment for the self and one's dependence. This requirement also extends to the responsibility of inculcating religious-discipline and spiritual orientation in self as well as among the family members. In practice, to smoothly entertain these requisites, physical, mental and financial efforts have to be exerted.

The *Shariah* ethos indicate the desirability of an inclusive development at community and then at society level. For this, *Shariah* envisions the responsibility of development of community being shouldered by the community itself. For this, an atmosphere of shared responsibility is created by commanding that each one is responsible for other. Be it in a material or spiritual term, the affluent and enlightened group of the community is envisaged to share and redistribute a portion of their resources among the deprived ones. Adoption of such sharing mechanism ensures that privileged is considerate to impoverished and developed are concerned about underdeveloped. This in turn entails an atmosphere of harmony and cohesiveness, bringing about a shared prosperity which eventually benefits all.

This study classifies the salient features and key pillars of Islamic framework of development in four major clusters. These clusters comprise four major themes of development consisting of belief system and individual discipline, physical efforts, social responsibility and the wider role of custodianship. The ingredients of these 4 clusters are further sub-divided into 6 each and thus making cumulatively 24 sub-themes.

Finally, the study delineated some standing points of conflict between Islamic and modern framework of development. It found that conflict on issues such as gender equality and women empowerment can be simply resolved by putting the Islamic position into a right perspective, as the rift between the two paradigms on women and their right-related issues is more artificial than being genuine. The cause of divergence on this issue is mainly fanned by the differences in philosophies of the two paradigms. Whereas, considering the biological, emotional and physical differences of men and women, *Shariah* treats the dignity and honour of women in line with their natural peculiarities, the secular approach insists on achieving equality and impartiality for them with the opposite gender. If deliberated, discussed and dissected in a proper manner, perhaps a middle path for the two approaches can be struck.

However, the conflict persists between the Islamic and modern paradigms of development where the fundamental values of *Shariah* are exposed to damage. For example, a clash between Shariah underpinnings and the modern approach arises on the issue of whether to condone or condemn the promotion of unnatural sexual orientation. Though in the modern context there may be discussion on being tolerant to this, *Shariah* can neither provide an acceptability to this phenomenon nor can it engage in endorsing or promoting this simply due to the fact that this falls under the category of a direct clash with the fundamentals of *Shariah*. Similarly, for being against the basic tenets and ethos of *Shariah*, promotion of concepts such as live-in relationship, having mistress or indulging in extra marital affairs is completely indefensible and is destined to be resisted. In the same vein, a development scheme which eventually ends up promoting commoditization of women's body or encouraging nudity, vulgarity or obscenity, etc. is bound to invite vigorous opposition from the religion, be it in the name of art, skills or talent development.

To sum up, it is critical to understand that there are certain unanimously agreed upon fundamental values and principles of Islam which cannot be either changed or be compromised in the name of development. Thus, the scope of discussion and collaboration between Islamic and modern developmental paradigms are open so far as the later does not directly collide with the globally agreed basics of the former. Other than the unanimously accepted fundamentals of *Shariah*, there may be possibility of tweaking, re-interpretation, realignment and at occasion's change of opinion on certain Islamic rulings in order to accommodate necessary developmental programmes and initiatives.

Notes

1 The Quranic verse 49/13 states 'O mankind, indeed We have created you from male and female and made you peoples and tribes that you may know one another. Indeed, the most noble of you in the sight of Allah is the most righteous of you'.

2 The Quranic verse 49/13 directs 'O you who have believed, be persistently standing firm in justice, witnesses for Allah, even if it be against yourselves or parents and relatives. Whether one is rich or poor, Allah is more worthy of both. So follow not [personal] inclination, lest you not be just'.

3 The Quranic verse 17/32 admonishes '*Do not go near adultery. It is truly a shameful deed and an evil way'.*

4 The Quranic verse 7/33 instructs 'Say, My Lord has only forbidden immoralities - what is apparent of them and what is concealed'.

5 The Quranic verse 2/201 instructs the believers to pray for good of both the worlds, as it teaches the following Dua: 'Our Lord! Give us in this world that which is good and in the Hereafter that which is good, and save us from the torment of the Fire!'.

6 The two Quranic verses 2/132/33 hold 'Allah has chosen for you the (true) Deen (religion), then die not except as Muslims (in submission to Him)'.

7 The Quranic verse 2/153 instructs 'O you who have believed, seek help through patience and prayer. Indeed, Allah is with the patient'.

8 The Quranic verse 5/48 holds 'To Allah is your return all together, and He will [then] inform you concerning that over which you used to differ'.

9 The Quranic verse 2/155 informs "And We will surely test you with something of fear and hunger and a loss of wealth and lives and fruits, but give good tidings to the patient"

10 The Quranic verse 12/87 advises "and never give up hope of Allah's Mercy. Certainly no one despairs of Allah's Mercy, except the people who disbelieve".

11 The two Quranic verses 57/22-23 explicate "No misfortune ever befalls on earth, nor on yourselves but We have inscribed it in the Book before We make it manifest. Surely that is easy for Allah. (We do so) that you may not grieve over the loss you suffer, nor exult over what He gave you. Allah does not love the vainglorious, the boastful."

12 The Prophet (PBUH) said: 'No believer is pricked by a thorn or more but that Allah will raise him one degree in status or erase a sin' (al-Bukhari: 5317). Another Hadith holds 'No calamity befalls a Muslim but that Allah expiates some of his sins because of it, even though it were the prick he receives from a thorn' (al-Bukhari: 5640).

13 The Quranic verse 2/233 states 'but the father of the child shall bear the cost of the mother's food and clothing on a reasonable basis'.

14 The Prophet (PBUH) instructed 'When a man spends on his family, hoping for reward, that is (counted as) an act of charity for him' (al-Bukhari/Hadith 55).

15 The Hadith states, 'There is no gift a father gives his child more virtuous than good manners (by providing him good education and upbringing)' (Tirmidhi Hadith No. 4977).

16 The Quranic verse 2/233 states 'And that there is not for man except that [good] for which he strives'.

17 The Prophet (PBUH) said 'Every one of you is a shepherd and is responsible for his flock. The leader of people is a guardian and is responsible for his subjects. A man is the guardian of his family and he is responsible for them. A woman is the guardian of her husband's home and his children and she is responsible for them. The servant of a man is a guardian of the property of his master and he is responsible for it. No doubt, every one of you is a shepherd and is responsible for his flock' (Muslim, Hadith No. 1829).

References

AAOIFI (2015). Shariah Standards for Islamic Financial Institutions. Bahrain: Accounting and Auditing Organisation for Islamic Financial Institution.

Abdullah, M. (2015). Analysing the moral aspect of qard: A shariah perspective. *International Journal of Islamic and Middle Eastern Finance and Management* 8(2), 171–184.

Abdullah, M. (2015a). A new framework of corporate governance of *waqf*: A preliminary proposal. *Islam and Civilisational Renewal 6*(3), 353–370.

Abdullah, M. (2018). Waqf, sustainable development goals (SDGs) and Maqasid al-shariah. *International Journal of Social Economics 45*(1), 158–172.

Abdul Muthaliff, M. (2019). Iman, the Islamic belief system. In Encyclopedia of Indian Religions (1st ed.). The Netherlands: Springer.

Abdullah, M. (2020a). Islamic endowment (Waqf) in India: Towards poverty reduction of Muslims in the country. *Journal of Research in Emerging Markets 2*(2), 48–60.

Abdullah, M. (2020b). Waqf, social responsibility, and real economy. In Saiti, B. & Sarea, A. (Eds.), Challenges and Impacts of Religious Endowments on Global Economics and Finance. USA: IGI Global, pp. 23–36.

Abdullah, M. (2020c) Objectives of Awqaf within the Classical Discourse and their Modern Implications. In Masum Billah. M. (Ed.) Awqaf-led Islamic Social Finance, Innovative Solutions to Modern Applications. UK : Routledge, pp. 23–38.

Afkhami, M. (1997). Promoting women's rights in the Muslim world. *Journal of Democracy 8*(1), 157–66.

Ahmad, K. (1994). Economic Development in an Islamic Framework. Leicester: The Islamic Foundation.

Ahsan, A. (2015). Monograph of Islamic contributions to global sustainable development. *Pegasus V*(XI), 4–22.

Allen, T. & Thomas, A. (eds.) (2000). Poverty and Development in the 21st Century. Oxford: Oxford University Press.

al-Bukhari (1999). Mawsuah al-Hadith al-Sharif. Riyadh: Darussalam.

Chapra, M.U. (2008). The Islamic Vision of Development in the Light of Maqasid al-Shariah. London: The International Institute of Islamic Thought (Occasinal Paper).

Clarke, M. & Tittensor, D. (2016). Islam and Development: Exploring the Invisible Aid Economy . London: Routledge.

Clarke, M. & Islam, S. (2004). Contemporary development issues and economic growth. In Clarke, M. & Islam, S. (Eds.), Economic Growth and Social Welfare: Operationalising Normative Social Choice Theory (Contributions to Economic Analysis, Vol. 262). Bingley: Emerald Group Publishing Limited, pp. 181–202.

Dien, M. (2000). The Environmental Dimensions of Islam. Cambridge: The Lutterworth Press.

Deneulin, S. & Bano, M. (2013). Religion in Development: Rewriting the Secular Script. London: Zed Books.

Deneulin, S. & Rakodi, C. (2011). Revisiting religion: Development studies thirty years on. *World Development* 39(1), 45–54.

DFID (2012). Faith Partnership Principles: Working effectively with Faith Groups to Fight Global Poverty. London: Department for International Development.

Golnaz, G. & Albert, J. (2013). Unveiling the myth of the Muslim woman: A post-colonial critique. *Equality, Diversity and Inclusion: An International Journal 32*(2), 157–172.

Gunthen, S. & Lawson, T. (2017). Roads to Paradise: Eschatology and Concepts of the Hereafter in Islam. The Netherlands: Brill.

Haar, G. & Ellis, S. (2006). The role of religion in development: Towards a new relationship between the European Union and Africa. *The European Journal of Development Research 18*(3), 351–367.

Hasan R. (2017). Islam and Development, in Religion and Development in the Global South. UK, Palgrave Macmillan, pp. 41–78.

Haynes, J. (2007). Religion and Development: Conflict or Cooperation. New York: Palgrave MacMillan.

Iqbal, Z. & Mirakhor, A. (2010). An Islamic perspective on economic development. In El-Ansary, W. & Linnan, D.K. (Eds.), Muslim and Christian Understanding. New York: Palgrave Macmillan.

James, R. (2016). Religion and Development, Professional Development Reading Pack No. 35. Available at: https://gsdrc.org/wp-content/uploads/2016/03/Religion-and-development_RP.pdf.

James, R. (2011). Handle with care: Engaging with faith-based organisations in development. *Development in Practice 21*(1), 109–117.

Jawad, S. (2010). An historical perspective on Islamic modesty and its implications for female employment. *Equality, Diversity and Inclusion: An International Journal 29*(2), 150–166.

Jones, B. & Petersen, M. (2011). Instrumental, narrow, normative? Reviewing recent work on religion and development. *Third World Quarterly 32*(7), 1291–1306.

Kahf, M. (2002) Sustainable Development in the Muslim Countries, Available at: http://monzer.kahf.com/papers/english/Sustainable_development_Revised_First_Draft.pdf, accessed on 10 October 2015.

Kamali, H.M. (2012). Maqasid al-Shariah, Ijtihad and Civilisational Renewal. London: The International Institute of Islamic Thought (Occasional Paper Series 20).

Kamali, H. (2010). Islam and sustainable development. *Islam and Civilizational Renewal 7*(1), 8–26.

Kates, R., Parris, T., & Leiserowitz, A. (2005). What is sustainable development? Goals, indicators, values and practice. *Environment: Science and Policy for Sustainable Development 47*(3), 8–21.

Kenneth, P. (2012). Contemporary development and economic history: How do we know what matters? *Economic History of Developing Regions, 27*(sup1), S136–S148.

Lunn, J. (2009). The role of religion, spirituality and faith in development: A critical theory approach. *Third World Quarterly 30*(5), 937–951.

Madrueño, R. & Vázquez, S. (2018). The contemporary development discourse: Analysing the influence of development studies. *Journals, World Development* 109, 334–345.

Mirakhor, A. & Askari, H. (2010). Islam and the Path to Human and Economic Development. New York: Palgrave MacMillan.

Mirakhor, A. & Hamid, S. (2009). Islam and Development: The Institutional Framework. New York, NY: Global Scholarly Publications.

al-Muslim (1999). Mawsuah al-Hadith al-Sharif. Riyadh: Darussalam.

Al-Qaradawi, Y. (2010). Islam an Intorduction. Kuala Lumpur: Islamic Book Trust (translated by Kashmiri, S.).

Sadeq, A. (1987). Economic development in Islam. *Journal of Islamic Economics 1*(1), 35–45.

Sachs, J.D. (2012). From Millennium Development Goals to Sustainable Development Goals. Available at: www.thelancet.com/journals/a/article/PIIS0140-6736%2812%2960685-0/fulltext, accessed on 20 September, 2015.

Saeed, A. (2018). Human Rights and Islam: An Introduction to Key Debates Between Islamic Law and International Human Rights Law. Gloucestershaire: Edward Elgar Publishing.

Sen, A. (1999). Development as Freedom. Oxford: Oxford University Press.

Selinger, L. (2004). The forgotten factor: The uneasy relationship between religion and development. *Social Compass 51*(4), 523–543.

Tahir, S. (1995). Islamic perspectives on economic development. *Pakistan Development Review 34*(4), 845–856.

al-Tirmidzi (1999). Mawsuah al-Hadith al-Sharif. Riyadh: Darussalam.

Tomalin, E. (2018). Religions, poverty reduction and global development institutions. *Palgrave Communications 4*, 132.

Tomalin, E. (2012). Thinking about faith-based organisations in development: Where have we got to and what next? *Development in Practice 22*(5–6), 689–703.

Tyndale, W. (2003). Idealism and practicality: The role of religion in development. *Development 46*, 22–28.

10

ACCOUNTABILITY AND SUSTAINABILITY IN ISLAMIC ACCOUNTING LITERATURE

Murniati Mukhlisin and Rifka Mustafida

Accounting is the most important aspect of business because it collects, processes, analyses and communicates information to the both internal and external users who make their important decisions (Sultana 2015). Accounting has been getting recognition on its role in development of Islamic finance. Increasing claims on operating Islamic finance products and services leads the formation of Islamic accounting (Lahrash 2015). Today, accounting which is transformed, one way, in form of accounting standards has been very much debatable on which standards that fit to the Islamic finance industry. Accounting as technology has also been proposed to replace the current role of accounting, which is merely to serve the Islamic finance industry. Thus, accounting should become a traffic light for the Islamic finance to develop (Warsono 2011).

Islamic accounting is an alternative accounting system to replace the conventional accounting system which aims to provide information to clients enabling them to invest to project, operate business according to Islamic law (Yousef 2004). The need for Islamic accounting is emphasized in the Quran. It has been clearly stated in the following verses: "*Never get bored with recording it, however small or large, up to its maturity date, for this is seen by Allah closer to justice, more supportive to testimony and more resolving to doubt*" (QS Al-Baqarah (2), p. 282). The role of Islamic accounting then questions the term of testimony of accountability as raised in the above verses. There is necessity to perform religious accounting when producing financial reports for the purpose of ensuring the accountability and sustainability of Islamic financial institutions and their stakeholders, which is the motivation of this study. This therefore leads to a research question "To what extent have accountability and sustainability been well discussed in the context of Islamic accounting?"

The aim of this research is to familiarize Islamic accounting researchers in defining accountability and sustainability so they will be able to make more contribution to the academic and practice. The finding shows that the academic literature on the meaning and application of accountability has been very limited. Thus it is important for the researchers to develop new ideas on how to ensure it will be more well discussed and presented and applied in accounting practices. Likewise, the term sustainability has not been discussed in the current literatures that should become a potential area of research to contribute to the development of Islamic finance that has been considered as a fast-growing industry to date. However, as the industry carries the title of religion, many critiques that demand the industry to be more accountable (both in the framework of professional and religious practices) so that they will become more financially sustainable in the future.

The paper is organized as follows. Section 10.2 presents the meaning of accountability and sustainability while Section 10.3 offers mapping method. Section 10.4 draws mapping analysis of Islamic accounting, accountability and sustainability, followed by Section 10.5 that wraps discussion and conclusion as well as recommendation for future research.

10.1 The meaning of accountability and sustainability

Accountability describes internal control of an accounting by management to assist in the efficiency of resources by providing information, either for ex post monitoring of performance or for ex ante decision-making by those responsible for making investment decisions (Whittington 1992). Accountability can be proven through transparency and disclosure as Allah SWT states in the following verse: "*And O my people, give full measure and weight in justice and do not deprive the people of their due and do not commit abuse on the earth, spreading corruption*" (QS Hud (11), p. 85). In the Quran, accountability is called *hisab*. The word of *hisab* is repeated more than eight times in different verses (Askary and Clarke 1997). *Hisab* is the root of accounting and in Quran, it is related to one's obligation to account to God on all matters pertaining to human endeavor for which every Muslim is accountable (Lewis 2006). Similarly in business, all stakeholders are accountable for their actions both within and outside their firm. Although in the conventional practice, the accountability is only towards humans while in Islam the accountability is to humans, society and ultimately to God who will judge all worldly affairs during the Day of Judgment. Disclosure is an important aspect of the accountability function of Islamic finance to its stakeholders (El-Halaby 2015).

The Islamic Financial Institution (IFI) accountability mechanism reveals two types of accountability applicable to international organizations. Vertical accountability refers to the power of oversight held by the stakeholders of international organizations. Horizontal accountability refers to international organizations to determine whether they are acting properly (Carrington *et al.* 2008).

Sustainability on the other hand is associated with social and environmental impact of business (Adam and Gonzalez 2007). The social and environmental reporting theory was first developed without involving the companies that did not prepare sustainability reporting. Nevertheless, it was found that the process of reporting, the attitude of participants and corporate culture play an important role determining in the extents of disclosure discharged through corporate accountability (Adam 2002).

By definition, sustainability in accounting related to both present and future generations and it requires that all needs are met. It is common to refer to the needs of the USA for instance, for eco-justice, eco-efficiency and eco-effectiveness (Gray and Bebbington 2000; Gray 2006). Sustainability accounting has many perspectives, it is reflected in different names used for the concept, such as accounting and carbon accounting (Bebbington and Gray 2001; Gray 2010; De and Van 2014). Sustainability accounting is also defined by as a process for information collection and communication to support internal decision-making to implement corporate sustainability (Burritt and Schaltegger 2010). Both accounting and sustainability are related and have common objectives. According to Rubenstein (1992, p. 506), accounting not only measures consuming resources in producing goods and services for trade but it also preserves wealth created for future use. The later also refers to the meaning of sustainability.

According to Hasan (2006), sustainability implies maintaining the long-run rate of economic growth, achieving intergenerational equity in the use of the natural resources and restricting as far as possible the increase in pollution for maintaining the present quality of environment. Sustainability in Islam is extension of ensuring intergenerational equity in the distribution of wealth and prosperity, conservation of resources and substance of the environment (Hasan 2006; Killawi 2014). To make resources sustainable is a duty of every mankind that has been stipulated under QS Ar-Rad (13:3): *And it is He who spread the earth and placed therein firmly set mountains and rivers; and from all of the fruits He made therein two mates; He causes the night to cover the day. Indeed in that are signs for a people who give thought.* The implied understanding on sustainability is stated in this verse, which is to order mankind to take a good care of what has been created for them.

10.2 Supporting studies and mapping method

Khlif and Chalmers (2015) in Journal of Accounting Literature (3*) highlights that meta-analytic method are being applied and accepted to answer complex questions concerning the moderating effects of country level variables such as national culture, economic conditions and institutional characteristics. This study identifies 27 meta-analytical studies over 1985–2014 with financial reporting topic.

Haynes (2017) in Critical Perspectives on Accounting (3*) reviewed of 25 years of critical accounting research on gender. The paper addresses what readers have learned to date and what are the most challenging areas to be investigated in the future. It also outlines the contribution of feminist theory to accounting research on gender and challenges for further research on the interaction of gender relations with global capitalism. The study finds that accounting acts both a gendered and gendering institution in relation to career hierarchies, motherhood, work-life debates, feminization, segmentation, interacts with gendered identity, embodiment and sexuality.

Apostolou and Dorminey (2017) in Journal of Accounting Education (2*) analysed publication trends in six accounting education journals published during the 20-year period 1997–2016. The paper shows that the number of articles per year has increased over time and the proportion of articles in four categories (empirical, descriptive, instructional resources and cases) has changed over the 20 years.

Brierley and Cowton (2000) in Journal of Business Ethics (3*) show how meta-analysis can make a valuable contribution. The paper covers social journals for the years 1981–1995, searching articles that described the empirical correlations between organizational-professional conflict and other work environment variables. This study concludes that meta-analysis can make a contribution even when the substantive findings are limited.

Mukhlisin (2017) in Journal of Islamic Accounting and Business Research (1*) reviews 1* to 4* relevant peer-reviewed journal in the academic journal guide 2015 of the Association of Business School from the period 2005 to 2012. The paper finds that studies emphasis not only on the technical matters related to financial reporting standard but also on the complex arrangement in different country settings.

After examining previous studies and the aim of the research that substantially composed the meaning of accountability and sustainability therefore the suitable methodology for this paper is meta-analysis. The scope of this article covers research papers ranked in Academic Journal Guide, Association of Business School (ABS) 2015 version. The guide is specific on business school studies unlike Scopus List or Thomson & Reuters that index and rank papers from various disciplines. The ABS rank journals through six steps such as: 1. Assessing the need of business and management research community; 2. Ranking from 1 to 4*(read: star/s) after consulting at least three out of five international journal listings; 3. Classifying the journals through several reviews; 4. Drawing comprehensive coverage of research; 5. Finalizing process from editors and 6. Stating justification from editors on the methodology.

The method of this research is first, the authors list down 1–4* journals published in ABS under the "Accounting" heading then search the subject with keywords: "Islamic Accounting." There are 150 papers from 38 journals that have published papers on Islamic accounting including two Islamic journals (International Journal of Islamic and Middle Eastern Finance & Management/IJIMEFM and Journal of Islamic Accounting and Business Research/JIABR). Details of the 38 journals are as follows:

1. Journal of Business Finance & Accounting (JBFA), 3*, 2 Papers
2. Accounting, Auditing & Accountability Journal (AAAJ) 3*, 2 Papers
3. Accounting and Business Research (ABR), 3*, 2 Papers
4. Financial Accountability & Management (FAM), 3*, 2 Paper
5. Abacus, 3*, 4 Papers
6. International Journal of Bank Marketing (IJBM), 1*, 1 Paper
7. European Accounting Review (EAR), 3*, 1 Paper,
8. Journal of International Accounting, Auditing & Taxation (JIAAT), 3*, 5 Papers
9. Journal of Business Ethics (JBE), 3*, 8 Papers
10. Journal of Management and Governance (JMG), 1*, 1 Paper
11. International Journal of Theoretical and Applied Finance (IJTAF), 2*, 1 Paper
12. Asian Review of Accounting (ARA), 2*, 6 Papers
13. International Journal of Accounting (IJA), 3*, 1 Paper
14. Managerial Auditing Journal (MAJ), 2*, 14 Papers
15. Managerial Finance (MF), 1*, 1 Paper
16. Journal of Accounting and Economics (JAE), 4*, 1 Paper
17. Accounting Historians Journal (AHJ), 2*, 1 Paper
18. Research in Accounting Regulation (RAR), 2*, 3 Papers
19. Advances in International Accounting (AIA), 2*, 13 Papers
20. Accounting Research Journal (ARJ), 2*, 9 Papers
21. Journal of Contemporary Accounting & Economics (JCAE), 2*, 3 Papers
22. Journal of Accounting & Organizational Change (JAOC), 2*, 1 Paper
23. Journal of Applied Accounting Research (JAAR), 2*, 7 Papers
24. Accounting Forum (AF), 3*, 3 Papers
25. Journal of Banking Regulation (JBR), 2*, 2 Papers
26. Critical Perspectives on Accounting (CPA), 3*, 4 Papers
27. Journal of Islamic Accounting and Business Research (JIABR), 1*, 21 Papers
28. International Journal of Auditing (IJA), 2*, 2 Papers
29. International Journal of Islamic and Middle Eastern Finance and Management (IJIMEFM) 1*, 11 Papers
30. International Journal of Disclosure and Governance (IJDG), 2*, 9 Papers
31. Meditari Accountancy Research (MAR), 1*, 1 Papers
32. Journal of International Financial Management & Accounting (JIFMA), 2*, 2 Papers
33. Journal of Accounting in Emerging Economies (JAEE), 2*, 1 Paper
34. Journal of Economic Issues (JEI), 2*, 1 Paper
35. British Accounting Review (BAR), 3*, 1 Paper
36. Accounting in Europe (AE), 2*, 1 Paper
37. Australian Accounting Review, 2*, 1 Paper
38. Social and Environmental Accountability Journal, 1*, 1 Paper

From the above journals, major countries under study are Malaysia, GCC countries, Bahrain and 92 papers focus on accountability issues, while 58 papers focus on sustainability issues. Section 10.4 elaborates the depth of each study per period of time.

10.3 Mapping analysis of Islamic accounting, accountability and sustainability

This analysis aims to explore how far Islamic accounting studies have given priority to discuss accountability and sustainability issues. With recent rapid growth of IFIs in 1990s, there was still inconclusive stance regarding the specificity of accounting standards for IFIs such as the ones issued by Accounting and Auditing for Islamic Financial Institution (AAOIFI) (Mohammed, Fahmi, Ahmad, and Asyaari 2015). It is acknowledged that the establishment of AAOIFI has influenced reporting system of IFIs. Islamic Financial Institution transactions are prepared under a variety of accounting standards, which pose a threat to its unique accounting and reporting system. Therefore the papers below are grouped before the establishment period of AAOIFI as to whether they have contribution to the formation of the standard body (see Table 10.1).

The first paper categorized under "Islamic accounting" found in the journal was written in 1986. The two words: accountability and sustainability are not directly termed in the papers within this period although the finding shows that the authors impliedly state the meaning of the two words. Karim, a student of Gambling and Tomkins seems to dominate the publication during this period. It becomes apparent that he justified the publication to support the establishment of AAOIFI or known before as Financial Accounting Organization for Islamic Banks and Financial Institutions/FAOIBFI) in 1990, which aims to convince the world that there was a need of Islamic financial reporting set of standards.

All papers above did not mention the clear methodology on how to develop standards for Islamic banks/institutions. It turned out that the *hybrid methodology* was adopted by AAOIFI as it offers an express way which is to imitate the current practices and edit them according to Shariah law. As a result, the accounting framework and standards produced by AAOIFI have been criticized due to its similarities with that of International Accounting Standards issued by Financial Accounting Standards Board that was based in the USA.

The next examination is on the period after the formation of AAOIFI to see if AAOIFI in its presence could stimulate researchers to write more papers relating to Islamic accounting (see Table 10.2).

Period from 1990 to 2000 was considered as the emerging development of Islamic finance that was noted with the establishment of several Islamic financial institutions. This section focuses on the meaning of accountability and sustainability that have been discussed during this decade.

Table 10.1 Empirical research of Islamic accounting before AAOIFI (1986–1990)

Year, Author; Journal	*Country, Sample, Method, Paradigm*	*Finding*
1986, Gambling and Karim; JBFA	N/A, Literature Review, Interpretativism, Sustainability	The traditional Western double-entry based accounting technology is well suited to an orthodox, positivist society of any kind, and it is proving inadequate for an integrated Islamic world views.
1989, Karim and Ali; JBFA	Sudan and Kuwait, Faisal Islamic Bank of Sudan (FIBS) and Kuwait Finance House (KFH). Data 1979–1985, Descriptive Statistic, Interpretivism, Sustainability	This paper attempts to shed light on that important aspect of Islamic banks.
1990a, Karim; AAAJ	N/A, Literature Review, Critical, Accountability	It is necessary that through joint forces, SSB and external auditors are perceived to be independent to ensure the credibility of financial statements.
1990b, Karim; ABR	N/A, Literature Review, Interpretivism, Accountability	The fear of Islamic banks of possible future intervention by their regulatory agencies in their current accounting practices seems to be the predominant factor that has motivated Islamic banks to establish a standard setting body to regulate their financial accounting and reporting.

The development of International Institute of Financing and Accounting (IIFA) can be traced to as far back as the sixth century, during which the fundamental principles of Islamic finance such as strict prohibition of usury (*riba*), were established through Qur'anic revelations and the traditions (i.e., *hadith*)

Table 10.2 Empirical research of Islamic accounting after AAOIFI establishment (1993–2001)

Year, Author; Journal	*Country, Sample, Method, Paradigm*	*Finding*
1993, Gambling, Jones, and Karim; FAM	N/A, Literature Review, Interpretivism, Sustainability	The common feature of accounting for charities, Islamic banks, and governments, is the absence of agreement over the inherent moral justification of their financial activities, thus requires assurance.
1993, Hamid, Craig, and Clarke; Abacus	N/A, Literature Review, Interpretivism, Sustainability	Its potential for influencing accounting policy is illustrative of religion as a confounding element in the analysis of national idiosyncrasies in accounting practice and in deconstructing the impediments to international harmonization.
1995, Karim; ABR	N/A, Literature Review, Interpretivism, Sustainability	The ambiguities that may arise from different interpretations of the religious rules will require resolutions primarily by reference to religious rather than accounting authority.
1996, Karim; IJBM	N/A, Literature Review, Intepretivism, Accountability	It develops four possible scenarios for the treatment of profit sharing accounts.
1996, Cooke and Cürük; EAR	N/A, Turkey, Literature Review, Interpretivism, Accountability	The results of the empirical part of this paper show that, except for three requirements stated in IAS 17, all the principles set out in that standard are acceptable to accountants in Turkey.
1997, Pomeranz; JIAAT	N/A, Literature Review, Critical, Sustainability	Increased communication between the West and the nations of Islam will help mankind to follow the ethical and moral precepts of the revealed religions.
1997, Zaid; JBE	Australia, 303 Accountant and auditor, Observation, Poststructurialism, Sustainability	The examination revealed the lack of such general agreement and further indicated that the perceptual differences are subjective in nature and not influenced by the participant's qualifications, income, experience, gender or marital status.

Table 10.2 (Cont.)

Year, Author; Journal	*Country, Sample, Method, Paradigm*	*Finding*
1998, Archer, Karim, and Al-Deehani; JMG	N/A, Literature Review, Intepretivism, Accountability	Three main ways to mitigate deficiencies in IAH governance; reduce Islamic Banks' discretion to manage IAH's return; increase monitoring; generalization of hostage posting.
1998, Rahman and Goddard; FAM	N/A, 12 Islamic banks, Observation, Poststructurialism, Sustainability	The emergent theoretical perspective stage is an important but far from terminal stage. More theorizing and testing is required both within the organizations studied in this research and in new case studies before a grounded theory can be proposed.
1999, Al-Deehani, Karim, and Murinde; IJTAF	N/A, Bahrain, 52 accountants, Interview, Poststructurialism, Accountability	It provides new dimension to the theory of capital structure.
1999, Joshi and Al-Basteki; ARA	N/A, Malaysia, Literature Review, Interpretivism, Accountability	It is found that the need for compliance with IASs will better enhance users' understanding of accounting concepts and financial statements.
2000, Iskandar and Pourjalali; ARA	N/A, Literature Review, Critical, Accountability	The development of IAS continues to help the advancement of accounting practices in Malaysia as the MASB continues to support and adapt the IASs.
2000, Baydoun and Willett; Abacus	N/A, Literature Review, Interpretivism, Accountability	The specific recommendations are that ICRs should contain a value-added statement as the focus of performance of the accounting entity and a current value balance sheet in addition to the historic cost balance sheet. It is argued that ICRs, extended in this way, would better serve the needs of users wishing to act in accordance with the Islamic code.

(*continued*)

Table 10.2 (Cont.)

Year, Author, Journal	*Country, Sample, Method, Paradigm*	*Finding*
2000, Naughton and Naughton; JBE	N/A, Literature Review, Interpretivism, Accountability	The use of stock index and equity futures and options are also unlikely to be acceptable within an Islamic market. Regulatory authorities in Muslim countries will therefore find a vast array of problems in attempting to structure a trading system that will be acceptable.
2000, Karim; IJA	N/A, Literature Review, Critical, Accountability	Islamic banks casts light on the need to develop and implement accounting standards that specifically cater for the unique characteristics of the contracts.
2001, Ataur Rahman Belal; MAJ	Bangladesh, 30 annual reports, Statistic Descriptive, Accountability	In addition to measuring the extent and volume of disclosures by using content analysis, it explores the socio-political and economic context in which these disclosures take place.

of Prophet Muhammad (peace be upon him). By the end of the 19th century, however, much of the Muslim world had become subject to Western colonial powers, who introduced commercial banking into the local economy. This had been met with strong criticisms by Muslim scholars during the 1900s–1930s who considered lending with interest as a form of usury that goes against the Islamic principles. Discontents that grew rapidly within the Muslim world in the 1950s and 1960s had then become the impetus for the development of a modern framework for Islamic finance, leading to the establishment of Islamic financial institutions during the 1970s. The creation of the Islamic Development Bank (IDB) in 1975 arguably marked the turning point in the development of IIFA, as it paved the way towards the establishment of various other organizations within the architecture. To date, the IDB has continued to play a central role in supporting the development of Islamic finance.[1]

Rapid growth of the Islamic finance sector since 1990s has created the need for a more resilient supporting architecture in order to deal with issues such as risk management, corporate governance, accountability and sustainability. During the period of 1990–2000, the authors tend to discuss the meaning of accountability (eight papers) instead of sustainability (six papers).

Accountability is crucial for every organization. In general, holding international organization accountable means to ensure that (1) international policies and procedures are lawful and reflect the best interests of its stakeholders and (2) the organization acts according to its particular governance arrangement. The international financial institutions (conventional and Islamic) have implemented various mechanisms such as transparency initiatives and inspection panels to hold themselves accountable for their actions (Carrington *et al.* 2008). The reporting of sustainability issues by corporations is one of the most important parts of sustainability reporting. Recently, several initiatives by independent and governmental organizations have provided guidance to assist organizations with sustainability reporting (Adams and Narayanan 2007). Corporate sustainability has been gaining importance in practice (Ernst and Young 2010). Numerous recent studies reveal that companies seem to have realized the contribution of tackling sustainability issues towards their long-term success (Schaltegger *et al.* 2005; Schaltegger and Wagner 2006, 2011).

In 2002, the Islamic Financial Services Board (IFSB) was established. IFSB serves as an international standard-setting of regulatory and supervisory agencies that have vested interest in ensuring the soundness and stability of the Islamic financial services industry through introducing new, or adapting existing international standards consisting of Shariah principles and recommend them for adoption. This establishment benefits for accountability and quality disclosure of IFIs (Tessema, Garas, and Tee 2017). The summary of the papers collected from 2002 to 2017 follows the assumption that after International Financial Reporting Standard (IFRS), more researchers are motivated to write IFRS and Islamic finance (see Table 10.3).

The journals that have published more papers on the meaning of accountability and sustainability are JIABR (21 papers), MAJ (14 papers), AIA (13 papers) and IJIMEFM (11 papers). JIABR focuses on Islamic accounting research thus it published the highest number of papers that discuss the extent and extant meaning of accountability and sustainability. The finding shows that the meaning of accountability has been discussed in 81 papers, higher than the meaning of sustainability that has been discussed in 51 papers during the period. The focus on "accountability" indicates that the Islamic financial institutions are very concerned with the role of Islamic accounting as a medium of accountability to God and society as claimed by the Islamic financial institutions whenever they call themselves as "Islamic."

10.4 Conclusion and recommendation for future research

This paper aims to address "To what extent have accountability and sustainability been well discussed in the context of Islamic accounting?" and finds the meaning of accountability has been discussed more frequently than the meaning of sustainability. It shows that the understanding and application of accountability is still in the emerging trend as compared to sustainability. Sustainability itself portrays a message that the Islamic financial

Table 10.3 Empirical research of Islamic accounting during AAOIFI-IFRS period (2002–2017)

Year, Author; Journal	*Country, Sample, Method, Paradigm*	*Finding*
2002, Haniffa and Cooke; Abacus	Malaysia, 167 companies that published their annual reports during the year ended 31 December 1995, Regression, Positivism, Accountability	This finding has implications for corporate governance policy formulation by the Malaysian Institute of Corporate Governance (MISG). One cultural factor (proportion of Malay directors on the board) is significantly associated (at the 5% level) with the extent of voluntary disclosure suggesting that governmental focus on culture may solicit a response to secrecy from those who feel threatened.
2003, Harahap; MF	Indonesia, Bank Muamalat, comparative and analytical, Interpretivism, Accountability	The standard issued by AAOIFI are not binding but can be used as a guideline to be followed by Islamic financial institutions when preparing their financial statements. It is also argued that the BMI annual report places primary emphasis on local regulations and in particular, those decreed by Indonesia's central bank, Bank Indonesia.
2003, Ahmad, Sulaiman, and Alwi; MAJ	N/s, Malaysia, 62 companies in two sectors; industrial products 104 companies) and consumer products 58 companies), questionnaire survey, Poststructurialism, Accountability	The companies in Malaysia appear to use flexible budgets more than those in the UK and New Zealand.
2003, Robin and Wu; JAE	Hong Kong, Malaysia, Thailand, Singapore, Literature Review, Interpretivism, Accountability	The paper shows their financial reporting quality is not higher than under code law, with quality operationalized as timely

Table 10.3 (Cont.)

Year, Author; Journal	*Country, Sample, Method, Paradigm*	*Finding*
		recognition of economic income (particularly losses). It is misleading to classify countries by standards, ignoring incentives, as is common in international accounting texts, transparency indexes, and IAS advocacy.
2004, Zaid; AHJ	Arab World, Literature Review, Interpretivism, Accountability	This paper argues that the accounting systems and recording procedures practiced in Muslim society commenced before the invention of the Arabic numerals in response to religious requirements, especially zakat, a mandatory religious levy imposed on Muslims the year 2 H.
2004, Joshi and Amal Wakil; MAJ	N/A, Bahrain, 30 companies listed on the Bahrain stock exchange, Descriptive Statistic, Positivism, Accountability	ACs do not report their findings to shareholders, but other functions seem to accord with the BRC's recommendations. However, some perceptions of audit firms negate the claims of the companies to comply with BRC recommendations.
2005, Mirshekary and Saudagaran; IAAT	Iran, 55 bank loan officers, 35 academics, 40 stockbrokers, 40 bank investment officers, 55 institutional investor representatives, 95 auditors, and 180 tax officers, Kruskal–Wallis and Mann–Whitney U tests, Positivism, Accountability	There is a weak level of consensus among bank loan officers, tax officers and auditor groups about the importance of several information items. The overall results showed that they ranked the income statement, the auditors' report and the balance sheet as the three most important parts of the annual report (in that order).

(*continued*)

Table 10.3 (Cont.)

Year, Author, Journal	*Country, Sample, Method, Paradigm*	*Finding*
2005, Hassan & Christopher; ARA	N/A, Malaysia, Literature Review, Interpretivism, Sustainability	Being an Islamic organization (by virtue of label attached to and/or the nature of its operations) and/or having Malaysia/Muslim directors leading such Islamic organization have not resulted in better corporate governance practices and disclosure relative to other secular banking institutions that have fewer Malaysia/ Muslims directors.
2005, Shankaraiah and Rao; RAR	Oman, 2001–2002 annual reports of 10 top Omani companies, Literature Review, Interpretivism, Accountability	To strengthen accounting standards and improve financial reporting and corporate governance in Oman, the Capital Market Authority in Oman, in consultation with other appropriate professionals and regulatory bodies, should develop some mechanism to limit the scope of alternative methods available by focusing on appropriate disclosures under Oman's domestic conditions to improve the relevance and indigenisation of accounting standards.
2005, Bakar, Rahman, and Rashid; MAJ	Malaysia, 86 officers of commercial Banks, Survey, Poststructurialism, Accountability	Audit firm size appears to be the most important factor that affects the auditor independence, followed by tenure, competition, audit committee, audit firms providing managerial advisory services and size of audit fee.

Table 10.3 (Cont.)

Year, Author; Journal	*Country, Sample, Method, Paradigm*	*Finding*
2005, Sulaiman, Ahmad, and Alwi; MAJ	Malaysia, 66 companies, Descriptive Statistic, Postivism, Accountability	Despite its various criticisms, the empirical findings suggest that standard costing is still being used by a large majority of firms in Malaysia. Thus, Malaysian companies (both Japanese and local) perceive that the basic principles of standard costing remain sound.
2005, Beekun and Badawi; JBE	N/A, Literature Review, Interpretivism, Sustainability	The Islamic ethical system is balanced, fair, just and benevolent, and seeks to respect the rights of both primary and derivative stakeholders without allowing for exploitation, nepotism and other human ills. Islam advocates a tiered, multi-fiduciary stakeholder approach that calibrates what various stakeholders of a business receive in proportion to their inputs.
2006, Rahman and Ali; MAJ	N/A, Malaysia, 100 top companies, for the period January 2002 to December 2003, Regression, Positivism, Accountability	The study reveals that earnings management is positively related to the size of the board of directors.
2006, Naser, Hussaini, Kwari, and Nuseibeh; AIA	Qatar, Annual reports from 22 listed companies for the year 1999/ 2000, Regression, Postivism, Accountability	The outcome of the study lends partial support to agency theory, political economy theory, legitimacy theory, stakeholder theory as well as the accountability approach.

(*continued*)

Table 10.3 (Cont.)

Year, Author; Journal	*Country, Sample, Method, Paradigm*	*Finding*
2006, Auyeung, Dagwell, Ng, and Sands; ARA	Australia, Hong Kong, Malaysia and Singapore, Participants were accounting academics, Observation, Poststructurialism, Sustainability	Results suggest that Australian and Malaysian accounting educators differed significantly in their epistemological beliefs on the source of knowledge as well as the acquisition of knowledge.
2006, Maali, Casson, and Napier; Abacus	N/A, 200 financial institutions around the world offering Islamic banking, disclosure index, Interpretivism, Sustainability	The results of the analysis also suggest that banks required to pay the Islamic religious tax *Zakah* provide more social disclosures than banks not subject to *Zakah*.
2007, Haniffa and Hudaib; JIAAT	Arab Saudi, 48 respondents, the questionnaire using a Likert scale, Positivism, Sustainability	The "performance gap" arises from four factors in the environment within which auditing is practiced: licensing policy, recruitment process, the political and legal structure, and dominant societal values.
2007, Perera and Baydoun; AIA	Indonesia, Literature Review, Interpretivism, Accountability	The possibility that the use of IFRSs in Indonesia might trigger a change from a "credit-insider" to an "equity-outsider" financing system should not be ruled out.
2007, Kamla; AIA	Middle East, Literature Review, Critical, Accountability	Pursuing a critical and postcolonial perspective that is sensitive to the context of the AME, it is concluded that social accounting manifestations in the AME are largely orientated towards "repressive/counter radical" positions of accounting.

Table 10.3 (Cont.)

Year, Author; Journal	*Country, Sample, Method, Paradigm*	*Finding*
2007, Waha, How, and Verhoeven; JCAE	Malaysia, 440 firms from 1999 to 2002, Panel data, Positivism, Accountability	The implementation of MCCG has had a substantial effect on shareholders' wealth, increasing stock prices by an average of about 4.8%. Although there is no evidence that politically connected firms perform better, political connections do have a significantly negative effect on corporate governance, which is mitigated by institutional ownership.
2007, Ali and Ahmed; RAR	South Asia, Literature Review, Interpretivism, Accountability	The paper concludes that the prevailing similarities in political, legal, economic, business ownership, accounting profession, culture and institutional structures in the three countries should have facilitated regional accounting harmonization.
2007, Haniffa and Hudaib; JBE	The Arabian Gulf region, 24 annual reports for the years 2002-2004, content analysis, Interpretivism, Sustainability	The study founds the largest incongruence to be related to four dimensions: commitments to society; disclosure of corporate vision and mission; contribution to and management of zakah, charity and benevolent loans; and information regarding top management.
2008, Hassan; JAOC	Egypt, 12 individuals, Interview, Poststructurialism, Accountability	The paper finds that the EFAR have had a constitutive tendency during the Egyptian transformation towards a market-based economy.

(*continued*)

Table 10.3 (Cont.)

Year, Author; Journal	*Country, Sample, Method, Paradigm*	*Finding*
2008, Mashayekhi and Azaz; JCAE	Iran, companies listed in the Tehran Stock Exchange (TSE) for the years 2005–2006, Regression, Positivism, Accountability	There is no relationship between leadership structure and firm performance. Likewise, the presence of institutional investors on the board of directors is not positively associated with firm performance.
2008, Dey, Grinyer, Sinclair, and El-Habashy; JAAR	Egypt, 320 firms, multivariate analysis, Positivism, Accountability	The evidence of the study is consistent with the validity of the conventional "bonus" and "debt" hypotheses and the new "taxation" hypothesis. These conclusions are also consistent with recent empirical studies of cultural and socio-economic change in Egypt.
2008, Joshi, Bremser, and Ajmi; AIA	Bahrain, 52 listed companies, Survey, Poststructurialism, Accountability	The survey findings suggest that there will be a growing demand for detailed application guidance for IFRS. Also, it appears that nationalism may well continue to be a major impediment to global adoption of IFRS.
2008, Irvine; AF	UAE, Literature Review, Interpretivism, Accountability	This paper identifies some of the global coercive, normative and mimetic pressures which have contributed to this widespread adoption. The challenge for emerging economies such as that of the UAE is whether the reality of IFRS implementation can match the image of IFRS adoption.

Table 10.3 (Cont.)

Year, Author; Journal	*Country, Sample, Method, Paradigm*	*Finding*
2009, Ariffin, Archer, and Karim; JBR	14 different countries, including Malaysia, Sudan, Bangladesh, Pakistan and Middle East count ries, 28 Islamic banks, a questionnaire survey, Poststructurialism, Accountability	The findings show policy implications for the issue of transparency, with particular reference to risk reporting in Islamic banks.
2009, Archer and Karim; JBR	Middle East, Asia, Jordan, Malaysia, Qatar and Bahrain, Literature Review, Interpretivism, Accountability	It explains problems of and offers solution to profit-sharing investment account holders.
2009, Tapanjeh; CPA	N/A, Literature Review, Interpretivism, Accountability	The OECD principles have been successfully implemented and considered a very effective tool of corporate governance as compared to Islamic principles of corporate governance.
2009, Joshi, Ajmi, and Bremser; AIA	Bahrain, 87 clients, Survey, Poststructurialism, Accountability	The audit process and evidence problems reported indicate possible audit quality problems faced by audit firms in Bahraini environment when conducting external audits, indicating the need for future research on auditor–client relationships in emerging economies.
2009, Dey, Grinyer, Sinclair, and El-Habashy; JAAR	Egypt, 320 Egyptian firms with the largest net asset, Survey, Poststructurialism, Accountability	The paper finds that technical reasons were frequently given in survey responses from managers. However, the available evidence on the actual depreciation methods used by their firms and industries is in fact more consistent with PAT-based theories of accounting

(*continued*)

Table 10.3 (Cont.)

Year, Author; Journal	*Country, Sample, Method, Paradigm*	*Finding*
		choice than with such alternatives. This suggests that the responses to the survey reflected managers' rationalisations of decisions made for self-interested purposes.
2009, Al-Ajmi; AIA	Bahrain, 300 credit and financial analysts, Survey, Poststructurialism, Sustainability	Non-audit services were found to affect auditor's independence and hence impair audit quality. Effective audit committee enhances the quality of audit reports. Financial analysts perceive financial statements to be more credible than do credit analysts.
2009, Wahab, Zain, James, and Haron; ARJ	Malaysia, 390 Malaysian firms from 1999 to 2003, Panel Analysis, Positivism, Accountability	Based on a panel analysis of 390 Malaysian firms from 1999 to 2003, a positive relationship between institutional ownership and audit fees is found, although the economic impact is minimal. Further, the authors find that audit fees are higher for politically connected firms.
2009, Al-Ajmi; MAJ	Bahrain, 800 individual investors, Survey, Positivism, Accountability	The study found that individual investors perceived corporate financial statements as the most important source of information for their investment decisions. The results also show a relatively high degree of agreement within the groups (both large and small) as to the ranking in terms of the importance of the topics.

Table 10.3 (Cont.)

Year, Author; Journal	*Country, Sample, Method, Paradigm*	*Finding*
2009, Hossain and Hammami; AIA	Qatar, 42 Annual reports for the year 2007, Regression, Positivism, Accountability	The users of financial reporting including investors need confidence of financial markets and information disclosure is a vital element to fulfil this confidence and in this case this study would provide a communication bridge to the various stakeholders in the society.
2010, Maali and Napier; JIABR	Jordan, Literature Review, Interpretivism, Sustainability	The paper shows that creating a new type of organisation – an Islamic bank – in Jordan required special legislation. A study of the development of this legislation reveals that the bank's founder needed to convince both the religious and political authorities and potential investors that the bank would comply with *Shari'a* principles while at the same time generating profitable business.
2010, Sufian; JIABR	Malaysia, 11 domestic window Islamic banks, and four foreign window Islamic banks during the period of 2001–2007, Regression, Positivism, Sustainability	The empirical findings suggest that overhead cost is negatively related to Malaysian Islamic banks' profitability. On the other hand, Islamic banks which are better capitalized and have a higher level of liquidity tend to be more profitable
2010, Archer and Karim; JIABR	N/A, Literature Review, Interpretivism, Accountability	The characteristics of PSIA can vary from being a deposit like product (fixed return, capital certain, all risks borne by shareholders) to an investment product (variable return, bearing the risk of losses in underlying investments),

(*continued*)

Table 10.3 (Cont.)

Year, Author; Journal	*Country, Sample, Method, Paradigm*	*Finding*
		depending upon the extent to which the balance sheet risks get shifted ("displaced") from investment account holders to shareholders through various techniques available to Islamic banks' management. Second, the paper finds that this DCR has a major impact on Islamic bank's economic and regulatory capital requirements, asset liability management and product pricing.
2010 Haniffa and Hudaib; JIABR	N/A, Literature Review, Interpretivism, Accountability	Islamic accounting research is still at the infancy stage compared to Islamic banking and finance.
2010, Abdullatif and Khadash; IJA	Jordan, Literature Review, Interpretivism, Accountability	The results of the study show that the business risk approach has been generally adopted by the larger Jordanian audit firms to varying extents, especially those which are full members of an international audit firm network.
2010, Vinnicombe; AIA	N/A, Literature Review, Critical, Accountability	The findings of the study show compliance to be very high with respect to the governance standard relating to the in-house supervisory boards of Islamic banks, and reporting the Islamic murabaha contract. In contrast, compliance with the AAOIFI's requirements regarding the zakah religious tax and the mudaraba contract is relatively low.

Table 10.3 (Cont.)

Year, Author; Journal	*Country, Sample, Method, Paradigm*	*Finding*
2010, Menassa; JAAR	Lebanon, annual report social disclosures of 24 Lebanese commercial banks, Correlation, Postivism, Sustainability	The findings provide evidence of the widespread use of this phenomenon by these banks as a means to communicate with their stakeholders. Moreover, results reveal that these banks attribute a greater importance to human resource and product and customers disclosures, whereas the availability and extent of environmental disclosure is still weak.
2010, Hassan and Harahap; IJIMEFM	Bahrain, Bangladesh, Indonesia, Malaysia, Saudi Arabia, Kuwait, and the United Arab Emirates, annual reports of seven Islamic banks, content analysis, Intepretivism, Sustainability	The results show the overall mean CSR disclosure index of one Islamic bank out of seven to be above average and the issues of CSR are not of major concern for most Islamic banks.
2010, Kamil, Abdullah, Shahimi, and Ismail; IJIMEFM	N/A, Descriptive, analytical, and comparative analyses, Interpretivism, Accountability	The paper reveals that although sukuk are structured in a similar way to conventional asset-backed securities, they can have significantly different underlying structures, provisions and shariah-compliant.
2011, Gallhofer, Haslamb, and Kamla; CPA	Syria, 10 respondents, Interview, Poststructurialism, Sustainability	The critical understanding of Syrian accountants and their appreciation of the ambiguity of the accounting–globalisation interrelation for Syria is a particular form of resistance to globalisation's problematics. Concurrently, given the significance of local influences in Syria, it is somewhat surprising that interviewees evidenced so little resistance.

(*continued*)

Table 10.3 (Cont.)

Year, Author; Journal	*Country, Sample, Method, Paradigm*	*Finding*
2011, Amin, Rahman, Sondoh Jr, and Hwa; JIABR	Malaysia, 150 customers, Regression, Positivism, Sustainability	The study found three determinants to be significant in influencing the intention to use Islamic personal financing, namely, attitude, social influence and pricing of Islamic personal financing. Religious obligation and government support were found to be insignificant predictors.
2011, Al-Janadi, Rahman, and Normah Omar; IJDG	Arab Saudi and UAE, Analytical Descriptive, 150 companies, Intepretivism, Sustainability	The results indicate that voluntary disclosure has been found lacking for most of the items of social and environmental information. In comparing the results of voluntary disclosure between the two countries, it was found that UAE companies have significantly higher voluntary disclosure than Saudi companies, with an average of around 42% for UAE companies and 32% for Saudi companies.
2011, Haji and Ghazali; IJDG	Malaysia, companies listed on the Main Market of Bursa Malaysia for the years 2006 and 2009, Wilcoxon signed-ranks test, Positivism, Sustainability	The results reveal that based on the category of information (that is, strategic, financial, CSR), CSR information was the most widely disclosed category following the financial crisis.
2011, Ariff and Fah; AIA	40 largest banks in the four countries, Australia, Korea, Malaysia and Thailand. The data set spans over eight years across 2000–2007 (before world financial crisis), OLS Regression, Positivism, Sustainability	The investors in Malaysia and South Korea appear to consider changes in fee income as bad news with negative price impact, anomalous to theory. The Australian investors appear to regard both total and fee incomes as equally important

Table 10.3 (Cont.)

Year, Author; Journal	*Country, Sample, Method, Paradigm*	*Finding*
		whereas investors in other markets either ignore or consider changes in fee income as bad news for share valuation.
2011, Al-Ajmi, Al-Saleh, and Hussain; AIA	Gulf Cooperation Council (GCC), 105 conventional and Islamic financial institutions, t tests and interview, Positivism, Sustainability	The decisions to select particular capital budgeting techniques, cost of capital estimation methods, and risk assessments are partly related to the characteristics of the chief financial officers.
2011, Aribi and Gao; MAJ	The Gulf region, he annual reports of 21 fully Shari'a approved IFIs, Content Analysis, Intepretivism, Sustainability	This study provides evidence of Islamic influence on the CSRD of IFIs. It finds that the largest part of CSRD produced by the IFIs is the disclosure of reports of the Shari'a Supervisory Board. IFIs also disclose other Islamic information (e.g., "Zakah" and charity donation, and free interest loan) and report on their compliance with Islam along with information of philanthropy, employees and community.
2012, Atmeh and Ramadan; JIABR	N/A, Literature Review, Critical, Accountability	The paper finds that presenting UIAHS in a separate category in the financial position statement (balance sheet), without reclassifying the assets in the financial position statement to reflect the assets attributable to UIAHS, suggests undue bias in the financial statements.
2012, Zainol and Kassim; JIABR	N/A, Literature Review, Critical, Sustainability	One of the major issues highlighted is the sensitivity of Islamic banks to the changes in the conventional

(*continued*)

Table 10.3 (Cont.)

Year, Author; Journal	*Country, Sample, Method, Paradigm*	*Finding*
		interest rate due to the fact that many Islamic banking products are benchmarked against the conventional interest rate. Moreover, the limited techniques and instruments available to mitigate the rate of return risk also need serious attention by the regulators.
2012, Ika and Ghazali; MAJ	Indonesia, 211 non-financial Indonesian listed companies, Multivariate Regression, Positivism, Accountability	The findings show that timeliness of reporting is associated with audit committee effectiveness. This result suggests that audit committee effectiveness is likely to reduce the financial reporting lead time, i.e., the time taken by companies to publicly release audited financial statements to the stock exchange.
2012, Mohammadrezaei, Banimahd, and Saleh; IJDG	Iran, Literature Review, Interpretivism, Accountability	Thus, it can be concluded that, first, due to the aforementioned reasons, full adoption of IS by Iran seems very difficult. Second, if Iran fully adopts the standards due to the less-developed infrastructure, there is no guarantee of successful implementation and *de facto* convergence.
2012, Baydoun, Maguire, Ryan, and Willett; MAJ	Gulf Countries, Survey data reported by the OECD (2005), Intepretivism, Accountability	Based on the corporate governance measurement scale, Oman is the clear leader among the five countries, followed by Kuwait and the United Arab Emirates. Bahrain and Qatar rank fourth and fifth, respectively.

Table 10.3 (Cont.)

Year, Author; Journal	*Country, Sample, Method, Paradigm*	*Finding*
2012, Al-Saidi and Al-Shammari; IJDG	Kuwait, Interview, Academic and investor, Poststructurialism, Accountability	The findings suggest that the corporate governance concept is well known, yet current laws are irrelevant; several obstacles need to be addressed to implement corporate governance in Kuwait.
2012, Muniandy and Ali; RAR	Malaysia, Literature Review, Intepretivism, Sustainability	The conclusion suggests the necessity to improve the quality of financial reporting practices and to build the confidence of stakeholders and potential investors.
2012, Pellegrina; ARJ	GCC, conventional and Islamic banks[6] has been extracted from the database Bankscope for the period 2001–2011, Panel Regression, Positivism, Accountability	Results provide evidence that more capitalized Islamic banks are associated to less risky positions in terms of their asset structure. In particular, the latter exhibit higher liquidity standards and a lower incidence of non-performing loans compared to other banks.
2012, Yunos, Ismail, and Smith; ARA	Malaysia, 300 Malaysian listed firms between 2001 and 2007, Panel Data Regression, Positivism, Sustainability	The analysis shows that the ethnic groups influence the adoption of conservatism, but that the evidence is mixed, implying that there could be factors other than ethnicity which explained the directors' behaviour.
2012, Cebeci; ARJ	Literature Review, Critical, Sustainability	Concepts of SR and corporate social responsibility (CSR) are not enough to describe Islamic Banks' responsibilities. Also, this failure cannot be understood only with reference to the "external environment," i.e., competition-driven,

(*continued*)

Table 10.3 (Cont.)

Year, Author; Journal	*Country, Sample, Method, Paradigm*	*Finding*
		capitalistic market conditions; but it is also closely related to the transformation of Islamic finance into an almost exclusively murabaha-based Islamic banking, which promotes more individual maslahah than social maslahah.
2012, Grassa; ARJ	GCC Countries, Data from 2002-2008 for 42 Islamic banks, Regression, Positivism, Accountability	This article reveals that greater reliance on the income share of the profit-loss-sharing products is associated with higher risk and higher insolvency risk for both listed Islamic banks and non-listed Islamic banks.
2012, Hassan; IJDG	UAE, the annual reports of 23 UAE financial institutions, Content Analysis, Intepretivism, Sustainability	The article findings show that UAE financial institutions utilize "assertive" and "defensive" disclosure tactics to gain, maintain and restore their social legitimacy. The article is one of the first studies to examine how financial institutions, operating in emerging economies, use narrative disclosures to pursue organizational legitimacy.
2013, Kamla and Rammal; AAAJ	Selected Muslim Countries, annual reports and web sites of 19 Islamic banks, Content Analysis, Critical, Sustainability	The disclosures do not indicate that the banks have serious schemes targeting poverty elimination or enhancing equitable redistribution of wealth in society.
2013, Naim, Isa, and Hamid; JIABR	Content analysis, interviews, observations and descriptive, Interpretivism and Poststructurialism, Accountability	The findings showed that there were negligible changes on the principle term and condition (PTC) of the Sukuk after the pronouncement, thus it

Table 10.3 (Cont.)

Year, Author; Journal	*Country, Sample, Method, Paradigm*	*Finding*
		did not have much effect in changing the Shariah Advisors and industry players when deciding more authentic principles and decisions.
2013, Taylor; MAR	South Africa, quasi-experimental, three former studies, Poststructurialism, Sustainability	The results indicate that the business ethics course was indeed effective in increasing the ethical sensitivity of accounting students. Students' demographic characteristics, in terms of accounting specialisation area and years of work experience, did play a role in the extent of their changes in ethical sensitivity. However, gender and previous ethics education as influencing factor in ethical sensitivity was negated.
2013, Noghondari and Foong; MAJ	Malaysia, 212 Loan Officers, structural equation modelling (SEM), Positivism, Sustainability	The findings indicate that the knowledge/experience factors could significantly mitigate the audit expectation gap. More importantly, the audit expectation gap is found to adversely affect the loan decision quality. The mediating role of the audit expectation gap is also supported.
2013, Al-Saidi and Al-Shammari; MAJ	Kuwait, nine listed Kuwait banks over the 2006–2010 period, ordinary least squares (OLS) and two-stage-least squares (2SLS), Positivism, Sustainability	The results provide some evidence that board composition of banks relates to their performance. According to the OLS regression results, only board size and proportion of non-executive directors negatively

(*continued*)

Table 10.3 (Cont.)

Year, Author; Journal	*Country, Sample, Method, Paradigm*	*Finding*
		affect bank performance. Meanwhile, the 2SLS results indicate that role duality positively affects a bank's performance while board size affects a bank's performance negatively.
2013, Ismail, Kamarudin, Zijl, and Dunstan; ARA	Malaysia, 4,010 observations, OLS, Positivism, Accountability	The results show that IFRS adoption is associated with higher quality of reported earnings. It is found that earnings reported during the period after the adoption of IFRS is associated with lower earnings management and higher value relevant.
2013, Johl, Johl, Subramaniam, and Cooper; MAJ	Malaysia, 620 firms listed, Regression and Interview, Positivism, Accountability	This paper finds although the lower ordered variables board quality and internal audit quality coefficients are negatively related to abnormal accruals, the interaction variable between these two variables is positively associated with abnormal accruals, indicating the possibility of a substitution relationship between board quality and internal audit quality.
2013, Quttainah, Song, and Wu; JIFMA	Bahrain, Bangladesh, Egypt, Indonesia, Iran, Jordan, Kuwait, Lebanon, Malaysia, Pakistan, Qatar, Saudi Arabia, Sudan, Turkey, and the United Arab Emirates, 84 Islamic banks in 15 countries, Dummy Regression, Positivism, Accountability	First, Islamic banks are less likely to conduct earnings management as measured by both earnings' loss avoidance and abnormal loan loss provisions. Second, there are no significantly different earnings management behaviours between Islamic banks with and without Shari'ah Supervisory Boards. Third, several

Table 10.3 (Cont.)

Year, Author; Journal	*Country, Sample, Method, Paradigm*	*Finding*
		Shari'ah Supervisory Board characteristics, such as size and the presence of members from Auditing Organization for Islamic Financial Institutions, are important determinants of the earnings management of Islamic banks who have Shari'ah Supervisory Boards.
2013, Fooladi, Shukor, Saleh, and Jaffar; IJDG	Malaysia, 400 companies listed on Bursa Malaysia, Regression, Positivism, Accountability	It is found that high quality audit firms can mitigate the agency problems in firms with divergence between cash flow and control rights.
2013, Hayat, Butter, and Kock; JBE	Muslim Countries, Literature Review, Critical, Accountability	As the financial product become increasingly complex, the credibility of these sharia scholars become ever more questionable.
2014, Echchabi, Olorogun, and Azouzi; JIABR	Tunisia, Hundred Tunisian customers, SEM, Postivism, Sustainability	The results indicate that the Tunisian customers are willing to adopt Islamic insurance services.
2014, Velayutham; JIABR	N/A, Literature Review, Intepretivism, Sustainability	It is shown that this belief of incompatibility can be traced to misconceptions about the assumptions underlying conventional accounting. It is then argued that the neglect of Islamic accounting in Islamic countries could be attributed to Islamic accounting not meeting the needs of users rather than acculturation or economic dependency.
2014, Al-Kayed, Zain, and Duasa; JIABR	N/A, 85 IBs covering banking systems in 19 countries, a two-stage least squares, Positivism, Sustainability	The result is consistent with the signalling theory which predicts that banks expected to have better performance credibly transmit this

(*continued*)

Table 10.3 (Cont.)

Year, Author, Journal	*Country, Sample, Method, Paradigm*	*Finding*
		information through higher capital. Optimal capital structure results of the IBs found a non-monotonic U-shaped relationship between the capital-asset ratio and profitability, supporting the efficiency risk and franchise value hypotheses.
2014, Salihin, Fatima, and Ousama; JIABR	N/A, Literature Review, Intepretivism, Accountability	The paper found that the TFVO is relevant and applicable in Islamic accounting and auditing and not contradictory to the rules of the Shari'ah. Therefore, the concept is acceptable for use in Islamic accounting. Moreover, based on the several roles played by the TFVO, in the Islamic context, the practicality of this concept in Islamic accounting provides further justification for its continued usage.
2014, El-Firjani, Menacere, and Pegum; JAEE	Libya, 470 questionnaires, Survey, Poststructurialism, Accountability	This paper found general agreement that the accounting regulation of public corporations and banks is strongly influenced by the Libyan Commercial Code and the Income Tax Law.
2014, Alzeban and Gwilliam; JIAAT	Arab Saudi, 203 managers and 239 internal auditors, OLS, Positivism, Sustainability	Results suggest that management support for IAE drives perceived effectiveness of the internal audit function from both management's and the internal auditors' perspective.
2014, Muttakin and Khan; JEI	Bangladesh, 135 manufacturing companies listed, Regression, Positivism, Sustainability	The study finds that CSR disclosure has positive and significant relationships with export-oriented sector, firm size and types of industries.

Table 10.3 (Cont.)

Year, Author; Journal	*Country, Sample, Method, Paradigm*	*Finding*
2014, Ismail; ARA	Malaysia, 396 Questionnaires, Regression, Positivism, Sustainability	The study discovered a significant impact of ethical ideology on judgments regardless of the legality of the cases. In addition, the study found a significant positive and negative impact of idealism and relativism, respectively, on ethical judgment. Moreover, the study reported that absolutists are stricter whilst situationists are more lenient in making ethical judgments compared to other ideologies.
2014, Mohdali and Pope; ARJ	Malaysia, 302 Respondent, Survey, Poststructurialism, Sustainability	Religiosity is found to have a minimal but statistically significantly positive impact on voluntary tax compliance. This probably can be explained by the strong religious values held by many Malaysians, as well as the concept of giving which has been emphasised in almost all religions.
2014, Ringim; IJIMEFM	Nigeria, 385 respondents, PLS, Positivism, Accountability	The results revealed that perception was positively associated with a Muslim account holder's decision to patronize Islamic banking products.
2014, Mulcahy; IJIMEFM	N/A, Literature Review, Intepretivism, Accountability	Purification is a pivotal element of the Islamic investment process, yet Standard 21 permits a loose interpretation which causes portfolios to be under-purified. Standard 21 also makes no mention of the interest tax shield from debt even though the benefits are at odds with the principles of social justice in Islam.

(*continued*)

Table 10.3 (Cont.)

Year, Author; Journal	*Country, Sample, Method, Paradigm*	*Finding*
2014, Suzuki and Uddin; IJIMEFM	Bangladesh, 16 available banks during the period 2007-2012, Content Analysis, Intepretivism, Accountability	The asset-based nuancing gives the Bangladeshi Islamic banks relatively higher Islamic bank rent opportunity for protecting their "franchise value" as Shari'ah-compliant lenders, while responding to the periodic volatility in transaction costs of pro t-and-loss sharing.
2015, Gupta; IJIMEFM	UAE, Literature Review, Intepretivism, Accountability	The author has found that the accounting treatment of Ijarah practiced by four UAE Islamic banks, it is clear that all of them are following IAS-17 and not FAS-8 of AAOIFI.
2015, Belal, Abdelsalam, and Nizamee; JBE	Bangladesh, annual reports over a period of 28 years (1983–2010) of Islami Bank Bangladesh Limited's (IBBL hereafter), Interview and content Analysis, Poststructurialism, Accountability	The bank is still failing to provide full disclosure on certain significant categories such as sources and uses of disposable income, thereby contradicting the principles of full and comprehensive disclosure and accountability.
2015, Rosman and Rahman; JIABR	MENA, Asian, 32 Islamic banks from 16 different countries, Mann–Whitney U test, Positivism, Accountability	A significant difference was found between the Islamic banks in the Middle Eastern and North African (MENA) and Asian countries concerning the practice of both displaced commercial risk and operational risk/ Shari'ah non-compliance risk management.
2015, Kamla and Alsoufi; AF	N/A, Literature Review, Critical, Sustainability	So far, the limited and technical Islamic accounting agenda has ignored issues of poverty and environmental tragedies in the Muslim world and beyond.

Table 10.3 (Cont.)

Year, Author; Journal	*Country, Sample, Method, Paradigm*	*Finding*
2015, Abdullah, Perc, and Stewart; JCAE	Southeast Asian and Gulf Cooperation Council regions, 67 Islamic banks, Regression, Positivism, Accountability	The results inform the global debate on the need for corporate governance reform by Islamic banks by providing insights on the part played by corporate governance mechanisms in encouraging enhanced disclosure in the annual reports of Islamic banks.
2015, Kamla, Gallhofer, and Haslam; AF	N/A, Literature Review, Intepretivism, Sustainability	In concluding, we point, among other things, to the irony whereby Western transnational corporations have sought to promote their particular brand of corporate social (and environmental) responsibility accounting in Arab countries, variously influenced by Islam, with little to no mention of a notion of accounting for the environment integral to and deeply rooted in Islam.
2015, Sensoy and Guvemli; BAR	Middle East, Literature Review, Intepretivism, Accountability	Risalei Felekiyye is seen as an excellent example of a written doctrine of accounting book with explanations of an accounting system and advanced level of accounting understanding.
2015, Mukhlisin and Hudaib; IJIMEFM	Indonesia, 160 respondents, survey, Poststructurialism, Accountability	The respondents differ in their opinion on the possibility of Shariah harmonization, both *de jure* and *de facto*. The role of various actors involved in the financial reporting standardization may impede Shariah harmonization to take place.

(*continued*)

Table 10.3 (Cont.)

Year, Author; Journal	*Country, Sample, Method, Paradigm*	*Finding*
2016, Rezaei, Saleh, Jaffar, and Hassan; IJA	Iran, the annual reports of firms listed on the TSE between 1999 and 2010, Probit Regression, Positivism, Accountability	The findings suggest that increased competition in the audit market is more likely to decrease the relative bargaining power of auditors and that there is a significant concern regarding audit opinions when both auditee and auditor are state-controlled entities.
2016, Al-Hadi *et al.*; JIFMA	GCC, logistic regression, 553 firm-year observations over the 2007–2011 period, Positivism, Sustainability	This study finds that MRDs are significantly and negatively associated with both underinvestment and overinvestment and that this association is more pronounced for larger firms.
2016, Moume, Othman, and Hussainey; AIA	MENA, 320 listed firms in nine MENA emerging markets (789 observations) over the period from 2007 to 2009, Regression, Positivism, Sustainability	Our findings suggest that the composition of the board and its size enhance the informativeness of risk disclosure as it allows investors to better predict future earnings growth. A further finding is that a CEO/Chairperson duality does not impact the way investors trust risk disclosures.
2016, Mathuva and Kiweu; AIA	Kenya, 1272 observations for 212 deposit-taking SACCOs in Kenya over the period 2008–2013, OLS, Positivism, Accountability	The results reveal a relatively low level of CSED by deposit-taking SACCOs in Kenya at 29.3%. As a departure from findings in mainstream studies, the study reveals a negative association between CSED and financial performance.
2016, Alotaibi and Hussainey; IJDG	Saudi Arabia, annual reports of Saudi Arabian firms listed in the Tadawul Stock Exchange over the period 2013–2014, Regression, Positivism, Sustainability	The results suggest that Saudi Arabia provides higher levels of disclosure with a lower quality. In addition, the levels of CSR disclosure quantity and quality have different drivers.

Table 10.3 (Cont.)

Year, Author; Journal	*Country, Sample, Method, Paradigm*	*Finding*
2016, Alzoubi; ARJ	Jordan, 86 industrial companies in the period of the years from 2007 to 2010, OLS Regression, Positivism, Accountability	The result produces evidence on the negative association between DQ and EM. The result also evidences the view that as the level of the disclosure is high, the magnitude of the EM reduces and, in turn, increases the financial reporting quality.
2016, Al-Akr, Qader, and Billah; JIAAT	MENA, Literature Review, Intepretivism, Accountability	We find that while the majority of the region has introduced reforms to the IA function, more needs to be done to (1) insure independence and objectivity and (2) involve IA in consulting services, particularly with respect to risk management, control and governance.
2016, Tahat, Dunne, Fifield, and Power; ARJ	Jordan, 82 Jordanian listed companies, Survey, Poststructurialism, Accountability	The study finds that a larger number of Jordanian listed companies provided a greater level of FI-related information after IFRS 7 was implemented.
2016, Haji; ARJ	Malaysia, annual reports of 153 firm-year observations across a three-year period (2008–2010), Regression, Positivism, Sustainability	The overall amount of IC disclosures, and in particular human capital information, has a significant positive association with hidden values and, consequently, the market value of the companies.
2016, Gharbi and Khamoussi; JIABR	GCC, annual Reports of 20 Islamic banks and 40 conventional banks, Regression, Positivism, Sustainability	Empirical evidence shows that there is a significant change in dynamic volatility in GCC banking sector because of financial crisis 2008.

(*continued*)

Table 10.3 (Cont.)

Year, Author; Journal	*Country, Sample, Method, Paradigm*	*Finding*
2016, Gundogdu; JIABR	N/A, Literature Review, Critical, Accountability	The author argues that the ECA export financing structures, or restricted Mudaraba if preferred, with an embedded supplier financing Wakala agreement can pave the way for Islamic FIs to support exporting companies. It is also concluded that development and support of the Takaful industry are vital for the success of Islamic export financing schemes because of its role in risk management.
2016, Al Shattarat and Atmeh; JFRA	N/A, Literature Review, Critical, Accountability	The paper proves that implementing the Mudarabah contract by banks imposes several problems among which are the following: difficulty in the determination of total profit resulting from Mudarabah and in allocating this profit to the multiple parties involved in Mudarabah; usage of reserves to cater against future losses may undermine the concept of Mudarabah profit-loss sharing and lead to earnings management; corporate governance is also a major problem in Mudarabah contract, as the depositors are exposed to risks but have no governance rights; and Mudarabah may also lessen the fair presentation of financial reporting.

Table 10.3 (Cont.)

Year, Author; Journal	*Country, Sample, Method, Paradigm*	*Finding*
2016, Shafii and Rahman; JIABR	N/A, Literature Review, Intepretivism, Accountability	The paper found that the classification and measurement of equity-based Islamic financial assets do not fit into the "default" classification category of amortised cost, as the future cash flow receivable does not constitute solely the payment of principal and interest (fixed rate payment)
2016, Nainggolan, How, and Verhoeven; JBE	MENA and GCC, Islamic equity funds (IEFs) from 1984 to 2010, Regression, Positivism, Sustainability	The study finds no such out-performance for other crises or high volatility periods. Based on fund holdings-based data, we provide evidence of a negative curvilinear relation between fund performance and ethical screening intensity, consistent with a return trade-off to being more ethical.
2016, Abdullah; IJIMEFM	N/A, Literature Review, Intepretivism, Accountability	The research found that in assessing economic substance over legal form, each of the three products involved risk-free transactions and interest.
2016, Platonova, Asutay, Rob Dixon, and Mohammad; JBE	Bahrain, Saudi Arabia, Qatar, Kuwait and the United Arab Emirates (UAE), 24 fully fledged Islamic banks from five GCC countries, Panel Data Regression, Positivism, Sustainability	The findings show no statistically significant relationship between the individual dimensions of the CSR disclosure index and the current financial performance measure except for "mission and vision" and "products and services."
2017, Atmeh and Maali; JIABR	N/A, Literature Review, Intepretivism, Sustainability	This ambiguity may hinder the faithful representation of financial statements. The Tabarru contract is used to justify the risk-shifting practices by Islamic banks.

(*continued*)

Table 10.3 (Cont.)

Year, Author, Journal	*Country, Sample, Method, Paradigm*	*Finding*
		The accounting effects of such contracts may result in failure to recognize assets or liabilities in the financial reports, earnings management and incomplete financial information for the users of the financial reports.
2017, Fakhfakh; JIABR	Bahrain, Bangladesh, Britain, Malaysia, Pakistan, Kingdom of Saudi Arabia, the Republic of the Sudan, Tunisia, Palestine, Jordan and Oman, 27 auditing reports signed in 2012 and 2013, t-test, Postivism, Accountability	The results show lack of harmonization in several elements related to the form of the auditor's report and in all elements related to the content of the auditor's report among the Islamic banks.
2017, Abdul-Baki and Uthman; JIABR	N/A, Literature Review, Intepretivism, Sustainability	The paper concludes that despite the unfavourable environment, the social ideals of the Islamic banking system may still be met, to an extent, through investment in microfinance and waqf.
2017, Nawaz and Haniffa; JIABR	World, 64 IFIs operating in 18 of three main groupings, namely, Asia, Europe and the Middle-East, Panel Data, Positivism, Sustainability	The results suggest that value creation capability of IFIs is highly influenced by HCE and CEE.
2017, Kamla and Haque; CPA	N/A, Literature Review, Intepretivism, Accountability	The paper showed that AAOIFI's role in sustaining the accounting-imperialism nexus was mainly performed through providing narrow intellectual challenge to the Anglo-American logic under IAH. Alternatives suggested by AAOIFI were mainly limited to technical notes to the accounts on interest-ban and Zakat calculations.

Table 10.3 (Cont.)

Year, Author; Journal	*Country, Sample, Method, Paradigm*	*Finding*
2017, Garas and Tee; IJDG	Kuwait, firms listed in Kuwait over the period of 2000–2013, OLS Regression, Positivism, Accountability	This suggests that IFAB-3 is more important for Islamic than conventional institutions. Accordingly, this study conclude that corporate governance guideline (IFAB-3) has improved the corporate governance structure of firms listed in the Kuwait stock market. In this context, the study increases the awareness of standard setters, academics, investors, regulators and many other stakeholders about the effect of IFAB-3 in the region.
2017, Montenegro; AE	N/A, Literature Review, Intepretivism, Sustainability	It demonstrates that accounting and capitalism have religious roots, and highlights how the four main monotheistic religions viewed and incorporated accounting historically. This book can be used in the PhD curriculum, but I think that it is too challenging to be included in the master-level curriculum.
2017, Mihret, Alshareef, and Bazhair; CPA	Saudi Arabia, Literature Review, Intepretivism, Accountability	Professional closure in accounting takes multiple forms, and is contingent upon the socio-historical context in which it occurs. This study has illustrated that hybridization enables an occupational group to form alliances with the state, and other potentially competing groups to secure entry controls, despite lacking demonstrated capacity as a professional body.

(*continued*)

Table 10.3 (Cont.)

Year, Author, Journal	*Country, Sample, Method, Paradigm*	*Finding*
2017, Muttakin, Khan, and Mihret; MAJ	Bangladesh, 917 firm-year observations listed on the Dhaka Stock Exchange from 2005 to 2013, OLS Regression, Positivism, Sustainability	Results showed that the level of discretionary accruals is positively associated with business group affiliation status, and higher audit quality reduces this association. This suggests that in environments without strong investor protection, complex ownership structures create opportunities for controlling shareholders to expropriate minority shareholders.
2017, Juhmani; JAAR	Bahrain, 44 Bahraini companies, Regression, Positivism, Accountability	The results show that three of the CG mechanisms (i.e., board independence, audit committee independence, and Chief Executive Officer duality) are associated with the level of IFRS disclosure. This suggests that CG mechanisms are effective in the financial reporting practices.
2017, Sellami and Tahari; JAAR	MENA, 38 Islamic banks with disclosure accounting standards during the 2011-2013 period, Regression, Positivism, Accountability	The results show a wide variation in compliance levels among the disclosure accounting standards and reveal that compliance is positively related to the listing status, the existence of an audit committee, the bank's age and the country of domicile.
2017, Mohammed and Muhammed; JAAR	Developing Countries, 34 Islamic banks annual financial information from the year 2007 to 2010, Panel Data Regression, Positivism, Sustainability	The authors of this paper found that the macroeconomic factors reflected in gross domestic product, gross domestic product growth, and inflation rate have a significant positive relationship with the return on assets.

Table 10.3 (Cont.)

Year, Author; Journal	*Country, Sample, Method, Paradigm*	*Finding*
2017, Al-Htaybat; AAR	Jordan, Literature Review, Intepretivism, Accountability	The four significant elements that emerge as particularly relevant regarding country and corporation-level adoption of IFRS are reflected in the four central pillars of the model. These are institutional push and uncertainty at the country level, and corporations' need to pull and ramp up their disclosure levels and deal with corporate deterrents.
2017, Nurunnabi; IJDG	Saudi Arabia, Literature Review, Intepretivism, Accountability	The findings are innovative and will be helpful to local standard setters (SOCPA), international standard setters (IASB), and preparers and investors. The findings suggest that urgent training is required for the effective implementation of IFRS in Saudi Arabia.
2017, Al-Amri, Al Shidi, Al Busaidi, and Akguc; JAAR	GCC, 7,960 firm-year observations and 796 distinct firms, Regression, Positivism, Accountability	The paper documents evidence consistent with private and public firms using real earnings management to influence their earnings figures. The paper also shows that the level of real earnings management is higher for private firms compared to public firms when cash flow management and discretionary expenses management models are used.
2017, Perkiss and Tweedie; SEAJ	N/A, Literature Review, Intepretivism, Sustainability	There are many alternative hyper goods on which social accounting could draw. However, whatever goods and sources one chooses,

(*continued*)

Table 10.3 (Cont.)

Year, Author, Journal	*Country, Sample, Method, Paradigm*	*Finding*
		the critical challenge we identify is the need to articulate and defend hyper goods and moral sources commensurate with the scale of contemporary social and ecological sustainability challenges.
2017, Mukhlisin; JIABR	Indonesia, 1* to 4* relevant peer-reviewed journals in the academic journal guide 2015, Meta-Analysis, Intepretivism, Accountability	Learning from Indonesian experience, the literature suggests that neo-liberalism is piercing through different parts of economic and political setting of the country's infrastructural powers leading up to the influence of financial reporting standardization process.
2017, Suandi; IJIMEFM	Asia, 63 Islamic banks from 15 countries, Literature Review, Intepretivism, Accountability	The results show heterogeneity of classification for PSIAs. Applying the same standards does not lead to the uniform classification of PSIAs when banks apply International Financial Reporting Standards, while financial statements applying Financial Accounting Standards by the Accounting and Auditing Organization for Islamic Financial Institutions are more similar.
2017, Tessema, Garas, and Tee; IJIMEFM	GCC, 395,670 firm-day observations, OLS Regression, Positivism, Accountability	The findings reveal that information asymmetry among investors is lower after the implementation of IFSB-4 than before, indicating that the standard has increased transparency. The results also reveal that information asymmetry after

Table 10.3 (Cont.)

Year, Author; Journal	*Country, Sample, Method, Paradigm*	*Finding*
		the implementation of IFSB-4 is lower for Islamic than for conventional financial institutions. This suggests that IFAB-4 promotes more transparency for Islamic than conventional institutions.
2017, Kolsi and Grassa; IJIMEFM	GCC, 223 firm-year observations and a nine-year period (2004-2012), Regression, Positivism, Accountability	Institutional ownership and bank size have no effect on earnings management through DLLPs (discretionary loan loss provision).

institutions should maintain its long-run rate of economic growth, measure natural resources used to support their growth and at the same time safeguard the environment. However, the sustainability in terms of supporting the current US$2.2 trillion fast-growing Islamic finance asset has not been deeply researched. Thus, both issues on accountability and sustainability are still considered as emerging topics that entail further research.

This chapter is not for generalization as 150 articles examined in this research are from journals ranked only in ABS ranking. Other journal ranking or index used in similar study may lead to different result. It is therefore recommended that other researchers adopt different ranking or index to conduct similar study. Different methodology to use content analysis and systematic literature review (see Tranfield *et al.* 2003) could be one way to improve the methodology of this research. The contribution from this study is to extend the debate on Islamic accounting and sustainability from the perspective of academic and practice.[2]

Notes

1 The term Islamic financial architecture was first introduced in 2000 by the then President of IDB, Dr Ahmad Ali Al-Madani, during his keynote speech at the 5th Harvard University Forum on Islamic Finance. The full text is available in Ali (2000).

2 Note: 150 references are not included in the reference list for convenience purposes, data will be supplied by the authors upon request.

References

Adams, C.A. (2002). Internal organisational factors influencing corporate social and ethical reporting: Beyond current theorizing. *Accounting, Auditing & Accountability Journal 15*(2), 223–250.

Adams, C.A. & González, C.L. (2007). Engaging with organisations in pursuit of improved sustainability accounting and performance. *Accounting, Auditing & Accountability Journal 20*(3), 333–355.

Adams, C. & Narayanan, V. (2007). The standardization of sustainability reporting. In Unerman, J., Bebbington, J., & O'Dwyer, B. (Eds.), Sustainability Accounting and Accountability. London and New York, NY: Routledge, pp. 70–85.

Ali, A.M. (2000). The emerging Islamic financial architecture: The way ahead. Paper presented at the The Fifth Harvard University Forum on Islamic Finance: Islamic Finance: Dynamics and Development, Cambridge, Massachusetts.

Apostolou, B., Dorminey, J.W., Hassell, J.M., & Rebele, J.E. (2017). Analysis of trends in the accounting education literature (1997–2016). *Journal of Accounting Education,* 41(C), 1–14.

Askary, S. & Clarke, F. (1997). Accounting in the Koranic Verses. Proceedings of International Conference, The Vehicle for Exploring and Implementing Shariah Islami'ah in Accounting, Commerce and Finance . Macarthur: University of Western Sydney.

Bebbington, J. & Gray, R. (2001). Accounting for the Environment: Second Edition. Newbury Park, CA: Sage.

Brierley, J.A. & Cowton, C.J. (2000). Putting meta-analysis to work: Accountants' organizational-professional conflict. *Journal of Business Ethics 24*(4), 343–353.

Burritt, R.L. & Schaltegger, S. (2010). Sustainability accounting and reporting: fad or trend? *Accounting, Auditing & Accountability Journal 23*(7), 829–846.

Carrington, W., DeBuse, J., & Lee, H.J. (2008). The Theory of Governance & Accountability. Iowa: The University of Iowa Center for International Finance and Development.

De Villiers, C. & Van Staden, C. (2014). Special issue on sustainability accounting. *Pacific Accounting Review 26*(1/2), 54–74. https://doi.org/10.1108/PAR-09-2013-0090.

El-Halaby, Sherif Ismail Abdel-Rahman (2015). Accountability Practices of Islamic Banks: A Stakeholders' Perspective. A Doctoral Thesis of the Degree of Doctor of Philosophy in Accounting of Plymouth University Graduate School of Management United Kingdom.

Ernst and Young. (2010). Corporate Responsibility Report. https ://assets.ey.com/content/dam/ey-sites/ey-com/nl_nl/topics/corporate-responsibility/cr-reports/ey-nl-corporate-responsibility-report-2010-2011.pdf

Gray, R. & Bebbington, J. (2000). Environmental accounting, managerialism and sustainability: Is the planet safe in the hands of business and accounting? In Advances in Environmental Accounting and Management (Vol. 1). Bingley, West Yourk: Emerald Group Publishing Limited, pp.1–44.

Gray, R. (2006). Social, environmental and sustainability reporting and organisational value creation: Whose value? Whose creation? *Accounting, Auditing & Accountability Journal 19*(6), 793–819.

Gray, R. (2010). Is accounting for sustainability actually accounting for sustainability...and how would we know? An exploration of narratives of organisations and the planet. *Accounting, Organizations and Society 35*(1), 47–62.

Hasan, Z. (2006). Sustainable development from an Islamic perspective: Meaning implications and policy concerns. *Islamic Economics*, *19*(1), 3–18.

Haynes, K. (2017). Accounting as gendering and gendered: A review of 25 years of critical accounting research on gender. *Critical Perspectives on Accounting 43*, 110–124.

Khan, T. (2009). Islamic Financial Architecture and Infrastructures: Development and Challenges. Lecture. Jeddah: IRTI-GDLN World Bank.

Killawi, R.L. (2014). Islamic Development from Islamic Perspective. Islamic Affairs & Charitable Activities Department, Research Department, Dubai, ISBN 978-9948-455-08-0.

Khlif, H. & Chalmers, K. (2015). A review of meta-analytic research in accounting. *Journal of Accounting Literature 35*, 1–27.

Lahrash, Omar Mohammad Ali A. (2015). Accounting from the perspective of Islamic Sharia. *South East Asia Journal of Contemporary Business, Economics and Law 7*(1), 1–8.

Lewis, M.K. (2006). Accountability and Islam. Fourth International Conference on Accounting and Finance in Transition, Adelaide, April 10–12, 2006.

Mohammed, Nor Farizal., Fahmi, Fadzlina Mohd., Ahmad, Asyaari Elmiza. (2015). The influence of AAOIFI accounting standards in reporting Islamic financial institutions in Malaysia. *Procedia Economics and Finance 31*, 418–424.

Mukhlisin, M. (2017). Unveiling IASB standardization projects and its influence on the position of Takaful Industry in Indonesia. *Journal of Islamic Accounting and Business Research 8*(2), 229–247.

Rubenstein, D.B. (1992). Bridging the gap between green accounting and black ink. *Accounting, Organisations and Society 17*(5), 506.

Schaltegger, S., Burritt, R. (2005). Corporate sustainability. In Folmer, H., Tietenberg, T. (Eds.), *International yearbook of environmental and resource economics 2005/2006* (pp. 185–222). Cheltenham: Edward Elgar.

Schaltegger, S. and Wagner, M. (2006) Integrative Management of Sustainability Performance, Measurement and Reporting. *International Journal of Accounting, Auditing and Performance Evaluation*, 3, 1–19. http://dx.doi.org/10.1504/IJAAPE.2006.010098

Schaltegger, S. and Wagner, M. (2011). Sustainable entrepreneurship and sustainability innovation: categories and interactions. *Business Strategy and the Environment*, (20)4, 222–237. https://doi.org/10.1002/bse.682

Sultana, N. (2015). Contribution of Islamic accounting system to the commercial organizations. *Banglavision Research Journal 15*(1), 125–132.

Tranfield, D., Denyer, D., & Smart, P. (2003). Towards a methodology for developing evidence-informed management knowledge by means of systematic review. *British Journal of Management 14*. 207–222.

Tessema, A.M., Garas, S., & Tee, K. (2017). The impact of Islamic accounting standards on information asymmetry: The case of Gulf Cooperation Council (GCC) member countries. *International Journal of Islamic and Middle Eastern Finance and Management 10*(2), 170–185.

Warsono, S. (2011), Adopsi Standar Akuntansi IFRS Fakta, Dilema dan Matematika. Yogyakarta: ABPublisher.

Whittington, G. (1992). Accounting and Finance in The New Palgrave Dictionary of Money and Finance (Vol. 1), edited by Newman, P., Milgateand, M., & Eatwel, J. London: Macmilan, pp. 6–10.

Yousef, T.M. (2004). The murabaha syndrome in Islamic finance: Laws, institutions, and politics. In Henry, C.M. & Wilson, R (Eds.), The Politics of Islamic Finance. Edinburgh: Edinburgh University Press.

Note: 150 references are not included in the reference list for convenience purposes, data will be supplied by the authors upon request.

Part III

EMPIRICAL EVIDENCES

11

FINANCIAL DEVELOPMENT AND ECOLOGICAL FOOTPRINT NEXUS

A comparative analysis

Muhammad Tariq Majeed

Environmental degradation is one of the key issues that have great interest among researchers, politicians and policy makers. The overexploitation of nonrenewable natural resources is compromising the sustainability of current societies as well as the sustainability of future generations. According to the World Bank (2019), high-income countries create an average of 10.9 metric tons (MT) emissions of carbon dioxide (CO_2) per capita. These emissions exhibit almost three times that it is emitted by middle-income countries (3.9 MT) and almost 36 times as much as that which is emitted by low-income countries (0.3 MT). In such a situation, government intervention through regulation is essential, but businesses, international and non-profit organizations, and societies need to find ways to mitigate the accelerated process of environmental degradation.

In the recent years, the empirical studies have shown that financial development has significant impact on the quality of environment (Katircioglu and Taşpinar 2017; Destek and Sarkodie 2019). The studies in this respect provide an evidence of both positive and negative environmental effects of financial development. Zhang (2011) argued that developed financial sector can facilitate finance of such projects which are favorable for environmental quality through research and development (R&D) activities. Financial development can boost the investment in energy-efficient technologies such as renewable energy, that is, more environmentally friendly. Similarly, it can increase economic efficiencies by reducing the capital risk and financial costs, thereby minimizing the overall resource inefficiency.

In contrast, countries with high financial development provide credit facilities for electrical products, vehicles and homes. In such situation, business horizons expand, and new plants are installed, thereby increasing carbon emissions in the atmosphere (Zhang and Zhang 2018). Financially developed economies also attract inflows of foreign direct investment (FDI), which also increase ecological degradation (Sarkodie and Strezov 2019). Thus, empirical studies provide inconclusive results and suggest diverse policy implications.

One main issue with these studies is that they measure the quality of environment with CO_2 emissions. (Bekhet *et al.* 2017; Maji *et al.* 2017, Majeed and Mumtaz 2017; Majeed and Mazhar 2019). However, CO_2 emissions just represent one dimension of environmental deterioration triggered by non-renewable energy resources (Al-Mulali *et al.* 2015).

Some studies recently emphasize that ecological footprint (EFP) is a better measure of environment performance than CO_2 emissions because it is a more comprehensive indicator of ecological quality. EFP comprises environmental indicators into a single measure (Castellani and Sala 2012; Katircioglu *et al.* 2018; Aydin *et al.* 2019). The studies have pointed out certain advantages of using EFP as environmental measure. First, it is comprehensive and can be easily comprehended (Senbel *et al.* 2003). Second, it incorporates the necessary information of diverse natural resources, which are important for the balance of ecosystem (Katircioglu *et al.* 2018; Aydin *et al.* 2019). Third, it monitors the information on ecological imbalances (Castellani and Sala 2012). Fourth, it contains the information related to resource metabolism, which facilitates the state officials to track the imbalances between resource demand and supply and they can efficiently handle distributional process (Wackernagel *et al.* 2006).

Developing countries at different level of economic development experience wide variation in environmental and financial indicators. The relationship of financial development with the quality of environment can vary across different income groups. Consequently, financial development and environment nexus largely remains inconclusive. The available studies focus on geographical groups of countries but ignore income groups. The present study provides a comparative analysis of financial development and environment nexus using four groups of countries according to income level. Following World Bank (2019) country classification four groups of countries are analyzed. The classification of countries according to their income level is as follows: "low income ($995 and below), lower middle income ($996–$3,895), upper middle income ($3,896–12,055), and high income ($12,056 and above)."

Theory predicts diverse effects of financial development on ecological footprint. The earlier literature provides country-specific or case study-based evidence, which cannot be generalized globally. This research offers a comparative analysis using better measures of environmental degradation. The paper will also explore the validity of "pollution haven hypothesis" in a comparative setting. Additionally, this research employs three indicators of financial development to provide a more comprehensive picture of finance environment nexus.

The study attempts to address the following three research questions: (i) Does financial development increase ecological footprint; (ii) Is the impact of financial development on ecological footprint sensitive to the measures used to measure financial development; (iii) Does the effect of financial development on environmental quality vary depending upon the income group of countries. This study suggests that the impact of financial development on ecological footprint is conditional. If financial development helps to increase environmental-friendly projects and investment, then it causes the reduction in overall ecological footprint.

The rest of the chapter is structured as follows: Section 11.2 describes the review of relevant literature; Section 11.3 presents the data, methodology and statistical analysis; Section 11.4 delineates the estimated results and a detailed discussion on them; and final Section 11.5 concludes the study.

11.1 Financial development and ecological footprints: a literature review

In the recent decades, environmental quality is deteriorating as natural resources are being over exploited and depleted. Moreover, loss of biodiversity, weather variations, species extension and soil erosion have increased. Such loss is the consequence of diverse anthropogenic activities all over the world.

The theoretical literature in this respect dates back to the pioneer study of Grossman and Krueger (1995) who showed that the relationship between income per capita and environmental degradation is non-linear. That was later referred as environment Kuznets curve (EKC) by Panayotou (1995). The EKC suggests that economic development and environmental degradation move together at lower levels of economic development, but after a threshold level environmental quality tends to improve as society prefers better quality of environment.

The empirical literature largely supports the notion of EKC but also presents somewhat mixed results. The studies by Al-Mulali and Ozturk (2015), and Majeed (2018) suggest a dynamic relationship between GDP per capita and pollutant indicators by validating the inverted U-shaped EKC hypothesis. While N-shaped relationship was identified by Hill and Magnani(2002) and Majeed and Luni (2019), no relationship was found by Ozturk and Acaravci (2010).

Later on many studies explored diverse determinants of environmental quality. Henceforth, international trade (Shakeel *et al.* 2014), energy consumption (Stern *et al.* 2006; Siddique and Majeed 2015), urbanization (Zhang and Lin 2012) and foreign direct investment (Zarsky 1999; Asghari 2013) have hitherto been used as an important determinant of environmental degradation.

However, in the late 1980s Aufderheide and Rich (1988) argued that multilateral banks are also responsible for environmental pollutants. They claimed that World Bank's financial assistance programs do not consider the environmental consequences of financing and compromise the quality of environment. For example, in India, soil erosion increased because of the financing of energy capital, tropical forestland deteriorated because of the financing of Grand Bereby rubber project and micro-finance for the cotton production resulted in degradation of agricultural land because of soil erosion. Similarly, Schmidheiny and Zorraquin (1998) inferred that global financial institutes supported short-run objectives, ignoring the related environmental problems, thereby causing overexploitation of natural resources.

Following the leading studies of Aufderheide and Rich (1988) and Schmidheiny and Zorraquin (1998), the research related to finance and environment initiated in the late 2000 got momentum in the recent decade. The empirical literature in this respect analyzes the several potential channels through which financial development affects environmental quality and found mixed results.

Tadesse (2007) and Kumbaroglu *et al.* (2008) argued that financial development helps to control pollutant emissions by encouraging the technological innovations in the energy sector. Similarly Tamazian *et al.* (2009) consider well-developed financial system mainly capital markets as a major source of reducing greenhouse concentration from the atmosphere. Thus, increasing R&D expenditures on energy-efficient technology help to control carbon emissions and improve the environmental quality.

A study by Xiong and Qi (2018) exploits the STIRPAT model and spatial panel econometrics methods for analyzing the environmental effects of financial development for 30 Chinese provinces. The study covers the time period of 1997–2011. The findings revealed that financial development improves the environmental quality in Chinese provinces through the spatial spillover effect. Similarly, Dar and Asif (2018), using the annual data of Turkey from 1960 to 2013, also confirmed that the development in financial sector improved the environmental quality.

Similarly, a research conducted by Hamdan *et al.* (2018) examined the relationship between financial development and environmental degradation in ASIAN-5 economies, namely, Indonesia, Malaysia, Philippines, Singapore and Thailand over the period 2000–2014. Their results confirmed that financial development helps to improve the environmental quality by channelizing the technological transformation through higher FDI.

In the recent study, Mohammed *et al.* (2019) empirically tested the impact of financial development on environmental degradation using the time-series data of Venezuela economy from 1971 to 2013. They found out favorable and significant impact of financial development on environmental deterioration. Their finding suggested that well-developed financial institutions reduce the financing cost (i.e., information asymmetry) by channelizing the resource into new and energy-efficient technology that curb the intensity of CO_2 emissions. In the same way, Seetanah *et al.* (2019) scrutinized the impact of financial development on environmental degradation using the panel data of selected 12 Island developing economies from 2000 to 2016. Using the panel vector autoregressive model and cointegration analysis the study found that financial development improves the quality of environment although results are not statistically significant.

Apart from affirmative effects of financial development on environmental quality there are studies that have shown the detrimental impacts of financial development on the quality of environment. Moghadam and Lotfalipour (2014) pointed out undesirable effects of financial development on environmental quality of Iran. Using the Auto Regression Model Distributed Lag (ARDL) model over the period of 1970–2011, they concluded that higher financial development resulted in higher environmental degradation as the investor's motive is only to increase the size of investment. For the case of India, Sehrawat *et al.* (2015) reported that financial development degrades the overall environmental quality by increasing the environmental pollution.

Mesagan and Nwachukwu (2018) use the time-series data of Nigerian economy over the period of 1981–2016. They claimed that the higher financial development contributed to higher intensity of CO_2 emissions and particulate emissions. Similarly, Moghadam and Dehbashi (2018) investigated the effect of financial development and trade on environmental quality in Iran over the period 1970–2011. The results confirmed that financial development increases the pollutant emissions and deteriorates the environmental quality by increasing the industrial activities. In addition, detrimental effect of financial development on environmental quality of Pakistan is confirmed by Raza and Shah (2018).

Moving towards the most recent studies of financial development–environmental degradation nexus, Zakaria and Bibi (2019) validate the EKC hypothesis along with the devastating effect of financial development on environmental quality for South Asian economies over the period of 1984–2015. Likewise, using a panel data of OECD economies, Ganda (2019) concluded that the effect of financial development on environmental degradation differs depending on the measures used to gauge the impact of financial development. The results of static models and system generalized method of moments (GMM) reveal that the impact of domestic credit to private sector and FDI is worsening while the impact of "domestic credit to private sector by banks" is favorable for the environmental quality. Similarly, Bloach *et al.* (2019) showed the detrimental effect of financial development on environmental quality for Belt and Road Initiative (BRI) countries.

It can be concluded from the above discussion that the relationship of financial development with environment is inconclusive. The favorable environmental effect is pointed out by some studies along with the other studies that disagree with these findings and highlighted the undesirable role of financial development. Moreover, the literature highlighted the several channels through which financial development affect environmental degradation, i.e., high FDI inflows, development in R&D, technological advancement, and promotion of green technologies.

Moreover, the existing literature largely focused on CO_2 emissions to explain the relationship between finance and environment. CO_2 emissions, however, represent limited information on the loss of environment. In contrast, ecological footprint is a better measure of environmental loss because it tracks "*human requirements on the biosphere's regenerative capacity and human dependence on ecosystems*" (Wackernagel *et al.* 2002).

Ecological footprint is determined by the size of population in each area, quality of life, production level, consumption behavior and efficiency of ecosystem (Wackernagel *et al.* 1999). Ecological footprint represents a comprehensive understanding about the balance of ecosystem by utilizing the information of natural resource base used for production process. EFP comprises the information of overall environment by incorporating the amount of "carbon emissions, residential and grazing land, fishing grounds and forest products."

This chapter provides comprehensive understanding of environment and finance nexus by exploiting the comprehensive indicators of environmental quality and utilizing three measures of financial development over a long period of 1971–2017 for 131 countries. This chapter provides deeper insights by providing a comparative analysis of different groups of countries according to their income level. This chapter also resolves the issue of potential problem of endogeneity by using system GMM.

11.2 Data, econometric specification and methodology

11.2.1 The data

We have used the panel data over the period 1971–2017 for 131 countries. The data for ecological footprint is extracted from Global Footprint Network (2019). The data for remaining series is collected from World Bank (2019).

11.2.2 Econometric specification and data description

For empirical analysis, this study uses standard model, which is followed by many studies (Destek and Sarkodie 2019). However, the empirical studies use carbon emissions as a measure of environmental degradation, whereas this research uses ecological footprint as comprehensive indicator of environmental loss. The econometric model can be specified as follows:

$$\mathrm{EFP}_{i,t} = \gamma_0 + \gamma_1 \mathrm{FD}_{i,t} + \gamma_2 \mathrm{EC}_{i,t} + \gamma_3 \mathrm{GDP}_{i,t} + \gamma_4 \mathrm{UP}_{i,t} + \gamma_5 \mathrm{FDI}_{i,t} + v_i + \mu_t + \varepsilon_{it}. \quad (11.1)$$

Here, t represents the time span of the study from 1971 to 2017 and i represents the cross-sectional units. γ_0 stands for the constant term. The term EFP represents ecological footprint, FD shows financial development, GDP measures economic growth, UP represents urbanization and FDI shows foreign direct investment. The term v_i shows country-specific unobservable effects, μ_t shows temporal effects and ε_{it} represents error term.

Financial development is measured using three indicators that are "domestic credit to private sector (DCP)," "domestic credit to private sector by banks (DCB)" and "domestic credit to private sector provided by the financial sector (DCF)." Equations for these measures can be specified as follows:

$$\text{EFP}_{i,t} = g_0 + g_1\text{DCP}_{i,t} + g_2\text{EC}_{i,t} + g_3\text{GDP}_{i,t} + g_4\text{UP}_{i,t} + g_5\text{FDI}_{i,t} + n_i + m_t + e_{it} \quad (11.2)$$

$$\text{EFP}_{i,t} = \gamma_0 + \gamma_1\text{DCB}_{i,t} + \gamma_2\text{EC}_{i,t} + \gamma_3\text{GDP}_{i,t} + \gamma_4\text{UP}_{i,t} + \gamma_5\text{FDI}_{i,t} + v_i + \mu_t + \varepsilon_{it} \quad (11.3)$$

$$\text{EFP}_{i,t} = \gamma_0 + \gamma_1\text{DCF}_{i,t} + \gamma_2\text{EC}_{i,t} + \gamma_3\text{GDP}_{i,t} + \gamma_4\text{UP}_{i,t} + \gamma_5\text{FDI}_{i,t} + v_i + \mu_t + \varepsilon_{it}. \quad (11.4)$$

11.2.3 Construction of the variables

EFP shows ecological footprint measured in "global hectares (GHA) per person" (see Charfeddine and Mrabet 2017; Katircioglu *et al.* 2018). "*Ecological Footprint accounts act as balance sheets by documenting for a given population – a household, a district, a city, a region or humanity as a whole – the area of biologically productive land and sea required to produce the renewable resources this population consumes and assimilate the waste it generates, using prevailing technology. It documents the extent to which human economies stay within the regenerative capacity of the biosphere. Overall, it is the sum of built-up land, carbon, cropland, fishing grounds, forest products and grazing land.*"

The domestic credit to the private sector has direct impact on environmental quality. It is measured as percentage of GDP. "*It refers to financial resources provided to the private sector by financial corporations, such as through loans, purchases of nonequity securities, and trade credits and other accounts receivable, that establish a claim for repayment.*"

The second measure of financial development is "domestic credit to private sector by banks" as percentage of GDP. "*It refers to the financial resources provided to the private sector by other depository corporations (deposit taking corporations except central banks), such as through loans, purchases of nonequity securities, and trade credits and other accounts receivable, that establish a claim for repayment.*" Finally, the third measure of financial development is the "domestic credit to private sector provided by the financial sector" as percentage of GDP. "*It includes all credit to various sectors on a gross basis, with the exception of credit to the central government, which is net.*"

Energy consumption (EC) is measured in terms of "kg of oil equivalent per capita" and it is log transformed. "*It refers to use of primary energy before transformation to other end-use fuels, which is equal to indigenous production plus imports and stock changes, minus exports and fuels supplied to ships and aircraft engaged in international transport.*" The environmental impact of energy consumption can be positive as well as negative. If efficient use of energy is focused and its utilization is diverted towards green technologies than its favorable effects can be expected for environmental quality (Stern *et al.* 2006). If traditional sources of energy such as gas, oil and coal contribute more in energy consumption then environmental quality is compromised (Majeed and Luni 2019).

Economic growth is measured using the log of "GDP per capita constant 2010 US dollars" (GDP) which is the "*sum of gross value added by all resident producers in the economy plus any product taxes and minus any subsidies not included in the value of the products. It is calculated without making deductions for depreciation of fabricated assets or for depletion and degradation of natural resources.*" The relationship of GDP with environment can be explained through "scale, composite and technique effects." Scale effect refers high production with the expansion of the economy using traditional inputs. The economy transits from traditional agricultural sector to industrial sector. This effect causes negative effect on the environmental quality. Composite effect appears in the next stage of development when the economy transits from manufacturing sector to services sector. Finally, technological improvements support environmental quality by introducing green technologies (Stern 1998; Stokey 1998). Insofar as linear impacts of economic growth are concerned, economic growth results in the expansion of traditional and modern sectors, thereby increasing investment, production and consumption at the cost of environment.

Urbanization is also an important source of environment. It is measured as percentage of total population (UP). "*It refers to people living in urban areas as defined by national statistical offices.*" Zhang and Lin (2012) and Wang *et al.* (2016) claimed that urbanization increases the environmental degradation because it increases the energy demand and consumption. However, some studies argue that urbanization contributes positively to environmental quality in the context of high-income nations (Chikaraishi *et al.* 2015). Furthermore, increasing urbanization also leads to efficient utilization of transportation and space, thereby increasing economies of scale and improving quality of the environment (Arouri *et al.* 2013; Majeed and Gillani 2017).

Finally, FDI is considered an important factor of the environmental quality. It is measured as percentage of GDP and can be defined as "*These are the net inflows of investment to acquire a lasting management interest in an enterprise operating in an economy other than that of the investor. It is the sum of equity capital, reinvestment of earnings, other long-term capital, and short-term capital as shown in the balance of payments.*"

The relationship of FDI with environment can be described through two hypotheses, namely, pollution halo hypothesis and pollution haven hypothesis. First hypothesis claims a positive association between FDI inflows and environmental quality. Foreign firms prefer the use of clean technologies because of environmental laws. Moreover, they invest in R&D to promote energy-efficient technology. Consequently, quality of the environment improves in host economies (Zarsky 1999; Asghari 2013). In contrast, second hypothesis claims a negative association between FDI inflows and environmental quality. Foreign firms use cheap and inefficient technologies in countries with weak environmental regulations and poor institutional framework (Solarin *et al.* 2018).

11.2.4 Methodology

The empirical analysis is based on panel data estimators. Baseline results are obtained using pooled ordinary least squares (POLS) estimator. To account for country-specific effects and temporal effects, fixed- and random-effects models are employed. Finally, to address the issues of endogeneity, system GMM is also exploited in the current study for obtaining the robust estimates.

11.2.5 Descriptive statistics

Table 11.1 shows the descriptive statistics. The statistics show that the highest mean value of ecological footprint is 6.06, which belongs to high-income countries whereas the lowest mean value of ecological footprint is 1.28, which belongs to low-income countries. Among high-income countries EFP varies substantially from 1.43 to 42.71, whereas among low-income countries EFP varies from 0.50 to 3.77.

Table 11.2 reports correlation matrix of the variables used for empirical analysis. Financial development has positive correlation with ecological footprint across all groups of countries. High-income and low-income countries demonstrate low correlation, whereas middle-income countries exhibit high correlation.

Figure 11.1 suggests that more than 50% of global EFP belongs to high-income countries whereas just 11% belongs to low-income countries. Thus, these are the developed countries, which are mainly responsible for creating EFP. Figure 11.2 shows the "distribution of domestic credit to private sector" over the study period. The highest average value 46% belongs to high-income countries, where low-income countries just contribute 9% in global distribution. Similarly, Figures 11.3 and 11.4 represent similar patterns of financial development in terms of "domestic credit to private sector by banks" and "domestic credit to private sector by financial sector."

Table 11.1 Descriptive statistics

Variable	*Obs.*	*Mean*	*Std. Dev.*	*Min*	*Max*
		High-Income Countries			
EFP	1,773	6.060527	2.747243	1.427972	24.71293
DCP	1,773	69.88489	47.12291	.1858704	312.019
DCP	1,773	65.35187	43.80289	.1858528	312.019
DCB	1,773	85.71006	62.88069	–55.23498	347.4836
EC	1,773	8.155852	.7427713	4.718983	10.61423
GDP	1,773	10.08229	.7417938	7.583572	12.1631
UP	1,773	73.04423	19.95942	14.303	100
FDI	1,773	5.295838	25.38073	–58.32288	773.9002
		High Middle-Income Countries			
EFP	1,327	2.63814	1.066377	.7448617	10.30041
DCP	1,327	38.77742	29.27118	1.166062	166.5041
DCB	1,327	36.31147	26.16038	1.166062	166.5041
DCF	1,327	52.26995	42.69699	–79.09235	333.9872
EC	1,327	7.002302	.6189792	5.429423	8.687553
GDP	1,327	8.360131	.6086077	5.471488	9.920047
UP	1,327	54.17926	18.62393	8.998	100
FDI	1,327	3.835072	9.335184	–56.46446	217.9205
		Low Middle-Income Countries			
EFP	1,241	1.545012	1.064706	.428228	9.499869
DCP	1,241	24.39256	17.53852	.0046205	130.7218
DCB	1,241	23.29963	16.78321	.0046205	130.7218
DCF	1,241	34.90696	27.59545	–114.6937	248.9012
EC	1,241	6.195918	.6902375	2.260188	8.488091
GDP	1,241	7.272148	.6338462	5.116898	9.402658
UP	1,241	37.94673	17.62807	4.477	79.817
FDI	1,241	2.929513	4.800388	–37.15476	50.01802
		Low-Income Countries			
EFP	1,203	1.279114	.4883106	.5027919	3.772464
DCP	1,203	12.65877	9.327468	.4025806	103.6323
DCB	1,203	11.90066	8.978294	.4025806	84.05232
DCF	1,203	23.55477	20.51086	–6.338999	164.5591
EC	1,203	5.942885	.609835	3.769541	7.553293
GDP	1,203	6.273167	.481725	4.880119	7.317412
UP	1,203	26.60371	13.16019	2.97	61.678
FDI	1,203	2.278036	6.536103	–28.62426	103.3374

Table 11.2 Correlation matrix

	EFP	*DCP*	*EC*	*GDP*	*UP*	*FDI*
			High-Income Countries			
EFP	1.0000					
DCP	0.0536	1.0000				
EC	0.8025	0.0978	1.0000			
GDP	0.6542	0.4568	0.6751	1.0000		
UP	0.3375	0.1188	0.2899	0.3757	1.0000	
FDI	0.0369	0.0682	–0.0235	0.0315	0.1107	1.0000
			High Middle-Income Countries			
EFP	1.0000					
DCP	0.1583	1.0000				
EC	0.7200	0.2550	1.0000			
GDP	0.5253	0.0532	0.5775	1.0000		
UP	0.2530	–0.1340	0.3695	0.6114	1.0000	
FDI	0.1300	0.0615	0.1553	–0.0129	0.0287	1.0000
			Low Middle-Income Countries			
EFP	1.0000					
DCP	0.2292	1.0000				
EC	0.5131	0.2681	1.0000			
GDP	0.4358	0.3061	0.5735	1.0000		
UP	0.5160	0.2864	0.5546	0.7087	1.0000	
FDI	0.3485	0.0674	0.2122	0.1929	0.2964	1.0000
			Low-Income Countries			
EFP	1.0000					
DCP	0.1006	1.0000				
EC	0.0398	0.2861	1.0000			
GDP	0.1866	0.1439	0.1051	1.0000		
UP	0.0296	–0.0077	–0.0966	0.3666	1.0000	
FDI	0.0209	0.0602	–0.0775	–0.1855	0.1123	1.0000

Figure 11.5 displays time trend for EFP for all groups of countries. In the case of high-income countries, EFP exhibited fluctuating trend over the study period and it is increasing since 1990s. In the case of low middle-income countries and low-income countries, same trend is observed in the decades of 1970s and 1980s. However, since 1990s middle-income countries are experiencing upward trend of EFP than low-income countries. Figure 11.6 indicates time trend for DCP over the study period. All groups show stagnant trend in 1970s whereas high-income and high middle-income countries developed financial sector since 1980s while other groups of countries since 2000s.

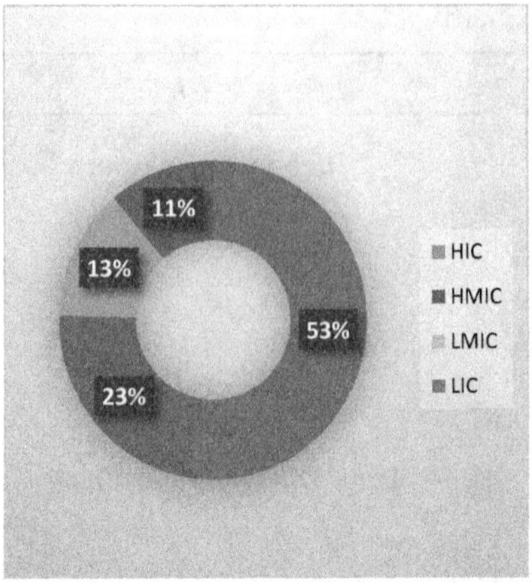

Figure 11.1 Ecological footprint.

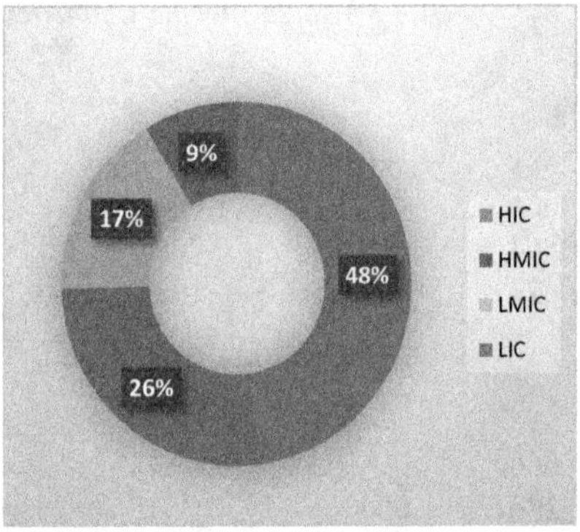

Figure 11.2 Domestic credit to private sector.

Figure 11.7 displays time trend for second measure of financial development. High-income countries experience rising trend throughout the study period except downward trend since 2008. This perhaps reflects the outcome of financial crisis during 2007–2008. The trends for all other groups of countries are smooth over the study period. Figure 11.8 shows the time trend for third measure of financial development. Low-income groups of countries show little improvement over the study period while high-income countries exhibit rising trend. Note the differences of levels of DCF are relatively lower in the case of this measure of financial development.

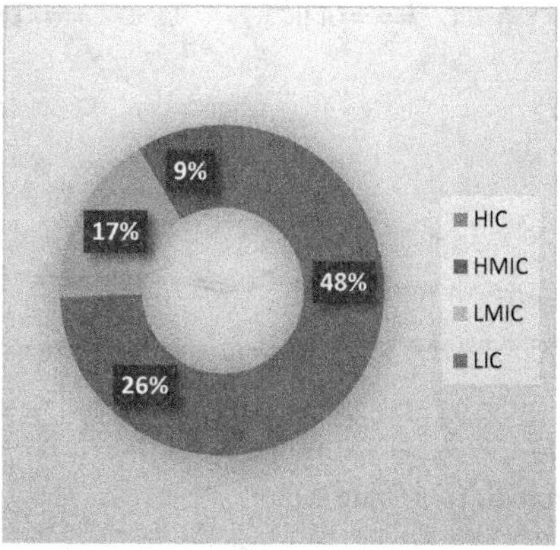

Figure 11.3 Domestic credit to private sector by banks.

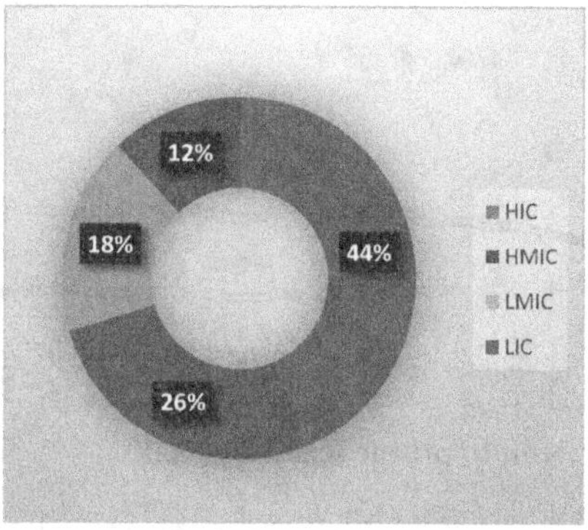

Figure 11.4 Domestic credit to private sector by financial sector.

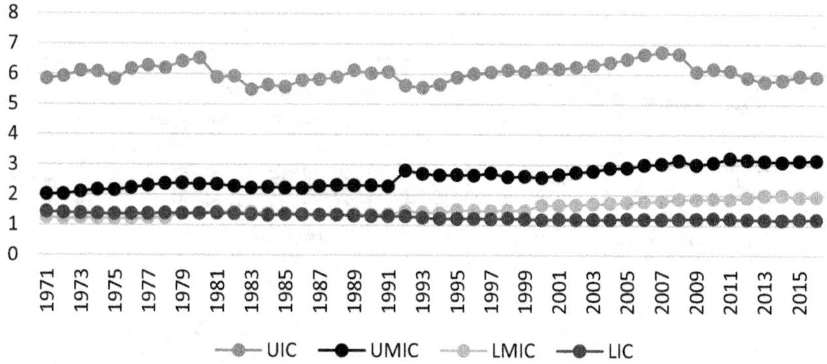

Figure 11.5 Ecological footprint trend.

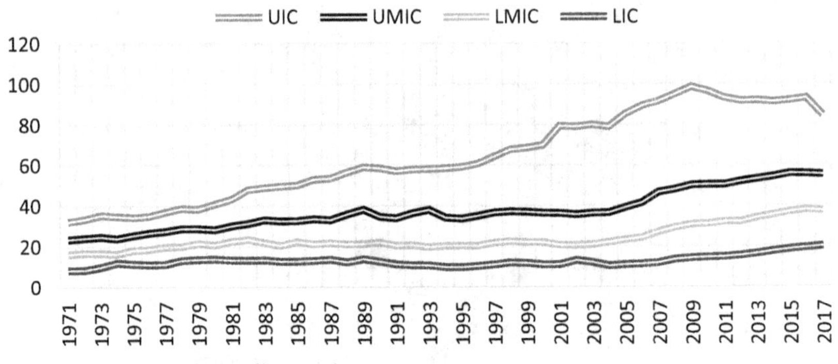

Figure 11.6 Domestic credit to private sector.

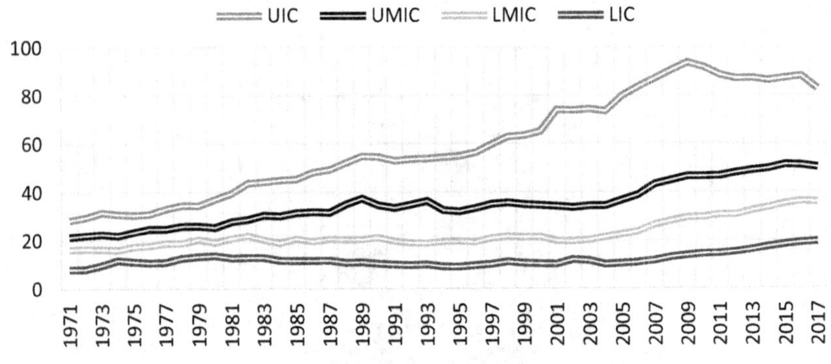

Figure 11.7 Domestic credit to private sector by banks.

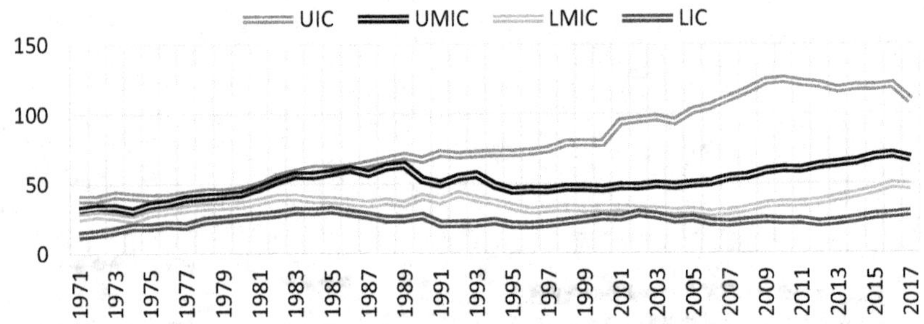

Figure 11.8 Domestic credit to private sector by financial sector.

11.3 Results and discussion

11.3.1 Results of pooled OLS

Table 11.3 provides the empirical results of pooled OLS. Columns 1–3 display the results for high-income countries and columns 4–6 exhibit the results for high middle-income countries. The results for high-income countries suggest that all measures of financial development negatively contribute to ecological footprint suggesting that financial development helps to improve the quality of environment. The estimated parameters suggest that 1% rise in DCP, DCB and DCF will lead to 0.009%, 0.001% and 0.005% drop in ecological footprint, respectively. These negative effects are statistically significant. Relatively, the impact of DCP is stronger than the effects of DCB and DCF.

These findings are consistent with the findings of Zhang (2011) and Mohammed *et al.* (2019) who assert that advanced financial structure supports the finance for energy-efficient and environmentally sustainable projects. Furthermore, it supports the industries for using the energy-efficient technologies such as renewable energy sources that release less emissions relative to non-renewable energy resources. In such scenario, the quality of environment tends to improve.

In the case of high middle-income countries, the direction of effect remains consistent, that is, all measures of financial development are negatively associated with EFP. However, this negative impact is only significant in the context of DCF. These findings infer that the strength of financial development in influencing environmental quality dissipates in the case of high middle-income countries.

The effect of energy consumption is significant and positive implying that energy consumption is an important factor that causes environmental degradation. The positive effect of energy consumption is consistently significant in high middle-income countries as well. The magnitudes of the effects (2.325–2.518) are comparatively large in the case of high-income countries. Our findings are in line with the studies of Al-Mulali and Ozturk (2015) and Siddique and Majeed (2015). Increasing energy consumption reflects high consumption of fossil fuels such as coal, gas and oil. Emissions also increase when energy intensive industry employs pollution intensive input for production (Suri and Chapman 1998).

Economic growth also influences ecological quality. The results confirm a positive and significant impact of economic growth on ecological footprint in both groups of countries. Comparatively, this positive effect is stronger in the case of high-income countries. This result is consistent with the studies of Suri and Chapman (1998) and Moghadam and Lotfalipour (2014). Economic growth indicates that opportunities for investment and production have increased that also put pressure on the utilization of resources at the cost of environmental quality. In addition, consumption levels and patterns also

Table 11.3 Results of pooled OLS for high-income countries

Variables	*(1)*	*(2)*	*(3)*	*(4)*	*(5)*	*(6)*
	High-Income Countries			*High Middle-Income Countries*		
DCP	–0.00877***			–0.00111		
	(0.00117)			(0.000700)		
DCB		–0.0135***			–0.000657	
		(0.00132)			(0.000780)	
DCF			–0.00529***			–0.00111**
			(0.000879)			(0.000498)
EC	2.512***	2.325***	2.518***	1.093***	1.081***	1.094***
	(0.0981)	(0.1000)	(0.101)	(0.0487)	(0.0483)	(0.0469)
GDP	1.034***	1.232***	0.986***	0.430***	0.432***	0.428***
	(0.0982)	(0.0999)	(0.101)	(0.0544)	(0.0557)	(0.0541)
UP	0.0144***	0.0140***	0.0147***	–0.00917***	–0.00887***	–0.00907***
	(0.00384)	(0.00376)	(0.00387)	(0.00187)	(0.00187)	(0.00182)
FDI	0.00523***	0.00615***	0.00534***	0.00845*	0.00845*	0.00761*
	(0.00195)	(0.00191)	(0.00197)	(0.00450)	(0.00453)	(0.00450)
Constant	–25.37***	–25.53***	–25.11***	–8.087***	–8.064***	–8.069***
	(0.662)	(0.643)	(0.667)	(0.364)	(0.368)	(0.359)
Observations	1,150	1,150	1,150	972	972	973
R-squared	0.689	0.702	0.684	0.549	0.547	0.553

Standard errors in parentheses (***p < 0.01, **p < 0.05, *p < 0.1).

change with increasing income levels of individuals that put pressure on natural resources such as air, water and soil.

Urbanization is another important cause of changes in environmental quality. Theoretical literature suggests mixed effects of urbanization on environmental quality. The results of this study suggest that the effect of urbanization on environment is positive in the context of high-income countries and the opposite effect is observed in the case of high middle-income countries. This is an important finding, which suggests that the effects of urbanization on the environment depends on the level of development. In the context of high middle-income countries, the results are consistent with the *compact city theory*. This theory implies that more urbanization leads to productive and efficient utilization of resources. Urbanization increases economies of scale, which facilitate efficient utilization of resources, thereby alleviating the burden on environments (Effiong 2016).

Finally, the results show that FDI inflows exert positive and significant influence on EFP. In the literature this positive impact is also justified by the pollution haven hypothesis, that is, FDI inflows tend to increase in pollutant-intensive industries because of weak environmental laws of host economies. Thus, such industries increase water pollution (i.e., chemicals), air pollution (i.e., fuel, transportation) and deforestation (i.e., cutting of forest for the requirement of wood). This relationship is supported by the following studies (Hitam and Borhan 2012; Solarin *et al.* 2018).

Table 11.4 presents the regression results for low middle-income (columns 1–3) and low-income (4–6) countries, respectively. The results indicate that financial development increases ecological footprint. The parameter estimates show that with 1% increase in DCP, DCB will bring 0.003 and 0.004 units increase in ecological footprint, respectively. This finding implies that the favorable effect of financial development on environment not only dissipates in the low-income groups of countries but also its effect is reversed. However, the effect of FDF remains negative in both low-middle income and low-income countries. This finding implies that the effect of FD also varies depending upon the measures of FD.

11.3.2 Results of fixed effects

Pooled OLS model considers all cross-sectional units as homogeneous and does not incorporate the cross-sectional heterogeneity in terms of temporal and cross-sectional unit specific effects. The results can be biased if significant temporal and cross-sectional unit specific effects prevail in the selected panel of countries. To incorporate the heterogeneity across countries, fixed-effects and random-effects models are also utilized.

Tables 11.5 and 11.6 provide the results of the fixed-effects model, which assumes that each cross section has its own intercept term that captures the cross-section differences. Here, the findings for high-income countries show

Table 11.4 Results of pooled OLS for low-income countries

Variables	*(1)*	*(2)*	*(3)*	*(4)*	*(5)*	*(6)*
	Low Middle-Income Countries			*Low-Income Countries*		
DCP	0.00318*			0.00164		
	(0.00164)			(0.00125)		
DCB		0.00428**			0.00205	
		(0.00174)			(0.00130)	
DCF			–0.00244**			–0.00163***
			(0.00106)			(0.000539)
EC	0.491***	0.488***	0.517***	–0.00101	–0.0241	0.0128
	(0.0549)	(0.0547)	(0.0547)	(0.0322)	(0.0322)	(0.0307)
GDP	0.0493	0.0464	0.0372	0.112***	0.0942***	0.134***
	(0.0678)	(0.0677)	(0.0682)	(0.0292)	(0.0292)	(0.0292)
UP	0.0172***	0.0173***	0.0187***	–0.00156	–0.00101	–0.00235
	(0.00265)	(0.00264)	(0.00267)	(0.00156)	(0.00155)	(0.00156)
FDI	0.0528***	0.0527***	0.0503***	0.00376	0.00354	0.00492
	(0.00724)	(0.00723)	(0.00727)	(0.00308)	(0.00305)	(0.00304)
Constant	–2.799***	–2.786***	–2.755***	0.345	0.567**	0.211
	(0.434)	(0.433)	(0.434)	(0.242)	(0.246)	(0.234)
Observations	912	913	916	420	415	420
R-squared	0.379	0.381	0.381	0.045	0.036	0.062

Standard errors in parentheses (***$p < 0.01$, **$p < 0.05$, *$p < 0.1$).

Table 11.5 Results of fixed effects for high-income countries

Variables	*(1)*	*(2)*	*(3)*	*(4)*	*(5)*	*(6)*
	High-Income Countries			*High Middle-Income Countries*		
DCP	–0.00452***			0.000311		
	(0.00111)			(0.000714)		
DCB		–0.00420***			0.00191**	
		(0.00108)			(0.000824)	
DCF			–0.00356***			–0.00108**
			(0.000917)			(0.000546)
EC	3.607***	3.681***	3.574***	1.190***	1.178***	1.242***
	(0.156)	(0.152)	(0.160)	(0.0704)	(0.0707)	(0.0694)
GDP	0.00496	–0.0583	–0.0693	0.368***	0.325***	0.381***
	(0.164)	(0.158)	(0.157)	(0.0570)	(0.0591)	(0.0548)
UP	–0.108***	–0.114***	–0.103***	–0.0109***	–0.0104***	–0.0113***
	(0.0103)	(0.0101)	(0.0108)	(0.00235)	(0.00237)	(0.00235)
FDI	0.000944	0.000941	0.000997	0.00920***	0.00847***	0.00840**
	(0.00139)	(0.00139)	(0.00139)	(0.00322)	(0.00322)	(0.00326)
Constant	–14.80***	–14.38***	–14.20***	–8.209***	–7.845***	–8.581***
	(1.135)	(1.096)	(1.077)	(0.443)	(0.460)	(0.411)
Observations	1,150	1,150	1,150	972	972	973
R-squared	0.443	0.442	0.442	0.547	0.545	0.545
Number of id	46	46	46	37	37	37

Standard errors in parentheses (***p < 0.01, **p < 0.05, *p < 0.1).

that all measures of financial development lead to improved ecological quality as coefficients are negative and highly significant. In the case of high middle-income countries only DCF is negatively associated with EFP, whereas other two measures of FD are positively associated with EFP. The result in the case of DCB turns out be significant suggesting that POLS underestimated the effect of DCB. The results for other variables are similar to baseline results implying that the results are robust to country-specific temporal and fixed effects.

Table 11.6 reports the fixed-effects results for low middle-income countries and low-income countries, respectively. The results are similar to the baseline findings, that is, DCP and DCB are positively and significantly associated with EFP, while the effect of DCF is negative and significant at 1% level of significance.

11.3.3 Results of random effects

Table 11.7 reports the regression results of the random-effects model that captures the cross-section difference in the error term. In the case of high-income countries, the results show that all measures of financial development improve ecological quality. On the contrary, the effects of DCP and DCB are positive in the case of high-middle-income countries, whereas the effect of DCP is negative and significant at 1% level of significance.

Table 11.8 reports the regression results of the random-effects model for low middle-income and low-income countries, respectively. The results are similar to the baseline findings. The results suggest that financial development increases ecological footprint. The parameter estimates show that with 1% increase in DCP, DCB will bring 0.002 and 0.001 units increase in ecological footprint, respectively, in low middle-income countries.

11.3.4 Results of system GMM

The likely presence of reverse causality between financial development indicators and ecological footprint creates the problem of endogeneity. The endogeneity problem is addressed using instruments and employing the system GMM estimator. The lag of dependent variable is used as independent variable and own lag variables of explanatory variables are used as instruments. The results are reported in Table 11.9. The baseline results for high-income countries remain intact. The results for other groups of countries differ from baseline results. Table 11.10 reports the system GMM results for low middle-income and low-income countries, respectively. The results are similar to the baseline findings that is DCP and DCB are positively associated with EFP, while the effect of DCF on EFP is negative in both group of countries. The effect of DCF, however, is mainly signficnt at 1 percent level of significance in low middle-income countries. Thus, overall the main conclusion remains

Table 11.6 Results of fixed effects for low-income countries

Variables	*(1)*	*(2)*	*(3)*	*(4)*	*(5)*	*(6)*
	Low Middle-Income Countries			*Low-Income Countries*		
DCP	0.00176**			6.97e–05		
	(0.000744)			(0.000519)		
DCB		0.00223***			0.000453	
		(0.000769)			(0.000551)	
DCF			–0.000688*			–0.000176
			(0.000404)			(0.000333)
EC	0.248***	0.241***	0.293***	0.250***	0.242***	0.248***
	(0.0571)	(0.0571)	(0.0573)	(0.0353)	(0.0345)	(0.0352)
GDP	0.405***	0.399***	0.441***	0.115***	0.110***	0.119***
	(0.0395)	(0.0392)	(0.0367)	(0.0194)	(0.0191)	(0.0191)
UP	0.00201	0.00201	0.00245	–0.00356***	–0.00346***	–0.00349***
	(0.00158)	(0.00158)	(0.00159)	(0.000810)	(0.000806)	(0.000799)
FDI	0.00334	0.00325	0.00319	0.000398	0.000323	0.000448
	(0.00221)	(0.00221)	(0.00222)	(0.00107)	(0.00104)	(0.00106)
Constant	–3.112***	–3.030***	–3.598***	–1.038***	–0.971***	–1.048***
	(0.301)	(0.301)	(0.268)	(0.220)	(0.214)	(0.210)
Observations	912	913	916	420	415	420
R-squared	0.383	0.385	0.382	0.254	0.257	0.254
Number of id	32	32	32	16	16	16

Standard errors in parentheses (***p < 0.01, **p < 0.05, *p < 0.1).

Table 11.7 Results of random effects for high-income countries

Variables	*(1)*	*(2)*	*(3)*	*(4)*	*(5)*	*(6)*
	High-Income Countries			*High Middle-Income Countries*		
DCP	–0.0061***			0.000341		
	(0.00110)			(0.000695)		
DCB		–0.0053***			0.00186**	
		(0.00109)			(0.000799)	
DCF			–0.00497***			–0.000952*
			(0.000902)			(0.000529)
EC	3.354***	3.442***	3.307***	1.182***	1.172***	1.229***
	(0.151)	(0.148)	(0.154)	(0.0670)	(0.0673)	(0.0660)
GDP	0.106	–0.00572	0.0362	0.370***	0.331***	0.382***
	(0.159)	(0.154)	(0.153)	(0.0553)	(0.0573)	(0.0533)
UP	–0.0704***	–0.0749***	–0.0649***	–0.0107***	–0.0103***	–0.0111***
	(0.00892)	(0.00879)	(0.00921)	(0.00225)	(0.00227)	(0.00225)
FDI	0.00149	0.00153	0.00155	0.00916***	0.00841***	0.00844***
	(0.00141)	(0.00142)	(0.00141)	(0.00317)	(0.00318)	(0.00321)
Constant	–16.67***	–16.01***	–15.97***	–8.162***	–7.831***	–8.494***
	(1.118)	(1.088)	(1.068)	(0.443)	(0.458)	(0.413)
Observations	1,150	1,150	1,150	972	972	973
Number of id	46	46	46	37	37	37

Standard errors in parentheses (***p < 0.01, **p < 0.05, *p < 0.1).

Table 11.8 Results of random effects for low-income countries

Variables	*(1)*	*(2)*	*(3)*	*(4)*	*(5)*	*(6)*
	Low Middle-Income Countries			*Low-Income Countries*		
DCP	0.00173**			9.16e–05		
	(0.000743)			(0.000520)		
DCB		0.00219***			0.000467	
		(0.000768)			(0.000553)	
DCF			–0.000712*			–0.000243
			(0.000404)			(0.000333)
EC	0.253***	0.247***	0.297***	0.222***	0.216***	0.219***
	(0.0558)	(0.0558)	(0.0559)	(0.0343)	(0.0334)	(0.0340)
GDP	0.404***	0.397***	0.439***	0.117***	0.112***	0.122***
	(0.0392)	(0.0389)	(0.0364)	(0.0193)	(0.0190)	(0.0190)
UP	0.00210	0.00210	0.00256	–0.00337***	–0.00326***	–0.00327***
	(0.00158)	(0.00157)	(0.00158)	(0.000807)	(0.000803)	(0.000796)
FDI	0.00349	0.00339	0.00333	0.000468	0.000390	0.000542
	(0.00221)	(0.00221)	(0.00222)	(0.00107)	(0.00105)	(0.00107)
Constant	–2.920***	–2.838***	–3.401***	–0.801***	–0.741***	–0.807***
	(0.359)	(0.359)	(0.331)	(0.226)	(0.221)	(0.216)
Observations	912	913	916	420	415	420
Number of id	32	32	32	16	16	16

Standard errors in parentheses (***p < 0.01, **p < 0.05, *p < 0.1).

Table 11.9 Results of system GMM for high-income countries

Variables	*(1)*	*(2)*	*(3)*	*(4)*	*(5)*	*(6)*
	High-Income Countries			*High-Middle-Income Countries*		
DCP	–0.0146***			–0.00361**		
	(0.000629)			(0.00137)		
DCB		–0.0184***			–0.00277**	
		(0.000568)			(0.00128)	
DCF			–0.0114***			–0.00245***
			(0.000329)			(0.000516)
EC	3.187***	3.128***	2.880***	1.759***	1.712***	1.700***
	(0.0792)	(0.0582)	(0.0531)	(0.144)	(0.126)	(0.0998)
GDP	1.096***	1.263***	1.491***	0.578***	0.556***	0.359***
	(0.111)	(0.0564)	(0.0855)	(0.102)	(0.109)	(0.120)
UP	–0.0146	–0.0163**	–0.0198***	–0.0360***	–0.0330***	–0.0262***
	(0.0102)	(0.00634)	(0.00497)	(0.00794)	(0.00679)	(0.00442)
FDI	0.0117***	0.0139***	0.0108***	–0.00205	–0.000927	–0.00408*
	(0.000803)	(0.000770)	(0.000758)	(0.00211)	(0.00213)	(0.00205)
Constant	–28.90***	–29.81***	–29.97***	–12.33***	–12.03***	–10.71***
	(0.635)	(0.387)	(0.466)	(0.927)	(0.901)	(0.953)
Observations	1,127	1,127	1,127	953	953	953
Number of id	46	46	46	37	37	37

Standard errors in parentheses (***p < 0.01, **p < 0.05, *p < 0.1).

Table 11.10 Results of system GMM for low-income countries

Variables	*(1)*	*(2)*	*(3)*	*(4)*	*(5)*	*(6)*
	Low Middle-Income Countries			*Low-Income Countries*		
DCP	0.00290			0.00242		
	(0.00253)			(0.00141)		
DCB		0.00170			0.00639***	
		(0.00340)			(0.00215)	
DCF			–0.00699***			–0.00219
			(0.000638)			(0.00126)
EC	0.750***	0.815***	0.655***	0.0191	0.0556	–0.351
	(0.0890)	(0.163)	(0.178)	(0.224)	(0.289)	(0.317)
GDP	–0.00203	0.0109	–0.0184	0.210	0.0302	0.427*
	(0.0448)	(0.0709)	(0.112)	(0.185)	(0.152)	(0.240)
UP	0.0285***	0.0265***	0.0296***	–0.00427	–0.00900*	0.00183
	(0.00711)	(0.00652)	(0.00536)	(0.00838)	(0.00506)	(0.00933)
FDI	0.114***	0.108***	0.107***	0.00533	0.00446	0.00858**
	(0.00424)	(0.00517)	(0.00446)	(0.00341)	(0.00419)	(0.00311)
Constant	–4.473***	–4.863***	–3.513***	–0.385	0.618	0.336
	(0.356)	(0.542)	(0.450)	(0.937)	(1.260)	(1.101)
Observations	892	893	896	408	403	408
Number of id	32	32	32	16	16	16

Standard errors in parentheses (***p < 0.01, **p < 0.05, *p < 0.1).

same, that is, financial development is good for the environment in the context of high-income countries, whereas in other groups of countries the effects of finance on the quality of environment are not certain as they are sensitive to the selection of financial measures and estimation approach. The p-values of Hansen test confirm the validity of instruments and the p-values of AR (2) confirm that the results do not suffer from the second-order serial correlation problem.

11.4 Conclusion

The role of financial sector in influencing ecological quality has been received considerable attention in the recent years. The available literature provides conflicting theories and evidence. The studies ignore the role of development stage in shaping the links of financial development with environmental quality. Moreover, the empirical studies largely use CO_2 emissions as proxy of environmental damage, which just explains a part of environmental degradation. In addition, the empirical studies provide country-specific or case study-based evidence, which cannot be extended for a large group of countries.

This research examines the effects of financial development on environmental quality using ecological footprint as a comprehensive measure of environmental loss. The analysis covers the data set of 131 economies for the period of 1971–2017. Quality of environment is measured using ecological footprint, whereas the financial sector's development is measured using three measures, namely, "domestic credit to private sector, domestic credit to private sector by banks and domestic credit provided by financial sector." The empirical analysis is carried out using the panel data estimators pooled OLS, fixed- and random-effects models along with the system GMM.

The findings show that all measures of financial development improve the ecological quality by reducing the overall ecological footprint in high-income countries. This implies that well-developed financial institution and capital markets help to control the overall carbon and GHG emission concentration from the atmosphere by providing the loans to the energy-saving industries and promoting the green technology usage. The endogeneity problem in the model is tackled through the utilization of system GMM. The system GMM is estimated by resolving the problem of endogeneity and heteroskedasticity.

One very important implication is drawn from the findings that if financial institutions are more concerned about environmental preservation, then they need to support the industries that adopt energy-efficient technologies. Furthermore, they need to facilitate the funds for research and development of green technologies. Financial institutions can help to mitigate environmental damage by providing loans and relaxation for the alternative clean energy usage.

References

Al-Mulali, U. & Ozturk, I. (2015). The effect of energy consumption, urbanization, trade openness, industrial output, and the political stability on the environmental degradation in the MENA (Middle East and North African) region. *Energy 84*, 382–389.

Al-Mulali, U., Saboori, B., & Ozturk, I. (2015a). Investigating the environmental Kuznets curve hypothesis in Vietnam. *Energy Policy 76*, 123–131.

Al-Mulali, U., Tang, C.F., & Ozturk, I. (2015b). Estimating the environment Kuznets curve hypothesis: Evidence from Latin America and the Caribbean countries. *Renewable and Sustainable Energy Reviews 50*, 918–924.

Arouri, M., Shahbaz, M., Onchang, R., Islam, F., & Teulon, F. (2013). Environmental Kuznets curve in Thailand: Cointegration and causality analysis. *The Journal of Energy and Development 39*(1/2), 149–170.

Asghari, M. (2013). Does FDI promote MENA region's environment quality? Pollution halo or pollution haven hypothesis. *International Journal of Scientific Research in Environmental Sciences 1*(6), 92–100.

Aufderheide, P. & Rich, B. (1988). Environmental reform and the multilateral banks. *World Policy Journal 5*(2), 301–321.

Aydin, C., Esen, Ö., & Aydin, R. (2019). Is the ecological footprint related to the Kuznets curve a real process or rationalizing the ecological consequences of the affluence? Evidence from PSTR approach. *Ecological Indicators 98*, 543–555.

Baloch, M.A., Zhang, J., Iqbal, K., & Iqbal, Z. (2019). The effect of financial development on ecological footprint in BRI countries: Evidence from panel data estimation. *Environmental Science and Pollution Research 26*(6), 6199–6208.

Bekhet, H.A., Matar, A., & Yasmin, T. (2017). CO_2 emissions, energy consumption, economic growth, and financial development in GCC countries: Dynamic simultaneous equation models. *Renewable and Sustainable Energy Reviews 70*, 117–132.

Castellani, V. & Sala, S. (2012). Ecological footprint and life cycle assessment in the sustainability assessment of tourism activities. *Ecological Indicators 16*, 135–147.

Charfeddine, L. & Mrabet, Z. (2017). The impact of economic development and social-political factors on ecological footprint: A panel data analysis for 15 MENA countries. *Renewable and Sustainable Energy Reviews 76*, 138–154.

Chikaraishi, M., Fujiwara, A., Kaneko, S., Poumanyvong, P., Komatsu, S., & Kalugin, A. (2015). The moderating effects of urbanization on carbon dioxide emissions: A latent class modeling approach. *Technological Forecasting and Social Change 90*, 302–317.

Dar, J.A. & Asif, M. (2018). Does financial development improve environmental quality in Turkey? An application of endogenous structural breaks based cointegration approach. *Management of Environmental Quality: An International Journal 29*(2), 368–384.

Destek, M.A. & Sarkodie, S.A. (2019). Investigation of environmental Kuznets curve for ecological footprint: The role of energy and financial development. *Science of the Total Environment 650*, 2483–2489.

Effiong, E. (2016). Urbanization and Environmental Quality in Africa (MPRA Paper No. 73224). Germany: University Library of Munich.

Ganda, F. (2019). The environmental impacts of financial development in OECD countries: A panel GMM approach. *Environmental Science and Pollution Research 26*, 6758–6772.

Global Footprint Network (2019). Living planet report. Species and spaces, people and places. [Online] Available at: http://data.footprintnetwork.org/#/analyzeTrends?type=EFCtot&cn=5001

Grossman, G.M. & Krueger, A.B. (1995). Economic growth and the environment. *The Quarterly Journal of Economics 110*(2), 353–377.

Hamdan, R., Ab-Rahim, R., & Fah, S.S. (2018). Financial development and environmental degradation in ASEAN-5. *International Journal of Academic Research in Business and Social Sciences 8*(12), 14–32.

Hill, R. J. & Magnani, E. (2002). An exploration of the conceptual and empirical basis of the environmental Kuznets curve. *Australian Economic Papers 41*(2), 239–254.

Hitam, M.B. & Borhan, H.B. (2012). FDI, growth and the environment: Impact on quality of life in Malaysia. *Procedia-Social and Behavioral Sciences 50*, 333–342.

Katircioglu, S.T. & Taşpinar, N. (2017). Testing the moderating role of financial development in an environmental Kuznets curve: Empirical evidence from Turkey. *Renewable and Sustainable Energy Reviews 68*(1), 572–586.

Katircioglu, S., Gokmenoglu, K.K., & Eren, B.M. (2018). Testing the role of tourism development in ecological footprint quality: Evidence from top 10 tourist destinations. *Environmental Science and Pollution Research 25*(33), 33611–33619.

Kumbaroglu, G., Karali, N., & Arıkan, Y. (2008). CO_2, GDP and RET: An aggregate economic equilibrium analysis for Turkey. *Energy Policy 36*(7), 2694–2708.

Majeed, M.T. (2018). Information and communication technology (ICT) and environmental sustainability in developed and developing countries. *Pakistan Journal of Commerce and Social Sciences 12*(3), 758–783.

Majeed, M. T., & Gillani, S. (2017). State capacity and health outcomes: An empirical Analysis. *Pakistan Journal of Commerce and Social Sciences, 11*(2), 671-697.

Majeed, M.T. & Luni, T. (2019). Renewable energy, water, and environmental degradation: A global panel data approach. *Pakistan Journal of Commerce and Social Sciences 13*(3), 749–778.

Majeed, M.T. & Mazhar, M. (2019). Environmental degradation and output volatility: A global perspective. *Pakistan Journal of Commerce and Social Sciences 13*(1), 180–208.

Majeed, M. T. & Mumtaz, S. (2017). Happiness and environmental degradation: A global analysis. *Pakistan Journal of Commerce and Social Sciences 11*(3), 753–772.

Maji, I.K., Habibullah, M.S., & Saari, M.Y. (2017). Financial development and sectoral CO_2 emissions in Malaysia. *Environmental Science and Pollution Research 24*(8), 7160–7176.

Mesagan, E.P. & Nwachukwu, M.I. (2018). Determinants of environmental quality in Nigeria: Assessing the role of financial development. *Econometric Research in Finance 3*(1), 55–78.

Moghadam, H.E. & Dehbashi, V. (2018). The impact of financial development and trade on environmental quality in Iran. *Empirical Economics 54*(4), 1777–1799.

Moghadam, H.E. & Lotfalipour, M.R. (2014). Impact of financial development on the environmental quality in Iran. *Chinese Business Review 13*(9), 537–551.

Mohammed, A.S.M., Guo, P., Haq, I.U., Pan, G., & Khan, A. (2019). Do government expenditure and financial development impede environmental degradation in Venezuela? *PloS One 14*(1), 1–13.

Ozturk, I. & Acaravci, A. (2010). CO_2 emissions, energy consumption and economic growth in Turkey. *Renewable and Sustainable Energy Reviews 14*(9), 3220–3225.

Panayotou, T. (1995). Environmental degradation at different stages of economic development. In Ahmed, I. & Doeleman, J.A. (Eds.), Beyond Rio: The Environmental Crisis and Sustainable Livelihoods in the Third World. London: International Labour Organization and Macmillan Press Ltd., pp. 13–36.

Raza, S.A. & Shah, N. (2018). Impact of Financial Development, Economic Growth and Energy Consumption on Environmental Degradation: Evidence from Pakistan (MPRA Paper No. 87095). Germany: University Library of Munich.

Siddique, H.M.A. & Majeed, M.T. (2015). Energy consumption, economic growth, trade and financial development nexus in South Asia. *Pakistan Journal of Commerce and Social Sciences 9*(2), 658–682.

Sarkodie, S.A. & Strezov, V. (2019). Effect of foreign direct investments, economic development and energy consumption on greenhouse gas emissions in developing countries. *Science of the Total Environment 646*(1), 862–871.

Schmidheiny, S. & Zorraquin, F.J. (1998). Financing Change: The Financial Community, Eco-Efficiency, and Sustainable Development. Cambridge, MA: MIT Press.

Seetanah, B., Sannassee, R.V., Fauzel, S., Soobaruth, Y., Giudici, G., & Nguyen, A.P.H. (2019). Impact of economic and financial development on environmental degradation: Evidence from small island developing states (SIDS). *Emerging Markets Finance and Trade 55*(2), 308–322.

Sehrawat, M., Giri, A.K., & Mohapatra, G. (2015). The impact of financial development, economic growth and energy consumption on environmental degradation: Evidence from India. *Management of Environmental Quality: An International Journal 26*(5), 666–682.

Senbel, M., McDaniels, T., & Dowlatabadi, H. (2003). The ecological footprint: A non-monetary metric of human consumption applied to North America. *Global Environmental Change 13*(2), 83–100.

Shakeel, M., Iqbal, M.M., & Majeed, M.T. (2014). Energy consumption, trade and GDP: A case study of south Asian countries. *The Pakistan Development Review 53*(4), 461–476.

Solarin, S. A., Al-Mulali, U., Gan, G. G. G., & Shahbaz, M. (2018). The impact of biomass energy consumption on pollution: Evidence from 80 developed and developing countries. *Environmental Science and Pollution Research*, 25(23), 22641–22657.

Stern, D. I. (1998). Progress on the environmental Kuznets curve? Environment and Development Economics, 3(2), 173–196.

Stern, N., Peters, S., Bakhshi, V., Bowen, A., Cameron, C., Catovsky, S., ... & Garbett, S.L. (2006). Economics, ethics and climate change. *Stern Review: The Economics of Climate Change*, 30, 23–40.

Stokey, N. L. (1998). Are there limits to growth? *International Economic Review*, 39(1), 1–31.

Suri, V. & Chapman, D. (1998). Economic growth, trade and energy: Implications for the environmental Kuznets curve. *Ecological Economics 25*(2), 195–208.

Tadesse, S. (2007). Financial Development and Technology (The William Davidson Institute Working Paper No. 879). University of Michigan.

Tamazian, A., Chousa, J.P., & Vadlamannati, K.C. (2009). Does higher economic and financial development lead to environmental degradation: Evidence from BRIC countries. *Energy Policy 37*(1), 246–253.

Wackernagel, M., Kitzes, J., Moran, D., Goldfinger, S., & Thomas, M. (2006). The ecological footprint of cities and regions: Comparing resource availability with resource demand. *Environment and Urbanization 18*(1), 103–112.

Wackernagel, M., Onisto, L., Bello, P., Linares, A.C., Falfán, I.S.L., Garcıa, J.M., ... & Guerrero, M.G.S. (1999). National natural capital accounting with the ecological footprint concept. *Ecological Economics 29*(3), 375–390.

Wackernagel, M., Schulz, N.B., Deumling, D., Linares, A.C., Jenkins, M., Kapos, V., ... & Randers, J. (2002). Tracking the ecological overshoot of the human economy. *Proceedings of the national Academy of Sciences 99*(14), 9266–9271.

Wang, Q., Zeng, Y.E., & Wu, B.W. (2016). Exploring the relationship between urbanization, energy consumption, and CO_2 emissions in different provinces of China. *Renewable and Sustainable Energy Reviews 54*, 1563–1579.

Wang, S.S., Zhou, D.Q., Zhou, P., & Wang, Q.W. (2011). CO_2 emissions, energy consumption and economic growth in China: A panel data analysis. *Energy Policy 39*(9), 4870–4875.

World Bank (2019). World Development Indicators. Washington, DC: World Bank. Available at http://data.worldbank.org/products/wdi.

Xiong, L. & Qi, S. (2018). Financial development and carbon emissions in Chinese provinces: A spatial panel data analysis. *The Singapore Economic Review 63*(02), 447–464.

Zakaria, M. & Bibi, S. (2019). Financial development and environment in South Asia: The role of institutional quality. *Environmental Science and Pollution Research 26*, 7926–7937.

Zarsky, L. (1999). Havens, halos and spaghetti: Untangling the evidence about foreign direct investment and the environment. *Foreign direct Investment and the Environment 13*(8), 47–74.

Zhang, C. & Lin, Y. (2012). Panel estimation for urbanization, energy consumption and CO_2 emissions: A regional analysis in China. *Energy Policy 49*, 488–498.

Zhang, Y.J. (2011). The impact of financial development on carbon emissions: An empirical analysis in China. *Energy Policy 39*(4), 2197–2203.

Zhang, Y. & Zhang, S. (2018). The impacts of GDP, trade structure, exchange rate and FDI inflows on China's carbon emissions. *Energy Policy 120*, 347–353.

World Bank. (2019). World Development Indicators. Washington, DC : World Bank.

Appendix

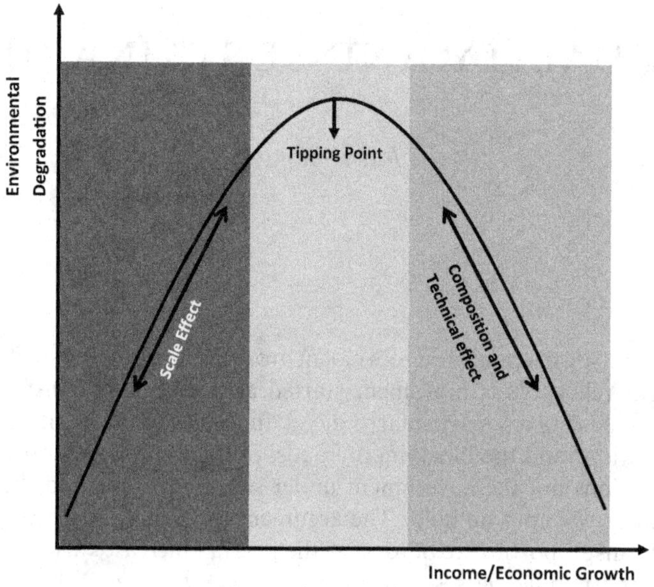

Figure 11.A1 Environmental Kuznets curve.

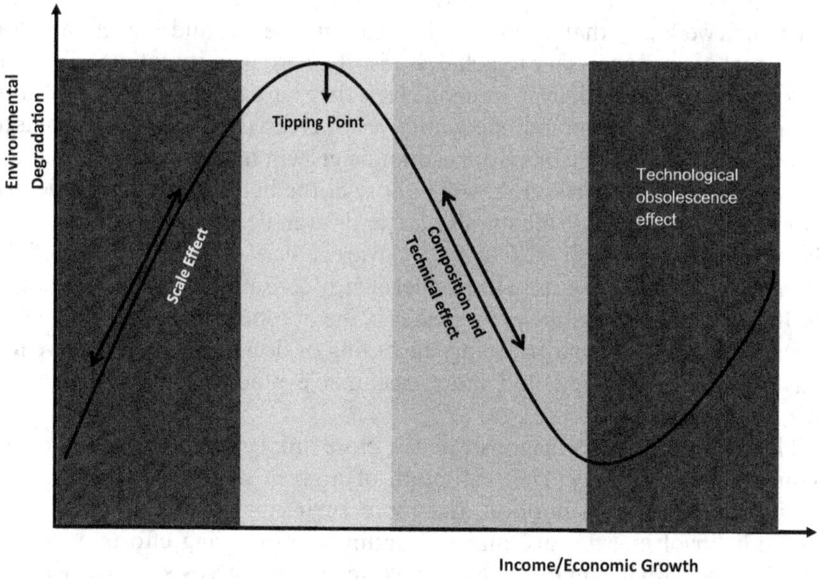

Figure 11.A2 N-shaped Kuznets curve.

12

INEQUALITY AND SUSTAINABILITY

Jon Reiersen

In October 2018, a new protest movement arose in France, the so-called Yellow Vests. The Yellow Vests movement started as a reaction against a planned increase in fuel taxes, particularly diesel fuel. The protests involved mass demonstrations and the blocking of roads, particularly in central Paris. The demonstrations put the government under severe pressure, and the planned tax increases were put on hold. The argument the Yellow Vests were making was that a disproportionate burden of the fuel tax increase was falling on the working and middle classes, particularly in remote areas. While the "rich" Parisians could take their bikes or the tube to work, the people in the rural areas had no choice but to drive their cars.

The Yellow Vests in France is just one example illustrating that social and environmental sustainability is closely linked. To meet the threat of global warming, we know that carbon emissions must be cut and higher taxes on fossil-fuel use are necessary to achieve this.[1] The problem is that it easily leads to social protest, especially if someone feels they have to bear others' cost. For the past 30 years, economic inequality has increased in most industrialised countries. Most of the gains from economic growth have gone to those at the top of the income distribution, while those at the bottom of the income distribution have seen their incomes stagnate or even decrease (e.g., Piketty and Saez 2006; Piketty 2014; OECD 2015; Alvaredo *et al.* 2017). Greening of the economy with massive cuts in fossil-fuel energy consumption is challenging in itself. The challenge will be even greater if the question of income inequality is not tackled. People experiencing stagnating or decreasing income have few reasons to embrace new and more sustainable practices, especially if this involves higher costs.

This chapter aims to demonstrate the close link between social and environmental sustainability. The realisation of a green transition, with reduced fossil-fuel energy consumption and more environment-friendly production methods, involves extensive and demanding restructuring efforts, which in the short term will impose considerable restructuring costs on individuals, groups and society. If peoples experience these costs are reasonably and fairly distributed, restructuring will be less difficult. In addition, innovative forces are more easily mobilised, and resistance to change is reduced by low-income inequality, high social trust levels, and collective risk-sharing. In this chapter, we will use the experience of the Nordic countries to support this claim.

As Acemoglu and Robinson (2012) show, major social and economic change usually take place as a result of a complex interplay between politics, markets, technology and social organisation. They provide several examples of cases where social and economic development, which could benefit society as a whole, is obstructed if dominant groups feel threatened by the changes brought about by the development process. Acemoglu and Robinson (2012) remind us that social and economic change tend to create winners and losers, and those who fear winding up on the losing side often have good reason for opposing change. Therefore, policies and institutions that ensure that the losers are compensated by the winners are essential to achieving successful economic restructuring. In the following, we will argue that the Nordic countries have come a long way in developing such arrangements. By reducing the resistance to change, the Nordic societal model therefore gives more leeway to policy makers as well as the business community with regard to developing more sustainable practices.

The rest of this chapter will expand on this idea by giving examples of how the Nordic model contributes to promoting sustainable development through high social trust, efficient handling of distributional conflicts, collective risk-sharing, and high employee participation and autonomy at the workplace. The overall objective is to show that societies that manage to keep income disparities down are also better equipped to cope with the transition to a greener economy.

12.1 Elements of the Nordic model

12.1.1 Creating and sharing wealth

The traditional picture of the Nordic model has been one of a generous welfare state offering social protection and delivering publicly provided services such as free healthcare and education. However, the Nordic model has also delivered high levels of productivity and income per capita in an international perspective.

According to the World Economic Forum, the Nordic countries constitute a global winning region (Schwab 2012; World Economic Forum 2018). The Nordic countries are open to international competition and trade, they are at the forefront of digital transformation, and the pace of innovation and technological modernisation is high. At the same time, the Nordic countries have the lowest income inequality among all industrialised countries. Viewed in a comparative perspective, the Nordic countries are both rich and egalitarian. Table 12.1 presents data that illustrates this further.

Table 12.1 Dimensions of economic and social performance

	GDP per capita[1]	*Gini coefficient*[2]	*Poverty rate*[3]
Nordic countries	**55,842**	**0.27**	**7.0**
Denmark	55,138	0.26	5.5
Finland	48,248	0.27	6.3
Iceland	57,453	0.26	5.4
Norway	65,603	0.26	8.4
Sweden	52,766	0.28	9.3
Continental Europe	**52,240**	**0.28**	**9.3**
Austria	55,529	0.28	9.8
Belgium	50,442	0.27	9.7
France	45,149	0.29	8.3
Germany	53,752	0.29	10.4
Netherlands	56,326	0.28	8.3
Southern Europe	**35,990**	**0.33**	**14.0**
Greece	29,592	0.33	14.4
Italy	41,426	0.33	13.7
Portugal	33,035	0.33	12.5
Spain	39,908	0.34	15.5
UK	**45,505**	**0.35**	**11.1**
USA	**62,480**	**0.39**	**17.8**

	GDP per hour worked[4]	*Competitiveness*[5]
Nordic countries	**111.7**	**79.1**
Denmark	122.2	80.6
Finland	97.6	80.3
Iceland	103.9	74.5
Norway	131.9	78.2
Sweden	102.7	81.7
Continental Europe	**111.8**	**77.6**
Austria	106.8	76.3
Belgium	122.0	76.6
France	111.5	70.0
Germany	114.8	82.8
Netherlands	113.9	82.4
Southern Europe	**81.4**	**69.3**
Greece	87.6	62.1
Italy	91.2	70.8
Portugal	59.1	70.2
Spain	87.6	74.2
UK	**88.5**	**82.0**
USA	**115.4**	**85.6**

Table 12.1 (Cont.)

Definition and sources:

1 PPP-adjusted GDP per capita in US dollar, 2018. OECD.
2 Gini coefficient, disposable income of households, 2017. The Gini coefficient can take on values between 0 (all households have the same income) and 1 (all income goes to only one household). OECD.
3 The number of people (in percent) whose income falls below half the median household income of the total population. OECD.
4 Gross domestic product at current process per hour worked, EU-15 = 100. Ameco.
5 Measures the microeconomic and macroeconomic foundations of national competitiveness, which is defined as the set of institutions, policies and factors that determine the level of productivity of a country. World Economic Forum.

Table 12.1 includes the Nordic countries as well as a selection of other European countries and the United States. Table 12.1 shows that the Nordic countries as a group show better results than all the other areas except the United States in terms of GDP per capita. The Nordic countries also have low-income inequality. The Nordics have the lowest income inequality of all countries in Table 12.1, measured both by the Gini coefficient and the poverty rate. Denmark, Iceland and Norway have the lowest Gini coefficients while Denmark, Finland and Iceland have the lowest poverty rates among all countries. The United Kingdom and the United States have the highest Gini coefficients (high-income inequality), while the United States has a particularly high poverty rate.

Labor productivity measured as GDP per hour worked is particularly high in Norway and Denmark, and higher than in all other countries listed in Table 12.1. This explains why Denmark and Norway together generate a GDP per capita almost on par with that of the United States, in spite of working less. The annual labour input per employee in 2018 in Denmark and Norway is 1,392 and 1,416 hours, respectively, while the corresponding figure in the United States is 1,786 hours. Various international organisations regularly compare and rank economies' competitiveness by constructing an index of several economic factors. The Nordic countries often rank highly in these comparisons, as also confirmed in Table 12.1.

Another noticeable characteristic of the Nordic countries is the high degree of organisational and technological change. This is illustrated by Figures 12.1 and 12.2.

Figure 12.1 ranks countries according to their digital competitiveness. The digital competitiveness ranking, produced by IMD World Competitiveness Center, measures the extent to which a country adopts digital technologies leading to transformation in government practices, business models and society in general (IMD 2018). The four largest Nordic countries rank at the top of the list, only beaten by the United States.

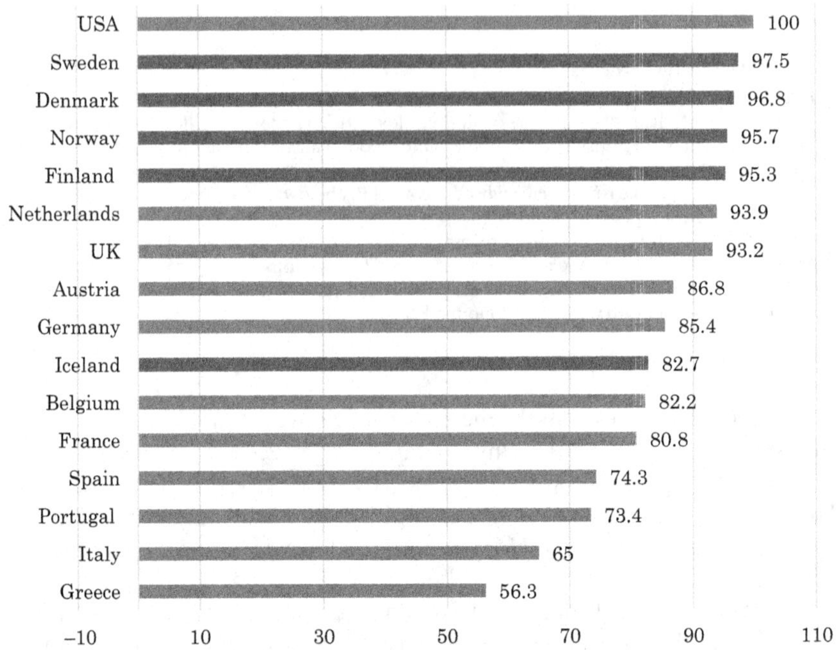

Figure 12.1 World digital competitiveness ranking.
Source: IMD (2018).

Figure 12.2 shows the percentage of employees reporting that they had been subject to substantial organisational and technological changes in their workplace and the percentage of employees reporting that they work with computers, laptops, smartphones, etc. Again, we see that the Nordic countries rank highly on both measures.

12.1.2 Two examples

We can look at two examples that illustrate the Nordic countries' ability to modernise and embrace more environmentally sustainable solutions: electric vehicles in Norway and wind turbines in Denmark.

Decarbonisation of transport, including the expansion of electric vehicles, is an important element of a transition consistent with limiting global warming (IPCC 2018). Around 50% of new cars sold in Norway during 2019 were entirely electric-powered. There are now far more electric vehicles on Norwegian roads as a proportion of total vehicles than anywhere else in the world. One of the main reasons is that the Norwegian government has implemented favourable financial incentives together with good charging infrastructure. The aim of the government is to stop sales of fossil-fuelled cars by 2025.

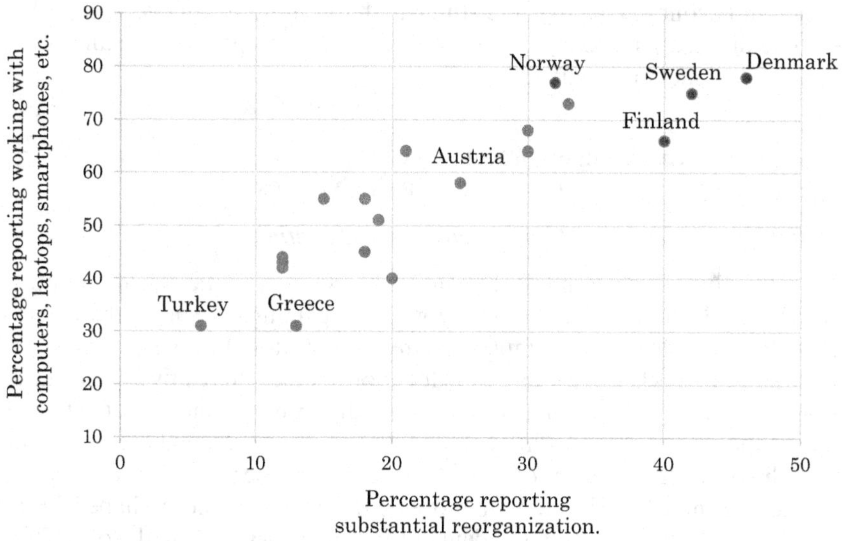

Figure 12.2 Organizational change and new technology.

Note: Substantial reorganization is defined as dismissals, reorganization of business units, closing of branch, etc.

Source: European Working Condition Survey (2015).

Solar and wind energy will form an important part of the transition away from fossil energy, and Denmark has been a pioneer in commercial wind energy development. Denmark has now the highest proportion of wind power in the world. Wind-generated electricity accounted for 34% of Denmark's total electricity consumption in 2014. In 2012, the Danish government adopted a plan to increase the share of electricity generation from wind to 50% in 2020, and to 84% in 2035.

12.1.3 Equality and prosperity are possible to combine

The Nordic experiences speak against the notion, often expressed by economists that efficiency and distribution are difficult to reconcile. Standard economic theory holds that there is a conflict between efficiency and equality. Redistribution of income from the relatively well-off to the relatively poor distorts market forces and weakens the incentives to innovate, save and work hard, thus reducing the overall economic pie. But the economic performance of the Nordic countries illustrates that this does not apply universally. The Nordic experiences show that equality and efficiency not only can be compatible, but that egalitarian redistribution can fuel technological modernisation, high productivity and necessary restructuring of the economy.

In the next section we outline some of the key elements of the Nordic equality–efficiency-driven economic strategy, followed by a discussion of why social and economic change are stimulated and more readily accepted when income disparity in society is not too great and when people have an acceptable level of income security.

12.2 Reaching low-income inequality and good economic performance in the Nordics

12.2.1 Small wage differentials

It is difficult to understand the low-income inequality in the Nordic countries without understanding the collective wage bargaining systems in these countries. Both employers and employees are well organised in the Nordic countries, and this has laid the foundation for coordinated and relatively centralised wage bargaining.[2] Coordinated wage bargaining has numerous effects, and one of them is small wage differentials. The lowest paid wages have been gradually lifted while the wages of the highest paid have been held down.

The Nordic countries' labour movement has always been shaped by an ideal of equality, especially the demand for equal pay for equal work. Thus, trade unions try to reduce wage inequality whenever they influence the determination of wages. As Barth *et al.* (2014) show:

- When wage negotiations are carried out at company level, the trade unions reduce wage differentials between employees of each company.
- When wage negotiations are carried out at the sector level, the trade unions reduce wage differentials between the employees of different companies within the same sector.
- When wage negotiations are carried out at the national level, the trade unions reduce wage differentials between companies, sectors and occupational groups.

The last point has historically been the situation in the Nordic countries. As a result, the Nordic countries have one of the most compressed wage structures among all industrialised countries (OECD 2015; Barth and Moene 2016). However, it is important to notice that the original motivation for collective bargaining in the Nordic countries was more closely linked to the need for economic efficiency than to considerations of equality (Moene and Wallerstein 1995; Erixon 2018).

12.2.2 Technological modernisation is stimulated by small wage differentials

Non-coordinated wage bargaining normally leads to a differentiation of wages adapted to local conditions. Wages increase in sectors and companies with high productivity and an ability to pay high wages, whereas wages remain low in sectors and companies with low productivity (Moene and Wallerstein 1997). Coordinated wage bargaining and equal pay for equal work, in contrast, pushes up wages in less productive companies, while keeping wages in highly productive ones lower than they otherwise would have been. This ensures good operating conditions and high profits in highly productive companies that apply modern technology, whereas less productive companies are forced out of the market at an earlier stage. In this way, creative destruction in the economy is stimulated by moving labour and resources away from less productive and less efficient companies to more efficiently operated ones. The overall economic performance and the pace of modernisation of business and industry thus increase.[3] This is just one example of how efficiency and equality can go hand in hand and mutually reinforce one another.

In addition to coordinated wage bargaining and wage compression, the welfare state plays a key role in holding income inequality low in the Nordic countries. But, as we will see in the following, the Nordic-type of welfare state also plays an important role (together with coordinated wage bargaining) in supporting risk-taking, technological modernisation and restructuring of the economy.

12.2.3 The welfare state support risk-taking and restructuring

The welfare state is not only an arrangement for redistribution of income. An essential, and sometimes overlooked, element of the welfare state is that it provides insurance against unforeseen loss of income, e.g., due to restructuring and unemployment. Since insurance is an important part of the welfare state, it should not be a surprise that the welfare state tends to be strongest in economies deeply integrated into the global economy (Katzenstein 1985; Rodrik 1997, 2018). The Nordic countries are small open economies, with a huge proportion of GDP generated from import and export (Calmfors 2014). Income based on globalisation and international trade is associated with a considerable risk, since open economies are vulnerable to external factors related to the international economy's ups and downs. This vulnerability increases citizens' interest in social security and income insurance.

An increasingly globalised economy is also increasing the pressure for competitiveness and the ability to restructure and modernise the economy. The welfare state contributes to the citizens being more willing to accept this pressure for constant restructuring. A strong welfare state implies that people's incomes are relatively well secured, however, without necessarily having any guarantee for keeping the same job throughout a person's career. Jobs disappear and new ones are created, perhaps requiring a different set of skills. If people feel that their income is fairly secure, such structural changes are more readily accepted and easier to implement, which in turn benefits society in the long run.

Thus, the welfare state helps to ensure broad social acceptance for openness, structural change and modernisation – again illustrating that redistribution helps secure long-term economic performance (Moene 2013).

12.2.4 The role of social trust

Social trust is an important factor behind the strong welfare states in the Nordic countries. The level of social trust varies widely across countries (Holmberg and Rothstein 2017). Data for social trust usually draws on responses to survey questions such as "Generally speaking, would you say that most people can be trusted, or that you can't be too careful when dealing with others?" Globally, an average of about 25% state that most people can be trusted. On top of the list we find three Nordic countries (Denmark, Norway and Sweden) and the Netherlands with scores of between 64% and 74%. The United States has a trust score of 38%, France and Spain have a score around 18%, while Turkey and Romania are down at 12% and 7%, respectively.

Why this considerable variation? Many scholars have noted the close correlation between trust and income inequality (Uslaner 2002; Rothstein and Uslaner 2005; Bjørnskov 2008; Bergh and Bjørnskov 2014; Barone and Mocetti 2016). Countries with high-income inequality tend to have much lower social trust levels than countries with less income inequality. High-income inequality increases the distance between individuals at different points on the income distribution, making the psychological distinction between those in "my group" and "the others" more noticeable. It becomes more difficult to identify with others, and this breaks down social trust (OECD 2015; Payne 2017; Hastings 2018; Wilkinson and Pickett 2018).

Others, however, claim that the relationship between inequality and trust runs the other way around – that trust creates low-income inequality (e.g., Bergh and Bjørnskov 2011; Rothstein *et al.* 2012; Bjørnskov and Svendsen 2013). The argument is that trust makes citizens more willing to support public policies for welfare spending. That is, trust allows a more encompassing and generous welfare state to develop, which in turn implies increased redistribution and lower income inequality.

In a Nordic context, there are strong reasons to believe that both perspectives noted above are important. That is, social trust is both a producer and a result of equality in the Nordic countries. Low wage and income inequality produce social trust, and high social trust creates political support among citizens for welfare state expansion. The equality created by the welfare state (together with an egalitarian wage policy) feeds back on even higher trust, and higher trust helps to generate even stronger political support for the welfare state, and so on. Over the long run, this feedback process has created a situation in which the Nordic countries have ended up with strong welfare states and high levels of social trust.[4]

12.3 Meeting the climate change challenge

The Nordic countries are both affluent and egalitarian, and they have been able to adapt well to the changing conditions of a constantly changing world. Today, the Nordic countries, together with the rest of the world, face a new fundamental challenge, as for example described in terrifying detail in the international bestseller "*The Uninhabitable Earth: A Story of the Future*" (Wallace-Wells 2019). Failure to reduce carbon emissions could threaten societies with food shortages, freshwater drain, heath deaths, refugee crisis, the flooding of major cities and economic collapse – just to name a few possible consequences of global warming. How prepared are the world's countries, including the Nordics, to respond to these threats?

As the Intergovernmental Panel on Climate Change (IPCC) noted in their latest report, limiting warming to 1.5°C above pre-industrial levels would require transformative systemic change. "*While transitions in energy efficiency, carbon intensity of fuels, electrification and land-use change are underway in various countries, limiting warming to 1.5°C will require a greater scale and pace of change to transform energy, land, urban and industrial systems globally.*" (IPCC 2018, p. 315). Limiting warming to 1.5°C is possible within the laws of chemistry and physics, but chemistry and physics are far from the only constraint. To enable a successful transition towards greater sustainability, policy makers and businesses are also dependent on the socio-economic system in which they are imbedded, as also noted in the introduction.

New technologies and production methods, new business models, regulation of fossil-fuel energy consumption, and a fundamental rethinking of how humans are connected to each other and nature only change if these initiatives do not meet too much social resistance and protest. Unfortunately, we seem not to be moving in that direction. The gap in income between rich and poor has increased sharply in most countries in recent years, and this has fuelled social and political tensions, making the transition towards more sustainable practices more difficult (Banarjee and Duflo 2019).[5] High-income inequality is not social sustainable, and societies that struggle with their social sustainability will also face immense difficulties in setting the course for a more environmentally friendly economy. Again, we will use examples from the Nordic countries to illustrate this point.

12.4 Trust and risk-sharing as instruments to counter climate change

12.4.1 The importance of trust

As shown in Section 3.4, the Nordic countries have high social trust levels compared to other countries. International comparisons show a positive correlation between trust, innovation and modernisation (Akcomak and ter Weel 2009; Algan and Cahuc 2013; Bjørnskov and Méon 2015).

Investments in new technology, production methods and organisational forms generally involve a considerable risk. The returns are often highly uncertain, particularly if the investments are about the development of technology and production methods that have never been tested before. Uncertainty and risk can be seen as a cost for the investors. Trust helps to reduce some of this risk and thereby the cost (La Porta *et al.* 1997; OECD 2001). Thus, trust makes room for more long-term and high-risk investments, which can again lay the foundation for more sustainable production methods, low-carbon energy technologies and energy-efficiency measures in transport and buildings.

Trust also enhances cooperation, and innovation often depends on individuals and companies that dare to cooperate. This applies especially to smaller firms with limited resources. These are often totally dependent on cooperating with external actors in order to succeed. Where there is trust, there is less need for protecting one's own interests through detailed agreements and contracts (La Porta *et al.* 1997). When the risk of opportunism goes down, transaction costs are reduced and innovative initiatives are faced with fewer obstacles.

The high level of trust in the Nordic countries also seems to foster greater employee autonomy. Thus, there is a high degree of involvement in the decision-making process at the firm level. When employers trust their employees, a social foundation is established that allows a more efficient organisation of the enterprise, without too much hierarchy, administration and surveillance.

Figure 12.3 shows some results from the most recent European Working Condition Survey. Sixty-eight percent of the Nordic countries' workers report that they work in teams, and 24% report that they work in teams with full autonomy. The corresponding figures from the other countries are much lower. Workers at the operative level ("the shopfloor") often know best where the shoe pinches. Where there is trust and decentralisation of power, the employees can exercise initiative, use their own problem-solving abilities and be actively involved in innovation and restructuring processes. Such bottom–up initiatives are going to play a vital role in the transition towards more sustainable practices in firms and industries.

Figure 12.3 shows that 82% of workers in the Nordic countries report that they can choose or change their work methods, while 57% report that they can influence decisions that are important for their work. The corresponding figures for the other countries are again much lower. The combination of trust, decentralised decision-making systems, and widespread employee participation is presumably a significant explanation for the high restructuring capacity of Nordic societies.

Trust also plays an important role in the coupling of resources. Societies marked by high social trust seem to be most successful in terms of combining resources, new ideas and talent (OECD 2001; Yamagishi 2011; Reiersen 2017). Trust often acts as a stepping-stone that enables actors to break out of

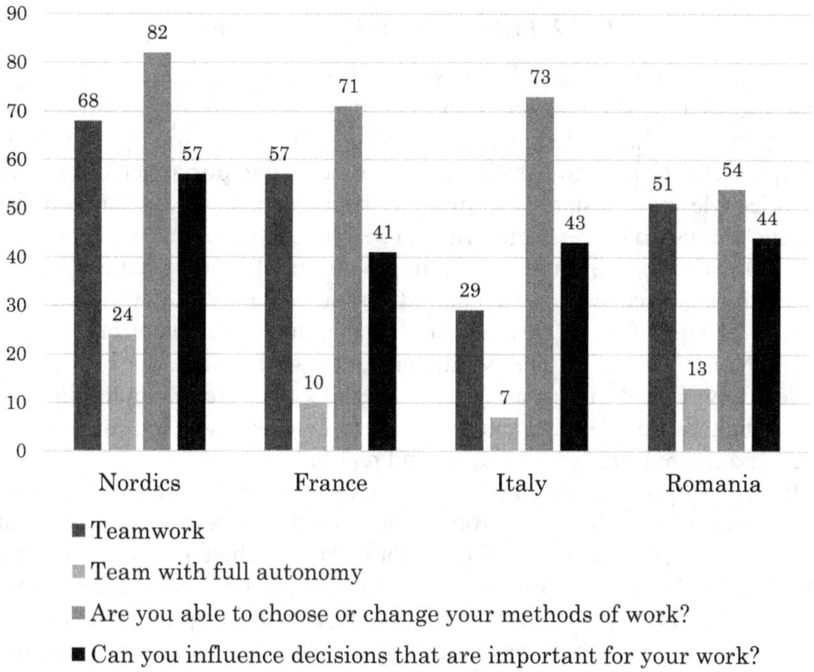

Figure 12.3 Teamwork and decision-making authority within firms.
Source: European Working Condition Survey, 2015.

established, secure relationships and to invest their resources in more uncertain but also more profitable projects. In societies where trust is limited to people you already know, and where individuals feel the need to secure their interests in closed networks and local communities it is harder to realise the benefits derived from innovation, spreading of ideas and the establishment of new alliances (Yamagishi 2011).

In much the same vein, Botsman (2017) shows that trust also lowers the threshold for introducing and using new technology and new products and services. Trusting others, we feel secure enough to take risks and allow ourselves to be vulnerable. Trust acts as a bridge between the known and the unknown, thereby helping us to take "trust leaps." Such a trust leap occurs when we take a risk to do something new or do it differently from how we've done it before. Trust leaps create new opportunities by breaking down barriers and helping us to "*mash up ideas … in unexpected ways; and … open up new markets, new networks and new alliances that would once have been unthinkable*" (Botsman 2017, p. 24). In this way, social trust is an immensely important asset in the transition towards a greener economy. However, social trust is difficult to build and sustain where income inequality is high and rising.

12.4.2 Risk-sharing and wealth-sharing

The Nordic countries have large, well-developed welfare states. Some argue that the welfare state weakens the incentive for innovation, restructuring and economic change (e.g., Acemoglu *et al.* 2012). But the opposite argument can also be applied. As already mentioned, an important element of the Nordic-style welfare state is to promote restructuring, innovation and risk-taking.[6] Access to universal, tax-funded welfare goods, such as free education, unemployment benefits and retraining support, contribute to reducing uncertainty during extensive adjustment and workforce reallocation processes. The risk of being "left out" without any income, due to restructuring, is small in the Nordic countries. The Nordic universal welfare state can be seen as a collectively funded insurance system. The safety net creates underpins both the willingness to take bigger risks and the willingness to accept the risk that accompanies repeated restructuring and renewal.

It is also important to bear in mind, as also noted in the introduction above, that even if innovations, new production methods and restructuring generate benefits for society at large, this does not mean that these processes are automatically embraced by everyone. A transition towards a greener economy creates winners and losers, and those who fear winding up on the losing end of this process have good reason for opposing change. Groups that are hurt may include people who lose their jobs, have their income reduced or whose education and skills become outdated. If these groups are not compensated and helped, the result could easily be a significant social and political backlash – as we already observe in many countries today (Goodhart 2017; Collier 2018; Rodrik 2018).

In countries with poorly developed welfare systems, people quickly take to the streets and protest if they feel threatened by major structural changes. The social reaction to restructuring and reallocation of resources are often much milder in the Nordic countries. However, this is not because structural change takes place without a cost. The restructuring costs for individuals can be considerable but are easier to accept when society takes collective responsibility for reducing personal sacrifices.

12.5 Conclusion

Social sustainability is about income disparity in society not becoming too large. High-income inequality deepens social and political conflicts and breaks down trust and solidarity (OECD 2015; Hastings 2018; Wilkinson and Pickett 2018). Environmental sustainability produces goods and services with less fossil-fuel energy and uses more environment-friendly production methods. If the global average temperature continues to rise, society's challenges could become formidable (Hjort 2016; Emanuel 2018; Wallace-Wells 2019).

A main objective of this chapter is to show that social and environmental sustainability are closely linked. By using experiences from the Nordic countries this chapter has tried to draw out two learning points:

- Implementing a more egalitarian distribution of income is possible without compromising economic efficiency. Under the right institutional circumstances, redistribution can even stimulate economic restructuring, modernisation and innovation.
- The realisation of a green transition, with reduced fossil-fuel energy consumption and more environment-friendly production methods, involves extensive and demanding restructuring efforts – which in the short term will impose considerable restructuring costs on individuals, groups and society. If people experience these costs as being reasonably and fairly distributed, restructuring will be less difficult. In addition, innovative forces are more easily mobilised, and resistance to change is reduced by low-income inequality, high social trust levels and collective risk-sharing.

It does not follow from these learning points that other countries should try to copy the Nordic societal model. Each country has its own unique history, culture and set of beliefs, which makes the idea of exporting societal models seem meaningless. But countries can learn from each other.

We know that limiting global warming require a deep transformative change in economy and society, with lower energy demand and greater penetration of low-emission and carbon-free technology. Such change will be massively challenging, and the challenge will be even greater if the rise in income inequality is not moderated. People experiencing stagnating or decreasing income have few reasons to embrace new and more sustainable practices, especially if this involves higher costs. Recent experiences from the Nordic countries show that economic restructuring and change has been eased by low-income inequality, social protection and high social trust.

Notes

1 According to the Intergovernmental Panel on Climate Change (IPCC 2018), CO_2 equivalent (CO_{2e}) emissions would need to be reduced by 45% by 2030, compared to the 2010 level, and go down to zero by 2050, in order to limit global warming to 1.5°C.

2 Trade union density is around 80% in Iceland and close to 70% in Denmark, Finland and Sweden. Norway has a trade union density of around 55%.

3 Moene and Wallerstein (1997) analyze these mechanisms in greater detail within the context of a formal economic model.

4 In other countries (e.g. the United States), the feedback process between trust and equality seems to have gone the other way around, producing a situation of smaller welfare states and lower levels of social trust.

5 As a result of a consistent growth of the global economy, and a more interconnected world with more international trade, the world has experienced a reduction in extreme poverty and the gap in income between poor and rich countries has been reduced. However, this trend has co-existed with rising inequality within each country (e.g., Piketty and Saez 2006; Piketty 2014; Alvaredo *et al.* 2018).

6 See Barth *et al.* (2014), Andersen *et al.* (2007), Moene (2013) and Stiglitz (2015) who argue along the same lines. Stiglitz (2015) argues for instance that "(...) *the US could increase the pace of innovation (and the level of economic welfare) by making some moves in the direction of the Nordic model*" (Stiglitz 2015, p. 8).

References

Acemoglu, D. & Robinson, J. (2012). Why Nations Fail: The Origins of Power, Prosperity, and Poverty. London: Profile Books.

Acemoglu, D., Robinson, J., & Verdier, T. (2012). Can't We All Be More Like Scandinavians? MIT Working Paper (March).

Akcomak, I.S. & ter Weel, B. (2009). Social capital, innovation and growth: Evidence from Europe. *European Economic Review 53*(5), 544–567.

Algan, Y. & Cahuc, P. (2013). Trust, growth and well-being: New Evidence and policy implications. In Aghion, P. & Durlauf, S. (Eds.), *Handbook of Economic Growth* (Vol. 2A). Amsterdam: Elsevier.

Alvaredo, F., Chancel, L., Piketty, T., Saez, E., & Zucman, G. (2017). *World Inequality Report 2018*. World Inequality Lab.

Andersen, T.M., Holmstrom, B., Honkapohja, S., Korkman, S., Soderstrom, H.T., & Vartiainen, J. (2007). *The Nordic Model: Embracing globalization and sharing risks*. The Reseerch Institute of the Finnish Economy: Taloustieto Oy.

Banarjee, A.V. & Duflo, E. (2019). Good Economics for Hard Times: Better Answers to Our Biggest Problems. London: Allen Lane.

Barone, G. & Mocetti, S. (2016). Inequality and trust: New evidence from panel data. *Economic Inquiry 54*(2), 794–809.

Barth, E. & Moene, K. (2016). The equality multiplier: How wage compression and welfare empowerment interact. *Journal of the European Economic Association 14*(5), 1011–1037.

Barth, E., Moene, K.O., & Willumsen, F. (2014). The Scandinavian model – an interpretation. *Journal of Public Economics* 117, 60–72.

Bergh, A., & Bjørnskov, C. (2011). Historical trust levels predict the current size of the welfare state. *Kyklos 64*, 1–19.

Botsman, R. (2017). Who Can You Trust? How Technology Brought Us Together – and Why It Could Drive Us Apart. London: Portfolio Penguin.

Bergh, A. & Bjørnskov, C. (2011). Historical trust levels predict the current size of the welfare state, *Kyklos 64*(1), 1–19.

Bergh, A. & Bjørnskov, C. (2014). Trust, welfare states and income equality: Sorting out the causality. *European Journal of Political Economy 35*, 183–199.

Bjørnskov, C. (2008). Social trust and fractionalization: A possible reinterpretation. *European Sociological Review 24*(3), 271–283.

Bjørnskov, C. & Méon, P.-G. (2015). The productivity of Trust. *World Development 70*, 317–331.

Bjørnskov, C. & Svendsen, G.T. (2013). Does social trust determine the size of the welfare state? Evidence using historical identification. *Public Choice 157*(1–2), 269–286.

Calmfors, L. (2014). How well is the Nordic model doing? Recent performance and future challenges. In Valkonen, T. & Vihriälä, V. (Eds.), The Nordic Model – Challenged but Capable of Reform. Nordic Council of Ministers: Rosendahls-Schultz Grafisk.

Collier, D. (2018). The Future of Capitalism: Facing the New Anxieties. London: Allen Lane.

Emanuel, K. (2018). What We Know about Climate Change. Cambridge, MA: The MIT Press.

Erixon, L. (2018). Progressive supply-side economics: an explanation and update of the Rehn-Meidner model. *Cambridge Journal of Economics 42*(3), 653–697.

Goodhart, D. (2017). The Road to Somewhere: The New Tribes Shaping British Politics. London: C Hurst.

Hastings, O.P. (2018). Less equal, less trusting? Longitudinal and cross-sectional effects of income inequality on trust in U.S. States, 1973–2012. *Social Science Research 74*(August), 77–95.

Hjort, I.C. (2016). Potential Climate Risks in Financial Markets: A Literature Overview. Memorandum. Department of Economics, University of Oslo.

Holmberg, S. & Rothstein, B. (2017). Trusting other people. *Journal of Public Affairs 16*(1–2).

IMD (2018). IMD World Competitiveness Ranking 2018. IMD World Competitiveness Center. www.imd.org/wcc/world-competitiveness-center/

Intergovernmental Panel on Climate Change (2018). Global Warming of 1.5°C. An IPCC Special Report on the impacts of global warming of 1.5°C above pre-industrial levels and related global greenhouse gas emission pathways, in the context of strengthening the global response to the threat of climate change, sustainable development, and efforts to eradicate poverty. www.ipcc.ch/sr15/

Katzenstein, P.J. (1985). Small States in World Markets: Industrial Policy in Europe. Itacha: Cornell University Press.

La Porta, R., Lopez-de-Silanes, F., Shleifer, A., & Vishny, R.W. (1997). Trust in large organizations. *American Economic Review Paper and Proceedings 87*, 333–338.

Moene, K. (2013). Scandinavian equality: A prime example of protection without protectionism. In Stiglitz, I.J. & Kaldor, M. (Eds.), The Quest for Security: Protection Without Protectionism and the Challenge of Global Governance. New York: Columbia University Press.

Moene, K. & Wallerstein, M. (1995). Solidaristic wage bargaining. *Nordic Journal of Political Economy 22*, 79–94.

Moene, K. & Wallerstein, M. (1997). Pay inequality. *Journal of Labor Economics 15*(3), 403–430.

OECD (2001). The Well-Being of Nations: The Role of Human and Social Capital. Paris: OECD Publishing.

OECD (2015). In It Together. Why Less Inequality Benefits All. Paris: OECD Publishing.

Payne, K. (2017). The Broken Ladder. How Inequality Changes the Way We Think, Live and Die. London: Weidenfeld & Nicolson.

Piketty, T. (2014). Capital in the Twenty-first Century. Cambridge, MA: Harvard University Press.

Piketty, T. & Saez, E. (2006). The evolution of top incomes: A historical and international perspective. *American Economic Review 96*(2), 200–205.

Reiersen, J. (2017). Trust as a booster. *Journal of Business Economics and Management 18*(4), 585–598.

Rodrik, D. (1997). Has Globalization Gone Too Far? Washington: Institute for International Economics.

Rodrik, D. (2018). Populism and the economics of globalization. *Journal of International Business Policy 1*(1–2), 12–33.

Rothstein, B. & Uslaner, E.M. (2005). Equality, corruption, and trust. *World Politics 58*(1), 41–72.

Rothstein, B, Samanni, M. & Teorell, J. (2012). Explaining the welfare state: Power resources vs. the quality of government. *European Political Science Review 4*(1), 1–28.

Schwab, K. (2012). The End of Capitalism – So What's Next? World Economic Forum. www.weforum.org/agenda/2012/04/the-end-of-capitalism-so-whats-next/

Stiglitz, J. (2015). Leaders and followers: Perspectives on the Nordic model and the economics of innovation. *Journal of Public Economics 127*(July), 3–16.

Uslaner, E.M. (2002). The Moral Foundation of Trust. Cambridge: Cambridge University Press.

Wallace-Wells, D. (2019). The Uninhabitable Earth: A Story of the Future. London: Allen Lane.

Wilkinson, R. & Pickett, K. (2018). The Inner Level: How More Equal Societies Reduce Stress, Restore Sanity and Improve Everyone's Well-being. London: Allen Lane.

World Economic Forum (2018). The Global Competitiveness Report 2018. Geneva: World Economic Forum.

Yamagishi, T. (2011). Trust. The Evolutionary Game of Mind and Society. London: Springer.

13

THE SOCIO-ECONOMIC METABOLISM OF CANADA

A case study of energy flows from 1990 to 2011

Abdullah Toseef, Umar Burki and Pervin Ersoy

13.1 Introduction

In this chapter technical energy will be considered as energy flows in order to understand the socio-economic metabolism of Canada as well as the relationship of technical energy to sustainable and environmentally friendly energy production. Canada is ranked as the sixth largest economy in terms of its primary technical energy production and the eighth largest in terms of technical energy consumption (IEA 2017). Being one of the largest exporters of crude oil and coal, non-renewable fossil fuels amount to approximately 20% of total Canadian exports by value (Statcan 2012). The high production volumes and exports of fossil fuels have had an adverse effect on Canada's commitment towards climate change. Since 1990, Canada's carbon emissions have increased by 20%, reflecting the heavy production and usage of fossil fuels.

In order to study the importance of energy flows in Canada, it is necessary to take a deep dive into the socio-economic metabolism. To do this, we will use the tools of material flow analysis (MFA) and energy flow analysis (EFA) to understand the role of Canada as a producer of energy, and the historic values of these flows at a disaggregated level to differentiate coal, crude oil, natural gas and renewable sources as sources of technical energy. In addition, with the help of EFA, a link will be established between the key energy flows of Canada and the possibilities of a transition to sustainability. The data available for technical energy comprises both renewable and non-renewable energy sources. The specific research questions addressed in this study are:

i) How has the metabolic profile of Canada changed over time?
ii) How does Canada compare to other nations such as the United States in terms of energy usage?
iii) Where is the potential for a transition to sustainability in the energy sector?

13.2 Social metabolism

Biology textbooks define metabolism as: "to sustain the process of life, a typical cell carries out thousands of biochemical reactions each second, the sum of all biological reactions constitute metabolism" (Purves 1992). The process of metabolism in living things is carried out systematically where raw material is obtained from the environment and converted into useful energy, becoming a building block for the organism. In the case of human beings, the term metabolism needs to be expanded to include the interactions human beings have amongst themselves and with their environment. This results in a different definition of metabolism, used widely in social science theory.

Sustainability is a term to explain the interactions between society and the natural environment; society extracts and inputs resources from nature, processes those resources and emits outputs back into the natural environment (Fischer-Kowalski and Weisz 2016). These processes have caused long-term problems of resource scarcity, the extraction of non-renewable resources on the input side of the production system, and waste and pollution emitted into the natural environment through industrial processes. Thus, a key emphasis for sustainable development is to consider the interface between society and nature in terms of the flow of materials and energy, i.e., the social metabolism (Fischer-Kowalski and Weisz 1999).

Marx (1867) first used the term "metabolism" in the sphere of the social sciences in the 19th century. After that, a number of studies have discussed social metabolism, for example Fischer-Kowalski (1998), Ayres and Kneese (1969), Baynes and Müller (2016), along with many others. Some of the most important major frameworks and models discussed in the literature are Boyden's human ecological model, Godelier's society-natural model, Ostrom's social ecological system (SES), the Frankfurt School's social ecology framework, the Dutch framework for societal transitions management and the Vienna social ecology framework (Fischer-Kowalski and Weisz 2016; Fischer-Kowalski and Weisz 1999). The focus of this study will be on the framework for societal–nature interactions developed by the Vienna social ecology school.

The interface between a society and its natural environment creates a socio-ecological system (Haberl *et al.* 2004; Fischer-Kowalski and Weisz 2016). These socio-ecological modes can be categorized into three major types: hunter and gatherer, agrarian and industrial regimes (Singh *et al.* 2010). Transition from one type to the other over a period can elicit challenges to sustainability such as climate change, resource scarcity, loss of biodiversity, etc. (Haberl *et al.* 2004). The transition from an agrarian to an industrialized society is demanding more material use from developing economies causing sustainability problems with respect to resource use and an overload on the ecosystem's ability to absorb waste and emissions (Schaffartzik *et al.* 2014; Schandl and Schulz 2002).

Socio-economic metabolism is a continuous process which involves the conversion of raw materials into products and services used by society, and ultimately into emissions and waste in a similar way to that of any other ecosystem (Fischer-Kowalski and Haberl 1998; Krausmann *et al.* 2009; Schandl and Schulz 2002; Ayres and Simonis 1994). Singh *et al.* (2010, p. 63) summarized it as follows:

> The concept is based on the premise that any social system not only reproduces itself culturally but also biophysically through a constant flow of materials and energy with its natural environment as well as with other social systems. The size of flows is intricately linked to the biophysical stocks of the social system and determined by the socio-metabolic regime it belongs to: every socio-metabolic regime has a different metabolic profile, i.e. quantity and quality of materials and energy used.

13.3 Material flow analysis (MFA), energetic metabolism and energy flow analysis (EFA)

MFA is an accounting framework for analyzing the biophysical aspects of a socio-economic system. MFA is based on the first law of thermodynamics (Weisz *et al.* 2001). The law of conservation allows the system to understand the inputs from the environment to the economy (natural resources) and the outputs from economy to the environment (waste) as well as the material that is accumulated in the economy (Eurostat 2001a). The MFA accounting concept can be put into words in the following way: Input = output + additions to stock – removals from stock = output + net stock changes.

The three main categories of stock accounted for in a MFA are: a) human population, i.e., the materials used in providing the human population with the required material security, b) the infrastructure built by humans to carry out economic activities and c) livestock and other domestic animals with economic value. Material flows are also classified into three main types: air, water and materials (Eurostat 2009; Fischer-Kowalski *et al.* 2011; Matthews *et al.* 2000). A number of studies use a MFA for their empirical analysis, for example, for Japan, Germany and Austria (Fischer-Kowalski *et al.* 2011), for Germany, Japan, the Netherlands and the United States for the period 1975–1996 (Krausmann *et al.* 2015), for the outputs of these same four major economies plus Austria over the same period (Matthews *et al.* 2000; Schandl et al 2006; Krausmann *et al.* 2009; Schaffartzik *et al.* 2014), for resource extraction and consumption (Giljum *et al.* 2014), to analyze the transition of developing countries from an agrarian to an industrial economy, for India (Singh *et al.* 2012), for Uzbekistan (Raupova, Kamahara, and Goto 2014), for the Czech Republic (Kuskovaa, Gingrich, and Krausmann 2008) and for Estonia (Oras and Grüner 2010). However, in order to properly consider the energy flows of societies, studies need to be compatible with the current MFA methodology (Haberl 2001a; Nishioka, Yanagisawa, and Spengler 2000; Haberl and Geissler 2000).

Keeping in mind the interdependence between the two entities, a society's true metabolism needs to be accounted for by incorporating its energy demand and consumption along with the material requirement. Using energy flows in a study provides a reflection of the energy-related environmental and social problems associated with both renewable and non-renewable sources of energy (Haberl 2001a). Haberl (2001) emphasizes that in order to be consistent in accounting for energy flows it is advisable to count all energetic materials in terms of their gross calorific value (GCV) rather than the net calorific value (NCV). GCV differs from NCV in that it not only accounts for the usable energy in a particular material but also for the latent heat of water vapor. Biomass, i.e., food and fodder, is generally represented in GCV to maintain consistency in data compilation and analysis. Energetic metabolism requires technical energy to be represented in GCV as well. Calculations based on GCV allow for comparisons to be made between technical drive power and human/domestic animal drive power. Evidently, today, technical drive power has largely superseded human/animal drive power but in order to make historical comparisons, i.e., the transition of society from a system of hunters and gatherers through to the agricultural revolution and subsequently to the industrial system, it is necessary to include all types of drive power (Haberl and Geissler 2000; Haberl 2001a).

13.4 Methodology

The methodology followed in this research to assess the energy metabolism of Canada includes the data compilation of material flows, the use of MFA indicators and the interpretation of the indicators used in the analysis. These methods are consistent with Eurostat (2013) guidelines and have been followed in procedures for calculating energy flows developed by Krausmann *et al.*, (2015) and Haberl (2001a). The primary data for technical energy have been calculated by the IEA (IEA 2017). The MFA and EFA methodologies have been quantified and analyze energy flows on both a global and national scale (Krausmann *et al.* 2015; EFA Haberl 2001a). The above approach was taken to compile data on energy flows for Canada for the selected time series of 1990–2011.

13.4.1 System boundary

To analyze the material flows of a socio-economic system, a system boundary must be defined (Fischer-Kowalski *et al.* 2011; Krausmann *et al.* 2015). In this MFA, the system boundary is the national economy under consideration. The flows that enter the economy either from other political boundaries (i.e., imports), or the natural environment, are referred to as input flows, whereas the output flows are the discharges to the environment and exports to other economies. Furthermore, MFA accounts for relevant flows should be consistent with national accounts (Krausmann *et al.* 2015) and follow the following principles:

i) Flows that occur between the national economy and natural environment, i.e., the primary extraction of materials from the natural environment (such as the extraction of crude oil) and the post-process discharges to the natural environment, i.e., emissions and wastes.
ii) Flows occurring between the political boundary of the national economy and the rest of the world (ROW) economy. These are the import and export flows. The system boundary for this research is the national economy of Canada and flows are categorized in two different ways: a) input flows of technical energy, i.e., the domestic extraction (primary production) of technical energy in Canada, plus the imports of the same from the ROW to Canada and b) output flows, i.e., the exports of technical energy from the national economy of Canada to the ROW economy and environment.

13.4.2 Indicators for energy flows

The energy flow analysis (EFA) in this study has been conducted using the methodology presented by (Haberl 2001a) and is in line with the MFA methodology. The basic data compilation for the EFA is the same as that used for the MFA with some changes in the nomenclature of the indicators.

13.4.2.1 Domestic extraction (DE)

In order to explain the energetic metabolism of a society it is necessary to analyze the following types of energy flows:

a. Biomass flows, including timber and crop residues (referred to as food and feed, the current study is not focused on it)
b. Coal
c. Crude oil
d. Natural gas
e. Nuclear
f. Hydro
g. Geothermal, solar and wind power
h. Biofuels and waste

Data for coal, crude oil, nuclear, hydro, geothermal, solar and wind power was compiled in units of ktoe (kilotonne of oil equivalent) and converted into a GCV for each fuel in joules in line with the convention of EFA the energy of each material is represented in GCV to maintain consistency between food and feed and the rest of the energy carriers, referred to collectively in this study as technical energy. Coal and crude oil are represented in NCV in the IEA database (IEA 2017), whereas electricity and nuclear energy has no latent heat created through vaporization and is always represented in GCV. Biofuels, waste and natural gas are reported in GCV in units of terajoules (TJ) by the IEA (2017).

13.4.2.2 Imports and exports

Imports and exports are the physical quantity of energy carriers entering and leaving the Canadian physical border from and to other economies. Data for technical energy were collected from the IEA (2017) compiled in ktoe and converted to GCV using appropriate factors. Biofuels, waste and natural gas were compiled in GCV in units of TJ as reported by the IEA (2017). The imports and exports studied for their technical energy use were coal, crude oil, oil products, natural gas, electricity, heat, nuclear, and biofuels and waste.

13.4.2.3 Direct energy input (DEI)

DEI is expressed in the unit of joules. It can be calculated as follows:

DEI = DE + Imports

13.4.2.4 Domestic energy consumption (DEC)

DEC is expressed in the unit of joules. It can be calculated as follows:

DEC: DEI – Exports or DE + Imports – Exports

13.4.2.5 DE to DEC ratio

The ratio of DE to DEC indicates the level of dependence that the physical economy has on domestic energy supply. Therefore, expressing the DE to DEC ratio indicates domestic resource dependency (Wiesz *et al.* 2006).

13.4.2.6 Physical trade balance (PTB)

The PTB is the difference between the import and export of energy carriers and is expressed in the unit of joules.

13.4.2.7 Renewable energy

Energy derived from natural processes (e.g., sunlight and wind) is replenished at a higher rate than it is consumed. Solar, wind, geothermal, hydro and biomass are common sources of renewable energy (IEA 2017).

13.5 Empirical findings

This section represents the main findings from the analysis of the socio-economic metabolism of Canada for the time series 1990–2011. The material and energy flow accounting (MEFA) indicators discussed and explained in the methodology are used to interpret the socio-economic flows for energy. Comparisons with the United States (Gierlinger and Krausmann 2012) for the relevant time series will also be discussed for some sub-categories. To understand Canada's role in the global energy market and impact on climate change, it is important to analyze the energy flows of Canada with respect to domestic extraction, imports, exports and domestic energy consumption.

13.5.1 Canada's Sankey representation

To analyze how societal energy flows changed over time, three points in time are analyzed, i.e., 1990, 2000 and 2011. With the help of Sankey diagrams, a visual representation of Canada's systemic energy flow is compared after each decade (Figure 13.1). In examining these three figures it is clear that only domestic extraction and exports have gone through a noticeable change as part of the whole metabolism of the system. Furthermore, the Sankey representation points towards more domestic extraction of non-renewable energy to provide for increasing exports. Also, negligible changes have been seen in the DE and DEC of renewable energy in the energetic metabolism of Canada, showing the huge reliance of Canada on fossil fuels. Looking at the overall energetic metabolism it can be concluded that Canada has transitioned towards a technical energy-based society as most of the energy required for building stocks and carrying out flows for getting work done is coming from non-renewable energy.

13.5.2 Metabolism of Canada

One of our aims is to understand the metabolism of Canada with respect to the production, consumption and trading of energy from 1990 to 2011. The metabolic profile of Canada depicts an industrial society as Canada shows a similar pattern of energy production and consumption to that of the United States and the EU-15.[1]

The average DE/capita of biomass for Canada is twice that of the United States and 2.5 times that of the EU-15. The average DMC/capita of biomass

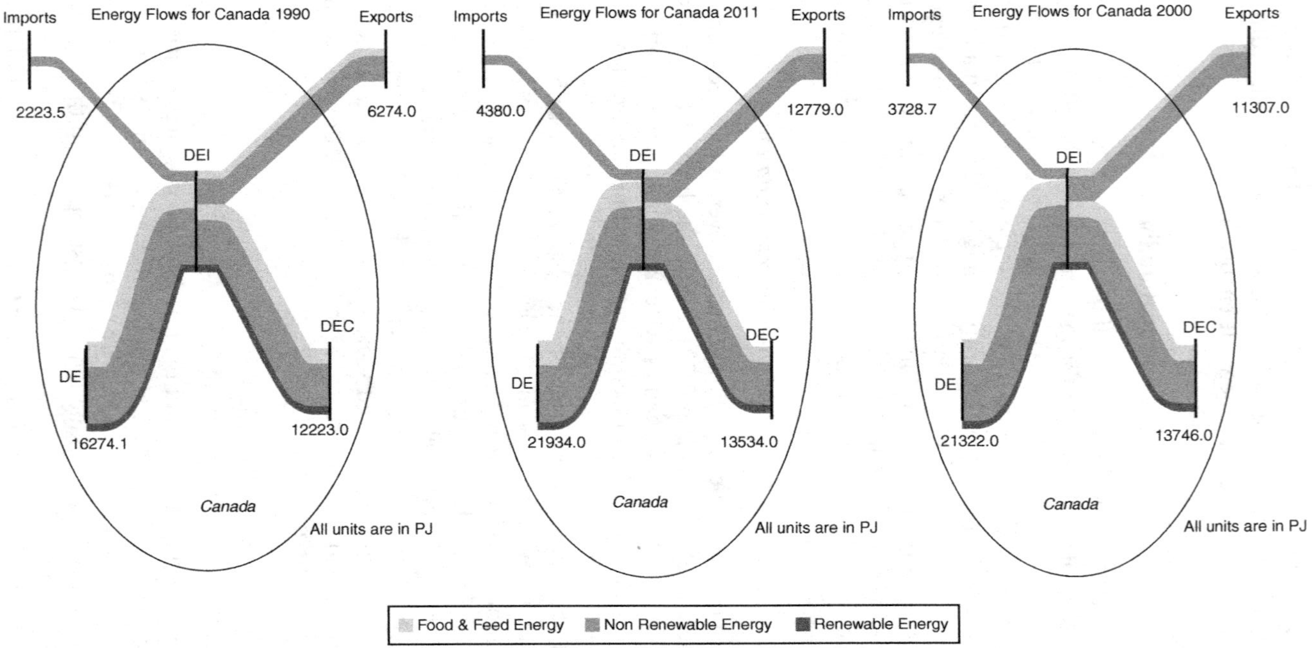

Figure 13.1 Energy Metabolic Profile for Canada represented in a Sankey diagram for the years 1990, 2000 and 2011.

for Canada has an average of 9.6 tons/capita/year which is approximately twice that of both the United States and EU-15 (Weisz *et al.* 2006) and is five times higher than developing and densely populated countries such as India and China. The average population density of Canada for the time period studies is 3.4 cap/km², far lower than the EU-15 average of 116.2 cap/km² but similar to countries with a high DE/capita and DMC/capita such as Finland, Sweden and Ireland which also have a low population density (Wiesz *et al.* 2006; Gierlinger and Krausmann 2012; Singh *et al.* 2012).

Animal feed comprises the largest share in Canada's DMC. This is consistent with countries having a high number of livestock head resulting in the production of animal feed and land for animal grazing. Ireland and Denmark, part of EU-15, also have a high share of animal feed because of their high number of livestock (Weisz et al 2006). Nonetheless, the feed efficiency of livestock, as well as the conversion of animal feed to secondary products such as meat, dairy, eggs, etc., has improved over time. The livestock conversion efficiency of Canada has been on average 9%, higher than the global average (3.2%), Western Europe (7.2%) and similar to that of Eastern Europe (9.2%) (Krausmann *et al.* 2008).

Other than animal feed, primary crops and forestry products also have a high share in both DE and DMC for Canada, together contributing to 47% of DE and 33% of DMC. However, the crop yields of Canada are less than the average for the EU-15 (Wiesz *et al.* 2006), likely because of climate differences, but have been improving in the past decade. Although fertilizer usage has increased it is still less than countries like Sweden and Finland that have similar crop yields to that of Canada (FAO 2017). Thus, Canada's biomass profile resonates with an industrial society, with efficiency gains in livestock conversion and yields when compared to other industrialized countries with a similar DE/capita and DMC/capita. The DE/DMC of Canada is greater than 1, indicating Canada's self-sufficiency for biomass. However, Canada still needs to import fruit and vegetables that make up 40% of total imports and are increasing year on year. A drop in the value of the Canadian dollar can increase the cost of fruits and vegetables (mostly imports). Areas like Nunavut, where the prices of fruit and vegetables are already higher than the Canadian average (Nunavut Bureau of Statistics 2016) is particularly vulnerable to price changes that can impact the daily intake of fresh fruit and vegetables for their communities.

Domestic energy consumption (DEC) in Canada showed similar growth rates to those in the United States, growing at 0.05–0.06% a year and at a similar average per-capita value of 445GJ/capita/year. However, the growth rate is twice that of the EU-15 for the same period (Haberl *et al.* 2006). At the same time, the share of non-renewable energy as a percentage of the DEC of Canada has been increasing, renewable energy consumption has slightly increased, and the average percentage of food and feed as a share of DEC has decreased, showing the pattern of an industrialized society shifting from solar based biomass to non-renewable energy sources (Haberl *et al.* 2006).

Fifty-four percent of the DE of energy for Canada is exported, but Canada still imports 29% of the energy locally consumed due to refinery economics (NRCAN 2013). This situation is particularly unique as the energy profile of Canada is similar to that of the United States and the EU-15 with respect to DEC and imports (Haberl *et al.* 2006) and similar to the Russian Federation with respect to exports and PTB (Krausmann *et al.* 2016). Canada meets its high demand of DEC from DE and imports, but exports of energy have been increasing, contributing 25% to total Canadian exports. The energy sector accounted for 10% of the total GDP for Canada in 2011 (NRCAN 2013) and largely consists of non-renewable fossil fuels. Furthermore, Canada has a high share of renewable energy consumption in DEC when compared to the United States and the EU-15, who, even though they are decreasing their share of fossil-fuel consumption are relying more on nuclear energy, a non-renewable resource, as a clean fuel (Haberl *et al.* 2006). However, the share of non-renewable fossil fuels as part of Canada's DEC is increasing each year and, given Canada's commitment to reduce its greenhouse gas (GHG) emissions to 523 MT by 2030, there is now a clear need for a transition to more sustainable energy sources in Canada.

13.5.3 Scope for a sustainability transition in the socio-economic metabolism of Canada

A sustainability transition is defined as a long-term transformation process through which a socio-economic system turns to a more sustainable means of production and consumption of materials (Markard, Raven, and Truffer 2012). The success of such a transition depends on the demographic, political, economic and social variables (Fischer-Kowalski 2011). Though it is beyond the scope of this study to analyze the factors behind transitions happening in the socio-economic system, the analysis of the metabolic profile suggests that Canada requires a sustainability transition with regard to energy.

Canada has committed itself to support the implementation of the United Nations' Sustainable Development Goals (SDGs). Three of the aims of the SDGs are to increase the percentage of global renewable energy, promote sustainable agriculture and take climate action. Canada has a high share of fossil-fuel energy in both its DE and DEC, which has an adverse effect on Canada's commitment to reduce GHG emissions. This also affects Canada's role in implementing the sustainable development goals of increasing renewable energy use and taking climate action, which therefore requires policy and technological interventions. Furthermore, the livestock conversion efficiency and high consumption of meat in the daily diets of Canadians suggests that there should also be efforts made for a sustainability transition in the biomass sector.

13.5.3.1 Transition towards a low carbon economy

A transition to a low carbon economy requires different policy and technological interventions in various economic and social sectors (Potvin 2017). However, in this study, the focus is only on GHG emissions from oil and gas, transportation and the building sector, i.e., the top three economic sectors in terms of their contributions to GHG emissions in 2015 and the possible transition of these sectors towards a low carbon economy (Toseef 2018).

The oil and gas sector is the largest source of GHG emissions in Canada (Government of Canada 2017). The major emissions from this sector have been from an increase in crude oil production mainly from new oil sands development. This increase in production has been due to high exports of crude oil and natural gas from Canada. The exports of fossils fuels have increased by about 10% every year from 1990 to 2011, twice the growth rate of other key trade commodities, which grew by about 5% (Statcan 2012). Given the considerable contribution of the carbon intensive oil and gas sector towards the overall GDP of Canada, a transition towards a low carbon economy may result in unemployment and a reduction in export revenues. To decouple oil production from economic growth and avoid negative impacts, policy interventions are required. Such interventions could incorporate multi-skill re-training of workers from the oil and gas sector. For example, a transition to a renewable energy infrastructure will require skilled workers and oil and gas manpower might be trained for such roles (Potvin *et al.* 2017). Other opportunities include transitioning to green building construction, providing financial services, green tourism and the development of new advanced technologies – such as nano-technology – to replace the loss of GDP from fossil fuels (Alberta Government 2016).

Transportation is the second largest sector responsible for GHG emissions in Canada. Major components for GHG emissions from this sector are passenger cars, passenger light trucks and freight vehicles (Government of Canada 2017). A shift towards low carbon transportation can be brought about by the increased usage of electric and plug-in hybrid vehicles (McKinsey 2012), and decarbonising local transit through the use of electric trains and autonomous cars (Schoitsch 2016). To move towards low carbon freight transportation, actions such as moving to hybrid-electric trucks for long-range distances, reserved truck lanes to reduce congestion for freight, and using right-sized vehicles for deliveries are required (Potvin *et al.* 2017). More use of electric trains for freight movements within the country is also potentially useful in reducing freight transportation emissions, as trains have been shown to be more energy efficient than trucks over their whole life cycle (Nahlik *et al.* 2015).

The third largest sector contributing towards GHG emissions in Canada is buildings. This sector includes both residential and commercial buildings that rely on natural gas for heating and electricity for power needs. While

80% of electricity in Canada is generated by non-carbon fuel (Government of Canada 2017), natural gas is mainly used for heating purposes. To reduce GHG emissions in this sector, greater energy efficiency and innovative renewable energy solutions are required. These may include reusing waste heat, developing carbon neutral building codes and renovating current buildings in line with these (Sandberg *et al.* 2016), and replacing natural gas (for heating purposes) with renewable fuels such as solar heaters, waste heat from sewage, geo-thermal, etc. (Pond *et al.* 2011). A new concept of net-zero energy housing is emerging in Canada, where such buildings are constructed with reduced energy requirements, on-site renewable energy systems and operated efficiently (CMHC 2018). All of these technological and policy changes can help to pave the way towards a low carbon economy for Canada and assist the country in achieving its goal of shifting to renewable energy and reducing GHG emissions, while maintaining jobs and GDP growth.

13.5.3.2 Transition to sustainable agriculture

When considering Canada's biomass material flows, the share of animal feed and animal products dominates the overall biomass metabolism (35% of DE and 47% of DMC). The average annual meat and dairy production in Canada is 12.2 Mt, of which 2.2 Mt is exported and 1.17 Mt is imported. The Canadian food balance data of 2011 also suggests a high share of animal products in the national diet, accounting for 34% in weight and 25% in nutritional energy (FAO 2017). From a sustainability perspective this is problematic, since the conversion of feed and fodder to secondary animal products such as meat, poultry and milk is highly inefficient (Krausmann *et al.* 2008). According to calculations for Canada during the study period, the conversion efficiency from feed and fodder to animal and dairy products is, on average, just 9%. However, the trends in the consumption of animal products per capita show a modest decline, from 35% to 34% in weight and 28% to 25% in energy supply during the study period (FAO 2017). This may be due to a combination of several factors, from health considerations to the increasing costs of animal and dairy products.

Along with the decreasing efficiency of the biomass food system, livestock systems account for 60% of the total direct GHG emissions by the agricultural sector, which in turn contribute 6% of total GHG emissions in Canada (Frenette, Bahn and Vaillancourt 2017). To improve the material intensity of food supply (Haas *et al.* 2005) and reduce GHG emissions from the agricultural sector, it is important to change dietary patterns and transition towards a smaller share for animal products in daily food uptake. Although direct animal GHG emissions may only be 3.6% of total Canadian emissions, on a life-cycle basis, the energy used to process, transport, store and prepare animal products was shown to contribute up to 65% of all GHG emissions in Ontario's dietary patterns (Veeramani *et al.* 2017). Of course, Canada has a cold climate and much of its land is not suitable for arable farming and so is used for grazing animals. Nonetheless, there could be a reduction in some types of farm animals (e.g., pigs or cattle that are not grass-fed) based on optimizing resource use (land, water, etc.) and adapting to local conditions and ecosystems. However, this sort of major transition from animal to plant food requires further research and understanding of the tradeoffs associated with it.

13.6 Discussion and conclusion

The aim of this study has been to understand socio-economic metabolism of Canada with respect to energy flows, as well as to provide insight into a potential sustainability transition in the energy sector. It has provided an analysis of the energy flows of Canada in the period from 1990 to 2011 consistent with MFA and EFA methodologies. In summarizing the socio-economic metabolism analysis of this study, Canada is a net exporter of energy and holds a strong global position in energy supply. When we consider the domestic extraction and consumption of these energy flows, Canada's metabolism is consistent with an industrial metabolism. Canada is a self-sufficient country with regard to energy flows. This study has also reflected the fact that the Canadian economy is highly dependent on the export of energy resources and receives large revenues as part of its total trade merchandise. Energy resources are extracted for both domestic and trade purposes. However, this reliance on energy production also highlights that Canada needs to exert a lot of effort into protecting the environment. As McArthur and Rasmussen (2017) have explained, despite the fact that Canada is a very advanced economy, its domestic trajectories with respect to the SDG targets show that Canada is not fully prepared to achieve the vast majority of targets by 2030. This research has endeavored to provide insights into the current energy structure of Canada with the aim of suggesting policies on a national and global scale with the potential for creating a sustainability transition in the energy sector. It has also provided inputs into a unique way of viewing the socio-economic system of Canada with respect to natural resources.

Note

1 The number of member countries in the European Union prior to the accession of ten candidate countries on 1 May 2004.

References

Alberta Government (2016). Highlights of the Alberta Economy: Alberta Economic Development and Trade, https://open.alberta.ca/dataset/10989a51-f3c2-4dcb-ac0f-f07ad88f9b3b/resource/a4037953-4c78-4550-b71f-cde59f7f1422/download/

6864680-2014-07-highlights-alberta-economy-presentation.pdf, July 2017: 33. Retrieved September 7, 2019.

Ayres, R.U. & Kneese, A.V. (1969). Production, Consumption and Externalities. *American Economic Review 59*(3), 282–297.

Ayres, R.U. & Simonis, U.E. (1994). Industrial Metabolism: Restructuring for Sustainable Development. Tokyo, New York, Paris: United Nations University Press.

Baynes, T.M. & Müller, D.B. (2016) A socio-economic metabolism approach to sustainable development and climate change mitigation. In: Clift, R. & Druckman, A. (Eds.), Taking Stock of Industrial Ecology. Cham: Springer, pp. 117–135. https://doi.org/10.1007/978-3-319-20571-7_6

CMHC (2018). Net-Zero Energy Housing. Retrieved from CANADA MORTGAGE AND HOUSING CORPORATION: www.cmhc-schl.gc.ca/en/co/grho/grho_020.cfm

Desai, R.M., Koto, H., Kharas, H., & McArthur, J.W (2018), Innovations in Implementing the Sustainable Development Goals: From Summit to Solutions. Washington, DC: The Brookings Institution.

Eurostat (2013). Economy-Wide Material Flow Accounts (EW-MFA). Compilation Guide 2013. Luxemborge: Eurostat.

Eurostat (2001a). Economy-Wide Material Flow Accounts and Derived Indicators: A Methodological Guide. Luxembourg: Eurostat, European Commission.

Eurostat (2009). Material Flow Data (MFA Data Collection 2007). Luxemburg: Eurostat.

FAO (2017). FAOSTAT. Retrieved from www.fao.org/faostat/en/#data

FAOSTAT (2010). Feeding the World Part 3. Retrieved from www.fao.org/docrep/018/i3107e/i3107e03.pdf

Fischer-Kowalski, M. & Haberl, H. (1998). Sustainable Development: Socio-Economic Metabolism and Colonization of Nature. Oxford: Blackwell Publishers.

Fischer-Kowalski, M. & Weisz, H. (1999). Society as hybrid between material and symbolic realms: Towards a theoretical framework of society-nature interaction. *Advances in Human Ecology 8*, 215–251.

Fischer-Kowalski, M. & Weisz, H. (2016). The archipelago of social ecology and the island of the Vienna school. In: Haberl, H. *et al.* (Eds.), Social Ecology: Society-Nature Relations Across Time and Space. Vienna: Springer, pp. 3–28.

Fischer-Kowalski, M. (1998). Society's metabolism the intellectual history of materials flow, Part I. *Journal of Industrial Ecology 2*(1), 61–78.

Fischer-Kowalski, M. (2011). Analyzing sustainability transitions as a shift between socio-metabolic regimes. *Environmental Innovation and Societal Transitions 1*(1), 152–159.

Fischer-Kowalski, M., Krausmann, F., Giljum, S., Lutter, S., Mayer, A., Bringezu, S., Moriguchi, Y., Sch¨utz, H., Schandl, H., & Weisz, H. (2011). Methodology and indicators of economy-wide material flow accounting. *Journal of Industrial Ecology 15*(6), 855–876.

Frenette, E., Bahn, O., & Vaillancourt, K. (2017). Meat, dairy and climate change: assessing the long-term mitigation potential of alternative agri-food consumption patterns in Canada. *Environ Model Assess 22*(1), 1–16.

Gierlinger, S. & Krausmann, F. (2012). The physical economy of the United States of America: Extraction, trade, and consumption of materials from 1870 to 2005. *Journal of Industrial Ecology 16*(3), 365–377.

Giljum, S., Dittrich, M., Lieber, M., & Lutter, S. (2014). Global patterns of material flows and their socio-economic and environmental implications: A MFA study on all countries world-wide from 1980 to 2009. *Resources 3*(1), 319–339.

Government of Canada (2017). Greenhouse Gas Emissions by Canadian Economic Sector. Retrieved from Government of Canada: www.canada.ca/en/environment-climate-change/services/environmental-indicators/greenhouse-gas-emissions/canadian-economic-sector.html

Haberl, H. & Geissler, S. (2000). Cascade utilization of biomass: How to cope with ecological limits to biomass use. *Ecological Engineering 16*(supplement), S111–S121.

Haberl, H. (2001). The energetic metabolism of societies Part II: Empirical examples. *Journal of Industrial Ecology* 5(2), 71–88.

Haberl, H. (2001a). The energetic metabolism of societies Part I: Accounting concepts. *Journal of Industrial Ecology* 5(1), 11–33.

Haberl, H., Fischer-Kowalski, M., Krausmann, F., Weisz, H., & Winiwarter, V. (2004). Progress towards sustainability? What the conceptual framework of material and energy flow accounting (MEFA) can offer. *Land Use Policy 21*(3), 199–213.

Haberl, H., Weisz, H., Amann, C., Bondeau, A., Eisenmenger, N., Erb, K.-H., Fischer-Kowalski, M., & Krausmann, F. (2006). The energetic metabolism of the European Union and the United States Decadal Energy Input Time-Series with an emphasis on biomass. *Journal of Industrial Ecology 10*(4), 151–171.

Haas, A. L, Laun, N. P and Begley, T. P. (2005) Thi20, a remarkable enzyme from Saccharomyces cerevisiae with dual thiamin biosynthetic and degradation activities. *Bioorg Chem* 33(4):338-44.

IEA (2017). International Energy Agency: Countries. Retrieved from International Energy Agency: www.iea.org/countries/

Krausmann, F., Weisz, H., Eisenmenger, N., Schütz, H., Haas, W., & Schaffartzik, A. (2015). Economy-Wide Material Flow Accounting Introduction and Guide Version 1.0, Social Ecology Working Paper 151. Vienna: Institute of Social Ecology.

Krausmann, F., Gaugl, B., West, J., & Schandl, H. (2016). The metabolic transition of a planned economy: Material flows in the USSR and the Russian Federation 1900 to 2010. *Ecolgical Economics 124*, 76–85.

Krausmann, F., Gingrich, S., Eisenmenger, N., Erb, K.-H., Haberl, H., & Fischer-Kowalski, M. (2009). Growth in global materials use. GDP and population during the 20th century. *Ecological Economics 68*(10), 2696–2705.

Krausmann, F., Erb, K.-H., Gingrich, S., Lauk, C., & Haberl, H. (2008). Global patterns of socioeconomic biomass flows in the year 2000: A comprehensive assessment of supply, consumption and constraints. *Ecological Economics 65*(3), 471–487.

Kuskovaa, P., Gingrich, S., & Krausmann, F. (2008). Long-term changes in social metabolism and land use in Czechoslovakia, 1830–2000: An energy transition under changing political regimes. *Ecological Economics 68*(1-2), 394–407.

Markard, J., Raven, R., & Truffer, B. (2012). Sustainability transitions: An emerging field of research and its prospects. *Research Policy 41*(6), 955–967.

Marx, K. A. (1867). Capital: A Critique of Political Economy (Volume I), The Process of Production of Capital (English edition first published in 1887 with some modernization of spelling). Moscow, USSR: Progress Publishers.

Matthews, E., Amann, C., Fischer-Kowalski, M., Bringezu, S., H¨uttler, W., Kleijn, R., Moriguchi, Y., *et al.* (2000). The Weight of Nations: Material Outflows from Industrial Economies. Washington, DC: World Resource Institute.

McArthur, J.W. & Rasmussen, K. (2017). Who and What Is Getting Left Behind? Canada's Domestic Status on the Sustainable Development Goals, Working Paper 108. October Brookings Global Economy and Development, Massachusetts Avenue, NW, Washington, DC, USA.

McKinsey & Company (2012). Opportunities for Canadian Energy. An analysis commissioned by Natural Resources Canada.

Nahlik, M.E. (2015). Goods Movement life cycle assessment for greenhouse gas reduction goals. *Journal of Industrial Ecology 20*(2), 317–328.

Nishioka, Y., Yanagisawa, Y., & Spengler, J.D. (2000). Saving energy versus saving materials. *Journal of Industrial Ecology 4*(1), 119–135.

NRCAN (2013). Energy Efficiency Trends in Canada 1990 to 2013. Retrieved from Natural Resources Canada: www.nrcan.gc.ca/energy/publications/19030

Nunavut Bureau of Statistics (2016). Nunavut Food Price Survey. Retrieved from Nunavut Bureau of Statistics: www.stats.gov.nu.ca/Publications/Historical/Prices/Food%20Price%20Survey%20StatsUpdate,%202016.pdf.

Oras, K. & Grüner, E. (2010). Economy Wide Material Flow Account. Estonia: Statistics Estonia.

Pond, E., Cavens, D., Miller, N., & Sheppard, S. (2011). The Retrofit Challenge: Re-thinking Existing Residential Neighbourhoods for Deep Greenhouse Gas Reductions. Collaborative for Advanced Landscape Planning, University of British Columbia, Canada.

Potvin, C.B. Burch, S. Layzell, D. Meadowcroft, J. Mousseau, N. Dale, A. Henriques, I. S. Margolis, Li. Matthews, H. D. Paquin, D. Ramos, H. Sharma, D. Sheppard, S. and Slawinski, N. (2017). Re-Energizing Canada: Pathways to a Low-Carbon Future. Sustainable Canada Dialogues, UNESCO.

Purves, W.K. (1992). The Science of Biology. Sunderland, MA: Sinauer Associates.

Raupova, O., Kamahara, H., & Goto, N. (2014). Assessment of physical economy through economy-wide material flow analysis in developing Uzbekistan. *Resources, Conservation and Recycling 89*(August), 76–85.

Sandberg, N.H. Heidrich, O. Dawson, R. J. Dascalaki, E. Dimitriou, S. Faidra, F. Stegnar, G. Zavrl, M. S. Brattebø, H. Sartori, I. and Vimmr, T. (2016). Dynamic building stock modelling: Application to 11 European countries to support the energy efficiency and retrofit ambitions of the EU. *Energy and Buildings 132*(January), 26–38.

Schaffartzik, A., Mayer, A., Gingrich, S., Eisenmenger, N., Loy, C., & Krausmann, F. (2014). The global metabolic transition: Regional patterns and trends of global material flows, 1950–2010. *Global Environmental Change 26*(May), 87–97.

Schandl, H. & Schulz, N. (2002). Changes in the United Kingdom's natural relations in terms of society's metabolism and land-use from 1850 to the present day. *Ecological Economics 41*(2), 203–221.

Schandl, H., Hobbes, M., & Kleijn, R. (Eds.) (2006). Local Material Flow Analysis in Social Context in Tat Hamlet, Northern Mountain Region, Vietnam, Social Ecology Working Paper 90, Institute of Social Ecology, IFF - Faculty for Interdisciplinary Studies, (Klagenfurt, Graz, Vienna), Klagenfurt University, Schottenfeldgasse Vienna.

Schoitsch, E. (2016). Autonomous Vehicles and Automated Driving Status, Perspectives and Societal Impact. *IDIMT 2016 Proceedings.* www.idimt.org/sites/default/files/IDIMT_proceedings_2016.pdf, *Trauner Verlag, Schriftenreihe Informatik 45, 2016, p. 405–423.*

Singh, S, J., Krausmann, F., Gingrich, S., Haberl, H., Erb, K.-H., & Lanz, P. (2012). India's biophysical economy, 1961–2008. Sustainability in a national and global context. *Ecological Economics 76*(April), 60–69.

Singh, S.J., Ringhofer, L., Haas, W., Krausmann, F., & Fischer-Kowalski, M. (2010). Local Studies Manual - A Researcher's Guide for Investigating the Social Metabolism of Local Rural Systems. VIenna: Social Ecology Working Paper 120, Institute of Social Ecology, IFF - Faculty for Interdisciplinary Studies (Klagenfurt, Graz, Vienna), Klagenfurt University Schottenfeldgasse, Vienna. Available from: www.researchgate.net/publication/28967415l_Local_Studies_Manual_A_researcher's_guide_for_investigating_the_social_metabolism_of_rural_systems [accessed Aug 21 2020].

Statcan (2007). *Stat Can.* Retrieved from CYB Overview 2007: www.statcan.gc.ca/pub/11-402-x/2007/1741/ceb1741_000-eng.htm

Statcan (2012). Manufacturing and Energy Division, Marketing and Dissemination Section, Management Division. Ottawa: Statistics Canada.

Toseef, A. (2018) Socio-economic Metabolism of Canada: A case study of Biomass and Energy flows from 1990 to 2011, presented to the University of Waterloo in fulfillment of the thesis requirement for the degree of Master of Environmental Studies in Sustainability Management, Waterloo, Ontario, Canada.

Veeramani, A., Dias, G., & Kirkpatrick, S. (2017). Carbon footprint of dietary patterns in Ontario, Canada: A case study based on actual food consumption. *Journal of Cleaner Production 162*(8),1398–1406.

Weisz, H., Krausmann, F., Amann, C., Eisenmenger, N., Erb, K.-H., Hubacek, K., & Fischer-Kowalski, M. (2006). The physical economy of the European Union: Cross-country comparison and determinants of material consumption. *Ecological Economics 58*(4), 676–698.

Weisz, H., Fischer-Kowalski, M., Grunbuhel, C.M., Haberl, H., Krausmann, F., & Winiwarter, V. (2001). Global environmental change and historical transitions. *Innovation 14*(2), 117–142.

14

ENVIRONMENTAL QUALITY AND HAPPINESS

A perspective of developed and developing countries

Muhammad Tariq Majeed

14.1 Introduction

The discontents from economic outcomes are mounting among environmentalists, academics and policy circles because increasing economic development and growth did not ensure human well-being and happiness across countries. As a result, the literature on happiness has attracted considerable attention in recent decades. Conceptually, happiness is traceable back to Aristippus's Hedonic view and Aristotle's views, who consider happiness as the fundamental purpose and intent of human existence.

Environmental quality has a distinctive association with psychological happiness (Wilson 1984). Does environmental quality matter equally for developed and developing countries? The answer to this question is not conclusive. Some researchers claim that the citizens of developed nations are more concerned about the environment than developing nations (Inglehart 1995; Bruneau and Echevarria 2009; Majeed 2018). Such differences are explainable from Maslow's (1954) hierarchy of needs theory. According to Inglehart's (1995) post-materialism hypothesis, economic struggles prioritize other concerns for people in developing nations, apart from environmental degradation, endanger human health and life. Besides, some scholars contend that ecological quality is a "luxury good" (Baumol and Oates 1979), implying that the poor are "too poor to green" (Bruneau and Echevarria 2009).

Nevertheless, some researchers discard the claim that environmental concerns are more significant in high-income countries than low-income countries (Broad 1994; Stern 2004; Fairbrother 2012, Sulemana *et al.* 2016). Dunlap and Mertig (1994) highlight that environmental quality has become a global issue and is not just limited to developed countries. Diekmann and Franzen (1999) show that whereas citizens of low-income countries do not rank environmental issues as among the most serious issues, pro-environmental problems are usually ranked high depending upon certain problems' seriousness such as water pollution. Since environmental priorities are linked with human well-being, it is vital to analyze the environment link with happiness in a comparative setting of developed and developing economies.

Pioneering studies (e.g., Easterlin 1974; Scitovsky 1976; Hirsch 1976) analyzed happiness determinants. The early research considered income as the primary source of happiness. However, the empirical evidence suggested that income causes an insignificant or minor effect on well-being and happiness. Income alone cannot ensure improved humankind's welfare (Easterlin 1974; Tukker *et al.* 2008). Attaining more considerable happiness requires to construct such economic modeling, which can guarantee human well-being and happiness.

Income is not enough to explain cross-country variations in happiness. Research identifies many non-income factors that explain happiness. The quality of the environment is a fundamental cause of happiness. The environment impacts people's psychology and, therefore, its relationship with happiness is intrinsic (Kellert and Wilson 1983). An individual living in an environment surrounded by green and natural scenes tends to be happier than an individual living in poor quality and grim environments.

To explore the relationship of the environment with health, Ulrich (1984) empirically examines the recovery rate of patients in the context of Pennsylvania. Using longitudinal data (1972–1982), his findings suggested that the patients with green views outside the windows of their rooms recovered much faster than having brick walls in their rooms. Besides, they used fewer medicines because they got a direct cure from nature. Furthermore, findings of a research report suggest that pretty sights enhance workers' productivity and improve their health status (California Energy Commission 2003). These findings underscore the need of nature in ensuring happiness.

The research on happiness is primarily concerned with the degrading quality of the natural environment. The literature has a consensus that degrading the environment poses a severe threat to health, happiness and life (McMichael 2003; Tiwari 2011; Majeed 2018). World Health Organization (2016) states that from 2030 to 2050, climate change is likely to cause 250,000 added deaths per year, from malaria, malnutrition, diarrhea and heat stress. According to the World Health Organization (2016), air pollution caused seven million deaths.

The quality of the environment is deteriorating with the increasing amount of greenhouse gases in the atmosphere. These gasses are considered responsible for lower-level human well-being and happiness. The research on the environment has mostly focused on economic, social and health losses. The relationship between greenhouse gases (GHG) and happiness has received little attention.

The extant literature on environment and happiness is limited in its scope. It is specific to country-specific studies or uses CO_2 emissions as the indicator of environmental degradation, or econometric evidence lacks valid estimators. For example, Lenzen and Cummins (2013) provide just survey-based evidence to explore the effect of carbon emissions on Australia's subjective well-being. Tiwari (2011) solely focused on a group of 20 countries to analyze environmental and happiness nexus. De Ribeiro Fiuza and Lele (2013) applied simple ordinary least squares (OLS) to determine the effect of the environment on happiness.

This chapter analyses the impact of total greenhouse gases on happiness. This research is unique as it provides evidence at global level, including separate groups of developed and developing economies. This research also uses the principal component analysis (PCA) on measuring three significant sources of emissions, namely, CO_2, nitrous oxide and methane emissions.

The rest of the chapter is as follows. Section 14.2 provides a brief literature review of the related studies. The research model and its variables are described in Section 14.3, followed by the data sources and description in Section 14.4. Section 14.5 reports the empirical results and their interpretation. Section 14.6 concludes the study.

14.2 Environment and happiness: a literature survey

The pioneering study on the importance of the environment for achieving happiness was conducted by Carson (1962). Subsequently, Ulrich (1984) has provided empirical evidence on the role of nature in curing human life in the context of Pennsylvania. He showed that the patients connected with nature recovered more rapidly during the period 1972–1982 than those isolated from the natural views. Besides, the patients relatively consumed less mediation because nature served to cure their health.

A parallel stream of studies focused on economic factors to explain the differences in happiness. These studies modeled income as the key variable to explain diverse happiness levels (Easterlin 1974; Daly 1987; Veenhoven 1991; Gardner and Oswald 2001). Easterlin (1974) was the first who modeled the role of income in explaining happiness. He showed that income explains happiness within nations but not across countries using the data over 1946–1970. In literature, this observation is referred to as the "Easterlin Paradox." This finding is also supported by Daly (1987), who also validated the minor role of income in securing happiness. In contrast, some later studies failed to confirm Easterlin claim that income does not buy happiness (Veenhoven 1991; Gardner and Oswald 2001).

In recent years, empirical studies provide evidence of environmental quality and life satisfaction. Welsch (2003) found out the negative effects of air pollution on well-being using the data of 10 European countries from 1990 to 1997. The quality of air is measured by using nitrogen dioxide and lead pollutant levels. Brereton *et al.* (2006) found evidence of the negative effects of noise pollution on happiness. They showed that people residing near to coast report high satisfaction levels than people living to near big transport points.

Similarly, Ferrer-i-Carbonell and Gowdy (2007) confirmed the negative impact of environmental degradation on subjective well-being using the data from the "British Household Panel Survey." Recently, using the panel of 21 countries from 1970 to 2005, Tiwari (2011) also reported favorable effects on the well-being of policies that care for the environment. Using panel data for Germany from 1984 to 2012, Binder and Blankenberg (2016) provided evidence that environmental concerns have positive effects on the tendency to volunteer work, increasing individuals' well-being.

The available studies highlighted the importance of the environment for happiness, but these studies' evidence is limited in terms of period, sample size and methodology. For example, De Ribeiro Fiuza and Lele (2013) estimated CO_2 emissions on happiness using OLS. This study's results compromise the OLS reliability as the model suffers from the problems of heteroskedasticity and endogeneity.

14.3 Methodology

This study follows the pioneering work of Easterlin (1974, 1995), who modeled income as a source of happiness and concluded that income alone is not enough to buy happiness. The present study models economic and non-economic factors to explain happiness levels of developed and developing economies. The study's model is as follows:

$$\mathrm{HP}_{i,t} = \beta_0 + \beta_1 G_{i,t} + \beta_2 \log \mathrm{GDP}_{it} + \beta_3 \mathrm{Un}_{it} + \beta_4 \mathrm{Urb}_{it} + \beta_5 \mathrm{Age}_{i,t} + \mu_{i,t}$$

Borrowing from Easterlin's pioneering work (1974, 1995), this study uses the subscripts i,t, which represent cross-sectional units and study time, respectively. $\mathrm{HP}_{i,t}$ represents happiness, $G_{i,t}$ denotes total greenhouse gases, GDP_{it} represents GDP per capita at constant prices, Un_{it} indicate unemployment level, Urb_{it} indicates urban population, $\mathrm{Age}_{i,t}$ refers to the population 65 years and above and finally $\mu_{i,t}$ shows an error term. The indicator of GDP, unemployment, urban population and age represent socioeconomic and demographic controls. To assess the robustness of results, the study constructed another measure of environmental quality by using PCA of carbon, nitrous and methane emissions. Equation (14.2) incorporates this measure of PCA.

$$\mathrm{HP}_{i,t} = \beta_0 + \beta_1 \mathrm{GPCA}_{i,t} + \beta_2 \log \mathrm{GDP}_{it} + \beta_3 \mathrm{Un}_{it} + \beta_4 \mathrm{Urb}_{it} + \beta_5 \mathrm{Age}_{i,t} + \mu_{i,t}$$

Table 14.1 Descriptive statistics

Variables	*Obs.*	*Mean*	*Std. Dev.*	*Min*	*Max*
		Global Sample			
Happiness	95	4.124506	.826334	2.7875	7.22
Income	95	9.137377	1.081568	6.472439	11.0018
Un	95	8.689912	5.406004	.6	32.67083
Urban	95	60.45304	21.74013	9.587139	100
Age	95	8.953943	4.88349	2.375252	17.63407
GHG	95	11.32666	1.634317	7.735046	15.6708
		Developed Countries			
Happiness	42	3.975849	.5144091	2.7875	5.255714
Income	42	10.09539	.3930371	9.326535	11.0018
Un	42	8.067361	3.334499	3.2375	17.3625
Urban	42	74.90086	16.24762	9.587139	100
Age	42	13.13413	3.144047	2.810107	17.63407
GHG	42	11.3598	1.649548	7.735046	15.6708
		Developing Countries			
Happiness	53	4.242309	.9968496	2.88	7.22
Income	53	8.378193	.8149082	6.472439	9.571973
Un	53	9.183255	6.59558	.6	32.67083
Urban	53	49.00383	18.54806	11.88342	85.96028
Age	53	5.641338	3.165241	2.375252	15.44205
GHG	53	11.3004	1.637477	8.288012	15.45403

14.3.1 Data and variables description

The selected data was form developed and developing countries. However, the data for happiness is missing for many countries. After screening, the sample includes 42 developed and 53 developing countries. The study covers the time from 1980 to 2015. The data for happiness is derived from the World Database of Happiness (2016). Tables 14.1 and 14.2 present the descriptive statistics and correlation matrix for the data used. Tables 14.A1–14.A3 provide the detailed description of the data used for the analysis in the appendix.

Figure 14.1 displays average happiness over the study period for developed and developing countries. The figure shows that the developing countries are experiencing higher levels of happiness as compared to developed countries. Figure 14.2 displays the regional classification of average happiness over the study period. The region of Europe and Central Asia (ECA) is experiencing the highest happiness level whereas the region of Latin American (LA) countries is experiencing the lowest level of happiness.

Table 14.2 Correlation matrix

	Happiness	*Income*	*Un*	*Urban*	*Age*	*GHG*
			Global Sample			
Happiness	1.0000					
Income	0.1205	1.0000				
Un	–0.0789	–0.0748	1.0000			
Urban	0.0110	0.7860	0.0479	1.0000		
Age	–0.0092	0.6663	–0.0430	0.5323	1.0000	
GHG	–0.0580	0.2056	–0.2084	0.0894	0.0849	1.0000
			Developed Countries			
Happiness	1.0000					
Income	0.2999	1.0000				
Un	–0.1460	–0.5216	1.0000			
Urban	0.0399	0.2723	–0.1808	1.0000		
Age	0.0243	0.2418	–0.0236	–0.0167	1.0000	
GHG	–0.0515	0.2775	–0.1003	0.0168	0.2390	1.0000
			Developing Countries			
Happiness	1.0000					
Income	0.0026	1.0000				
Un	–0.0326	0.2557	1.0000			
Urban	–0.0857	0.8190	0.3010	1.0000		
Age	–0.1673	0.2697	0.1584	0.3393	1.0000	
GHG	–0.0646	0.3373	–0.2674	0.1556	0.0369	1.0000

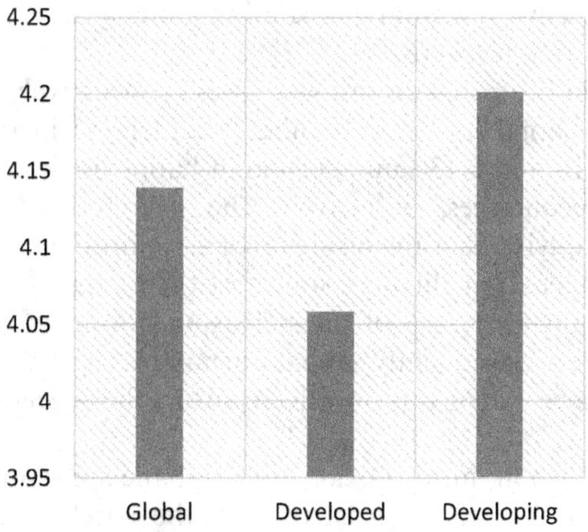

Figure 14.1 Global happiness.

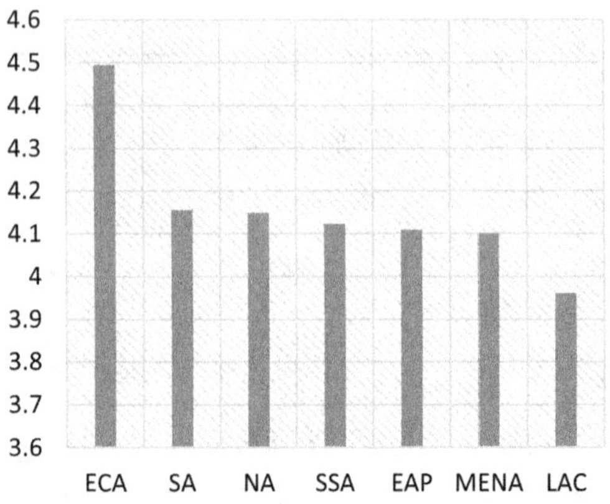

Figure 14.2 Regional happiness.

14.4 Empirical analysis and results

The empirical results are obtained using two greenhouse gas measures, i.e., first, total greenhouse gases in the atmosphere, and second, the measure by using PCA of carbon, nitrous oxide and methane emissions. Initially, global sample results are estimated, and then results for developed and developing economies are assessed. Different panel estimators are applied to maintain robustness and consistency in our results.

Table 14.3 reports pooled ordinary least squares (POLS) results. Columns 1–3 present results using total greenhouse gas emissions to measure environmental degradation for global, developed and developing countries, respectively. Columns 4–6 report the results using PCA of different greenhouse gases to measure environmental degradation globally and for developed and developing countries, respectively.

Columns 1–3 indicate that greenhouse gases are negatively and significantly associated with happiness. In particular, 1% increase in greenhouse gases leads to 0.13, 0.16 and 0.13 units decline in happiness in global, developed and developing economies, respectively. The magnitude of developed economies is high, implying that the residents of developed economies give more value to environmental quality as a source of their happiness. Environmental quality is worsening as a result of the increasing amount of greenhouse gases in the atmosphere. Consequently, global warming is negatively influencing the ecosystem's balance. All of this negatively affects the psychological health of humans.

The index of carbon, nitrous oxide and methane are reported in Columns 4–6. These results are also consistent with the baseline findings. That is, carbon, nitrous oxide and methane are significantly lowing global happiness. Notably, 1% increase in the index of greenhouse gases leads to 0.25, 0.34 and

Table 14.3 Pooled OLS regression results

Variables	*(1)*	*(2)*	*(3)*	*(4)*	*(5)*	*(6)*
	Global	*Developed*	*Developing*	*Global*	*Developed*	*Developing*
Income	0.723***	1.402***	0.665***	0.653***	1.347***	0.633***
	(0.0999)	(0.215)	(0.174)	(0.0989)	(0.220)	(0.174)
Un	–0.0211**	0.0110	–0.0120	–0.0199**	0.0260	–0.0136
	(0.00967)	(0.0238)	(0.0118)	(0.00987)	(0.0263)	(0.0125)
Urban	–0.0192***	–0.00730	–0.0230***	–0.0182***	–0.00404	–0.0232***
	(0.00447)	(0.00613)	(0.00712)	(0.00452)	(0.00635)	(0.00725)
Age	–0.0619***	–0.0197	–0.0725***	–0.0592***	–0.0213	–0.0725***
	(0.0153)	(0.0291)	(0.0212)	(0.0154)	(0.0298)	(0.0215)
GHG	–0.131***	–0.160***	–0.133***			
	(0.0337)	(0.0529)	(0.0481)			
GHG-PCA				–0.255***	–0.347***	–0.319**
				(0.0841)	(0.133)	(0.127)
Constant	1.132	–6.997***	1.842*	0.295	–8.469***	0.811
	(0.713)	(2.065)	(1.052)	(0.667)	(2.210)	(1.104)
Observations	983	442	541	961	429	532
R-squared	0.063	0.114	0.058	0.056	0.107	0.053

Standard errors in parentheses (***p < 0.01, **p < 0.05, *p < 0.1).

0.32 units decline in happiness globally, and for developed and developing economies, respectively. These findings augment previous studies (Tiwari 2011; De Ribeiro Fiuza and Lele 2013).

The effect of income on happiness is positive and significant across all regressions and samples. The parameter estimates on income reported in Columns 1–3 imply that 1% increase in income leads to 0.72, 1.40 and 0.67 units increase in the global and developing countries' happiness levels, respectively. Relatively, this effect is more robust in developed economies. This finding differs from that of Easterlin (1974), who found out that income does not buy happiness and does not explain differences in happiness across nations. Tiwari (2011) found out a favorable effect of income in explaining happiness. The results for income reported in Columns 4–6 also suggest the same conclusion. An increase in income enhances better life prospects in terms of living standards and purchasing power (Oswald 1997; Inglehart 1995).

The effect of urbanization on happiness is negative and significant in all models. The results indicate that 1% increase in urbanization leads to 0.019, 0.0073 and 0.023 decreases in happiness globally and in developed and developing countries, respectively. Comparatively, this effect is more substantial in the case of developing economies. One percent increase in urbanization increases almost three times more happiness in the context of developing economies. In the case of developed economies, urbanization is less damaging to happiness. Urbanization in developed countries mitigates the adverse effects of urbanization on citizens' mental well-being. Urbanization lowers psychological well-being because of removing natural greenery (White *et al.* 2013). The results are consistent with Duroy (2005), who argues that people living in urban areas compromise the natural environment, which lowers their quality of life. The effect of unemployment on happiness is negative and significant in a global sample, while this effect turns insignificant in developed economies. The negative effect is consistent with the study of Clark and Oswald (1994). The positive effects in developed economies suggest that unemployment perhaps does not affect happiness as unemployment allowances and other welfare programs support the unemployed people.

Age, a demographic indicator, negatively affects happiness globally, and in developed and developing economies. The magnitudes of coefficients indicate that a one-year increase in age leads to 0.062, 0.020 and 0.073 decreases in happiness globally and in developed and developing countries. The effect is more significant in the case of developing economies. The likely reason could be a lack of old-age benefits and security systems in developing economies. People over the age of 65 years have a dismal effect on mental well-being.

By applying limited information maximum likelihood (LIML) estimator, the problem of endogeneity is resolved. LIML approach uses instrumental variables to remove the bias of endogeneity and provides efficient results. Table 14.4 reports the results with LIML estimator. The results show that 1% increase in greenhouse gases leads to 0.12, 0.16 and 0.12 units decline in

Table 14.4 LIML regression results

Variables	*(1)*	*(2)*	*(3)*	*(4)*	*(5)*	*(6)*
	Global	*Developed*	*Developing*	*Global*	*Developed*	*Developing*
Income	0.718***	1.399***	0.643***	0.636***	1.320***	0.619***
	(0.0996)	(0.214)	(0.173)	(0.0998)	(0.221)	(0.176)
Un	–0.0207**	0.0110	–0.0106	–0.0196**	0.0226	–0.0138
	(0.00965)	(0.0236)	(0.0118)	(0.00995)	(0.0263)	(0.0126)
Urban	–0.0191***	–0.00729	–0.0226***	–0.0178***	–0.00442	–0.0226***
	(0.00446)	(0.00609)	(0.00708)	(0.00454)	(0.00633)	(0.00733)
Age	–0.0616***	–0.0200	–0.0726***	–0.0574***	–0.0225	–0.0700***
	(0.0152)	(0.0289)	(0.0211)	(0.0155)	(0.0297)	(0.0216)
GHG	–0.122***	–0.157***	–0.118**			
	(0.0337)	(0.0525)	(0.0483)			
GHG-PCA				–0.245***	–0.307**	–0.331**
				(0.0850)	(0.134)	(0.129)
Constant	1.064	–7.003***	1.811*	0.416	–8.151***	0.910
	(0.711)	(2.051)	(1.047)	(0.674)	(2.226)	(1.116)
Observations	983	442	541	949	426	523
R-squared	0.063	0.114	0.058	0.054	0.104	0.050

Standard errors in parentheses (***p < 0.01, **p < 0.05, *p < 0.1).

happiness in global, developed and developing economies, respectively. The magnitude for developed economies is high, implying that the residents of developed economies give more value to environmental quality as a source of their happiness. The results are similar to the baseline results. Thus, the results are not sensitive to the problem of endogeneity.

The pooled OLS model considers all cross-sectional units as homogeneous and does not incorporate the cross-sectional heterogeneity in terms of temporal and cross-sectional unit-specific effects. The results can be biased if significant temporal and cross-sectional units' specific effects prevail in countries' selected panel. To incorporate heterogeneity across countries, the study utilized fixed-effects and random-effects models. Table 14.5 reports the results of fixed-effects model. The effect of greenhouse gases on happiness remains negative. However, its significance level drops in the case of the fixed-effects model. Table 14.6 reports the results for the random-effects model. The results remain intact.

Table 14.7 illustrates the regression results of the *Driscoll–Kraay Standard Errors* approach for pooled OLS that deals with the issue of temporal and cross-sectional dependence. The findings confirm that 1% increase in greenhouse gases results in 0.13, 0.16 and 0.13 units decline in happiness in global, developed and developing economies, respectively.

The likely presence of reverse causality between greenhouse gases and happiness creates the problem of endogeneity. The endogeneity problem is addressed by using instruments and employing the system GMM estimator. The lag of the dependent variable is used as the independent variable, and own lag variables of explanatory variables are used as instruments. The results are reported in Table 14.8. The effect of greenhouse gases on happiness remains negative and significant in all models.

14.5 Conclusion

Earlier research on happiness and quality of life focused on economic indicators to explain variations in cross-country happiness levels. The current researchers focus on non-economic indicators. In this perspective, many research studies have realized the importance of quality of environment for health, happiness and quality of life. Wilson (1984) suggests that environmental quality has a distinctive association with psychological happiness. Therefore, maintaining a good environment is essential for human well-being. However, as countries prosper, ecological quality is compromised. Climate change has negative effects on the ecosystem and human life. This study explores the environment–happiness nexus using two proxies of environmental quality: total greenhouse gases and a principal component index of carbon emissions, methane and nitrous oxide over the period 1980–2015. This research is not limited to country-specific experience or a case study.

Table 14.5 FE regression results

Variables	*(1)*	*(2)*	*(3)*	*(4)*	*(5)*	*(6)*
	Global	*Developed*	*Developing*	*Global*	*Developed*	*Developing*
Income	2.325***	4.265***	0.146	2.258***	4.141***	0.191
	(0.392)	(0.582)	(0.544)	(0.401)	(0.590)	(0.570)
Un	0.0447	–0.0123	0.140***	0.0610**	0.0198	0.140***
	(0.0280)	(0.0430)	(0.0374)	(0.0285)	(0.0434)	(0.0379)
Urban	–0.0312	–0.0353	0.00197	–0.0460	–0.0531	0.0118
	(0.0395)	(0.0772)	(0.0452)	(0.0394)	(0.0782)	(0.0463)
Age	0.306***	0.0760	0.717***	0.289***	0.0443	0.686***
	(0.101)	(0.135)	(0.165)	(0.106)	(0.136)	(0.187)
GHG	–0.804**	–1.664**	0.138			
	(0.320)	(0.658)	(0.391)			
GHG-PCA				–1.042	0.164	–0.865
				(0.859)	(1.221)	(1.276)
Constant	–8.740**	–16.68*	–4.850	–15.89***	–33.47***	–3.306
	(3.627)	(8.785)	(3.851)	(2.737)	(6.137)	(3.210)
Observations	983	442	541	961	429	532
R-squared	0.135	0.233	0.122	0.128	0.214	0.121
Number of id	95	42	53	94	41	53

Standard errors in parentheses (***p < 0.01, **p < 0.05, *p < 0.1).

Table 14.6 EE regression results

Variables	*(1)*	*(2)*	*(3)*	*(4)*	*(5)*	*(6)*
	Global	*Developed*	*Developing*	*Global*	*Developed*	*Developing*
Income	0.836***	1.402***	0.994***	0.777***	1.347***	0.982***
	(0.125)	(0.215)	(0.232)	(0.126)	(0.220)	(0.234)
Un	–0.0191	0.0110	–0.00616	–0.0163	0.0260	–0.00690
	(0.0121)	(0.0238)	(0.0170)	(0.0125)	(0.0263)	(0.0180)
Urban	–0.0235***	–0.00730	–0.0348***	–0.0230***	–0.00404	–0.0364***
	(0.00564)	(0.00613)	(0.0104)	(0.00582)	(0.00635)	(0.0107)
Age	–0.0607***	–0.0197	–0.0441	–0.0586***	–0.0213	–0.0456
	(0.0198)	(0.0291)	(0.0345)	(0.0204)	(0.0298)	(0.0355)
GHG	–0.150***	–0.160***	–0.199***			
	(0.0444)	(0.0529)	(0.0742)			
GHG-PCA				–0.270**	–0.347***	–0.446**
				(0.112)	(0.133)	(0.200)
Constant	0.615	–6.997***	0.367	–0.499	–8.469***	–1.426
	(0.901)	(2.065)	(1.451)	(0.852)	(2.210)	(1.480)
Observations	983	442	541	961	429	532
Number of id	95	42	53	94	41	53

Standard errors in parentheses (***p < 0.01, **p < 0.05, *p < 0.1).

Table 14.7 Driscoll–Kraay standard errors regression results

Variables	*(1)*	*(2)*	*(3)*	*(4)*	*(5)*	*(6)*
	Global	*Developed*	*Developing*	*Global*	*Developed*	*Developing*
Income	0.723**	1.402**	0.665*	0.653**	1.347**	0.633*
	(0.274)	(0.571)	(0.338)	(0.269)	(0.584)	(0.360)
Un	–0.0211***	0.0110	–0.0120	–0.0199***	0.0260	–0.0136
	(0.00598)	(0.0136)	(0.00803)	(0.00659)	(0.0171)	(0.00963)
Urban	–0.0192*	–0.00730	–0.0230*	–0.0182*	–0.00404	–0.0232*
	(0.0103)	(0.00738)	(0.0123)	(0.0101)	(0.00633)	(0.0129)
Age	–0.0619**	–0.0197	–0.0725***	–0.0592**	–0.0213	–0.0725***
	(0.0212)	(0.0206)	(0.0178)	(0.0222)	(0.0234)	(0.0187)
GHG	–0.131**	–0.160**	–0.133**			
	(0.0467)	(0.0668)	(0.0462)			
GHG-PCA				–0.255**	–0.347*	–0.319**
				(0.103)	(0.167)	(0.126)
Constant	1.132	–6.997	1.842	0.295	–8.469	0.811
	(1.363)	(4.074)	(1.825)	(1.324)	(4.932)	(2.026)
Observations	983	442	541	961	429	532
R-squared	0.063	0.114	0.058	0.056	0.107	0.053
Number of groups	95	42	53	94	41	53

Standard errors in parentheses (***p < 0.01, **p < 0.05, *p < 0.1).

Table 14.8 Regression results of system GMM

Variables	*(1)*	*(2)*	*(3)*	*(4)*	*(5)*	*(6)*
	Global	*Developed*	*Developing*	*Global*	*Developed*	*Developing*
Happiness$_{(t-1)}$	0.409***	0.621***	0.430***	0.563***	0.752***	0.470***
	(0.0152)	(0.0131)	(0.00743)	(0.0159)	(0.0311)	(0.00789)
Income	0.337***	0.0673***	–0.0795***	0.129***	0.248***	0.0220***
	(0.0220)	(0.0176)	(0.00728)	(0.0131)	(0.0461)	(0.00765)
Un	–0.00506***	0.00178*	0.00721***	–0.0170***	0.0522***	–0.0171***
	(0.000462)	(0.000962)	(0.000365)	(0.00193)	(0.00475)	(0.000629)
Urban	–0.00601***	0.00816***	0.00712***	–0.00135*	–0.00265*	0.00275***
	(0.00139)	(0.00133)	(0.000577)	(0.000781)	(0.00142)	(0.000516)
Age	–0.0265***	–0.000469	–0.0551***	–0.0184***	–0.0168***	–0.0396***
	(0.00314)	(0.00392)	(0.00116)	(0.00338)	(0.00588)	(0.00591)
GHG	–0.164***	–0.0126*	–0.0664***			
	(0.0117)	(0.00730)	(0.00296)			
GHG-PCA				–0.112***	–0.0619***	–0.172***
				(0.00747)	(0.0193)	(0.00668)
Constant	1.779***	0.332***	3.345***	0.930***	–1.498***	2.094***
	(0.0691)	(0.123)	(0.0774)	(0.0941)	(0.347)	(0.0394)
Observations	540	243	297	524	234	290
Number of id	92	42	50	91	41	50

Standard errors in parentheses (***p < 0.01, **p < 0.05, *p < 0.1).

It considers the global scenario in focusing on developed and developing economies.

This research concludes that total greenhouse gases have a negative and significant association with happiness. In particular, 1% inline in greenhouse gases leads to 0.13, 0.16 and 0.13 units decline in happiness in global, developed and developing economies, respectively. The magnitude of developed economies is high, implying that the residents of developed economies give more value to environmental quality as a source of their happiness. This research provides additional evidence of the harmful impacts of environmental pollutants on human well-being. This research recommends that more green policies need to be focused all over the world. The global institutions and national governments need to formulate such laws that can protect the environment worldwide. Environmental awareness is essential for the happiness and well-being of current and future generations.

References

Baumol, W.J. & Oates, W.E. (1979). Economics, Environmental Policy, and the Quality of Life. Englewood Cliffs, NJ: Prentice Hall.

Binder, M. & Blankenberg, A. (2016). Environmental concerns, volunteering and subjective well-being: Antecedents and outcomes of environmental activism in Germany. *Ecological Economics 124*, 1–16.

Brereton, F., Clinch, J.P., & Ferreira, S. (2006). Happiness, geography and the environment. *Ecological Economics 65*, 386–396.

Broad, R. (1994). The poor and the environment: friends or foes? *World Development 22*(6), 811–822.

Bruneau, J. & Echevarria, C. (2009). The poor are green too. *Journal of International Cooperation Studies 16*(3), 1–22.

California Energy Commission (2003). Windows and offices: A study of office worker performance and the indoor environment, Technical Report P500-03-082-A-9, Fair Oaks, California, CA.

Carson, R. (1962). Silent Spring. Harmondsworth: Penguin.

Clark, A.E. & Oswald, A.J. (1994). Unhappiness and unemployment. *The Economic Journal 104*(424), 648–659.

Daly, H.E. (1987). The economic growth debate: What some economists have learned but many have not. *Journal of Environmental Economics and Management 14*(4), 323–336.

De Ribeiro Fiuza, A.F. & Lele, C. (2013). Happiness and the environment: Finding out a relationship. (Doctoral dissertation)

Diekmann, A. & Franzen, A. (1999). The wealth of nations and environmental concern. *Environment and Behavior 31*(4), 540–549.

Dolan, P., Peasgood, T., & White, M. (2008). Do we really know what makes us happy? A review of the economic literature on the factors associated with subjective well-being. *Journal of economic psychology 29*(1), 94–122.

Dunlap, R., Mertig, A., (1994), 'Global Environmental Concern: A Challenge to the Post-Materialism Thesis', in Estet, P., Schluter, W., (eds) Social Dimensions of Contemporary Environmental Issues, Tilburg: Tilburg University press.

Duroy, M.Q. (2005). The determinants of environmental awareness and behavior. *Working Papers in Economics* 0501, 1–25.
Easterlin, R.A. (1995). Will raising the incomes of all increase the happiness of all? *Journal of Economic Behavior and Organization 27*, 35–47.
Easterlin, R.A. (1974). Does economic growth improve the human lot? Some empirical evidence. *Nations and Households in Economic Growth 89*, 89–125.
Fairbrother, M. (2012). Rich people, poor people, and environmental concern: Evidence across nations and time. *European Sociological Review 29*(5), 910–922.
Ferrer-i-Carbonell, A. & Gowdy, J.M. (2007). Environmental degradation and happiness. *Ecological Economics 60,* 509–516.
Gardner, J. & Oswald, A. (2001). Does money buy happiness? A longitudinal study using data on windfalls. In *Royal economic society annual conference 2002*. Warwick University, Mimeo.
Hirsch, F. (1976), Social Limits to Growth. New York, NY: Harvard University Press.
Inglehart, R. (1995). Public support for environmental protection: Objective problems and subjective values in 43 societies. *Political Science & Politics 28*(01), 57–72.
Kellert, S. & Wilson, E.O. (1983), The Biophilia Hypothesis. Washington, DC: Island Press.
Lenzen, M. & Cummins, R.A. (2013). Happiness versus the Environment—A case study of Australian lifestyles. *Challenges 4*, 56–74.
Majeed, M.T. (2018). Information and communication technology (ICT) and environmental sustainability in developed and developing countries. *Pakistan Journal of Commerce and Social Sciences 12*(3), 758–783.
Maslow, A. H. (1954). Motivation and personality. New York: Harper and Row.
McMichael, A. J. (2003). Global Climate Change and Health: An Old Story Writ Large. Climate Change and Human Health: Risks and Responses. Geneva, Switzerland: World Health organization.
Oswald, A. J. (1997). Happiness and economic performance. *The Economic Journal 107*(445), 1815–1831.
Scitovsky, T. (1976). The joyless economy: An inquiry into human satisfaction and consumer dissatisfaction. *The Journal of Consumer Affairs 11*(2), 147–149.
Stern, D.I. (2004). The rise and fall of the environmental Kuznets curve. *World Development 32*(8), 1419–1439.
Sulemana, I., McCann, L., & James Jr, H.S. (2016). Perceived environmental quality and subjective well-being: Are African countries different from developed countries? *International Journal of Happiness and Development 3*(1), 64–87.
Tiwari, A.K. (2011). Happiness and environmental degradation: What determines happiness? *Economics Bulletin 31*(4), 3192–3210.
Tukker, A., Emmert, S., Charter, M., Vezzoli, C., Sto, E., Andersen, M.M., Geerken, T., Tischner, U., & Lahlou, S. (2008). Fostering change to sustainable consumption and production: An evidence based view. *Journal of Cleaner Production 16*, 1218–1225.
Ulrich, R. (1984). View through a window may influence recovery. *Science 224*(4647), 224–225.
Veenhoven, R. (1991). Is happiness relative? *Social Indicators Research 24*(1), 1–34.
Welsch, H. (2003). Environment and Happiness: Valuation of Air Pollution in Ten European Countries (No. 356). DIW Discussion Papers.

White, M.P., Alcock, I., Wheeler, B.W., & Depledge, M.H. (2013). Would you be happier living in a greener urban area? A fixed-effects analysis of panel data. *Psychological Science*, 24(6), 920–928.
Wilson, E.O. (1984). Biophilia. Cambridge: Harvard University Press.
World Bank (2016). World Development Indicators. Retrieved from The World Bank: http://data.worldbank.org/indicator.
World Health Organization (2016). Air Quality and Health, Fact Sheet N°313 [online] www.who.int/mediacentre/factsheets/fs313/en/ (accessed 26 November 2018).

Table 14.A1 Data and variables description

Variables	*Definition*	*Construction*	*Sources*
Happiness	*Happiness is mental state characterized by positive feelings ranging from satisfaction to delight.*	0 (least happy) to 10 (most happy)	[1]
GDP per capita	*GDP is the sum of gross value added by all resident producers in the economy.*	(Current US$)	[2]
Unemployment	*Unemployment refers to the share of the labor force that is without work but available for and seeking employment.*	(% of total labor force)	[2]
Urban Population	*Urban population refers to people living in urban areas.*	(% of actual population)	[2]
Age	*Population ages 65 and above as a percentage of the total population.*	(% of total)	[2]
Greenhouse Gas Emissions	*Total greenhouse gas emissions in kt of CO_2 equivalent are composed of CO_2 totals excluding short-cycle biomass burning (such as agricultural waste burning and Savannah burning) but including other biomass burning (such as forest fires, post-burn decay, peat fires and decay of drained peat lands), all anthropogenic CH_4 sources, N_2O sources and F-gases (HFCs, PFCs and SF6).*	*(kt of CO_2 equivalent)*	[2]
Carbon Dioxide (CO_2) Emissions	*Carbon dioxide is one of the greenhouse gases and released into atmosphere through human activities like fossil-fuel burning.*	(Metric tons per capita)	[2]

[1] World Database of Happiness (2016); [2] World Development indicators (2016).

Table 14.A2 Cross-sectional data of developed countries

No.	*Code*	*Country*	*Happiness*	*Income*	*Un*	*Urban*	*Age*	*GHG*
1	AUS	Australia	3.8037	10.27712	6.79583	86.9297	12.0443	13.40202
2	AUT	Austria	4.705	10.36512	4.19167	65.7502	15.781	11.33357
3	BEL	Belgium	4.02778	10.30865	8.03333	96.8385	16.0571	11.86037
4	CAN	Canada	4.05861	10.34257	8.07917	78.5544	12.2713	13.52741
5	CHE	Switzerland	4.10647	10.56185	3.64167	70.9843	15.3262	10.90598
6	CHL	Chile	3.72451	9.326535	7.80833	85.4419	7.74969	11.1435
7	CYP	Cyprus	4.97571	10.03453	6.04583	66.7508	10.4864	8.730083
8	CZE	Czech Rep.	3.85051	9.871175	6.16667	74.3186	13.8341	12.04817
9	DEU	Germany	3.93231	10.31015	7.9375	73.4439	17.0264	13.9278
10	DNK	Denmark	4.10194	10.34683	6.18333	85.3812	15.6538	11.20377
11	ESP	Spain	3.47741	10.06744	17.3625	76.2341	15.0606	12.69967
12	EST	Estonia	3.54231	9.620636	9.15417	69.585	14.5776	10.45222
13	FIN	Finland	3.9151	10.23551	9.9125	80.3491	14.9211	11.2376
14	FRA	France	3.74727	10.22164	10.0125	75.7782	15.4488	13.23284
15	GBR	UK	3.78463	10.26373	6.94583	79.3564	15.8918	13.46807
16	GRC	Greece	4.38	9.963765	12.0083	73.0598	16.2883	11.49659
17	HKG	Hong Kong	4.40857	10.3768	4.1375	98.3653	10.3264	10.5577
18	HRV	Croatia	2.7875	9.606077	12.5292	55.0485	14.5249	10.37357
19	HUN	Hungary	3.28594	9.595235	8.7	66.2671	14.7876	11.36138
20	IRL	Ireland	4.08111	10.31479	9.53333	58.8491	10.9703	11.08299
21	ISL	Iceland	3.40333	10.36365	4.1	91.7374	11.3207	9.168888
22	ISR	Israel	4.47875	10.06121	8.23333	90.8595	9.64625	10.81272
23	ITA	Italy	3.48682	10.22407	9.74167	67.3814	17.1859	13.13329
24	JPN	Japan	3.58259	10.23264	4.02083	81.8512	16.3213	14.08085
25	LTU	Lithuania	3.48564	9.545765	12.775	66.2944	13.7823	10.72548
26	LUX	Luxembourg	4.94375	11.0018	3.69167	84.1226	13.8484	9.40167

27	LVA	Latvia	3.53923	9.466063	12.3417	68.1941	14.9459	10.12308
28	MLT	Malta	3.75056	9.840025	6.77917	92.0811	12.3545	7.735046
29	NLD	Netherlands	3.95705	10.39548	4.7875	76.1061	13.6895	12.29365
30	NOR	Norway	3.70957	10.55781	3.975	75.0325	15.4672	11.12545
31	NZL	New Zealand	4.11588	10.06956	6.36667	85.212	11.7121	11.15927
32	POL	Poland	3.59725	9.414934	12.9667	60.8552	11.7639	13.0469
33	PRI	Puerto Rico	4.46	10.18831	13.6333	90.4823	10.9254	7.96286
34	PRT	Portugal	4.45437	9.862193	7.70417	52.8507	15.5998	11.07489
35	SAU	Saudi Arabia	4.65125	10.40846	5.6	77.8846	2.81011	12.56295
36	SGP	Singapore	4.87625	10.74194	3.2375	100	7.15027	10.47073
37	SVK	Slovak Rep.	3.61205	9.616519	14.0375	55.1493	11.1586	10.96926
38	SVN	Slovenia	3.6098	10.01307	6.91667	50.1198	13.4245	9.90624
39	SWE	Sweden	3.79741	10.34594	7.4625	83.9939	17.6341	11.27242
40	TTO	Trinidad and Tobago	5.25571	9.752159	10.7125	9.58714	6.71881	10.04777
41	URY	Uruguay	3.75077	9.345611	8.32917	90.9719	12.5991	10.3221
42	USA	United States	3.77123	10.54922	6.2375	77.7831	12.5472	15.6708

Table 14.A3 Cross-sectional data of developing countries

No.	*Country*	*Country*	*Happiness*	*Income*	*Un*	*Urban*	*Age*	*GHG*
1	ALB	Albania	3.11962	8.515161	14.8	42.4337	7.56221	9.056746
2	ARM	Armenia	3.42462	8.143745	21.9875	65.3369	8.54186	9.297238
3	AZE	Azerbaijan	2.88	8.772135	6.95833	52.9174	5.32018	10.84983
4	BFA	Burkina Faso	3.01	6.862418	2.81667	17.9549	2.90014	9.939666
5	BGD	Bangladesh	3.83115	7.360013	3.77083	23.5336	3.77047	11.83017
6	BGR	Bulgaria	3.02882	9.08073	13.3042	68.3673	15.4421	11.34941
7	BIH	Bosnia	3.89385	8.577069	26.525	38.8001	9.8316	9.912989
8	BLR	Belarus	3.29974	9.006824	6.32083	68.4596	12.5324	11.76855
9	BOL	Bolivia	5.16	8.282137	4.24167	59.2487	4.96469	12.05759
10	BRA	Brazil	3.77912	9.232624	7.75	77.8589	5.10794	14.32906
11	CHN	China	3.63373	8.281443	4.41667	35.1186	6.52603	15.45403
12	COL	Colombia	4.00529	8.97003	12.5458	70.6046	4.80639	12.0087
13	CRI	Costa Rica	7.22	9.064498	6.10833	58.1098	5.76077	9.165488
14	DOM	Dominican Republic	3.80654	8.861944	16.0458	62.1761	4.80034	10.01039
15	DZA	Algeria	4.42625	9.149922	19.3333	57.7791	4.2847	11.71863
16	ECU	Ecuador	5.67	8.87185	5.95833	57.7033	4.99601	10.50858
17	EGY	Egypt	3.9875	8.802384	10.1708	43.2281	4.89134	12.02423
18	ETH	Ethiopia	4.39286	6.472439	6.00833	14.3675	3.16189	11.52531
19	GEO	Georgia	3.71462	8.267659	13.5583	53.4453	11.7877	9.953111
20	GHA	Ghana	5.02429	7.670987	6.07917	41.99	3.05555	10.79768
21	GTM	Guatemala	6.79	8.550027	2.86667	44.2059	3.7954	10.02628
22	HND	Honduras	6.49	8.073586	3.90833	44.5243	3.82037	9.668781
23	IDN	Indonesia	4.24	8.645302	6.875	38.328	4.35385	13.9484
24	IND	India	3.67922	7.817477	3.99167	27.4754	4.37757	14.32257
25	IRN	Iran	3.78083	9.31988	12.0875	61.9616	4.01342	12.77811
26	IRQ	Iraq	3.77	9.040164	18.575	68.7328	3.59144	11.56768

27	JOR	Jordan	4.02333	8.880605	14.0583	76.2082	3.38111	9.601643
28	KGZ	Kyrgyz Rep.	4.5775	7.630243	8.63333	36.5185	5.18027	9.531259
29	MAR	Morocco	4.03083	8.372831	11.8917	51.656	4.80745	10.73212
30	MDA	Moldova	2.97618	7.957986	6.55833	45.1118	9.05133	9.948184
31	MEX	Mexico	3.92549	9.300434	3.9375	73.6123	4.88345	13.184
32	MKD	Macedonia	3.65731	8.915285	32.6708	57.3175	8.81239	9.409065
33	MLI	Mali	4.99143	6.982871	8.4125	27.9401	3.26025	10.70774
34	MYS	Malaysia	5.22571	9.571973	3.2625	58.4476	4.16901	12.22994
35	NER	Niger	4.43615	6.531251	5.075	16.0351	2.37525	9.06855
36	NIC	Nicaragua	5.89	8.014806	5.675	54.1852	3.77561	9.408062
37	PAK	Pakistan	3.86654	8.062716	5.8	32.8159	4.10893	12.27605
38	PER	Peru	3.47176	8.743859	5.1375	71.9062	4.87596	11.02448
39	PHL	Philippines	4.21308	8.286378	8.65	45.6742	3.45526	11.70965
40	PRY	Paraguay	6.3	8.626216	6.0625	52.4957	4.56168	11.04207
41	ROM	Romania	3.10392	9.100779	7.125	52.3994	12.9275	12.10193
42	RUS	Russia	3.24412	9.287	8.19583	73.002	11.9413	14.89119
43	RWA	Rwanda	4.63429	6.729268	0.6	13.6568	2.53307	8.288012
44	SLV	El Salvador	4.17846	8.607894	7.02917	55.7166	5.4631	9.066714
45	THA	Thailand	5.22714	9.096566	1.52917	34.3019	6.32613	12.46104
46	TUR	Turkey	3.71745	9.17892	9.225	62.1352	5.68078	12.48169
47	TZA	Tanzania	5.25125	7.279687	3.67083	22.0874	2.86172	11.74302
48	UGA	Uganda	4.5	6.897255	3.1875	11.8834	2.64173	10.75843
49	UKR	Ukraine	3.16794	8.651244	8.28333	66.8099	13.7341	13.24656
50	VEN	Venezuela	4.34538	9.453443	10.3833	85.9603	4.36859	12.33245
51	ZAF	South Africa	3.76784	9.116495	23.9583	55.8934	3.9289	12.86646
52	ZMB	Zambia	4.22	7.658691	15.2	38.1497	2.77351	12.34284
53	ZWE	Zimbabwe	3.84125	7.417089	5.49583	30.6213	3.11617	10.59892

15

ALTRUISM A CRITICAL PREREQUISITE FOR SUSTAINABLE DEVELOPMENT

Implications for Waqf Institutions in the Islamic Republic of Iran

Mohammad Soleimani and Hasan Kiaee

15.1 Introduction

Development as a multidimensional process requires sweeping changes in social structure, public beliefs and formal institutions. It must accelerate economic growth, reduce inequality and alleviate poverty to move society from an unfavorable situation to a materially and spiritually desirable situation. Therefore, over time, the development economy has shifted its focus to human and non-material issues such as human dignity, decent living, intergenerational justice and environmental protection. Addressing sustainable development in the literature in recent years shows that insights and perspectives on development have deepened between researchers and policy makers. Sustainable development is defined as a combination of economic, social and environmental goals to maximize the well-being of the current human being without damaging future generations' ability to meet their needs.

The Millennium Development Goals (MDGs) and the goals listed at the Rio + 20 Conference are two key examples of a set of goals for sustainable development. At the Rio + 20 Conference, a document entitled "The Future We Want" was adopted, setting out a set of Sustainable Development Goals (17 goals). Re-focusing on these goals, many of which are a repetition of the MDGs, shows countries fail to achieve sustainable development goals. People suffering from poverty, hunger, malnutrition, poor health services, illiteracy, discrimination against women in developing countries and environmental crises (e.g., air pollution, greenhouse gas emissions, depletion of water resources, etc.) is a sign of failure to achieve the goals of sustainable development in developed and developing countries. It is, therefore, critical to look at the current approach and to design a new path. Although purposeful interventions by governments and programs of international organizations alongside popular movements in NGOs have some positive effects on poverty alleviation, health improvement, environmental protection, etc., there are still many problems and obstacles to fulfill sustainable development goals.

In the same direction as the mainstream economics, development economics seems to have adopted an analytical approach that does not consider all the dimensions and capacities of human beings and cannot fully achieve its goals. Motivating people to change the status quo requires intrinsic rather than extrinsic motivations. This chapter highlights the sense of altruism and its effects on improving the human condition through inherent incentives.

Altruism could be defined as the principle and moral practice of concern for other human beings' happiness, resulting in a quality of life both material and spiritual. In short, altruism is the unselfish concern for other people (Kendra Cherry 2019). For many sociologists, including Auguste Comte, altruism has been seen as the opposite of egoism. Secchi (2007) has shown that to build a peaceful society; altruism must be the basis of social interaction; however, he emphasizes that selfish individuals are not eliminated in all situations and times. Carter and Castillo (2003) have also shown that altruism, like trust and honesty, is part of social capital and has an undeniable effect on economic well-being.

Humankind always has a sense of altruism. In all places and times, it is present in different forms and symbols. Numerous formal and informal institutions have been set up to achieve this goal. Especially in Islamic countries, institutions like charity, waqf, zakat, teachings about good interaction with women and environmental conservation are all tried to strengthen altruism in society. In this chapter, we focus on some evidence observed in the Islamic Republic of Iran on the Waqf institution's implication in achieving development goals.

The rest of chapter is organized as follows. The second section deals with the relationship between sustainable development and altruism. The third section addresses the role of intrinsic motivation in sustainable development. The fourth section focuses on the relationship between Islam, altruism and sustainable development. It introduces the Waqf institution as one of the manifestations of altruism to achieve sustainable development goals. The fifth section represents some facts and figures about the Waqf and its effects on Iran's Islamic Republic's development goal. The sixth section provides a summary and concluding remarks.

15.2 Altruism and development

Economics assumes that individuals act according to their self-interest; economic development is viewed as an individual free play outcome. But some other researchers believe that individuals have some cooperative spirit, which allows them often to work in the collective interest, even when that may not be in their self-interest (Basu 2006). Considering that the realization of public welfare is dependent on social life, one may think of altruism as an ethical basis of development.

In an abstract world of mainstream economics, the best economic situation would be focusing on individual interests, since in this abstract world (1) all persons have equal opportunities and facilities for flourishing their talents and capabilities, (2) there are no information problems like the agency problems and the conflict of interest issues, (3) individual decision-making units use the best possible mechanism for collective decision-making, and collective action problem does not exist and (4) economic agents fully incorporate the results and consequences of their activity into their analysis and decisions, and so there is no externality problem. But in the real world, many of the above conditions are not exist, and optimal social status is not achievable by focusing on the individual interest. On the other hand, in the modern world, where the adverse effects of the capitalist approach can cause damages to a large part of society, external control is complicated and, in many cases, not possible. Hence, we need internal components to alleviate the problems to achieve social optimal. One of the critical internal elements is altruism. Social theorists such as Parsons, Sorokin and Riesman show that altruism is a socially relevant concept and an important issue in understanding human behavior.

Altruism, self-sacrifice and forgiveness are the drivers of social life. Such behaviors facilitate social relationships and reduce the burden of daily living created by people's formal interaction. The principle of altruism behavior is based on the lack of self-interest or preference of other interests to self-interest. Altruism affects sustainable development in the following ways:

- Altruism reduces the negative side effects of production. Lusk, Nilsson, and Foster (2007) showed that more altruistic individuals are willing to pay more for pork products with certifications related to the environment, animal welfare and antibiotics than less altruistic individuals. In other words, altruistic people's behavior prevents from harming animals and spreading environmental pollution. On the other hand, the existence of altruism among individuals positively affects producing goods with positive side effects. Arana and León (2002) have shown that altruism is a positive component in the value of reducing the probability of flu. Also, Chami and Fischer (1996) have provided the same result in the insurance market. In this way, coinsurance is above the socially optimal level if individuals place greater weight on their utility than their partners.
- Altruism is effective in resolving the problem of collective action. Suppose there is a spirit of altruism in the community and some people are willing to sacrifice for others. In that case, one can expect that an altruistic agent would do the corrective actions that must be done collectively and at high expense for a fee or at a lower cost (Elster 1985). Similarly, consider

intrinsic motivations for self-sacrifice and altruism within some community since people work according to their personality and beliefs. In that case, their cooperation will solve collective action. Using the game theory concepts, when a player behaves according to his characteristic, his behavior is independent of other players' choices in their cooperation to supply a public good (Neuteleers and Engelen 2015). For example, people who are motivated externally by some regulation stop helping save various animal and plant species if other people meet that goal or if that goal is no longer achievable. However, internally motivated people are concerned about the wildlife and diversity of animal species and will try to care for them, regardless of whether others have succeeded in that goal. The fundamental difference is that intrinsic motivation can enhance behaviors that reflect one's personality and belief; such a person behaves in any circumstance vital to him (Hargreaves-Heap 1989).

- Altruism seeks to remove the barriers and flourishes the talents and abilities of those who face obstacles in their living (for example, the disabled or people with disasters). If the sense of philanthropy is reinforced in a society, one can expect to see more efforts to solve fellow citizens (Mirakhor and Ng 2015). Under these circumstances, helping others would be internalized in the community to facilitate education, prevent malnutrition and promote health.

The study of various researches shows that altruism, or at least the willingness to consider others in personal living, is natural to humanity. Second, altruism has an undeniable role in society's social and economic well-being and is vital for building a healthy and peaceful community (Kahana. *et al.* 2013; Music 2014; Schwartz, Keyl, Marcum, and Bode 2009).

15.3 Sustainable development and intrinsic motivation

Motivations can be economic, social and ethical. Under the general classification, motivations include intrinsic and extrinsic motivation. Intrinsic motivation occurs when a person does something because of its value to himself and not because of its independent consequences. Conversely, extrinsic motivation is when one does something to achieve an independent outcome (Frey 1997; Ryan and Deci 2000). The primary reliance on economic analysis is on the effects of human external and monetary motives on changing their behaviors and decisions. The intrinsic motivations in this analytical system are neglected (Benabou and Tirole 2003).

Accordingly, the economic analysis assumes that human beings are self-seeking and pursuing personal interests, and relying on these personal interests without considering public benefit would be the reason for social order (Barry,1982). In these circumstances, external motivations (e.g., reward or punishment) should motivate a person to do something outside their interests.

The consequence of this approach would be to focus only on price policies to encourage change in economic behavior. For example, economists suggest that policy makers increase taxes for reducing drug addiction or exempt non-profit activities from taxes to improve people's motivation to help others.

It seems that a mere focus on extrinsic motivations can have adverse effects. Based on the crowding-out effect (Frey 1997) as well as empirical evidence (Sandel 2012), increasing external incentives reduces the intrinsic motivation and correspondingly decreases the activities based on intrinsic motivation such as altruism (charity, benevolent participation, etc.). These are the internal elements that give a person the power to do extraordinary works. In other words, given that intrinsic motivations play a unique role in increasing the supply of specific jobs and services such as education, innovation, creativity-based work, entrepreneurship, etc., neglecting intrinsic motivation diminishes attention to all of these issues. In the absence of intrinsic incentives, the cost of providing certain services and social measures (such as transitional payments under specific circumstances, participation in the supply of certain public goods, and so on) increases.

If extrinsic motives are in line with intrinsic motives, the status quo will change. Otherwise, friction between internal and external motives will reduce correction speed (Frey 1997). Researchers often use the crowding-out theory to describe this situation. The crowding-out effect refers to how external motives lead to a decrease in internal incentives (Frey 2001; Frey and Jegen 2001; Goodin 1994). It is a psychological mechanism that can be referred to as motivational corruption due to the destruction of people's internal motives to support specific issues. Conflicts occur when changes in a motivating factor (such as a punishment or financial reward or regulation) that stimulate external motivations decrease people's intrinsic motivation (Neuteleers and Engelen 2015). In particular, if considered a controller, external motivations lead to a regress of intrinsic motivation, and if deemed a supporter, it leads to an increase in intrinsic motivation (Frey 2001).

For example, a lack of attention to intrinsic motivation can put environmental sustainability goals at serious risk. Neuteleers and Engelen (2015) have addressed the topic of environmental phenomena. They argue that creating an external incentive system and the use of price-dependent analysis may erode people's positive attitudes towards environmental phenomena and their reasons for supporting them. Gómez-Baggethun and Ruiz-Pérez (2011) also argued that a growing number of environmental scientists have supported the economic valuation of environmental services as a short-term and operational strategy in the last decade. This study pointed out that market incentives can undermine the environment's perception as a value in people's minds and hinder maximum efforts to protect the environment.

Education is another example. When education becomes a commodity and people try to value it according to market mechanism, it would have negative effects on the level of educational services provided and the sanctification of science and teacher status. In this way, teaching and ignorance elimination at the human level is out of all people's common goals and tasks (see Ball 2004; Williams 2002). Overall, altruism changes individuals' minds so that they consider others' interests in their utility functions. It also enhances the motivation to pursue social benefit and prosperity, thus helping to stabilize every country's development path.

15.4 Islam, altruism and sustainable development

From the Islamic point of view, the concept of sustainable development implies the creation of a prosperous, egalitarian and equitable economic and social structure. Economic development, economic growth and social justice are essential elements of an Islamic economic system. All members of the Islamic community must have equal opportunities for growth and excellence. Islam has introduced a rule-based system for guiding the individual in all aspects of life, including economic and business activities (Askari *et al.* 2012). The concept of development in Islam has three dimensions: (1) individual self-development, (2) the physical development and (3) the development of human society, which includes the first two dimensions. The first dimension specifies the dynamic process of human growth towards perfection. The second dimension introduces the ways to exploit natural resources to meet all individuals' and human beings' living needs. The third dimension of development refers to human society's progress towards complete unity (Askari *et al.* 2012). The most important element of development, which plays a central role in the Islamic conception of development, is individuals' efforts for their growth and excellence. Without one's transcendence, balanced progress towards the other two development dimensions would be impossible. Happiness and a sense of accomplishment in one's life are not only achieved by increasing income but by growing in all three dimensions (Al-Hakimi *et al.* 1989). Therefore, the Islamic perspective does not ignore altruistic attention to others in achieving sustainable development.

Many of Islam's social teachings focus on altruism and concern for other Muslims' affairs and even humanity. In the Islamic framework, a set of formal and informal institutions together encourage altruism and pave the way for achieving an optimal situation. In the Hadith of the great Prophet of Islam, he says: "We are not motivated to raise money but to spend it" (Tabarsi 2001). Concerning the people's sense of benevolence, Islam emphasizes on Waqf, Habs, Wassiah, Sadaqah, Nadhr and Kaffarah, and Qard al-Hasan, and on the power of faith and sacrifice instead of selfishness, luxury, which encourages the rich to use their surplus property in the way of God and the public interest.

15.5 Waqf: as an institution

One of the important institutions among those mentioned is Waqf, the main focus of this chapter. The word of Waqf means to stop, and in jurisprudence is the concept of confining the principle of property and releasing its profit and spending it in the predetermined ways. Waqf typically involves donating an asset for any charitable purposes with no intention of reclaiming the assets. Although the word waqf is not explicitly mentioned in the Qur'an, it is interpreted as continuous Sadaqah in religious texts. All the verses in the Qur'an concerning Sadaqah can be related in some way to the concept of Waqf (Bakhtiari 2002). The economic definition of Waqf can be seen as a shift in the use of resources, from individual exploitation to social benefit for the present and future generations whose services or benefits are widely used. Waqf, therefore, can be viewed as altruistic virtue. Because of its benevolent nature, the Waqf institution strengthens social foundations and the spirit of co-operation in society, which promotes social capital and increases the efficiency of the overall economy.

15.5.1 Waqf and development in the Islamic Republic of Iran

Waqf is one of the institutions that significantly impact development goals (particularly poverty alleviation, education and health). Under the rule of Islamic doctrine in Iran, the Waqf institution is undoubtedly centered on the altruism principle. Waqf in Iran has a long and brilliant history. But, Safavid[1] era can be considered the peak of development and growth of Waqf in Iran. Most land and residential houses in Iran cities were either fully or partially devoted to Waqf at the end of the Safavid period (Bakhtiari 2002; Eshkevari 1998).

Three different institutions manage Waqf properties in Iran. The first institution is the Auqaf and Charity Organization. The second institution is called Waqf Administration, which manages the Prophet's progeny members' holy shrines. These institutions are autonomous, and their mission is to advance Islamic Shari'ah and provide service to pilgrims. The most prominent among them is the Astan Quds Razavi of Imam Reza (AS), the eighth grandson of the Prophet (SAAS). The third administrative institution manages private trustees or joint private–public custodians. Two notable examples are Namazi Hospital and Afshar Cultural Foundations (Sadr and Karbalaei 2016).

15.5.2 The role of Waqf in health development in Iran

Islamic civilization is inseparably linked to Waqf with establishing hospitals and managing them. Since the early period of Muslim history, Muslims had acquainted with medical science, and to this day, hospitals are built in Islamic lands under Waqf. In Iran, the main focus of Waqf is to provide health facilities to patients and medical research. About 25% of medical centers in the country are currently endowed, and there are more than 1,400 treatment facilities based on Waqf.

In Iran, Waqf is not only limited to the field of treatment. One of these endowments is the Pasteur Institute of Iran, which has been dedicated by charities to carry out their services in diagnosis, vaccine production and research aimed at controlling and preventing infectious diseases. Pasteur Institute of Iran seeks to expand applied research on biological products, developing research on basic sciences with the underlying aim of introducing and optimizing new techniques and methods for use in applied research with particular emphasis on infections.[2] The Institute is an example of scientific endowment in the Qajar[3] era, which results from changing the traditional approach to endowment and charity. It is located in Tehran and was built by the late Mirza Abdolhossein Farmanfarmayian in 1920. A review of the deed of endowment of the Pasteur Institute of Iran also shows that he was aware of the contagious disease outbreak's impact and its associated problems. The Pasteur Institute has critical roles in health and medical research and specialist training, and is very important in the human development process, especially the health index (Alizadeh and Fatemi 2018). During its nearly hundred years of service, the Institute has taken significant steps to prevent and control infectious diseases in Iran and the world by conducting various researches related to the control of contagious diseases and producing vaccines and biological products.

15.5.3 The role of Waqf in education and science in Iran

Another area of Waqf is scientific and education endowment. This endowment aims to pave the way for the scientific and cultural advancement of Islamic society. Academic Waqf has various forms, from the endowment to building science centers such as schools and universities, book endowments or covering the deprived people's education cost. Lowering the cost of education for young people, especially those living in disadvantaged areas, and the cost of living and studying for religious scholars, through Waqf, contributes to the discovery and flourishing of talents. In the case of clergy, it will lead to the stability, independence of practice and financial freedom of the religious sciences in government credits (Adel 2004).

Alborz Cultural Foundation is one of the cultural Waqf of contemporary Iran. In 1973, the Alborz Cultural Foundation was founded with the personal capital of the late Hossein Ali Alborz in Tehran. The purpose of this charity is to spread Islamic culture. The foundation services include giving awards to graduates across the country, granting innovations awards to innovators, publishing books and researching Islamic culture. It also gives long-term interest-free loans to scholars, the construction or purchase of suitable buildings to establish schools with the priority of deprived areas, the formation of various scientific and research centers. Alborz Cultural Foundation also pays loans to students from the proceeds of its business units. Each year, the foundation awards special grants to students at different education levels at universities and educational centers.[4]

Since 2015, all the physical and intellectual property rights and income of the Qalamchi Cultural and Educational Complex are dedicated to the Cultural Foundation of Education. This Waqf is endowed to focus on spreading of knowledge and education for the public interest. The part of this Waqf covers the cost of education of at least 1,000 talented high school students from deprived areas. The earnings of the Qalamchi Cultural Foundation are used priority wise for (1) providing scholarships and supporting talented students in deprived areas, (2) construction of school and library and (3) any other cultural activity that has contributed to the spread of knowledge and education.[5]

15.6 Conclusion

Development as a multidimensional process is purposed to accelerate economic growth, reduce inequality and alleviate poverty. In mainstream economics, human beings are considered self-seeking and pursue personal interests. So it is believed that relying on these personal interests without considering public benefit would be the reason for social order. Some phenomena like information problems, collective action problems and externalities show that individual interests cannot achieve optimal social status. Development economics do not consider all the dimensions and capacities of human beings, and thus this approach cannot fully achieve sustainable development goals.

It seems that motivating people to change the status quo requires intrinsic alongside with extrinsic incentives. While the conventional approach in economics has focused on extrinsic motivation, this chapter sheds light on the sense of altruism and its effects on improving the human condition through intrinsic incentives. Altruism uses a set of internal components to alleviate a self-interest economy's mentioned problems and drive it to achieve social optimal and sustainable development goals.

In many ways, altruism (1) prevents altruistic people reducing the adverse side effects of pollution in the environment that harm people (and animals), (2) resolves the problem of collective action as people are willing to sacrifice for the benefit of others due to altruistic community and (3) removes the barriers to flourish the talents and abilities of those who face obstacles in their living. In other words, altruism changes individuals' mental framework and they start considering others' interest in their utility functions. It also enhances the incentive to pursue social benefit and prosperity, thus stabilizing every country's development path.

From the Islamic point of view, the concept of sustainable development implies the creation of a prosperous, egalitarian and equitable economic and social structure. Economic development and economic growth and social justice are essential elements of an Islamic economic system. All members of the Islamic community must have equal opportunities for growth and excellence. Therefore, paying attention to altruism in sustainable development from an Islamic perspective cannot be ignored. Islam's social teachings focus on altruism and concern for other Muslims' affairs and even humanity.

In the Islamic framework, a set of formal and informal institutions together encourage altruism and pave the way for achieving an optimal situation. One of the important institutions among them is Waqf, which involves donating an asset for any charitable purposes with no intention of reclaiming the assets. Because of its benevolent nature, the Waqf institution strengthens social foundations and the spirit of co-operation in society, which promotes social capital and increases the efficiency of the overall economy.

Like many Muslim countries, Waqf has great impacts on the achievement of development goals, particularly poverty alleviation, education and health in the Islamic Republic of Iran. Waqf's main focus in health in Iran has been on treatments and medical research and less attention has been paid in areas such as financing poor patient costs. The Pasteur Institute of Iran has been dedicated to carrying out its services in diagnosis, vaccine production and research to control and prevent communicable diseases. The endowment deed of the Pasteur Institute of Iran also shows that the endower was aware of the impact of the contagious disease outbreak and its associated problems. Another area of Waqf in Iran is scientific and education endowment. The purpose of these endowments is to pave the way for Islamic society's scientific and cultural advancement. Academic Waqf has various forms of endowment building such as science centers, schools and universities to book endowments or cover the deprived people's cost of education. Two famous educational Waqf in Iran are Alborz Cultural Foundation and Qalamchi Cultural Foundation.

Notes

1 The Safavid dynasty ruled from 1501 to 1736 in Iran.
2 http://en.pasteur.ac.ir/pages.aspx?id=848
3 The Qajar dynasty ruled from 1876 to 1925 in Iran.
4 http://bf-alborz.ir/index.aspx
5 http://www.kanoon.ir/

References

Adel m. (2004). Waqf, a Lasting Legacy. Sabzevar (Iran): Omide Mehr Press (In Persian).

Al-Hakimi, M.R., Al-Hakimi, M., & Al-Hakimi, A. (1989). Al-Hayat, Tehran: Maktab Nashr Al-Thaqrafa Al-Islamiyyeh (Arabic).

Alizade, z. & fatemi, f. (2018). Determining the Main Factor of Establishment and Development of Pasteur Institute of Iran, first national conference on WAQF function in human development, emphasizing scientific waqf, Birjand University (In Persian).

Arana, J.E. & León, C.J. (2002). Willingness to pay for health risk reduction in the context of altruism. *Health Economics 11*(7), 623–635.

Askari, H., Iqbal, Z., Krichene, N., & Mirakhor, A. (2012). Risk-sharing in Finance: The Islamic Finance Alternative. Singapore: John Wiley Sons (Asia).

Bakhtiari, S. (2002). Waqf and its role in socio-economic development. *The Journal of Waqf (Mirath-e-Javedan) 40*, 26–54 (In Persian).

Ball, S.J. (2004). Education for Sale! The Commodification of Everything? King's Annual Education Lecture, University of London.

Barry, N. (1982). The Tradition of Spontaneous Order: A Bibliographical Essay, [w:] LP Liggio (red.), Literature of Liberty: A Review of Contemporary Liberal Thought, Vol. V, No. 2, Summer 1982, Cato Institute.

Basu, K. (2006). Identity, Trust and Altruism: Sociological Clues to Economics Development (August 2006). CAE Working Paper, Available at SSRN: https://ssrn.com/abstract=956080 or http://dx.doi.org/10.2139/ssrn.956080

Benabou, R. & Tirole, J. (2003). Intrinsic and extrinsic motivation. *The Review of Economic Studies 70*(3), 489–520.

Frey, B. (1997). Not Just for the Money: An Economic Theory of Personal Motivation. Cheltenham: Edward Elgar Publishing.

Carter, M.R. & Castillo, M. (2003). The Economic Impacts of Trust and Altruism: An Experimental Approach to Social Capital. Working Paper.

Chami, R. & Fischer, J.H. (1996). Altruism, matching, and nonmarket insurance. *Economic Inquiry 34*, 630–647. doi:10.1111/j.1465-7295.1996.tb01401.x

Elster, J. (1985). Rationality, morality, and collective action. *Ethics 96*(1), 136–155.

Eshkevari, S.M. (1998). Moqufat of Imam Ali (PBUH). *The Journal of Waqf (Mirath-e-Javedan) 8*, 65–84 (In Persian).

Frey, B.S. & Jegen, R. (2001). Motivation crowding theory. *Journal of Economic Surveys 15*(5), 589–611.

Frey, B.S. (2001). Inspiring Economics: Human Motivation in Political Economy. Cheltenham: Edward Elgar Publishing.

Gómez-Baggethun, E. & Ruiz-Pérez, M. (2011). Economic valuation and the commodification of ecosystem services. *Progress in Physical Geography 35*(5), 613–628.

Goodin, R.E. (1994).Selling environmental indulgences. *Kyklos 47*(4), 573–596.

Hargreaves Heap, S. (1989). Rationality in Economics. New York: Blackwell.

Kahana, E., Bhatta, T., Lovegreen, L.D., Kahana, B., & Midlarsky, E. (2013). Altruism, helping, and volunteering: Pathways to well-being in late life. *Journal of Aging and Health 25*(1), 159–187.

Cherry, K. (2019). How Psychologists Explain Altruistic Helpful Behaviors. Available at: www.verywellmind.com/what-is-altruism-279482

Lusk, J.L., Nilsson, T., & Foster, K. (2007). Public preferences and private choices: Effect of altruism and free riding on demand for environmentally certified pork. *Environmental and Resource Economics 36*, 499–521.

Mirakhor A., Ng, A., & Ibrahim, M.H. (2015). Social Capital and Risk Sharing: An Islamic Finance Paradigm. Berlin, Germany: Springer.

Music, G. (2014). The Good Life: Wellbeing and the New Science of Altruism, Selfishness and Immorality. London: Routledge.

Neuteleers, S. & Engelen, B. (2015). Talking money: How market-based valuation can undermine environmental protection. *Ecological Economics 117*, 253–260.

Ryan, R.M. & Deci, E.L. (2000). Intrinsic and extrinsic motivations: Classic definitions and new directions. *Contemporary Educational Psychology 25*(1), 54–67.

Sadr, K. & Karbalaei, A. (2016). Muktamar Waqf Iqlimi III Conference, Central Mosque. Songkla, Thailand.

Sandel, M.J. (2012). What Money Can't Buy: The Moral Limits of Markets. New York: Macmillan.

Schwartz, C.E., Keyl, P.M., Marcum, J.P., & Bode, R. (2009). Helping others shows differential benefits on health and well-being for male and female teens. *Journal of Happiness Studies 10*(4), 431–448.

Secchi, D. (2007), Theory of docile society: A role of altruism in human behavior. *Journal of Academy of Business and Economics VII*(2), 146–160.

Tabarsi, A. (2001). MESHKAT-AL-ANVAR, Qom (Iran), Dar-al-Thaghalayn Press (In Persian).

Williams, C.C. (2002). A critical evaluation of the commodification thesis. *The Sociological Review 50*(4), 525–542.

16

SOCIAL ENTERPRISE AND WAQF

An alternative sustainable vehicle for Islamic social finance

Noor Suhaida Kasri (PhD) and Siti Fariha Adilah Ismail

Islamic social finance is one of the subsections in Islamic financial system that integrates economic activities with social value. Their activities enable communal socio-economic issues addressed hence results to positive socio-economic impact (Mahomed 2017). On that premise, social finance, as the third sector provides the community with basic necessities when government and market, being the first and second sector, have failed or are unable to provide such facilities to the public (Anheier 2019). The same with Islamic social finance where activities and instruments involving *waqf*, *zakat* and *sadaqa* are used to deliver activities with socio-economic impact (Mahomed 2017). At a larger scale, organization and enterprises like cooperatives, mutual benefit societies, associations, foundations and social enterprises are established as vehicles to execute the social economic activities (ILO Social Economy 2010).

While the need and demand for social economic activities persist particularly in the current state of global economy, sustaining these vehicles remain a fundamental issue. Sustainability aids these establishments to continuously deliver their social key performance targets. With the right and strategic sustainable structure and governance model, the survival of these entities as well as their social economic activities can be guaranteed. Due to its significance, this chapter opts to explore social enterprise and waqf entities and discern from their best practices' aspect of sustainability and transparency. This chapter has selected one social enterprise, Bangladesh Rural Advancement Committee (BRAC) and two waqf entities, namely, Malaysia's Larkin Sentral Property Berhad (Larkin Sentral) and Indonesia's Pondok Modern Darussalam Gontor (Pondok Gontor). The reason for their selection is due to them being recognized as among the most sustainable and impactful entities by their local peers and abroad.

This chapter is structured as follows: Section 16.1 introduces the paper. Section 16.2 explains briefly the theoretical concept of Social Enterprise and Waqf while Section 16.3 describes the research methodology and method involved in this research. Section 16.4 showcases mini case studies of BRAC, Larkin Sentral and Pondok Gontor with the focus on their establishment, governance, transparency, business model and social impact. Section 16.5 concludes with recommendation.

16.1 Social enterprise and Waqf

16.1.1 What is social enterprise?

According to BRAC, social enterprise is a self-sustaining cause-driven business entity that creates social impact by offering solutions to social challenges and reinvesting their surpluses to sustain and generate greater impact (BRAC 2018). Besides striving to meet the need to maximize profit, social enterprise is also expected to tackle environmental and economic issues (Department Trade and Industry 2002). The origin behind the idea of non-state/non-private enterprise can be traced back to the 19th century. As capitalism advanced, there were growing calls by groups of people linked to religious, political-ideological and other organizations such as voluntary associations, charities and co-operatives to pacify the increased public unrest associated with the intensification of capitalist social relations of production and industrialization. The burgeoning need to address the social and economic need in the society was conspicuous. These developments propel the notion of "social economy," within the continental European tradition, and "non-profits" in the US tradition and "voluntary" and "charity" within the UK tradition (Sepulveda 2015). Today social enterprise have been duly recognized and their establishment are being implemented through legal structures like company limited by guarantee, industrial and provident societies, companies limited by shares, unincorporated organization or registered charities (Department of Trade and Industry 2002). Some examples of accoladed social enterprises are Ashoka, Grameen Danone, DC Design, Big Issue and BRAC.

16.1.2 What is Waqf?

Waqf is the locking up of title and ownership of an asset from disposition and allotment of its benefit for a specific purpose or purposes. The ownership of the waqf asset cannot be transferred (perpetuity), and the benefits are to be used in accordance with the direction or meeting the aim of the donor, which is (are) mainly charitable (Sadeq 2002). In a hadith of Prophet Muhammad (peace be upon him) whereby he directed Uthman Ibn Affan to purchase the well of Bi'r Rumah for 20,000 dirhams. Uthman Ibn Affan purchased the well and endowed it for the use and benefit of the Muslim and non-Muslim communities in Madina. Although centuries have passed, the waqf of Bi'r Rumah is still serving humankind today. This practice laid down the foundation for waqf funds being invested in serving and making social and economic impact on society. In this modern age, waqf is applied in many forms: liquid and illiquid assets, such as immovable and movable assets, including cash and shares. Institutions such as Waqaf An-Nur Corporation Berhad, Larkin Sentral, Warees Investment, Daarut Tauhid, Rumah Wakaf Indonesia, Tabung Wakaf Indonesia and Pondok Gontor follow these practices.

16.2 Research methodology

In terms of research methodology, this paper employs qualitative research using the textual analysis approach. We gathered data from online sources, particularly the respective entities' annual reports, reports, academic writings, newspapers, websites and others to understand these establishments' context and operation. The analysis made from these data accentuates these entities' sustainable operating model, including their best practices, governance, transparency and social impact made. BRAC's outstanding social economic accomplishment will be used as the benchmark for waqf institutions to adapt and emulate, particularly from the angle of sustainability and transparency. This study contributes to the literature on Islamic social finance, particularly waqf. It highlights viable, sustainable social enterprise best practices for waqf establishments to learn and adapt whenever applicable and practical.

16.3 BRAC, Larkin Sentral and Pondok Gontor

16.3.1 Establishment

The three selected organizations share several common factors. They are all located in the Asian region; while BRAC is located in South Asia, Larkin Sentral and Pondok Gontor are in South-east Asia. Due to that, they share more or less the same climate. The majority of the population in Bangladesh, Malaysia and Indonesia are Muslims. Yet the majority of ultra-poor or poor people are Muslims. This reality spurs the comparative analysis of these mini case studies in exploring the sustainable best practice models.

16.3.2 BRAC

BRAC is one of the largest NGO in the world, operating across 11 countries in Africa and Asia. BRAC was ranked first among the world's top 500 NGOs by Geneva-based "NGO Advisor" in terms of impact, innovation and sustainability (BRAC 2018). Established for almost half a century, BRAC started way back in 1972, in the aftermath of the Liberation War in Bangladesh. The original mission of BRAC was to act as a temporary relief organization for the millions of refugees as the government lacked the capacity to aid these refugees. During this period, BRAC witnessed a host of social problems at a national scale and the conspicuous failure of government agencies in providing sufficient relief. Due to this reality, in 1974, BRAC changed its name from "Bangladesh Rehabilitation Assistance Committee" to "Bangladesh Rural Advance Committee." They then changed their mission from merely providing humanitarian relief to addressing the fundamental underlying socio-economic problem – eradicating extreme poverty in Bangladesh (Seelos and Mair 2006).

16.3.3 Larkin Sentral

Larkin Sentral was originally a private limited company. In 2016, it was then changed to a public company limited by guarantee. The conversion of its legal status allowed it to issue waqf shares initial public offering (IPO) to the Malaysian market. The purpose of the IPO is to create awareness of the concept of waqf and provide opportunity for the public – Muslims and non-Muslims – to contribute to society's socio-development. The proceeds from the issuance of the waqf shares will primarily be used to support and facilitate the upgrading and refurbishment of Larkin Sentral Transportation Terminal and Wet Market in Larkin, Johor. Johor is located at the southern end of Peninsular Malaysia. The proceeds from the IPO exercise will be used to purchase a piece of land adjacent to the Larkin terminal for the purpose of developing it into the terminal's multi-story car park (Larkin Sentral Project) (Prospektus Larkin Sentral 2017).

Larkin Sentral is a subsidiary of Waqaf An-Nur Corporation (WANCorp). Both Larkin Sentral and WANCorp are under one parent company, Johor Corporation (Jcorp). WANCorp is the appointed the *nazir* (manager) to the shares and other securities endowed by JCorp. Besides managing the endowed assets and shares of Jcorp Group, WANCorp is also appointed as the *nazir khas* (private trustee) for Larkin Sentral's waqf shares. The management of these endowed shares and securities is supervised by Johor Islamic Religious Council (JIRC). In Malaysia, each of its State's Islamic Religious Council (SIRC) is the sole trustee of all waqf properties. They are referred to as *nazir am* (public trustee). Nonetheless in certain situations, private trustee can be appointed to manage and administer the waqf property under the supervision of the respective SIRC which is practiced in the case of WANCorp and Larkin Sentral (Prospektus Larkin Sentral 2017).

16.3.4 Pondok Gontor

Pondok Gontor is regarded as one of the oldest waqf institutions in Indonesia (Fasa 2017). It was initially known as Gontor Lama or Gontor Generasi Pertama (Masruchin 2014a). It has been built in the 18th century by one prominent Islamic scholar, Kyai Sulaiman Jamaludin, a student of the prominent Kyai Khalifah, the founder of Pondok Tegalsari. Kyai Sulaiman Jamaludin was trusted by Kyai Khalifah to set up his own pesantren in Gontor. Gontor is located in the southeast of Ponorogo, Indonesia. At the initial stage of its set-up, Gontor Lama received only 40 students though the number gradually increased. However during the third generation of the administration of Gontor Lama, this development got stagnated and the students' intake was significantly reduced. This led to the fourth generation known as Trimurti – Kyai Ahmad Sahal, Kyai Zainuddin Fannani and Kyai Imam Zarkasyi – revolutionary action that modernized Gontor Lama in 1926 (Dacholfany 2015). The name of Gontor Lama then changed to Pondok Modern Darussalam Gontor. The modernization affected the education system and its management (Aswirna *et al.* 2018). Today Pondok Gontor hosts about 26,000 students, having 17 *pondok cabang* (branches), one institution for male students (Kulliyyatu-l-Mu'allimin Al-Islamiyyah Gontor Putra), five institutions for female students (Kulliyatu-l-Mu'allimat Al-Islamiyah Gontor Putri) and one Darussalam Gontor University (Pondok Modern Gontor Darussalam 2019).

16.3.5 Governance and transparency

Governance plays a big role in ensuring the organization's strategic planning and successfully implementation. Organizations are led by forward-thinking, passionate and mature leaders that help instill a good working culture and drive an organization growth to a higher level. Transparency is also another best practice that is deemed compulsory for organizations that deal with public financing and donations. These prerequisites are visible in these selected case studies.

1.6.3.6 BRAC

BRAC is governed by a ten-member governing body that comprises distinguished professionals, activists and entrepreneurs of excellent repute. Their expertise, skills and experience have driven BRAC to a globally recognized reputable standard. BRAC has also networks outside Bangladesh and they are governed by BRAC International Supervisory Board. The successful implementation of BRAC's programmes and initiatives that are able to reduce extreme poverty and empower the poor have proven the stature of its governing body and management team. The credibility and quality of BRAC's governance is reinforced by the "AAA" rating by Credit Rating Agency of Bangladesh Ltd. The "AAA" rating reflects BRAC's extremely strong capacity and highest quality in meeting its financial commitments (BRAC 2018). The organizational structure of BRAC is further described in Figure 16.1.

In addition to BRAC's calibre leadership and management team, BRAC has also engaged key government stakeholders. The engagement and collaboration with the local and foreign ministries and organizations enabled BRAC's programmes to scale up and be more impactful. Among the local government ministries that BRAC is in alliance with are: Ministry of Education, Ministry

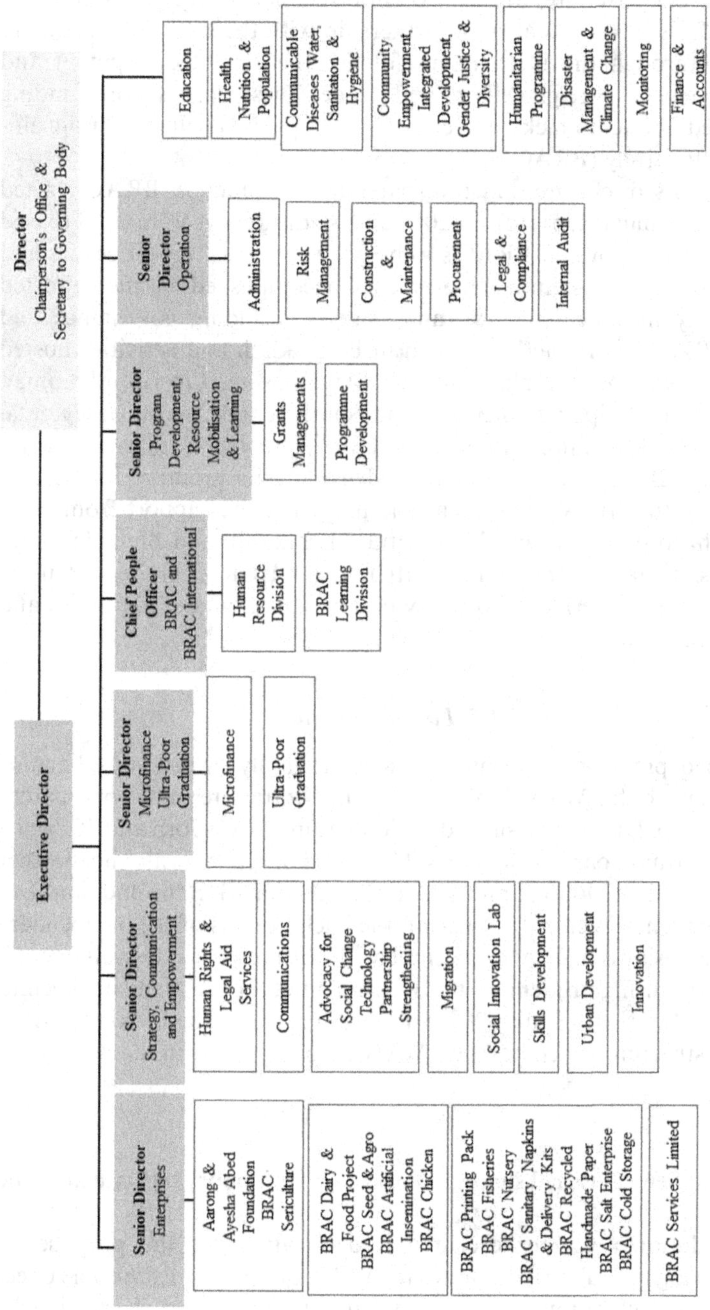

Figure 16.1 BRAC's organogram.

Source: BRAC (2018).

of Food, Ministry of Agriculture, Ministry of Health and Family Welfare, Ministry of Social Welfare, Ministry of Industries, Ministry of Women and Children Affairs. BRAC is also in partnership with the UK and Australian government through the Department for International Development and the Department of Foreign Affairs and Trade. These parties' core funding has facilitated BRAC to tackle the critical development challenges more efficiently and effectively (BRAC 2018).

As part of its disclosure and transparency best practice, BRAC started publishing its Annual Report from 2012 and Audit Report from 2008 (based on the uploaded reports in BRAC's website). The annual report covers and highlights the activities and achievements accomplished in the reported year especially meeting its vision and mission including governance and financial. BRAC reports activities held in Bangladesh and activities hosted by its networks across the globe, namely, Afghanistan, Liberia, Myanmar, Nepal, Pakistan, Philippines, Sierra Leone, South Sudan, Tanzania, Uganda, UK and USA. Key information shared in its report instills confidence and trust into BRAC's commitment to delivering its promise. Hence it is not surprising that BRAC has been able to garner the support from credible philanthropists and charitable institutions like Bill and Melinda Gates Foundations, Qatar Foundation, UNICEF, UNHCR, European Union, Kingdom of the Netherlands, Ministry of Foreign Affairs of Denmark and others (BRAC 2018).

16.3.7 Larkin Sentral

As mentioned previously, Larkin Sentral is a wholly owned subsidiary of WANCorp and both, WANCorp and Larkin Sentral are under one parent company, JCorp. Due to this subordination nature, WANCorp and JCorp sit on Larkin Sentral's board of directors. The board of directors also hosts other Jcorp's subsidiaries – Johor Land and TPM Technopark Sdn. Bhd, and two other independent directors. At present, the backgrounds of the independent directors are business management and law. Their presence adds value to the company by ensuring prudent and proper execution of the mandate given to the company (Kasri and Shukri 2020). Figure 16.2 shows the Larkin Sentral's governance structure which portrays WANCorp and JIRC in the waqf asset management.

Explanation:

1(a). Larkin Sentral issued shares and the *wāqif* or donors subscribed to the shares.

1(b). The donor/subscriber executed a declaration for the purpose of endowing the subscribed shares to WANCorp (*Waqfhujjah*). The effect of such declaration is that the status of the normal shares will be changed to *waqf* shares.

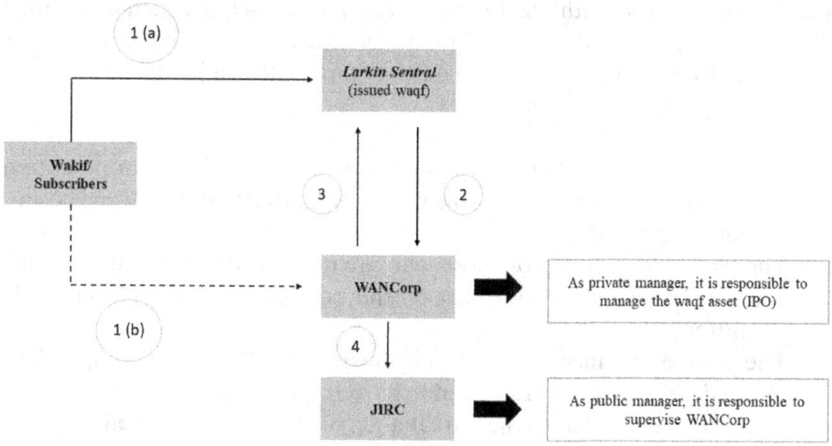

Figure 16.2 Larkin Sentral's waqf asset management.
Source: Ramli and Mahmud (2019) with adaptation.

2. 100% of the dividend declared by Larkin Sentral will be transferred to WANCorp as the private trustee cum beneficiaries to the waqf proceeds.
3. From the 100% transferred to WANCorp, 90% will be given back to Larkin Sentral for it to use for charity purposes.
4. The remaining 10% will be given to JIRC whereby 5% will be kept by JIRC and the remaining 5% will be distributed for charity in education, entrepreneurship and health sectors.

Another best practice of Larkin Sentral is its quarterly publication of report or statement that details out the Larkin Sentral Project's stage of performance or delivery including the collection and use of proceeds. Larkin Sentral has published several statements or reports in the form of advertisements in the local newspapers. Their quarterly reporting gave an update of the upgrading and refurbishment work of the Larkin Sentral Project, the amount of proceeds raised from the IPO and the corresponding use of proceeds on a quarterly basis. An accounting firm is hired to study and confirm the amount of revenue acquired and the amount utilized before these information are made available to the public (Kasri and Shukri 2020). This instill confidence in the public especially those who subscribed the waqf shares and assurance that the proceeds are utilized as per the commitment given in the Larkin Sentral's prospectus.

16.3.8 Pondok Gontor

In Indonesia, pesantren refers to the traditional Islamic school where customarily, the highest authority of pesantren remains with Kiyai (Islamic scholar/expert) as Kyai and his family solely owned the pesantren together with all its assets. Upon Kyai's death, the pesantren and all its assets are then bequeathed to his next generation. This hegemony system has attracted a number of criticisms. Masruchin (2014a) argued that this system inherits a number of disadvantages, among them:

1. Not all family members can comprehend inherent issues in pesantren. At the same time family problems could inadvertently be dragged into pesantren internal issues.
2. The lack of ownership of those who are not part of Kyai and his family could make them feel not part of the pondok but mere helper to the pesantren.
3. There were instances where family members of Kiyai who have been selected to lead pesantren do not have the required qualification. This factor unfailingly led to the retreat and collapse of a pesantren.

In fact, Gontor Lama was faced with these issues. Trimurti (Kyai Ahmad Sahal, Kyai Zainuddin Fannani and Kyai Imam Zarkasyi) (Dacholfany 2015) revolutionized the pesantren hegemony system by endowing (waqf) their pesantren ownership to the Muslim community. The effect of this revolutionary action is that the pesantren is no longer under the responsibility of Kyai and his family but the Muslim community. This differentiates them with other pesantren (Aswirna *et al.* 2018). The modernization impacted not only the management but its education and teaching system. The main authority now belongs to a Waqf Board. The Waqf Board acts as the *nazir* (trustee) to carry out duties towards their *waqif* (beneficiaries) and the Board members being elected every five years. The daily administrative duties and obligations are carried out by the leaders in Pondok Gontor. They are the senior teachers who devoted themselves in serving the pesantren with the help of junior teachers (Muzarie 2010). They too are chosen by Waqf Board and elected for every five years (Masruchin 2014a). Figure 16.3 describes the "modernized" governance structure of Pondok Gontor.

1. Waqif or founder of the Trimurti handed over all land assets along with the educational facilities and infrastructure to the Gontor Waqf Board which has 15 members.
2. The Waqf Board accepted waqf from the Waqif and managed and developed Gontor boarding schools. Its obligation is to execute the waqf mandate – to develop pesantren into a quality and meaningful Islamic university.
3. Islamic boarding school leaders form five institutions, where each institution undertakes separate and independent task but share the same goal, which is to help the Waqf Board and its leadership to realize the waqf mandate. The University of Darussalam (UNIDA), Ikatan Keluarga Pondok Modern (IKPM), Lembaga Pengasuhan Santri and Kulliyatul

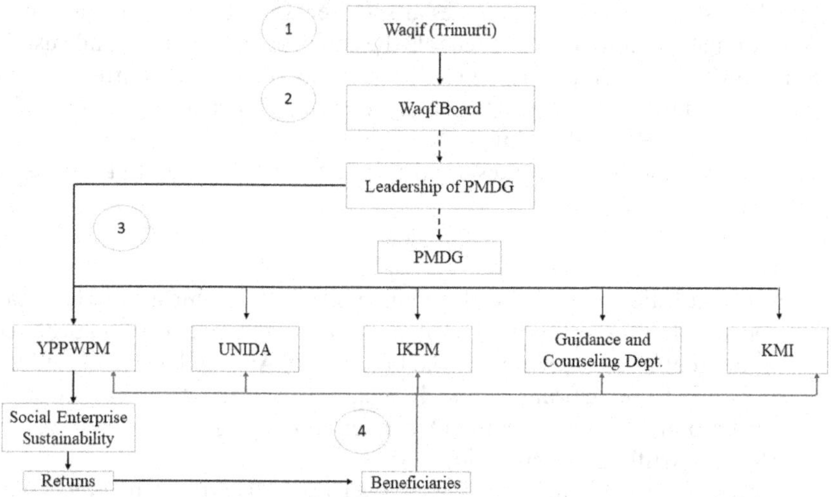

Figure 16.3 Governance structure of Pondok Gontor.

Source: Siahaan, Iswati and Zarkasyi (2019) with adaptation.

Mu'allimin / Mu'allimat Al-Islamiyyah (KMI) play the role of regulating, pursuing and running the field of education.

4. Yayasan Pemeliharaan dan Perluasan Wakaf Pondok Modern (YPPWPM) is an extension of the boarding school leadership that is being tasked with managing and developing waqf assets. The waqf assets centred around plantation, agriculture, livestock, services, trade and industry.

16.3.9 Sustainable Business Model

BRAC, Larkin Sentral and Pondok Gontor are all sustaining themselves by actively operating sustainable business models. Some have massive capacity and capability that enables them to diversify their business. This effectively allows them to benefit from economy of scale activities, cross-subsidies and natural hedging mechanism implementation.

16.3.10 BRAC

BRAC's social enterprises have facilitated the poor to overcome two major challenges – sustainable livelihood and market access. These major concerns, if left unattended, would hinder economic growth and social empowerment of the marginalized communities. BRAC's model of social enterprise leverages on traditional non-profit activities with business initiatives. The surpluses generated from the social enterprise business are reinvested back into BRAC's development projects that would further accelerate social impact (BRAC 2018).

BRAC's social enterprise activities are centred around agriculture and livestock commercial initiatives that enable the community to achieve and sustain food security. It developed value chains for individuals, microentrepreneurs, smallholder farmers and producers by combining capacity building and extension services, and linking them to markets for sustainability. The followings are the social business ventures that BRAC has undertaken as of 2018 (BRAC 2018):

1. Aarong
   Aarong is said to be one of the country's largest and most popular retail chains, with 3 sub-brands – HerStory, Taaga and Taaga Man that catered to different market segments. The business of Aarong has harnessed the skills of 65,000 artisans across Bangladesh through a vast network of rural production centres and independent producers.
2. BRAC's Artificial Insemination
   It provides insemination services to over 680,000 cattle farmers to boost the productivity of their livestock and optimize their gains as a result of higher-quality cow breeds. BRAC Artificial Insemination offers its services through 2,600 trained service providers across the country.
3. BRAC Chicken
   It processes and supplies high-quality dressed chicken and value-added frozen food products to a range of clients, from restaurants to retailers. BRAC Chicken processes around 8 metric tonnes of raw chicken and 2 metric tonnes of ready-to-cook frozen products every day.
4. BRAC Cold Storage
   It operates chill storage facilities for harvested yields of potato farmers to ensure that their products are kept fresh. BRAC Cold Storage also integrates farmers with the potato processing industry.
5. BRAC Dairy
   It provides a range of high-quality dairy products for urban consumers. BRAC Dairy is the third-largest milk processor in the country, collecting and processing on average 130,000 litres of milk every day. It also ensures fair prices and greater market access for over 50,000 dairy farmers across Bangladesh.
6. BRAC Fisheries
   It pioneered commercial aquaculture in Bangladesh and leverages on Bangladesh's water bodies to boost national fish production. BRAC Fisheries is one of the leading suppliers of fish spawn, prawn larvae and fingerlings. It also supplies fish food, operating ten hatcheries across seven locations nationwide.
7. BRAC Nursery
   It provides access to high-quality seedlings in order to promote tree plantation across the country. BRAC Nursery has been awarded first prize in

the National Tree Fair's NGO Category for the last 12 years. It operates 15 nurseries that are located across Bangladesh.

8. BRAC Printing Pack
   It provides flexible packaging material for food items, processed edibles and agricultural inputs. BRAC Printing Pack produces around 1,200 metric tonnes of packaging materials per year.
9. BRAC's Recycled Handmade Paper
   It recycles waste paper to make paper and paper products such as envelopes, gift boxes and photo frames. BRAC Recycled Handmade Paper recycles approximately 70 metric tonnes of waste paper in a year.
10. BRAC's Salt
   It provides a steady supply of iodized salt to help curb iodine deficiency of the rural population across the country. BRAC Salt has been able to reach approximately 1.5 million people through 380 salt dealers and around 40,000 community health workers.
11. BRAC's Seeds and Agro
   It produces and markets high-quality maize, potato, rice and vegetable seeds through an extensive network of farmers, dealers and retailers across Bangladesh. BRAC Seed and Agro is the largest private sector seed producer in the country, with 20 production centres and have employed 7,000 contract farmers.
12. BRAC's Sanitary Napkin and Delivery Kit
   It produces over 1.2 million safe and affordable sanitary napkins to allow suburban and rural women to attend work and school regularly. It also generates more than 73,000 delivery kits to facilitate safer births. BRAC Sanitary Napkin and Delivery Kit has created income-generating opportunities for almost 40,000 community health workers.
13. BRAC Silk
   It promotes silk production through its 19 production centres across Bangladesh by guiding rural women on the silk-making process. BRAC Silk promotes traditional silk reeling and spinning practices by supporting 3,700 women to engage in individual "charka" spinning within their homes. It has produced 900,000 yards of silk every year, which are sold through Aarong and trade fairs.

16.3.11 Larkin Sentral Property Berhad

As mentioned earlier, Larkin Sentral issued waqf shares to the Malaysian market. The offering aimed to raise RM85 million (USD21.25 million) for its Larkin Sentral Project. Larkin Sentral project consists of two phases. First is the upgrading and refurbishment of Larkin Sentral which involves upgrading the wet market and transport terminals as well as refurbishing shop lots. While the second phase includes the purchase of a piece of land, adjacent to the terminal and to develop on it a seven-story parking lot building. 42.6% from the RM85 million (USD21.25 million) will be allocated for the first phase and another 53.6% is allocated for the second phase. The remaining 3.5% is to cover the cost incurred in the public offering exercise (Kasri and Shukri 2020).

It was reported that at the closure of Larkin Sentral's public offering in May 2019, it has raised from the public about RM7.861 million (USD 1.97 million) out of RM85 million (USD 21.25 million) it planned to raise from its IPO exercise. Despite the meagre amount raised, the IPO exercise is seen as an important milestone in the development of innovative asset class for waqf sector. To facilitate the completion of the Larkin Sentral Project, Larkin Sentral applied and obtained financing for the project. The approval of the financing could be due to the creditworthiness of Larkin Sentral's parent company, JCorp which is the State of Johor's investment corporation (Kasri and Shukri 2020).

The Larkin Sentral Project is expected to garner steady and continuous income from the rental of the terminal bus, retail lots including the wet market and the parking. Currently, Larkin Sentral is one of the largest transportation terminals in Malaysia which attracted about 9 million visitors yearly or on average 26,000 visitors daily. It has direct bus services to and from various cities and towns in Peninsular Malaysia as well as Singapore and Hat Yai, Thailand. The installation of new e-ticketing system ticket, with waiting area equipped with air-conditioners together with QR Code system installed at the passenger entrances, made the bus terminal very convenient to all walks of life. Thus the upgrading and refurbishment work that Larkin Sentral is undertaking would bring more comfort to the users in using the facilities and indirectly increase the number of users and business to the retailers (Kasri and Shukri 2020).

16.3.12 Pondok Modern Darussalam Gontor

Pondok Gontor has able to survive and sustain due to its sustainable waqf management system (Siahaan et. al., 2019). Its waqf enlargement and economic enterprise initiatives in particular has enabled it to self-sustaining where surpluses made is channelled to its educational and operational purposes (Abdul Razak 2016). Among the activities are as follows:

(1) Development of La Tansa Kopontren Business Units.

Pondok Gontor established an institution called Yayasan Pemeliharaan dan Perluasan Wakaf Pondok Modern (YPPWPM) to administer and develop Pondok Gontor's waqf properties/assets. YPPWPM then formed an economic movement by opening business units/activities in the real sector under the establishment of Kopontren (Masruchin 2014b). Kopotren operates 32 units of economic activities with the total profit of Rp 124 billion (USD8.8 million) per year which have benefited its Islamic boarding schools, *santri* (students) and the wider community. Table 16.1 enumerates Kopotren economic activities.

Table 16.1 Economic activities under Kopotren

Unit Business	*Profit (in Rp)*	*Profit (in USD)*	*Unit Business*	*Profit (in Rp)*	*Profit (in USD)*
Printing	12,764,597,063	906,877	Bakery	1,514,020,100	107,520
Book store	12,544,965,417	891,273	Pharmacy	1,899,587,100	134,901
Mantingan Distribution Centre	17,515,221,000	1,244,392	Mineral water	2,094,132,934	148,738
Sport store	10,163,278,298	721,759	Gambia telephone	493,282,900	35,036
Confectionary	3,631,733,900	257,949	Roya	4,347,238,909	308,700
Building materials	20,521,212,500	1,457,598	Laundry	233,303,500	16,567
Al-Azhar telephone	1,206,540,000	85,699	Grocery	1,042,473,250	74,026
Selep	9,735,926,882	691,531	Latansa distributor centre	4,124,585,000	292,919
Latansa telephone	2,243,245,000	691,531	Restaurant	1,295,039,000	91,970
Sudan transportation	664,657,750	47,211	Chicken slaughter	1,592,778,500	113,115
Guesthouse IKPM	462,935,000	32,883	Chicken noodle	235,209,764	16,704
Azhar canteen	1,703,236,700	120,985	La-Tansa tea	235,541,000	16,727
Guesthouse	711,591,443	50,546	Ice cream	277,177,600	19,681
Asia photocopy	1,070,349,000	76,029	Computer centre	321,443,912	22,824
UKK Mini Market	8,059,056,103	572,454	TPS	140,301,000	9962
KUK Convenience Store	1,612,988,375	114,539	Catfish	58,232,000	4135
Total	**104,611,534,431**	**7,429,071**	**Total**	**19,904,346,469**	**1,413,523**

Source: Siahaan *et al.*, (2019).

(2) Waqf Land Management System.

Sawah (plantation) lands are managed by YPPWPM by planting crops food such as rice, corn and secondary crops. In managing these lands, YPPWPM is facilitated by a supervisor called the nazir. These lands are managed in three ways (Masruchin 2014b):

1. In the form of *Mukhabarah* Agreement where *tanah sawah* (padi field) is managed by the farmers and the profit sharing ratio is determined at the inception of the contract, based on the agreement between the farmers and YPPWPM. The profit distribution between farmers to YPPWPM is 40:60.
2. In the form of *Ijarah* Agreement where the waqf land is leased to the farmers and the farmers paid the rental according to the crop season.
3. In the form of rent which depends on the results of the plantation. The lessee will pay according to the amount of proceeds obtained.

The waqf lands cover 320 hectares and they continue to grow. Today 212 hectares of rice fields are harvested twice a year and have yielded Rp 726 million rupiahs (USD51,678) (Rumah Wakaf 2019).

16.3.13 Socio-Economic Impact

The social impact made by these three entities is tremendous considering their self-sustaining models and the end benefit that society and environment have enjoyed.

16.3.14 BRAC

In addition to the jobs created and capacity building developed through BRAC's social enterprises, BRAC has also made significant social impacts in its other programmes. Among them are BRAC's Ultra-Poor Graduation Program and Microfinance that have made positive social impact locally and abroad as follows (BRAC 2018):

i. 12.9% of the Bangladesh population lives in extreme poverty. It was reported in 2018 that via BRAC's Ultra-Poor Graduation Program, a total of 114,528 ultra-poor households have been enrolled into this programme. Out of which 43,682 households from the 2017 cohort graduated from ultra-poverty in 2018. Since its implementation in 2002, a total of 1.9 million households have emancipated from the cycle of ultra-poverty and have played active roles in the market economy. The exemplary model of this programme has been replicated by NGOs, governments and multilaterals from over 43 countries for example Uganda, Kenya, Lesotho, Philippines, Liberia, Egypt and Rwanda.

ii. 50% of adults in Bangladesh do not have access to formal financial services. Through BRAC's Microfinance, as of 2018, USD4 billion have been disbursed to 7.1 million clients of which 87% of its clients are women. Out of 7.1 million clients, 5.6 million are given loans and 84% thereof are given insurance coverage. By 2018, a total amount of USD828 million has been kept on saving. As part of its customers' protection, BRAC has put in place 2,100 customer service assistants in all its branches nationwide. They act as the first point of contact to attend to any queries and concerns by the customers as well as providing these customers pre-disbursement financial literacy training. This reflects BRAC's responsible financing policy and practice. BRAC has also offered Microfinancing to the poor outside Bangladesh. In 2018, a total of USD247.98 million in loans have been disbursed to 571,935 borrowers in Myanmar, Tanzania, Liberia, Sierra Leone and Uganda.

16.3.15 Larkin Sentral

The idea of issuing Larkin Sentral waqf shares publicly is due to the change in the corporate approach of WANCorp from being exclusive to inclusive. The IPO allows the public to participate in its waqf activities. Larkin Sentral Terminal is a rundown building where bus tickets are sold at the terminal counter with no availability of online ticketing system. The upgrading of the terminal is direly in need as it will cater for the lower and middle income people who travel within the country and to the neighbouring countries. The upgrading and refurbishment of the terminal provides ample parking space and online ticketing system as well as better retail facilities (Securities Commision 2018).

A total of 20 retail lots worth RM1.3 million (USD310,712) were distributed to 20 recipients consisting of single mothers, the disadvantaged and the disabled (BERNAMA 2019). The 100-square-foot bazaar lot which is equipped with water and electricity supply facilities, given to each recipient, are fully funded through the Larkin Sentral cash waqf shares. Eligible tenants are given a five year lease term of RM400 per month and among the businesses available in the lot are food, beauty and handicraft products (Hussein 2019). Guidance and assistance will be provided from time to time to ensure these recipients are self-sufficient and ultimately able to run their own business on the premises of their choice (BERNAMA 2019).

In addition to the above and as mentioned earlier, 90% of dividends received by WANCorp from the Larkin Sentral waqf shares will be used for the following charitable purposes:

1. Reasonable rental rate (by lowering the rental rate by up to 10% over the normal market rental rate) is imposed to selected Larkin Sentral tenants (excluding tenants with a stable business), subject to timely rental payment performance records.
2. Minimum rental rates for small shop lots created in Larkin Sentral for single mothers and low-income groups (which could be reduced to half the market rate per square feet).

While the balance of 10% dividend received by Johor Islamic Religious Council from the Larkin Sentral waqf shares will be used for itself as well as to be distributed for charity in education, entrepreneurship and health sectors (Waqaf Saham Larkin Sentral 2019).

16.3.16 Pondok Modern Darussalam Gontor

Pondok Gontor has health centres in each of its *pondok*. However, the health centres offer limited services and cater only for its students. Pondok Gontor decided to build a public hospital that would cater for the general public. The people of Ponorogo in the Mlarak region can then take advantage of the service offered by this public hospital. The plan is to build a three floor hospital with 100 beds. The construction of the hospital has reached 50% completion which is expected to be in operation by 2021. The budget for the construction of the hospital including the medical devices is estimated to reach about Rp 80 billion (USD5,681 billion). At the moment, the budget is funded solely by Pondok Gontor (Jalil 2019).

Pondok Gontor also conducts trainings to empower the local farmers, traders and small and medium (SME) businesses. It guides them on many respects particularly on growing their skills and mindset. Among the trainings given are instilling trading skills for traders and SMEs, and granting rice slips, rice milling and facilities for the farmers as well as the surrounding community (Kusumadewi 2016). Recently, Pondok Gontor entered into a Memorandum of Understanding with Bukalapak, a unicorn and one of the largest e-commerce companies in Indonesia, to do digital entrepreneurship training. The trainings are meant for the trainees from Pondok Gontor-assisted SMEs and Pondok Gontor alumni businesses to improve their business. The collaboration allows the use of Bukalapak online platform to market Pondok Gontor stakeholders' digital products and its e-ticketing technology for the collection of zakat funds, infaq and other charitable activities (Brito.Id 2019).

16.4 Conclusion

The three mini case studies deliberated in this paper disclosed and highlighted the sustainable operating model of these entities including their best practices, governance, transparency and social impact. These models have succeeded in sustaining these entities to where they are today. However, waqf institutions have much to learn from the success story of BRAC's sustainability and transparency. BRAC story demonstrated the importance of competent management team, transparency in reporting, disclosure and reliable database. This is important as waqf institutions deals with public money and public trust. In the meantime a number of recommendations can be proposed for consideration by waqf entities as well as waqf supervisory authorities, namely:

1. Publication of annual report annually. Among its key content are annual financial statement, mobilization of the waqf proceeds and returns from the investment, performance and delivery of the waqf projects, assessment of the waqf performance and effectiveness, and future plan to meet its missions.
2. Asset allocation, investment policy and strategy must be clearly stated and documented. The management team must clearly stipulate the apportionment that will go to cover the expenses of the waqf project and investment. This includes the operational and funding costs.
3. Qualified and competent professionals must be in the team of management. Human capital must be developed through theoretical and hands-on trainings, workshops and internships programmes.
4. Advanced technology like blockchain and smart contract can be adopted to address the transparency and accountability problems in the waqf mobilization and distribution structure. Through this advanced technology, the delivery and progress of the waqf project can be monitored on real time basis and alleviate any intended abuse of power and funds (Kasri and Shukri 2020).

References

Abdul Razak, D. *et al.* (2016). A study on sources of Waqf funds for higher education in selected countries. *Adam Akademi 6*(12016), 113–128.

Anheier, H. (N.D). What is The Third Sector. Available at: http://fathom.lse.ac.uk/Features/122549/. [Accessed: 18 October 2019]

Aswirna, P. *et al.* (2018). Paradigm changes of pesantren: Community based Islamic scholar perception about post-modernism pesantren based on android. *Asian Social Work Journal 3*(5), 31–38.

BERNAMA (2019). Dua puluh individu B40 ditawar premis perniagaan di Larkin Sentral. *BERNAMA*. 31 January 2019. Available at: www.bernama.com/state-news/beritabm.php?id=1690721 [Accessed: 19 October 2019]

BRAC (2018). BRAC Annual Report, 1(1), p. 108. Available at: www.brac.net/publications/annual-report/2018/. [Accessed:13 October 2019]

Brito. Id. (2019) Undang CEO Bukalapak, Pondok Gontor Rancang Ekonomi Umat Berbasis Digital. *Brito. Id.* 16 June 2019 Available at: www.brito.id/undang-ceo-bukalapak-pondok-gontor-rancang-ekonomi-umat-berbasis-digital [Accessed: 20 October 2019]

Dacholfany, M.I. (2015). Leadership style in character education at the Darussalam Gontor Islamic Boarding. *Al-Ulum 15*(2), 447. doi: 10.30603/au.v15i2.212.

Department Trade and Industry (2002). Social Enterprise: A Strategy for Success. Available at: www.dti.gov.uk/.[Accessed: 10 August 2019]

Fasa, M.I. (2017). Gontor as the learning contemporary Islamic Institution transformation toward the modernity. *HUNAFA: Jurnal Studia Islamika 14*(1), 141. doi: 10.24239/jsi.v14i1.462.141-174.

Hussein, I.N.A. (2019). OKU gigih berniaga bantu keluarga. *Harian Metro.* 01 February 2019 Available at: www.hmetro.com.my/mutakhir/2019/02/418553/oku-gigih-berniaga-bantu-keluarga [Accessed: 19 October 2019]

ILO Social Economy (2010). Operationalising the Action Plan for the Promotion of Social Economy Enterprises and Organisations in Africa. Available at: www.ilo.org/public/english/employment/ent/coop/africa/download/tf_se_final.pdf. [Accessed: 16 October 2019]

Jalil. A. (2019). Pondok Gontor Segera Miliki Rumah Sakit Senilai Rp80 Miliar. *Solopos.com* 08 October 2019 Available at: www.solopos.com/pondok-gontor-segera-miliki-rumah-sakit-senilai-rp80-miliar-1023661. [Accessed: 20 October 2019)

Kasri, N.S. & Shukri, M.H. (2020). International Best Practices in Existing Corporate Waqf Models: A Retrospective, *Challenges and Impact of Religious Endowments On Global Economics And Finance.* IGI Global

Kusumadewi, E.W. (2016). Selalu Libatkan Masyarakat Sekitar, Kunci Sukses Pesantren Gontor. *Merdeka.com* 24 January 2016 Available at: www.merdeka.com/peristiwa/selalu-libatkan-masyarakat-sekitar-kunci-sukses-pesantren-gontor.html [Accessed: 20 October 2019)

Mahomed, Z. (2017). The Islamic Social Finance & Investment Imperative. *Centre For Islamic Asset and Wealth Management*, pp. 29–31. Available at: www.inceif.org/archive/wp-content/uploads/2018/04/The-Islamic-Social-Finance-Investment-Imperative.pdf. [Accessed: 14 October 2019]

Masruchin. (2014a). Bab III Profil Pondok Modern Darussalam Gontor A Kemandirian Pondok Modern Darussalam Gontor. In *Wakaf Produktif dan Kemandirina Pesantren*, pp. 1–35. Available at: http://digilib.uinsby.ac.id/895/. [Accessed: 16 October 2019]

Masruchin. (2014b). Bab IV Hasil Analisis Data Dan Pembahasan A. Analisa Pengelolaan Wakaf Produktif Di Pondok Modern Darussalam Gontor 1. In *Wakaf Produktif dan Kemandirina Pesantren*, pp. 1–35. Available at: http://digilib.uinsby.ac.id/895/9/Bab%204.pdf [Accessed: 16 October 2019]

Muzarie, M. (2010). Hukum perwakafan dan implikasinya terhadap kesejahteraan masyarakat: implementasi wakaf di Pondok Modern Darussalam Gontor. Kementerian Agama RI, Indonesia.

Pondok Modern Darussalam Gontor (2019). [online] Available at: www.gontor.ac.id [Accessed 19 Oct. 2019]

Prospektus Larkin Sentral (2017). Larkin Sentral Property Berhad. Available at: www.waqafsahamlarkin.com/prospectus.pdf. [Accessed: 10 August 2019]

Ramli, R. & Mahmud, M.L. (2019). Waqaf Saham Larkin Sentral. Available at: www.at-mia.my/2019/02/15/waqaf-saham-larkin-sentral/. [Accessed: 20 August 2019)

Rumah Wakaf (2019). Rumah Wakaf.org Available at: www.rumahwakaf.org/ [Accessed 21 October 2019].

Sadeq, A.M. (2002). Waqf, perpetual charity and poverty alleviation. *International Journal of Social Economics 29*(1–2), 135–151. doi: 10.1108/03068290210413038.

Securities Commision (2018). *Proceedings of the SC-OCIS Roundtable 2018*. doi: 10.1017/CBO9781107415324.004.

Seelos, C. & Mair, J. (2006). BRAC – An Enabling Structure for Social and Economic Development, *3*(January), pp. 1–7.

Sepulveda, L. (2015). Social enterprise - a new phenomenon in the field of economic and social welfare? *Social Policy and Administration 49*(7), 842–861. doi: 10.1111/spol.12106.

Siahaan, D., Iswati, S., & Zarkasyi, A.F. (2019). Social enterprise: The alternatives financial support for educational institusion. *International Journal of Economics and Financial Issues 9*(3), 1–11. doi: 10.32479/ijefi.7626.

Waqafsahamlarkin.com (2019). *Waqaf Saham Larkin Sentral* [online] Available at: www.waqafsahamlarkin.com/pages.aspx?Content_Name=Soalan_Lazim [Accessed 23 October 2019].

17

SUSTAINABLE DEVELOPMENT AND THE WORK OF IBN KHALDUN

The case of Indonesia

Rahmi Edriyanti, Abu Umar Faruq Ahmad and Shafiqur Rahman

The high-tech industrialization that we are currently witnessing is resulting in potentially long-term harmful environmental and social impacts. Sustainability is an important phenomenon in economic development because it encompasses the management of resources, energy, economics, business development, environmental impacts, construction practices, social concerns and many other factors.[1] Consequently, in order to achieve sustainable development in any economy, it is a basic requirement that adverse impacts on the quality of natural resources such as air, water and biodiversity are minimized to sustain the overall integrity of the ecosystem.

The Stockholm declaration at the United Nations Conference on the Human Environment, June 5–16, 1972, marked a turning point in international *environmental* politics. It succeeded in opening a new paradigm in how economic, social and environmental issues were discussed.[2] The emergence of the concept of sustainable development put questions on how to ensure the perpetuity of the earth's resources at the center of international debate.

However, such questions have long been part of the discourse in Islam. In an attempt to explain the Islamic concept of sustainable development, Sharī'ah scholars have come up with a broad framework, called *maqāsid al-Sharī'ah*, or the higher objectives of the Sharī'ah. The 12th-century scholar, Al-Ghazzali initiated these, and broadly discussed in five categories of protection and preservation namely, religion or faith (*din*), self (*nafs*), intellect (*'aql*), progeny (*nasl*) and property (*māl*). Islam provided a guiding light for promoting sustainable development in Allah's vast universe by instructing its inhabitants to avoid committing mischief and wasting natural resources to protect the environment. Allah has given human beings, alone among his creatures, the right to exercise the proper use of natural resources based on its status on this earth as His vicegerent. This implies the right to use another person's property subject to a promise that it would not be damaged or destroyed. In other words, human beings are entitled to benefit from the resources of the earth without selfishly monopolizing them. Some contemporary Muslim scholars have attempted to define sustainable development from an Islamic perspective as a multi-dimensional process that seeks to balance economic and social development and preserve the environment. Sustainable development is, therefore, not a new phenomenon in Islam. The Qur'an and the Prophetic traditions (Sunnah) provided the framework for the welfare of humanity, whether spiritual or physical. Over 500 verses in the Qur'an provide Muslims with guidance on how to tackle environmental issues. The Prophet Mohammed's sayings and practice also provide a framework for justice and equity (Hassan and Cajee 2002). This chapter attempts to identify the indicators of sustainable development from the viewpoint of Ibn Khaldun, as described in his magnum opus, *Al-Muqaddimah*, to determine the differentiation between modern economists and Ibn Khaldun's concepts. It then addresses and discusses current issues related to sustainable development in Indonesia using the economic thought of Ibn Khaldun and its relevance today.

17.1 Differing definitions of sustainable development according to modern economists and Islamic scholars

Modern economists have promulgated several definitions of sustainable development. The most frequently quoted, provided by the Brundtland Commission in its report, *Our Common Future*, stated that it is "development that meets the needs of the present without compromising future generations' ability to meet their own needs" (Rogers, 2008).[3] In the same year, Goodland and Ledec (1987) defined sustainable development as the transformation (development) of economics, optimizing the economic and social benefit obtained at present without jeopardizing the possibilities for obtaining such benefit in the future.[4] On the other hand, according to Pirages (1977), sustainable growth is economic growth supported by the physical, social and the environment.[5] While Petkeviciute and Svirskaite (2001) consider sustainable development as the process of economic development and structural change that helps broaden human possibilities.[6]

Sughandy (2009) defined sustainable development as "a process of development that optimizes the benefit of natural and human resources on an ongoing basis, by connecting human activity with the ability of natural resources in the scope of land, sea and air as one unit".[7] According to Michel (2012), "the concept of sustainable development now means that the right to life and health of future generations must not be overlooked and measures that would be detrimental to them must not be adopted". This definition can be interpreted in the environmental area as speaking in favor of the principle of non-regression since it prohibits subjecting future generations to laws that would reduce environmental protection.[8] This notion in an essay arguing that sustainable development was born as a response to the discontinuity between three aspects: environmental, social and economical; when these aspects should interact with each other.[9] The definition of sustainable development has been developed into six points: first, it is oriented towards growth that supports ecological, social and economic purposes; second, it observes ecological constraints within material consumption and strengthens qualitative development in society and individuals through fair distribution; third, it requires government regulation, support and partnership with business to ensure the conservation and utilization of natural resources; fourth, it demands integrated policy and coordination at all levels and among all political jurisdictions to develop energy for human needs; fifth, it depends on education, planning and informed political processes for the transparent and equitable development and management of technology; and finally it requires the integration of social and environmental costs in economic calculations (Sughandy, 2009).[10]

Modern economists have also attempted to make quantitative determinations of sustainable development. Some of the notable examples include:

a. Gross domestic product (GDP): by calculating with two approaches, i.e., expenditure and income. Nevertheless, the expenditure approach is usually used by economists, with the formula GDP = consumption + investment + government expenditure + (export – import) without calculating for the depletion of natural resources and degradation of the environment (Mankiew, *2006*).[11]
b. Green gross domestic product (GGDP) or green gross national product (GGNP): by calculating the national income or output. The results of the larger number will indicate a higher level of sustainability (Harris and Fraser, 2002).[12]
c. Net investment or income: by calculating net national assets, which consist of natural resources and human capital. The results of the larger number will indicate a higher level of sustainability (Hamilton and Clemens, *1999*).[13]
d. Net development indicator: by calculating the change in human prosperity through 25 indicators such as consumption (a wider measure than GDP) and the value of the modal stock. The results of the larger number will indicate a higher level of sustainability.[14]
e. Human sustainable development index (HSDI): by calculating wealth, measured by per-capita national income and supplementing this by health, measured and quantified by citizens' longevity (life expectancy at birth), education, measured by a composite of the mean and expected years of schooling, the environment, measured by per-capita CO_2 emissions in reverse way. It is written in the formula, HSDI = wealth + health + education + environment.[15]

In the Islamic world, sustainable development is based on four principles, according to Al-Jayyousi (2012): 1) *'adl* (good governance and justice), 2) *ihsān* (beauty and sustainable development), 3) *arhām* (social capital) and 4) *fasād* (corruption). From an Islamic philosophical perspective, these concepts are not new. However, linking them together to address sustainability is a novel approach and now very much part of an emerging conversation within the Islamic world. From the Islamic perspective, it is the combination of the four key notions of *hikmah* (wisdom), *'adl* (justice), *maṣlahah* (public interest) and *ijtihād* (independent effort or reasoning). Concerning the first notion (wisdom), Al-Jayyousi saw this as the purposeful pursuit of acquiring and realizing wisdom from all countries. He meant this by justice in its broadest terms, which becomes the core of a sustainable rule based on rights. Public interest refers to a consensus reached by a group of individuals on what is good for all. Finally, independent effort appertains to the application of diligence and intellectual capital to solve current problems.[16]

17.2 A brief history of the concept of sustainable development

The concept of sustainable development aims to address the weaknesses of unmitigated economic growth, which cannot ensure the planet's economic, environmental and social sustainability. The notion was first discussed at the first UN Conference on the Human Environment in 1972 in Stockholm, Sweden. This conference attempted to explore the relationship between the quality of life and the environment and was addressed by many global leaders, including Dr. Emil Salim from Indonesia who went on to lead the newly established ministry of development. As a world-renowned expert in sustainability, Dr. Salim has always criticized the traditional development concept and promoted the tenets of sustainable development in Indonesia and many other developing nations.[17]

The concept of sustainable development has always been an evolving phenomenon, but concrete action has been slow to follow. The follow-up to Stockholm was held in 1984 under the auspices of the World Commission on Environment and Development (WCED), led by Gro Harlem Brundtland, the then Prime Minister of Norway. The WCED, became popularly known as the "Brundtland Commission" and was established to analyze global developmental problems and suggest ways forward, consistent with the concept of sustainable development (Siahaan, 2004).[18] The WCED resulted in the publication of the Brundtland Report (Our Common Future) in 1987, which comprehensively defined sustainable development for the first time.

The Brundtland Report led to the Earth Summit (officially called the United Nations Conference on Environment and Development) held in Rio de Janeiro in 1992, which adopted Agenda 21, a blueprint for environment and development in the 21st century. It set out to provide an agenda for local, national, regional and global action based on Brundtland's three-pillar concept of sustainable development – economic growth, social development and environment protection. The Rio Declaration on Environment and Development was adopted by more than 178 Governments and established the Commission on Sustainable Development (CSD) to support Agenda 21.[19]

Ten years later, world leaders, national delegates and leaders from non-governmental organizations (NGOs), businesses and other major groups convened again in Johannesburg, South Africa for the second Earth Summit: The World Summit on Sustainable Development. The aim of the Summit was to re-focus the world's attention on sustainable development and gain support for direct action to meet a host of difficult challenges, including improving global quality of life and conserving the world's natural resources amid exponential population growth, with ever-increasing demand for food, water, shelter, sanitation, energy, health services and economic security.[20] As far the regulatory framework for sustainable development from an Indonesian perspective is concerned, the government passed two laws regarding environmental sustainability which are stated in UU No. 23 in 1997 on the management of the living environment, and the government regulation Number 51 in 1993 on analyzing environmental impacts[21].

To assist countries' efforts to implement sustainable development, the CSD had compiled a set of 134 indicators in 1995 based on the OECD's environmental impact assessment model called driving force-state-response (DSR). Consequently, the CSD list was reduced to 58 indicators, embedded in a policy-oriented framework of themes and sub-themes. The CSD presented these indicators in 2001 and subsequently published as part of the second edition of the "blue book".[22] In 2005, the Division for Sustainable Development started a process to review the CSD Indicators. In 2007 it was revised again and reduced to 50 key indicators and 46 other indicators.[23] In 2008, Statistics Indonesia (2008) reviewed the indicators using compatible national data with guidance from the CSD. As a result, 62 indicators were adopted to guide sustainable development policy in Indonesia.[24]

On 25 September 2015 the United Nations General Assembly unanimously adopted the document "Transforming our World: the 2030 Agenda for Sustainable Development" under Resolution 70/1. This historic document lays out 17 sustainable development goals (SDGs) and 169 targets. These are renewed objectives and indicators for United Nations member countries' agreed universal targets from a previous agenda, i.e., the Millennium Development Goals (MDGs). The MDGs had been targets for all member countries until 2015 when they expired.[25] Achieving the SDGs can be summed up to mobilize global efforts to end poverty, eliminate hunger, maintain good health and well-being, ensure quality education, promote gender equality, support clean water and sanitation, and other human development goals.[26]

17.3 Ibn Khaldun and his contribution to economics

Born in Tunisia (AD 1332–1406), Abd al-Rahman Ibn Muhammad Ibn Khaldun al-Hadrami, commonly known as Ibn Khaldun, received his first education from famous teachers in the country. He learned Al-Qur'ān and Al-Qirā'at Al_Hasayiri from 'Abdullāh Muhammad ibn Sa'ad ibn Burr Al-Anṣāri, Arabic from Muhammad Shawwash Al-Zarlāli and Ahmad ibn Al-Qassār, knowledge of hadith and Fiqh from Sheikh Shamshuddin Abu 'Abdullāh Muhammad Al-Wadiyashi, kitab *Al-Muwatta'* from Abdullah Muhammad ibn 'Abdussalām, and philosophy and Islamic law from Sheikh Muhammad ibn Ibrahim Al-Abili and Sheikh Abd Al-Muhaimin ibn Al-Hadrami.[27]

From 751 to 776 A.H., he worked in administration positions as a secretary in Maghrib and Andalusia. From 776 until 784 A.H., he wrote his magnum opus, *The Muqaddimah* (also known as Prolegomena).[28]

Despite Ibn Khaldun's overall contribution to the field of economics, it is Adam Smith (1723–1790) who has been widely called the "father of economics". In fact, not only did Ibn Khaldun plant the first germinating seeds of classical economics, whether in production, supply, or costing, he also produced pioneering work on consumption, demand and utility, the cornerstones of modern economic theory. Ibn Khaldun used insightful empirical investigation to come to his analyses and produce original economic thought. He left a wealth of contributions in the field of economics that demonstrate incredible breadth and depth. Some of his most important accomplishments include his coverage of value and its relationship to labor; a theory of capital accumulation and its relationship to the rise and fall of dynasties; his perceptions of the dynamics of demand, supply, prices and profits; work on the subjects of money and the role of governments; a remarkable theory of taxation, as well as on other economic subjects. His distinctive contributions to the field should make him the father of economics (Siddiqi, 1976).[29]

In his book, *Muqaddimah*, Ibn Khaldun expounded on his ideas about taxation and how it impacted the economy and identified the market mechanism's concept.[30] He also clarified the concepts of profit, labor division, public finance, wealth management, money and prosperity.[31]

17.4 Sustainable development according to the ideas of Ibn Khaldun

A previous study conducted by Chapra (2008) considered whether Ibn Khaldun's theory of sustainable development explains the present-day Muslim world's relatively poor performance. In this regard, he summarizes his view on the variables in Ibn Khaldun's model, which he argues has triggered the Muslim decline and continues to be responsible for the inferior performance of many Muslim countries, as follows:

> *This theory [Ibn Khaldun's theory] argues that the development or decline of an economy or society does not depend on any one factor, but rather on the interaction of moral, social, economic, political and historical factors over a long period. One of these factors acts as the trigger mechanism and, if the others respond in the same direction, development or decline gains momentum through a chain reaction until it becomes difficult to distinguish the cause from the effect.*[32]

Chapra added that: "paying attention to only economic or even political variables for promoting economic development in Muslim countries may not be enough". We agree that considering only economic and political variables is not enough; crucially, the environmental variable is missing. In order to address this gap, this chapter seeks to identify this missing variable by reviewing the most critical factors – often discussed by Ibn Khaldun in *Muqaddimah* – relevant to sustainable development. According to Ibn Khaldun, the determinants of sustainable development are divided into five variables as summarized in the following.

17.4.1 The Sharīʻah

The Sharīʻah is the provision from Allah, which arranges all parts of the world to bring society prosperity in the *dunya* (world) and *ākhirah* (the hereafter).[33] This determinant is the main indicator and as it is law from Allah it controls all of the other determinants. Shariʻāh is the guidance given to humankind to follow the right path. The government and society as a whole practice Shariʻāh in a Muslim civilization. When both are of the same purpose and have strong faith, they will sacrifice themselves to protect the country from an enemy. But, if the faith is weakened, the country can be vulnerable to its enemies.[34]

17.4.2 Humankind

Humankind is the main actor in sustainable development. Ibn Khaldun places a great deal of attention on the human factor.[35] He explains that the main human duty is to act as the *khalifah* (trustee or vicegerent) of Allah on the earth. *Khalifah* means a human representative that acts as a leader for others in the scope of social organization.[36] Humankind's function is also to act as a guardian and supervisor for the world's sake and the hereafter. The *Khalifah* has a high position in governmental duties and a position and responsibility for the family and himself. Hence, Ibn Khaldun emphasizes that human beings should have a good education and the necessary skills to contribute to the country's welfare.[37]

17.4.3 Wealth

Ibn Khaldun defines wealth as a value derived from working and measured by money. Working is worship to Allah, which will bring rewards from Him. Several percent of the revenue earned by an individual is spent on the welfare of destitute people in the form of *zakāh, infāq, ṣadaqah,* tax and so forth, and important as part of a country's development.[38]

According to Ibn Khaldun, *zakāh, infāq* and *ṣadaqah* are Shari'āh's demands, which must be carried out by an individual in order to get closer to Allah. Meanwhile, tax is levied on an individual through rules that are subject to change by governments. The mandatory revenue earned by a country is for the development of infrastructure and to benefit society.[39]

17.4.4 Environment

The environment plays a pivotal role in human beings' health and well-being since it is their only home and provides all that they need. Their whole life support system depends on environmental factors. As social beings, humans depend on each other, and especially on a healthy environment.[40]

Humans cannot freely impact the environment as they wish as it is regulated and controlled by the Sharī'ah. They should utilize the environment without harming others while at the same time protecting and preserving it until the hereafter. This is what has been referred to in the Qur'ān as:

> *And when We [Allah] intend to destroy a city, We command its affluent but they defiantly disobey therein; so the word comes into effect upon it and We destroy it with (complete) destruction.*[41]

17.4.5. Justice

This is the most important goal after all of the other indicators are in action. Justice is a balance set up among humankind. All societies live in peace. Good leaders are also responsible as the arbiters and facilitators of distributing wealth and providing infrastructure.[42]

17.5 Sustainable development: the modern interpretation compared to Ibn Khaldun's era

The concept of sustainable development is in some ways understood in a remarkably similar fashion today as it was in the era of Ibn Khaldun. There is general agreement that the human factor is the most important indicator of sustainable development. Humans are social creatures and are highly dependent on the natural environment. From the natural environment humans can harness natural resources to develop new products. By educating themselves and specializing in a particular expertise, an individual can become a professional and expert in their discipline. When many people have such specializations, it will contribute to a higher quality of life through tax and, subsequently, the government's provision of infrastructural and societal benefits to simplify and improve human life. As a result, the impact of justice can be upheld.

Nevertheless, despite these similarities, differences are also apparent. In Islam, human beings are Allah's *khalīfah* (the caliphs) who are bound to obey His commands and create prosperity on the earth as His vicegerents. On the contrary, today, humans are free to opt out of secular practices and determine the course of their own lives.

Another difference lies in the Sharī'ah indicator. Ibn Khaldun's theory explains that every sub-indicator of sustainable development is subservient to the Sharī'ah in order to make the desired developments on the earth to earn salvation in the hereafter. However, the modern concept does not define or explain the human role and responsibility based on religion since it focuses only on the preservation of the physical world to protect future generations. It does not consider the *akhirah* or the eternal life after death as believed by faithful Muslims (Murad 1962).[43]

17.6 The relationship between sustainable development and Ibn Khaldun: an Indonesian perspective

Indonesia is the world's largest Muslim country with abundant natural resources. It is a leading producer of agricultural products. Located in Southeast Asia, Indonesia covers an overall area of around 191,378.68 km^2 and has 268,583,016 people (as per 2020 consensus). Indonesia has great potential to become a developed country. This chapter will now examine some of the key development issues in Indonesia and provide suggestions for how they might be addressed with reference to the work of Ibn Khaldun.

The issues are discussed in three key areas: economic, social and environmental, since they are all dependent on each other.

17.6.1 Economic aspects

Every human activity is connected to the economic system. Indonesia is a resource-rich country has still not been able to fulfill its inhabitants' basic needs. Poverty is the most serious problem facing the country. The United Nations' SDGs are aiming to reduce the number of people living on less than 1.25 dollars per day to mitigate and eventually eliminate poverty. In Indonesia, the poverty line is measured by the monthly average income per-capita, which, in 2016, amounted to 354,386 rupiahs. The government has undertaken

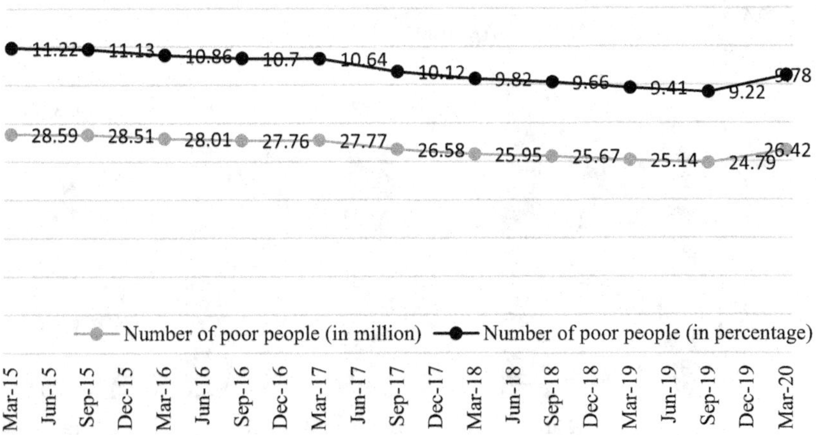

Figure 17.1 Number of poor people in Indonesia (in millions).

Source: BPS National Socio-Economic Survey.

several poverty alleviation programs to address the problem including cash transfers, family welfare cards, school operational assistance programs, credit for businesses, providing subsidized rice for the poor and so on.[44]

Poverty is connected to other problems, such as unemployment and the poor quality of human resources available to the country, all of which impact Indonesia's prosperity figures. Figure 17.1 illustrates that despite poverty alleviation programs, the number of people living below the poverty line remained stable from March 2016 to March 2019 with 9.22% (i.e., 24.79 million people) of its total population in poverty in March 2020.

Ibn Khaldun explained poverty and its key causes earlier than Karl Marx, Proudhon and Engels.[45] He stated that a large civilization can be achieved, which will yield large profits because of its great number of laborers.[46] So, as far as Indonesia is concerned, it is the government's responsibility to create jobs and provide employment opportunities to help all kinds of people in society, especially the poor and needy. This is because Indonesia has significant human capital that, if fully utilized, can create a huge amount of revenue. According to Ibn Khaldun, the ruling dynasty's tax revenues increased because of business prosperity, which flourishes with moderate, not excessive taxes. Therefore, he was the first scholar in history to lay the foundation for a theory of the optimum rate of taxation.[47]

The Gini ratio (or Gini coefficient) also provides us with statistics on economic inequality in Indonesia. The inequality in urban areas (a Gini coefficient of 0.392) was higher than in rural areas (0.317) in 2019. In general, the Gini ratio in Indonesia is at 0.382 (Statistics Indonesia, 2019) (Figure 17.2).[48]

The other factors that have a significant impact on sustainable development in Indonesia relate to economic development, measured by the country's

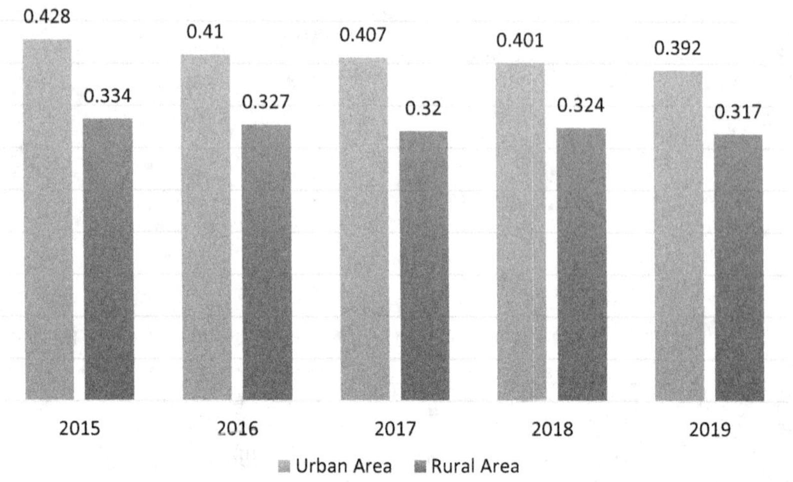

Figure 17.2 Gini ratio in Indonesia (percent).
Source: Statistics Indonesia.

economic growth and the effectiveness of regional economic partnerships such as the China-ASEAN Free Trade Area (CAFTA), ASEAN Economic Community (AEC), Asia-Pacific Economic Cooperation (APEC) and others. In reality, economic growth is the most powerful instrument for reducing poverty and improving GDP through the activities of a strong industrial sector. At the same time, trade partnerships are a source of increasing the scales of input. Currently, Indonesia emphasizes expanding its economic growth without considering its impact on natural resources in the future. Based on data from Statistics Indonesia (2016), Indonesia attained its growth target of 5.1% and at the third quarter of 2020, Indonesia experienced –5.32%. However, the country's economic growth cannot yet be considered the panacea for all of its problems. Therefore, GDP per-capita economic growth in Indonesia does not necessarily indicate the sustainability of the economy. Inflation and the ratio of external debt also denote more complex obstacles to Indonesia's economy's sustainability. Today, the price of almost all essential commodities is out of reach for many ordinary people. The government subsidizes its external debts to keep them under control. As a result, unemployment has risen precipitously and many companies saw no alternative other than but to lay off workers to decrease their inputs and maximize their profits.

Ibn Khaldun identified the causes of inequality in his famous book *Al-Muqaddimah*. In this work he compared the conditions of the inhabitants of regions with abundant civilizations with those living in insufficient ones. Ibn Khaldun evaluated the differences and came to conclusions similar to those drawn by Adam Smith in "The Wealth of Nations" hundreds of years earlier. "This may be exemplified by the experience of the eastern regions, such as Egypt, Syria, India and, China, and the whole northern regions, beyond the Mediterranean. When the development of their civilizations increased, the property of the inhabitants grew, and their dynasties became great. Their prosperity and affluence cannot be fully described because it is so great. The same applies to the merchants from the East and even more so to for the far Eastern merchants from the countries of the non-Arab Iraq, India, and China."[49]

17.6.2 Social aspects

The subject matter of society is human beings. The sociologist Peter Berger defines society as "a human product, and nothing but a human product, that yet continuously acts upon its producers". His view is therefore that although humans created society they are impacted and molded by it every day (Berger, 1967).[50] Humans are actors in all activities that form the social aspect of sustainable development because they determine whether a country is strong or weak. Human society greatly influences the natural environment and is especially important in fostering sustainable prosperity. Thus, there must be cooperation between governments and society to achieve sustainable prosperity. Nevertheless, in Indonesia, the relationship between the government and society is not conducive to sustainability. Political parties make promises during election campaigns to bring development to all sectors in Indonesia, but as soon as the election is over the government forgets these promises and continues its practice of corruption, conspiracies and nepotism. As a consequence, society has little faith in the governmental sector and the situation continually worsens.

Transparency International (TI) produces the corruption perception index (CPI), which reveals that Indonesia was ranked 85th of 180 measured countries in 2019. This ranking is a little higher than in 2014 when Indonesia was ranked 107th of 174 measured countries but remains extremely poor. Crime and corruption also present an obstacle to the implementation of sustainable development, presenting a threat to the region's stability and its educational, economic, social and perceived quality of life.[51]

Another issue that influences the social aspect of sustainability is education. Without knowledge, the population remains ignorant of the real value of natural resources, how to preserve them, and the threat posed to the planet should they become depleted. In Indonesia, the government encourages society to study for approximately 9 years or, for rural inhabitants, to at least be literate. Figure 17.3 shows the increase in the number of enrollments at elementary schools and junior high schools. It indicates that today's Indonesian society is more aware of the value of study and more students are asking their families to support them in attending higher education institutions to earn qualifications that can benefit them in the future. Through education,

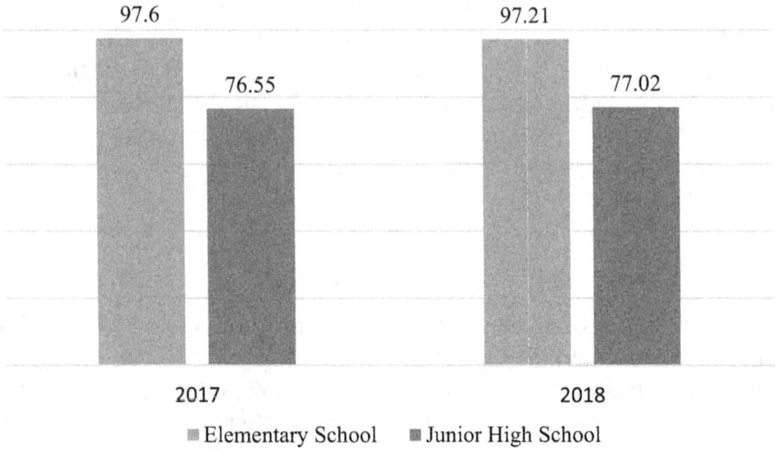

Figure 17.3 Net enrollment ratio of elementary schools and junior high schools in Indonesia.

Source: BPS National Socio-Economic.

individuals learn skills that improve their capabilities, consequently producing better tax revenues for the country and, as a result, increasing economic growth.[52]

Ibn Khaldun believed that teaching and learning are natural phenomena in the human sphere and education as a profession cannot be an abstract entity but should be based on experimentation, training and experiential practice, since one cannot acquire a craft without practicing it for a long time (Ibn-Khaldun 2001).[53] Given the fact that the root of a failing civilization is its lack of knowledge, in the *Al-Muqaddimah*, Ibn Khaldun explains the division of labor. Besides this, he also supported an increase in the population, provided that the specialization of skills accompanies it. To initiate a country's development and maintain its continuity, the governmental sector needs to encourage society to pursue quality education to build a healthier, more informed and skilled future generation. This will enable them to work on their passion and with a better attitude.[54]

Furthermore, he believed that when people have skill specializations, they make great contributions to their nations. For example, one part will go as a donation to the *zakāh* fund for faithful Muslims and a second as tax to improve society for every income earned. Thus, educated and skilled workers help the government create better facilities, infrastructure and provide other essential services. Ibn Khaldun sought social order in five ways: though the ruler, through the law, through the principles of justice, through the role of moral values and through the informal mechanism for justice (Mohammad,

2010).[55] In the determination of tax, he suggested that it should be of a small value in order to stimulate society to create businesses for development and growth. Otherwise, if the government determined higher taxes, business may be discouraged. In addition, he stated that tax administrators who are assigned to monitor the operation of system must be fair and honest to prevent fraud and deception.[56]

Another crucial issue is health. Without good health, people would not be in a position to carry out their daily economic activities in a normal way. Health is not only the state of being physically healthy; it also covers mental, spiritual and social well-being to enable people to live a socially and economically productive life. A healthy life is supported by water availability, access to healthcare, good nutrition and living in a pollution-free environment. If these factors are ignored, then the implementation of sustainable development is quite impossible. Key national indicators for societal health include overall life expectancy and the infant mortality rate; both are important ingredients in producing a healthy future generation. According to United Nations, the rate of infant mortality decreases each year in the country. As per the available data as in 2019, only 21.12% children died before celebrating their first birthday. This was far lower than in 2017 (22.62%). Malnutrition is an underlying cause of much infant mortality in Indonesia and is associated with diarrhea, pneumonia, malaria and measles. As for life expectancy, in 2019, Indonesian statistics expected that children born in that year would live an average of 69.3 years according data from World Health Ranking.

This phenomenon is relevant to Ibn Khaldun's thought as he argued: "medicine preserves the health of man and repels disease. It is a branch of physics. Its object is the human body".[57] He strengthens his argument by quoting the Prophetic tradition: "*The stomach is the home of disease. Dieting is the main medicine. The origin of every disease is indigestion*".[58]

17.6.3 Environmental Aspects

The environment is the most significant aspect of sustainable development in relation to the human need to establish a comfortable place to live. The concept of sustainable development attempts to integrate human beings' well-being with the well-being of the earth by ensuring the sustainability of natural resources, avoiding the over-exploitation of renewable resources, the depletion of non-renewable resources, and the availability of natural resources for future generations.[59]

Society tends to forget the value of the sustainability of the environment. Sustainability is the avoidance of the depletion of natural resources to maintain an ecological balance. Human beings must limit their exploitation of natural resources' benefits without compromising their availability to future generations. On many occasions during the past 20 years, every part of Indonesia has suffered natural disasters such as earthquakes in Aceh, Padang,

Bengkulu, Papua and Sulawesi, landslides in Java, floods in Jakarta and so on. On average, at least one major natural disaster has occurred in Indonesia every month since 2004 including earthquakes, tsunamis, volcanic eruptions and events that scientists argue have been caused by climate change. These disasters caused a plethora of problems. Many people died, key infrastructure was damaged and the health of society was under great threat. Moreover, rising CO_2 emissions have also caused obstacles to the economic development of Indonesia.[60]

Since human beings and nature are inseparable, the survival of mankind depends on the protection of the natural world and a healthy environment. To ensure that this is the case, there is a need to redouble efforts to protect nature from pollution and harmful *substances*.[61]

The glorious Qur'ān rightly refers to nature in this regard:

> It is Allah Who created the heavens and the earth and sent down rain from the sky and produced thereby some fruits as provision for you and subjected for you the ships to sail through the sea by His command and subjected for you the rivers. And He subjected for you the sun and the moon, continuous (in orbit), and subjected for you the night and the day. And He gave you from all you asked of Him. And if you should count the favor of Allah, you could not enumerate them. Indeed, mankind is (generally) most unjust and ungrateful.[62]

17.7 Conclusion

Ibn Khaldun is one of the most famous Islamic scholars to address human civilization in detail in his book *Al-Muqaddimah*. He considered five sustainable development variables in this work: Sharīʿah, human, wealth, environment and justice. Ibn Khaldun and modern economists agree that the most important variable is human beings' role, although in practical terms, Islamic scholars have a different worldview on moral value. Modern economics does have strong mechanisms that support and protect human actions, while Muslims have laws that have emerged from the Qur'an and the Sunnah.

What we have found and learned from the lessons from Ibn Khaldun's thoughts on sustainable development is that Indonesia, the world's largest Muslim country, must reconsider its trajectory of economic development. Even though Indonesia is not fully compliant with an Islam, it has the potential to make progress towards achieving sustainable development. This chapter suggests that Indonesia, being a densely populated Muslim country, must implement Ibn Khaldun's thoughts on sustainable development to benefit its people. A great civilization (justice) can be built in Indonesia if all parts of the governmental sector can work together with good intentions to achieve sustainable development.

Notes

1 Stephen A. Roosa, *Sustainable Development Handbook* (Lilburn: Fairmont Press, 2008), p. 2.
2 Sub Directorate of Environment Statistics, *Indicators of Sustainable Development* (Jakarta: Statistics Indonesia, 2012), p. 2.
3 Peter Rogers, Kazi F. Jalal and John A. Boyd, *An Introduction to Sustainable Development* (London: Earthscan, 2008), p. 42. See also, United Nations General Assembly (1987), p. 43.
4 Robert Goodland and George Ledec, *Neoclassical Economics and Principles of Sustainable Development. Ecological Modelling 38* (1987). p. 19.
5 Pirages, D.C. (1977). Social design for sustainable growth. In: *The Sustainable Society – Implications for Limited Growth*. New York: Praeger.
6 Petkeviciute, N., & Svirskaite, I. (2001). Ekonominis vystymasis ir žmogaus socialinė raida. Organizacijų vadyba: sisteminiai tyrimai(17).
7 Aca Sughandhy and Rustam Hakim, *Prinsip Dasar Kebijakan Pembangunan Berkelanjutan Berwawasan Lingkungan* (Jakarta: Bumi Aksara, 2009), p. 23.
8 Michel Prieur, "Non-regression in environmental law", *S.A.P.I.E.N.S* [Online], 5.2 | 2012, Online since 12 August 2012, connection on 03 October 2019. URL: http://journals.openedition.org/sapiens/1405.
9 Iwan J Azis, *Pembangunan Berkelanjutan: Peran dan Kontribusi Emil Salim* (Jakarta: PT. Gramedia, 2010), p. 23.
10 Aca Sughandy, Ibid, pp. 21–22.
11 Nicholas Gregory Mankiew, *Makroekonomi* (translated into Indonesian) (Jakarta: Erlangga, 2006), p. 25.
12 Michael Harris and Fraser, "Natural Resource Accounting in Theory and Practice: A Critical Assessment," *The Australian Journal of Agricultural and Resource Economics* (2002).
13 Kirk Hamilton and Michael Clemens, "Genuine savings rates in developing countries," *World Bank Economic Review,* no. 13 (1999), pp. 333–356.
14 Carl Hamilton, *Measuring Changes in Economic Welfare: The Genuine Progress Indicator for Australia*, In R. Eckersley, ed. *Measuring Progress: Is Life Getting Better?* (Australia: CSIRO Publishing, 1998) pp. 69–93.
15 Chuluun Togtokh, *Greening Human Development Index: Accounting Three Pillars of Sustainability,* presented at the conference Planet Under Pressure, slides of new knowledge towards solutions (2012), p. 3.
16 Rashed Al-Jayyousi, *Islam and Sustainable Development* (England: Gower, 2012), p. 15.
17 Iwan J Azis, *Pembangunan Berkelanjutan: Peran dan Kontribusi Emil Salim* (Jakarta: PT. Gramedia, 2010), pp. 1–2.
18 Nommy Horas Tombang Siahaan, *Hukum Lingkungan dan Ekologi Pembangunan* (Jakarta: PT. Gelora Aksara Pratama, 2004), p. 147.
19 Koesnadi Hardjasoemantri, *Perguruan Tinggi dan Pembangunan Berkelanjutan: Sebuah Tinjauan Aspek Hukum* (Jakarta: Direktorat Jenderal Perguruan Tinggi, 2001), p. 21.
20 Nommy Horas Tombang Siahaan, p. 150.
21 Santoso Soeroso, *Mengarusutamakan Pembangunan Berwawasan Kependudukan di Indonesia* (Jakarta: EGC, 2005), p. 27.

22 *United Nations, Indicators of Sustainable Development: Guidelines and Methodologies*, 2nd ed., UN Sales Publication No. E.01.II.A.6, September 2001.
23 Sub Directorate of Environment Statistics, *Indicators of Sustainable Development 2012*, p. 5.
24 *Ibid.*, p. 6.
25 Sub Directorate of Environment Statistics, *Indicators of Sustainable Development 2016*, p. 7.
26 Sustainable Development Goals. Retrieved 2 December 2019 from https://sustainabledevelopment.un.org/?menu=1300)
27 Ibn Khaldūn, *Mukaddimah Ibnu Khaldūn* (1st ed.). Translated into Indonesian by M. Irham, M. Supar and A. Zuhri (Jakarta Timur: Pustaka Al-Kautsar, 2011), p. 1082.
28 *Ibid.*, pp. 1082–1087.
29 Muhammad Nejatullah Shiddiqi, *Muslim Economic Thinking: A Survey of Contemporary Literature,* in the book of Studies in Islamic Economics (United Kingdom: International Centre for Research in Islamic Economics King Abdul Aziz Jeddah and The Islamic Foundation, 1976), p. 261.
30 Ibn Khaldūn, *Mukaddimah Ibnu Khaldūn* (1st ed.), p. 647.
31 Euis Amalia, *Sejarah Pemikiran Ekonomi Islam* (Depok: Gramata Publishing, 2010), pp. 235–249.
32 M. Umer Chapra, Ibn Khaldūn's theory of development: Does it help explain the low performance of the present-day Muslim world? *The Journal of Socio-Economics. 37* (2008), pp. 836–863.
33 Ibn Khaldūn, *Mukaddimah Ibn Khaldūn* (9th ed.). Translated into Indonesian by A. Toha (Jakarta: Pustaka Firdaus, 2011) p. 192.
34 Ibn Khaldūn, *Mukaddimah Ibnu Khaldūn* (1st ed.), p. 265.
35 p. 297.
36 Ibn Khaldūn, *Mukaddimah Ibn Khaldūn* (9th ed.), p. 74.
37 Euis Amalia, p. 242.
38 Ibn Khaldūn, *Mukaddimah Ibnu Khaldūn* (1st ed.) p. 643.
39 Ibn Khaldūn, *Mukaddimah Ibn Khaldūn* (9th ed.), p. 248.
40 *Ibid.,* p. 71.
41 Qur'ān 17:16.
42 Ibn Khaldūn, *Mukaddimah Ibn Khaldūn* (9th ed.), p. 192.
43 Murad, M.H. (1962). Abu al-Iqtiṣād, Ibn Khaldūn, in A'māl Mahrajan Ibn Khaldūn.
44 Sub Directorate of Environment Statistics, *Indicators of Sustainable Development 2016*, p. 50.
45 Waitlif Khalik Ibn Al-Sabil. See in Sheikh, Nasir Ahmad, "*Some Aspects of the Constitution and the Economic of Islam",* Working, England, The Working Mission & Literary Trust, (1957), p. 256.
46 Ibn Khaldūn, *The Muqaddimah,* (Translated by Franz Rosenthal), PDF E-book, p. 461.
47 I.M. Oweiss. "Ibn Khaldún, Father of Economics". In Arab Civilization: Challenges and Responses, edited by I.M. Oweiss, G.N. Atiyeh (New York: State University of New York Press, 1988).
48 Sub Directorate of Environment Statistics, *Indonesian Sustainable Development Goals (SDGs) Indicators* (Jakarta: Statistics Indonesia, 2019), p. 129.

49 Ibn Khaldūn, *The Muqaddimah* (Translated into English by Franz Rosenthal), PDF E-book, pp. 61–62.
50 Peter L. Berger, *The Sacred Canopy: Elements of a Sociological Theory of Religion* (Garden City, NYC: Doubleday & Company, Inc, 1967), p. 3.
51 Sub Directorate of Environment Statistics, *Indicators of Sustainable Development 2016*, pp. 64–65.
52 *Ibid.*, p. 85.
53 Ibn Khaldūn, *Mukaddimah Ibnu Khaldūn*.
54 Ibn Khaldūn, *Mukaddimah Ibnu Khaldūn* (1st ed.), p. 642.
55 Mohammad Tahir Sabit Haji Mohammad, Principles of sustainable development in Ibn Khaldūn's thought. *Malaysian Journal of Real Estate,* 5, no. 1 (2010), p. 13.
56 Ibn Khaldūn, *Mukaddimah Ibn Khaldūn* (9th ed.), p. 348.
57 Ibn Khaldūn, *The Muqaddimah* (Translated by Franz Rosenthal), PDF E-book, p. 513.
58 *Ibid.,* p. 526.
59 Mohammad Tahir Sabit Haji Mohammad, Principles of sustainable development in Ibn Khaldūn's thought. *Malaysian Journal of Real Estate,* 5, no. 1 (2010), p. 12.
60 Sub Directorate of Environment Statistics, *Indicators of Sustainable Development 2016*, pp. 101–103.
61 Ibn Khaldūn, *Mukaddimah Ibnu Khaldūn* (1st ed.), p. 684.
62 Qur'ān 14:34.

References

Al-Indunisi, S. (2011). Ensiklopedia Anak Muslim. Jakarta: PT. Elex Media Computindo.

Al-Jayyousi, R. (2012). Islam and Sustainable Development. England: Gower.

Amalia, E. (2010). Sejarah Pemikiran Ekonomi Islam. Depok: Gramata Publishing.

Azis, I.J. (2010). Pembangunan Berkelanjutan: Peran dan Kontribusi Emil Salim. Jakarta: PT. Gramedia.

Berger, P.L. (1967). The Sacred Canopy: Elements of a Sociological Theory of Religion. Garden City, NYC: Doubleday & Company. p. 3.

Chapra, M.U. (2008). Ibn Khaldūn's theory of development: Does it help explain the low performance of the present-day muslim world? *The Journal of Socio-Economics 37*, 836–863.

Goodland, R. & Ledec, G. (1987). Neoclassical economics and principles of sustainable development. *Ecological Modelling 38*, 19.

Hamilton, C. (1998). Measuring changes in economic welfare: The genuine progress indicator for Australia. In Eckersley, R. (Ed.), Measuring Progress: Is Life Getting Better? Australia: CSIRO Publishing.

Hamilton, K. & Clemens, M. (1999). Genuine savings rates in developing countries. *World Bank Economic Review, 13*(2), 333–356.

Hardjasoemantri, K. (2001). Perguruan Tinggi dan Pembangunan Berkelanjutan: Sebuah Tinjauan Aspek Hukum. Jakarta: Direktorat Jenderal Perguruan Tinggi.

Harris, M. & Fraser (2002). Natural resource accounting in theory and practice: A critical assesment. *The Australian Journal of Agricultural and Resource Economics, 46*(2), 139–192.

Hassan, A. and Cajee, Z.A (2002): Islam, Muslims, and Sustainable Development: The Message from Johannesburg, IMASE Web site. http://www.imase.org/details.php?articleid=1

Khaldūn, I. (2011). Mukaddimah Ibnu Khaldūn (1st ed.). (Translated into Indonesian by M. Irham, M. Supar, & A. Zuhri). Jakarta, Timur: Pustaka Al-Kautsar.

Khaldun, I. (n.d.). The Muqaddimah (F. Rosenthal, Trans.)

Mankiew, N.G. (2006). Makroekonomi (translated into Indonesian). Jakarta: Erlangga.

Mohammad, M.T. (2010). Principles of Sustainable Development in Ibn Khaldūn's Thought. *Malaysian Journal of Real Estate*.

Murad, M.H. (1962). Abu al-Iqtiṣād, Ibn Khaldūn, in A'māl Mahrajan Ibn Khaldūn. .Cairo: Markaz Al-Qawmi lil Buhuts al-Ijtimaiyah wa al-Jinaiyah.

Oweiss, I.M. (1988). Ibn Khaldún, Father of Economics. In Arab Civilization: Challenges and Responses. New York: State University of New York Press.

Petkeviciute, N., & Svirskaite, I. (2001). Ekonominis vystymasis ir žmogaus socialinė raida. Organizacijų vadyba: sisteminiai tyrimai (17).

Pirages, D.C. (1977). Social design for sustainable growth. In: The Sustainable Society – Implications for Limited Growth. New York: Praeger.

Prieur, M. (n.d.). Retrieved from http://journals.openedition.org/sapiens/1405.

Rogers, P., Jalal, K.F., & Boyd, J.A. (2008). An Introduction to Sustainable Development. London: Earthscan.

Roosa,S.A. (2008). Sustainable Development Handbook. Lilburn: Fairmont Press.

Sheikh, N.A. (1957). Some Aspects of the Constitution and the Economic of Islam. England: The Working Mission & Literary Trust.

Shiddiqy, M.N. (1976). Muslim Economic Thinking, A Survey of Contemporary Literature. Jeddah, Saudi Arabia and Leicester: International Centre for Research in Islamic Economics King Abdul Aziz Jeddah and The Islamic Foundation.

Siahaan, N.H. (2004). Hukum Lingkungan dan Ekologi Pembangunan. Jakarta: PT. Gelora Aksara Pratama.

Soeroso, S. (2005). Mengarusutamakan Pembangunan Berwawasan Kependudukan di Indonesia. Jakarta: EGC.

Sub Directorate of Environment Statistics (2012). Indicators of Sustainable Development 2012. Jakarta: Statistics Indonesia.

Sub Directorate of Environment Statistics (2016). Indicators of Sustainable Development. Jakarta: Statistics Indonesia.

Sub Directorate of Environment Statistics (2019). Indonesian Sustainable Development Goals (SDGs) Indicators. Jakarta: Statistics Indonesia.

Sughandhy, A. & Hakim, R. (2009). Prinsip Dasar Kebijakan Pembangunan Berkelanjutan Berwawasan Lingkungan. Jakarta: Bumi Aksara.

Sustainable Development Goals (2017, April 28). Retrieved from https://sustainabledevelopment.un.org/?menu=1300

Sustainable Development Goals (2019, December 2). Retrieved from https://sustainabledevelopment.un.org/?menu=1300)

Togtokh, C. (2012). Greening Human Development Index: Accounting Three Pillars of Sustainability. Greening human development index: accounting three pillars of sustainability. Retrieved 5 April, 2021 from https://ourworld.unu.edu/en/the-2010-human-sustainable-development-index.

United Nations (September 2001). Indicators of Sustainable Development: Guidelines and Methodologies (Vol. 2). UN Sales Publication No. E.01.II.A.6.

Waitlif Khalik Ibn Al-Sabil (1957). Some Aspects of the Constitution and the Economic of Islam. England: The Working Mission & Literary Trust.

World Bank Statistic Data (2017, February 18). Retrieved from http://data.worldbank.org/indicator/SL.UEM.TOTL.ZS?view=chart

18

PEOPLE, PLANET AND PROFITABILITY (3PS)

A gender management perspective

Eskil Sønju Le Bruyn Goldeng and Umar Burki

The global awareness and concern for climate change and the impact of environmental issues have gradually gained prominence in the last decades. Consequently, many commercial companies such as DHL (the courier company) and Patagonia (produces outdoor clothing) take a broader view of the responsibility for their actions and adopt a stakeholder approach. Such companies focus on negative externalities, i.e., how operations of a company may harmfully affect the external environment without reducing the profitability.

Under the shareholder perspective, enterprises focus mainly on economic outcomes such as profit or loss (Post, Preston, and Sachs 2002). Companies comply with formal rules and laws and focus primarily on economic benefits (profit). In contrast, the triple bottom line (TBL) approach focuses on a company's financial, social, and environmental aspects (Elkington 1998). TBL approach concentrates broadly on the effects of company operations beyond formal rules and regulations and how their business activities also affect social and environmental factors, also described as the 3Ps (people, planet, and profit) (e.g., Elkington 1998). The people dimension (*social bottom line*) refers to fair business practices towards employees and other individual stakeholders associated with the company's operations. The planet dimension (*the environmental bottom line*) denotes various sustainable ecological practices such as consuming and reusing and recycling natural and human-made resources. The profit dimension (*the economic bottom line*) signifies the economic value produced by a company's operations.

Measuring a company's performance using the traditional return on assets (ROA) approach fails to provide a full picture of a company's activities. In an ideal world, economic profitability should include the costs and benefits of social and environmental aspects. Companies considering these three dimensions vary in style. Decisions made by the management of companies reflect the attitudinal and personal characteristics of the decision-making hierarchy. One such feature may be gender.

Studies (e.g., Burke and Collins 2001; Ely 1995) show that women may have different upbringings, values, norms, and beliefs than men, which could affect their behavior and decisions. Men are generally considered assertive, controlling, confident, aggressive, and competitive, whereas women possess more communal traits and are more nurturing, helpful, kind, sympathetic, cooperative, sensitive, and gentle (Eagly and Johannesen-Schmidt 2001). Such distinctive gender differences may also manifest in men and women's approaches towards a more holistic view on operations, like the 3Ps.

In this chapter, we argue that gender explains management differences. We select a few indicators related to each of the three dimensions and then illustrate the management differences between men and women. For this purpose, we employ empirical data from one of the gender-neutral societies in Scandinavia (Norway) and identify variations related to people, planet, and profit.

18.1 Top management and gender

The role of top management is critical for business organizations. Top management in any firm formulate and execute strategic decisions and manage challenging issues with internal and external stakeholders (Hambrick and Mason 1984). Executive managers make vital decisions that significantly impact strategies and organizational outcomes (Finkelstein and Mooney 2003). Literature reports that when top executives support and provide sufficient human and financial resources to a cause, it directly affects a firm's strategic actions (Colbert 2004).

A business organization reflects the attitude or image of top managers (Hambrick and Mason 1984). While examining the determinants of voluntary environmental programs like ISO 14001 in India, Kumar and Shetty (2018) emphasize that the adoption of voluntary environmental programs is dependent on the willingness and the ability of a firm's top management. When top management fulfills a set of comprehensive sustainability demands, it has strategic and competitive implications. For instance, implementing sustainable practices differentiate between business firms and provide competitive advantages (Delmas and Pekovic 2013). Similarly, the adoption of ISO 14000 certification is a strategic initiative, which demands a substantial commitment from top management to integrate a firm's corporate strategies, functions, and operations.

The gender composition of the top management team may provide a meaningful predictor of a firm's strategy (Quintana-García and Benavides-Velasco 2016). For instance, studies show that the presence of women in top management affects strategic decision-making processes (Adams and Kirchmaier 2016; Nielsen and Huse 2010; Sonfield *et al.* 2001), strategic change (Naranjo-Giletal 2008), and strategic orientation (Escribá-Esteve *et al.* 2009). Literature also suggests that the top management team's composition plays a vital role in whether a firm implements environmental criteria in its operations (Naranjo-Gil 2016).

There is a visible surge of women represented in top management positions. For instance, Revlon recently appointed Debra Perelman as CEO; Airbnb appointed Belinda Johnson as Chief Operating Officer, and Arcadis appointed Sophie Brewitt as their Global Chief Marketing Officer. In Norway, women's representation in business firms' top management increased from 24% to 25.7% during 2006–2018 (Le Bruyn and Seierstad 2020). The following subsection argues about women's psychological role in the management and executive positions in comprehending ecologically based decisions.

18.1.1 Psychological attributes of women

Women show a higher degree of nurturance, affiliation to others, cooperation, and aversion to losses than men (Eagly and Carli 2003; Konrad, Corrigall, Lieb, and Ritchie Jr 2000). Women are considered to be "understanding, helpful, sophisticated, aware of the feelings of others, intuitive, creative and cheerful" (Ryan and Haslam 2007). Studies show women as more conservative and risk-averse than men in some contexts (Jianakoplos and Bernasek 1998; Johnson and Powell 1994). Other studies, like Nielsen and Huse (2010) suggest that women influence group decision-making, which increases the quality of said group decision-making. Having different communication styles, superior listening, and negotiation skills enable women to change the board dynamics and behaviors (Bilimoria and Wheeler 2000; Bradshaw and Wicks 2000; Huse and Solberg 2006). For instance, women introduce a different dynamic in the decision-making process, making group-decision more civilized and sensible to other perspectives and renewing the atmosphere (Huse and Solberg 2006; Zelechowski and Bilimoria 2004). Other studies underscore that women are ideologically different than men and have a greater sense of morality (Beutel and Marini 1995).

Women executives tend to be more risk-averse than men and may change a company's risk profile (Barber and Odean 2001; Beckmann and Menkhoff 2008; Eckel and Grossman 2002). For instance, when a firm CEO (chief executive officer) is a woman, its risk level is generally lower than when the CEO is a man (Khan and Vieito 2013; Rigolini, *et al.*, 2021). Female traits such as caring, sophistication, empathy, intuition, creativity and cheerfulness impact a company's risk profile (Ryan and Haslam 2007; Ryan, Haslam, and Postmes 2007). Literature associate women CEOs with lower levels of risk and a lower willingness to undertake financial investments and new acquisitions (Faccio, Marchica, and Mura 2016; Palvia, Vähämaa, and Vähämaa 2015; Huang and Kisgen 2013).

Top women managers follow ethical considerations and altruistic characteristics that provide a solid base for their unique leadership. For instance, cognitive biases, values, and perceptions influence women's decision frameworks (Eagly and Carli 2003). Hence, women executives' resilient ethical dispositions become mirrored in business organizations' strategies, which may provide a strong moral stance towards environmental sustainability.

Earlier studies show that women's presence had little effect on influencing a firm's strategic discussions (Ragins and Sundstrom 1989). Research reports that power plays a critical role in exerting top managers' influence in strategic decisions as all managers do not have the same degree of power in business organizations (Vander Vegtetal 2010). For instance, male senior management members are considered to be more influential than their female counterparts, a factor also visible in classrooms, businesses, and experiments in laboratories (Kimmel 2000; Ritter and Yoder 2004). However, this has varied with time and context.

18.1.2 Gender approaches in Scandinavia/Norway

Firm strategic decisions also reflect a society's structure and institutional norms (North 1990). In some nations, female managers have less power even when they are a part of the management team owing to gender biases in social relations (Rudman and Glick 1999). Societies with greater gender parity increase the say of women executives in making strategic decisions. Gender parity refers to the degree of female empowerment in a country. It can be measured in terms of the number of female representatives in the national parliament and executive positions in local business companies.

Norway is one of the most egalitarian societies in the world concerning race, religion, sexuality, and gender (Klugman 2011). Since the 1970s, numerous political initiatives have strengthened gender equality in Norway in all the major societal areas such as politics, education, and management boards in the public sector (Teigen 2000). Norway is internationally acknowledged as the first country to introduce a gender representation regulation on corporate boards for public limited companies (Goldeng *et al.* 2019). The Norwegian context is especially interesting as one can argue that women have more power in Norway than in other developed societies. Examining women's status in Norway and women-specific traits may help us make predictions about their participation tendencies, workplace behavior, and the arising consequences from these women-specific behaviors and preferences.

As discussed earlier, women are nurturing, helpful, kind, sympathetic, sensitive, and gentle. Such women-specific skills supplement social contact and reflect human compassion. Moreover, women have a greater sense of morality and tend to be more risk-averse than men. Consequently, the flip side of risk-averse behavior may be lower profits. Women being more risk-averse than men, we expect lower profits among companies that have female CEOs. Further, we assume women are more engaged than men in activities coping with ecological threats.

Based on the above arguments, we made two propositions. First, we expect that women's community approach and affiliation with others result in less discrepancy in companies' salaries with a female CEO. Second, we assume that women are more often engaged in industries that require more substantial human contact and have direct relations to end customers.

18.2 Linking empirical evidence with the 3Ps

We utilize two data sources to highlight gender differences. The first dataset is from the National Register of Company Accounts (NRCA) in Norway (Brønnøysundregisterne) and contains information about companies' accounting values, salaries, and CEOs' industrial affiliation in Norway. The second data covers the Norwegian companies' whole population, which we acquired through Dun and Bradstreet and Menon Economics AS. First, we use this data to calculate salary disparities in each company and then reflect on the employees' fairness of economic outcomes. And second, we employ this data to provide an overview of gender distribution in relatively socially oriented industries. This approach will help reveal the differences between men and women associated with the people dimension. We further expect to find a lower degree of salary disparity in companies with women CEOs and see a higher share of women as CEOs in industries that involve direct contact with end consumers.

With the accounting data's help, we calculate the profitability of companies with, respectively, male and female CEOs. Return on assets (ROA) is measured to calculate profitability as it captures the return on capital invested by a company. This is a traditional measure of performance that focuses on the returns to equity and debt. This measure is too narrow to capture the essence of profitability in the 3Ps framework but examining gender differences related to this measure will shed light on the difference in focus by men and women concerning myopic profit. We included value creation as a broader measure of performance, which captures the values created in each company that is shared between the owners and lenders and between employees (salaries) and the authorities (taxes). Such a measure of profit, or economic bottom line, fits better with the profit dimension in the 3P framework.

The second dataset is from the Ethical Trading Initiative (IEH), a Norwegian cooperation that promotes human rights, workers' rights, development, and environmental standards in their value chains (IEH 2019). IEH members have a total of 100,000 suppliers, with a total of 4 million employees that are affected by the guiding principles of the IEH. We accessed the names and gender of the IEH contact persons from each member company. The gender of the contact persons will be used as a proxy to reflect the difference in environmental and ethical focus between men and women.

18.2.1 The people dimension

18.2.1.1 Salary disparities

We investigate two proxies for people-orientation to reveal potential gender differences. As argued previously, we expect that women's collective attitude will influence the salary disparity in companies where the CEO is a woman. Using the NRCA data, we calculated the difference in salary disparities in companies having male and female CEOs. We divided the salary of the company's CEO with the total salaries in each company. As a result, this calculation shows the CEO salary proportion to all the salaries in a company. The reviewed literature proposed that male CEOs are more often viewed as assertive, controlling, confident, aggressive, competitive, and self-confident. Based on such masculine traits, male CEOs are more likely to negotiate a higher salary for themselves (see, e.g., Amanatullah and Morris 2010), even if it comes at their co-workers' expense.

Several factors strongly influence salaries for CEOs, with the most prominent factor being company size. Larger companies require more human capital and usually have more layers in their organizational hierarchy. Both these factors are responsible for a higher salary structure for the top managers and the CEOs (Tosi, Werner, Katz, and Gomez-Mejia 2000). To control for an association between companies' size and the distribution of men and women as CEOs, we have restricted this analysis by turnover. We only include those companies with an annual turnover higher than 100 million Norwegian kroner (NOK) but less than 1 billion NOK. We also restricted our sample by filtering out all companies whose CEOs received a salary less than 500.000 NOK (equals app. 50.000 Euros), and less than 10 million NOK in total salaries.

The data from the 3,181 companies reveals (see Table 18.1) that male CEOs tend to have a higher share of the total salaries in the selected companies. Both the mean and median percentage of salaries among male CEOs were substantially higher. These fractions show that male CEOs, in general, are considerably better remunerated than female CEOs in comparison to their co-workers and subordinates.

Table 18.1 CEO share of salaries in companies managed by women versus men CEOs

CEOs	*N*	*Mean*	*Median*
Women	256	3.4%	2.6%
Men	2823	4.1%	3.1%
Total	**3,181**	**4.0%**	**3.0%**

18.2.1.2 Share of women in different industries

Next, we examined our assumption that women are more often engaged in industries where the operations imply direct contact with people and the end consumer. By utilizing the NRCA data, we calculated the proportion of female CEOs in different industries. We followed the Statistical Classification of Economic Activities in the European Community (NACE) for the classification of industries. We included only those industries that had more than 200 companies (see Tables 18.2 and 18.3).

A general overview from the Statistics Norway (SSB) shows that the share of all female employees among organizations engaged in the health and social services sector was 79% in 2018, and 68% in the education sector (SSB 2019). Accordingly, women more often tend to be engaged in industries where interpersonal skills are essential. Similarly, this tendency is valid concerning women CEOs.

To compare female CEOs' share, we included the top five industries and the bottom five industries. There is a clear distinction between the top and bottom industries. In the top five industries, the operations involve direct interaction with the end consumer. This feature indirectly reflects the social dimension, i.e., all industries that require excellent interpersonal skills and need employees to be "people persons." The top industries focus on taking care of children, personal appearance, and gifts (flowers). The bottom five industries are related to the construction sector, usually having less or no interaction with end consumers. In these industries, being helpful, kind, sympathetic, sensitive, and gentle is not required at the same level as among the top five industries.

Table 18.2 Share of female CEOs in the top five (5) industries

Share of Women CEOs – Top 5 Industries	*Share of Female CEOs*
Kindergartens	86%
Hairdressing and beauty salons	84%
Cosmetics shops	79%
Clothing shops	78%
Flower shops	70%

Table 18.3 Share of female CEOs in the bottom five (5) industries

Share of Women CEOs – Bottom Five (5) Industries	*Share of Female CEOs*
Tinning	1.6%
Forestry services	1.9%
Sawing, planning, and impregnating of wood	2.1%
Manufacturing of builder's supplies	2.5%
Specialized construction businesses	2.5%

Table 18.4 Share of women as IEH contact person

Type of Member	*Number of Companies*	*Share of Women*
Commercial companies (Ltds)	57	48.70%
Other and non-profit companies	113	56.10%
Total	**170**	**51.20%**

18.2.2 *The planet dimension*

The IEH is a non-profit organization that helps its members to promote environmental and sustainability awareness in their supply chains and supports ethical trade. Small and medium-sized companies and a few of the largest companies in Norway, branches of public authority, industrial organizations, and NGOs are members of IEH. In 2019, IEH had 170 members who had to report their status and progress regarding environmental issues and ethical standards. All members of IEH have a dedicated contact person in their organization. Employees in the member companies which work is connected to IEH should be expected to have a stronger preference for ethical and ecological aspects.

Men's overall share in workplaces is higher; we would expect to find more men than women as contact persons if employees were stochastically allocated to positions and engagements. However, unlike most other Norwegian private and public sectors, we find that the majority of contact persons were women. The share of women among the contact persons in all organizations was 51%. To control for possible gender differences between the commercial companies and other organizations among the members of IEH, we divided the members into two groups; one with all the private business companies and one for NGOs, public authorities, etc.

The share of women associated with non-profit organizations among the members is higher than among the business companies. Still, among the business companies, we find (see Table 18.4) a substantially higher share of women than we usually do in most other positions and industries in the commercial sector in Norway. Interestingly, the percentage share of women is slightly higher among non-profit organizations, which may indicate that that women are less occupied with commercial and economic profit in general.

18.2.3 *The profit dimension*

18.2.3.1 *Value creation*

Value creation is an alternative measure of economic performance that includes the total economic gains of a company's operations that are to be shared between a company's critical stakeholders. We calculated the value creation divided by the total turnover. This is not a measure of profit per se, but

Table 18.5 Value creation share of turnover in companies with a female versus male CEO

CEO	*Number*	*Mean Share*	*Median Share*
Women	4,519	42.6%	39.1%
Men	31,494	33.9%	32.1%
Total	**36,013**	**35.0%**	**32.7%**

Table 18.6 Return of assets in companies with a female versus male CEO

CEO	*Number*	*Mean ROA*	*Median ROA*
Women	4,516	8.1%	6.0%
Men	31,485	8.7%	6.5%
Total	**36,001**	**8.5%**	**6.2%**

rather a measure that reveals how much of the company's turnover can be attributed to values created by the people working in the company, versus the share of the turnover that is outsourced and delivered through the market. A higher percentage reflects that the company's employees produce a greater share of the company's end product (see Table 18.5).

Our calculations only consider those companies having more than 10 million NOK in turnover because the volatility of smaller firms' operations often has a larger impact on their profits. Moreover, reporting errors are common among smaller firms (Goldeng, Grünfeld, and Benito 2008). Consequently, smaller firms introduce substantially more noise.

Women tend to be CEOs of those companies with a higher share of value creation per NOK of turnover. This underscores that women are managing companies with fewer outsourced operations, thus generating more value by bringing people to work together in a company. Contrastingly, men tend to be CEOs of companies with more of the value of their end products outsourced and, consequently, less value contribution from the company's people. Thus, women manage relatively more value creation from people in their companies in comparison to men.

18.2.3.2 ROA

Return on assets (ROA) is a robust measure for profit because it captures the yield to the company's total capital base. ROA is also influenced by the risk associated with the operations and the decisions of the top management. Like the earlier examination, we also put a 10 million NOK turnover as a limit (see Table 18.6).

The difference between female and male CEOs is seemingly not dramatic but dependent on the company's gearing and the expectations from the owners, these differences may be crucial. In general, men have a higher return on the asset in the companies they are responsible for. The difference between the mean and the median is approximately 0.5%-points. Male CEOs manage companies that seemingly focus more on profits in favor of the shareholders.

18.3 Discussion and conclusion

Privately owned companies are essential in maintaining the production and distribution of goods and services in societies. They represent a vital piece of the welfare and value creation puzzle. Furthermore, they perform efficiently and effectively to foster innovation and risk-taking to benefit the society at large.

Company owners are the residual claimants of the operations of the companies. The commercial interests, often measured in economic returns, play a crucial role in the activities and engagements of companies, and arguments have been made that a company's primary responsibility is to maximize profits to its shareholders as long as it stays within the rules of the game (Friedman 1970). However, the game rules vary between industries, due to various prevailing challenges, and can change at a slower pace. Consequently, formal rules cannot be trusted to capture all possible issues, e.g., negative externalities that may confront companies' operations. Williamson (2000) suggests that changes in the institutional environment, like lawmaking, bureaucracy, and organizations' policies, may take 10–100 years. If we apply the shareholder perspective as a guiding principle, and companies make decisions primarily to comply with laws and regulations, which may involve considerable negative externalities, this directs managers to maximize yield to the owners and, in worst case, disregard negative externalities. Ignoring sustainability and equality issues that are not regulated by the authorities and are not directly harmful to a company's profits might result in exploitation and misuse of people and natural resources. Lawmakers can't keep up with the various challenges' businesses face related to issues that may harm people and the environment (but not profit). Thus lawmakers will lag in many circumstances. Consequently, companies need to take social and environmental responsibility for their actions.

We introduced gender as an explaining variable to show the differences in attitude towards people, planet and profit. Using this as a guiding principle, companies need to focus and consider society when it concerns maximizing economic benefits.

Our analyses do not constitute a formal test on how and why women tend to end up in certain positions in different industries. However, the people, planet, and profit perspectives reveal interesting workplace gender differences. First, we find a clear pattern that indicates that women are more inclined to care for *the people dimension* in the workplace. Our modest data analysis shows that women tend to engage themselves in specific types of industries.

Women are usually people persons and therefore work in those industries that mandate direct contact and interaction with the end consumers, like working in kindergartens, the education sector, health and social services, hairdressers, and beauty salons.

In large companies, the salary differences between the CEO/top executive and the rest of the organization's employees are smaller when a woman is a CEO. A low salary difference between women CEOs and the rest of the employees in an organization demonstrates that women are less inclined to negotiate a high salary for themselves at the rest of the employees' cost. The consequence is that they, to a greater extent than men, share the economic outcome earned by all individuals' joint efforts in the company. Such a tendency is a sign of equality in an organization.

Second, women are seemingly more occupied with *the planet dimension* in the operations of organizations. Judging from the contact information among the members of the IEH, women have a better compliance approach towards sustainability issues and ethical standards. In the private sector, the share of female participation overall is 36.6%, while among the IEH member companies, 48.7% of the contact persons are women.

Third, we find that women do not solely watch investors and creditors; the traditional *profit* approach. As presumed under the shareholder perspective, men focus more on economic profit as women are more risk-averse decision-makers. That may be why the ROA is higher for those companies that have male CEOs. Women CEOs have a higher percentage of value creation per unit of turnover. Value creation is our alternative measure of economic performance. Women CEOs manage companies with less outsourcing and create more value-added benefits for employees and managers, credit lending institutions and authorities, and owners.

This chapter focuses on the different approaches followed by men and women in management positions based on specific female traits. With empirical evidence, our arguments suggest that women tend to focus more on people and the planet than their male peers. The economic bottom line, profit, showed a somewhat more nuanced result; men as CEOs seemingly focus more on financial return, whereas women focus on the joint product and value creation in their companies. At a later point, this finding should consider controlling for the industry. We demonstrated considerable differences in women CEOs' rates across industries and that the economic indicators we utilized may be somewhat industry-specific.

The empirical analysis identifies exciting patterns about the Norwegian gender approaches regarding 3Ps. In terms of limitations, we may have missed some working environment preferences and opportunities that affect women CEOs' tendencies to put a greater emphasis on people and environmental issues, along with economic profitability. We need more comprehensive research to understand the role of gender in the triple bottom line context. Qualitative studies could have given us in-depth knowledge about the differences between male and female managers' and employees' mindset. Moreover, we have only employed cross-sectional data, so there is a clear limit to our conclusions, our findings are based on associations and correlations. Later studies should also consider employing time-series data with more industry control, ownership, size, etc. Interesting findings could also have been harvested from experiments to reveal gender differences in attitudes towards moral and ethical dilemmas related to people, planet, and profitability.

References

Adams, R.B. & Kirchmaier, T. (2016). Women on boards in finance and STEM industries. *American Economic Review 106*(5), 277–281.

Amanatullah, E.T. & Morris, M.W. (2010). Negotiating gender roles: Gender differences in assertive negotiating are mediated by women's fear of backlash and attenuated when negotiating on behalf of others. *Journal of Personality and Social Psychology 98*(2), 256.

Barber, B.M. & Odean, T. (2001). Boys will be boys: Gender, overconfidence, and common stock investment. *The Quarterly Journal of Economics 116*(1), 261–292.

Beckmann, D. & Menkhoff, L. (2008). Will women be women? Analyzing the gender difference among financial experts. *Kyklos 61*(3), 364–384.

Beutel, A.M. & Marini, M.M. (1995). Gender and values. *American Sociological Review 60(3)*, 436–448.

Bilimoria, D. & Wheeler, J.V. (2000). Women corporate directors: Current research and future directions. *Women in Management: Current Research Issues 2*(10), 138–163.

Bradshaw P., Wicks D. (2000) The Experiences of White Women on Corporate Boards in Canada. In: Burke R.J., Mattis M.C. (eds) Women on Corporate Boards of Directors. Issues in Business Ethics, vol. 14, pp. 197–212. Dordrecht: Springer.

Burke, S. & Collins, K.M. (2001). Gender differences in leadership styles and management skills. *Women in Management Review 16*(5), 244–257.

Colbert, B.A. (2004). The complex resource-based view: Implications for theory and practice in strategic human resource management. *Academy of Management Review 29*(3), 341–358.

Delmas, M.A. & Pekovic, S. (2013). Environmental standards and labor productivity: Understanding the mechanisms that sustain sustainability. *Journal of Organizational Behavior 34*(2), 230–252.

Kumar, S. & Shetty, S. (2018). Corporate participation in voluntary environmental programs in India: Determinants and deterrence. *Ecological Economics 147*, 1–10.

Eagly, A.H. & Carli, L.L. (2003). The female leadership advantage: An evaluation of the evidence. *The Leadership Quarterly 14*(6), 807–834.

Eagly, A.H. & Johannesen-Schmidt, M.C. (2001). The leadership styles of women and men. *Journal of Social Issues 57*(4), 781–797.

Eckel, C.C. & Grossman, P.J. (2002). Sex differences and statistical stereotyping in attitudes toward financial risk. *Evolution and Human Behavior 23*(4), 281–295.

Elkington, J. (1998). Partnerships from cannibals with forks: The triple bottom line of 21st-century business. *Environmental Quality Management 8*(1), 37–51.

Ely, R.J. (1995). The power in demography: Women's social constructions of gender identity at work. *Academy of Management Journal 38*(3), 589–634.

Escribá-Esteve, A., Sánchez-Peinado, L., & Sánchez-Peinado, E. (2009). The influence of top management teams in the strategic orientation and performance of small and medium-sized enterprises. *British Journal of Management 20*(4), 581–597.

Faccio, M., Marchica, M.-T., & Mura, R. (2016). CEO gender, corporate risk-taking, and the efficiency of capital allocation. *Journal of Corporate Finance 39*, 193–209.

Finkelstein, S. & Mooney, A.C. (2003). Not the usual suspects: How to use board process to make boards better. *Academy of Management Perspectives 17*(2), 101–113.

Friedman, M. (1970). The social responsibility of business is to increase its profits. *New York Times Magazine*. September 13, 1970.

Goldeng, E., Grünfeld, L.A., & Benito, G.R.G. (2008). The performance differential between private and state owned enterprises: The roles of ownership, management and market structure. *Journal of Management Studies 45*(7), 1244–1273.

Goldeng, E.S.L.B., Rigolini, A., & Gabaldon, P. (2019). The effect of the introduction of the gender quota regulation among public limited companies' boards in Norway: Taking stock, looking ahead. In: Gabrielsson J., Khlif W., Yamak S. (eds) Research Handbook on Boards of Directors. Cheltenham: Edward Elgar Publishing.

Hambrick, D.C. & Mason, P.A. (1984). Upper echelons: The organization as a reflection of its top managers. *Academy of Management Review 9*(2), 193–206.

Huang, J. & Kisgen, D.J. (2013). Gender and corporate finance: Are male executives overconfident relative to female executives? *Journal of Financial Economics 108*(3), 822–839.

Huse, M. & Solberg, A.G. (2006). Gender-related boardroom dynamics: How Scandinavian women make and can make contributions on corporate boards. *Women in Management Review 21*(2), 113–130.

IEH (2019). Dette er Etisk handel Norge. Retrieved from https://etiskhandel.no/om-oss/ April 29, 2020.https://etiskhandel.no/om-oss/

Jianakoplos, N.A. & Bernasek, A. (1998). Are women more risk averse? *Economic inquiry 36*(4), 620–630.

Johnson, J.E.V. & Powell, P.L. (1994). Decision making, risk and gender: Are managers different? *British Journal of Management 5*, 123–138.

Khan, W.A. & Vieito, J.P. (2013). CEO gender and firm performance. *Journal of Economics and Business 67*, 55–66.

Kimmel, M.S. (2000). The Gendered Society. Oxford: Oxford University Press.

Klugman, J. (2011). *Sustainability and Equity: A Better Future for All (November 2, 2011). UNDP-HDRO Human Development Reports.*

Konrad, A.M., Corrigall, E., Lieb, P., & Ritchie Jr, J.E. (2000). Sex differences in job attribute preferences among managers and business students. *Group & Organization Management 25*(2), 108–131.

Le Bruyn, E.S. & Seierstad, C. (2020). Kjønnsbalanse blant ledere i Norge. Oslo: Magma.

Naranjo-Gil, D., Hartmann, F., & Maas, V.S. (2008). Top management team heterogeneity, strategic change and operational performance. *British Journal of Management 19*(3), 222–234.

Naranjo-Gil, D. (2016). The role of management control systems and top teams in implementing environmental sustainability policies. *Sustainability 8*(4), 359.

Nielsen, S. & Huse, M. (2010). Women directors' contribution to board decision-making and strategic involvement: The role of equality perception. *European Management Review 7*(1), 16–29.

North, D.C. (1990). A transaction cost theory of politics. *Journal of Theoretical Politics 2*(4), 355–367.

Palvia, A., Vähämaa, E., & Vähämaa, S. (2015). Are female CEOs and chairwomen more conservative and risk averse? Evidence from the banking industry during the financial crisis. *Journal of Business Ethics 131*(3), 577–594.

Post, J.E., Preston, L.E., & Sachs, S. (2002). Managing the extended enterprise: The new stakeholder view. *California Management Review 45*(1), 6–28.

Ragins, B.R. & Sundstrom, E. (1989). Gender and power in organizations: A longitudinal perspective. *Psychological Bulletin 105*(1), 51.

Rigolini, A., Gabaldon, P., & Goldeng, E. L. B. (2021). CEO succession with gender change in troubled companies: The effect of a new woman CEO on firm risk and firm risk perceived. *Scandinavian Journal of Management 37*(1), 101–138.

Ritter, B.A. & Yoder, J.D. (2004). Gender differences in leader emergence persist even for dominant women: An updated confirmation of role congruity theory. *Psychology of Women Quarterly 28*(3), 187–193.

Rudman, L.A. & Glick, P. (1999). Feminized management and backlash toward agentic women: The hidden costs to women of a kinder, gentler image of middle managers. *Journal of Personality and Social Psychology 77*(5), 1004.

Ryan, M.K. & Haslam, S.A. (2007). The glass cliff: Exploring the dynamics surrounding the appointment of women to precarious leadership positions. *Academy of Management Review 32*(2), 549–572.

Ryan, M.K., Haslam, S.A., & Postmes, T. (2007). Reactions to the glass cliff: Gender differences in the explanations for the precariousness of women's leadership positions. *Journal of Organizational Change Management 20*(2), 182–197.

Sonfield, M., Lussier, R., Corman, J., & McKinney, M. (2001). Gender comparisons in strategic decision-making: An empirical analysis of the entrepreneurial strategy matrix. *Journal of Small Business Management 39*(2), 165–173.

SSB-Statistisk Sentralbyrå/Statistics Norway (2019). Fakta om likestilling. Retrieved from www.ssb.no/befolkning/faktaside/likestilling, April 29, 2020.

Teigen, M. (2000). The affirmative action controversy. *Nora: Nordic Journal of Women's Studies 8*(2), 63–77.

Tosi, H.L., Werner, S., Katz, J.P., & Gomez-Mejia, L.R. (2000). How much does performance matter? A meta-analysis of CEO pay studies. *Journal of Management 26*(2), 301–339.

Van der Vegt, G.S., De Jong, S.B., Bunderson, J.S., & Molleman, E. (2010). Power asymmetry and learning in teams: The moderating role of performance feedback. *Organization Science 21*(2), 347–361.

Williamson, O.E. (2000). The new institutional economics: Taking stock, looking ahead. *Journal of Economic Literature 38*(3), 595–613.

Quintana-García, C. & Benavides-Velasco, C.A. (2016). Gender diversity in top management teams and innovation capabilities: The initial public offerings of biotechnology firms. *Long Range Planning 49*(4), 507–518.

Zelechowski, D.D. & Bilimoria, D. (2004). Characteristics of women and men corporate inside directors in the US. *Corporate Governance: An International Review 12*(3), 337–342.

19

CHALLENGES AND OPPORTUNITIES

Toseef Azid, Umar Burki and Robert Francis Dahlstrom

Our world is facing perpetual environmental challenges due to climate change. After the 2015 Paris Agreement, the world societies are serious about the consequences of climate change. Environmental challenges and sustainable development are more prominent in our daily lives. Businesses corporations are undertaking a massive transformation by adopting green technologies in their critical operations to improve the traditional consumption–production link on the environment. If the world stays determined and continues to take appropriate steps in the right direction, achieving environmental sustainability objectives and the SDGs 2030 is conceivable. However, managing the global environmental challenges and achieving SDGs necessitates a strong collaboration between the world nations and a united front for actions. Our academic work (Chapters 1–18) provides a sincere effort to underscore the role of moral and religious dimensions in mitigating the looming environmental threat and achieving SDGs 2030.

Successive UN Sustainable Development reports (e.g., from 2016 to 2020) identify the necessary policy measures for achieving environmental sustainability and SDGs. However, several governments still lag in their response. In conjunction with pertinent stakeholders, governments must highlight climate change; identify adverse effects of environmental pollution on human health, the environment, social equalities, and the requisite to adopt environmentally friendly technologies and innovations. Further, Governments need to develop and implement clear, rational, logical, consistent, and legally embedded policy frameworks. If necessary, redefine and transform old policy frameworks to integrate the multidimensional nature of sustainability. Government policies should demonstrate an absolute commitment towards reducing socio-economic disparities among the different segments of society, such as poverty and gender disparity related areas, particularly in the least developed countries. Without such an inclusive approach, it is hard to accomplish 5Ps, reduce poverty, and attain global human prosperity.

Religious and moral foundations are an essential part of human psychology and have a significant potential to contribute to healing the earth and achieving sustainability targets. Further, religious and moral values affect positively on the collective behavior of people. There is consensus that every religion and its guiding foundations improve the standards of living, enhance individual and mutual economic prosperity, protect the Mother Nature, and result in maintaining peace and partnership at the local and global levels. In addition to economic, social, environmental factors, moral, and religious components play a critical role in achieving environmental goals globally and locally. People follow moral values in their everyday life (e.g., honesty, avoiding lies) that contribute to their socio-economic welfare and help them prevent destructive vices such as greed and corruption. Therefore, it is critical to integrate religious and moral aspects to achieve SDGs and save our planet earth.

Religion has a prominent role in determining its followers' moral behavior and closely interwoven with charity and social welfare. All faiths have common morals values and teach their followers to protect every form of life in our universe. Similarly, all religions appreciate charity deeds. For instance, *Zakat* is one of the five pillars of Islam, which a practicing follower of Islam (*Musalman*) must perform unconditionally. This sacred pillar is absolutely focused on charity and contributes to improving the marginalized segments' socio-economic well-being in an Islamic society. Such religions and moral values ensure that humans should respect and help fellow humans, when possible, in physical and monetary terms. Concisely, every religion focuses on increasing man's welfare, protecting the planet, striving for economic prosperity, and strengthening human partnerships to maintain peace at the local and global levels.

Buddhism has the belief about the other creatures of the planet, as narrated by Dalai Lama, spiritual leader of Buddhism, "Life is as dear to a mute creature as it is to man. Just as one wants happiness and fears pain, just as one wants to live and not die, so do other creatures" (Singh and Clark 2016, p. 27). The book of Genesis (2:15) guides the follower of Christianity about the protection of the planet, "The Lord God took the man and placed him in the Garden of Eden to work it and take care of it." Similarly, the old scripture of Hinduism, Mahabharata narrates (109.10), "Dharma exists for the welfare of all beings. Hence, by which the welfare of all beings is sustained, that for sure is dharma." Judaism emphasizes, "The Earth is the Lord's, and the fullness thereof; the world, and they that dwell therein" (Psalm 24:1). In the Holy Quran (30:41), God says,

> Corruption has appeared throughout the land and sea by [reason of] what the hands of people have earned so He may let them taste part of [the consequence of] what they have done that perhaps they will return [to righteousness].

It is clear from the above quotations from the different major religions that every religion teaches supporting the agenda of sustainable development 2030.

Integrating FBOs (faith-based organizations) should be a welcoming step to counter climate change. Almost every country on this planet relies in one way or another on local and international FBOs to fight socio-economic disparities, most recently, contribute with excellent results to support efforts at the local levels to mitigate the adverse effects of climate change. For instance, the COVID-19 pandemic demonstrated the significant and contributory role of FBOs in providing health, education, and subsistence food requirements to masses at the grass root levels. FBOs such as *Catholic Faith*, Art of Living, *Jamaat-I-Islami Hind, All India Muslim Personal Law Board, Jamate-e-Ulema*, All India Ulema Council, ISKCON, Isha Foundation, Rama Krishna Math, Al Khidmat, etc. worked closely with governments and international organizations (UNICEF, WHO, etc.) in the fight against COVID-19. In the USA, Catholic Charities USA and Jewish Funders Network contribute prominently in serving society's poor segment. UK Oxfam, Red Cross, and Barnardo's are the best examples in the United Kingdom. In Pakistan, FBOs such as Al Khidmat serve the communities, especially during disasters. Buddhist Welfare Association work for the welfare of people and the planet. Buddha Dharma Education Association, Ecological Buddhism, and the International Network of Engaged Buddhists (INEB) are Buddhist organizations responding to global warming.

Religious harmony and inter-faith cooperation among the world nations would ultimately provide the impetus to mitigate climate change's harmful effects and achieve the 2030 SDGs. One can suggest that achieving SDGs 2030 and protecting the planet would become more manageable by employing religious foundations and moral values. Accomplishing "no one is left behind" demands a holistic and universal approach for building sustainable human societies. It is equally essential for governments to involve and support faith-based organizations in highlighting and combating climate change bearings.

The world nations still have to make more wholehearted concrete pledges to reduce GHG emissions to diminish environmental degradation processes and their impact on human health. One of the catalysts in augmenting climate change's enormity is the new dimensions of consumer metabolism, which has brought a fundamental shift in socio-economic settings and negatively impact human health and other socio-economic relationships. For instance, a better income level in developing and emerging economies has increased the demand phenomenally, one of the significant sources of GHG emissions. Similarly, insatiable consumer demand is responsible for processed foods in plastic packing, which creates plastic and, eventually, responsible for micro-plastic presence in the human food chain. Increasing mountains of food tins, plastic bottles, and textiles in garbage dump visible signs of innumerable pollution that the human race face. Collectively, all such pollution contributes to negatively affecting human health. The world experiences a continuous deterioration in human health as chronic diseases such as heart diseases (e.g., heart attack, hypertension, etc.), diabetes 2, asthma, and stress are on the rise.

Several emerging economies leaders show far-sighted commitments to mitigate adverse environmental effects and develop judicious future development policies. This good rationale behavior demonstrates the vital paradigm shift and responsibility at the top national levels to achieve sustainability goals.

Similarly, the financial sector began to owe the impact of its policies on the environment and SDGs 2030. Financial institutions are partners in investment projects. Therefore, it is the responsibility of financial institutions to examine whether a project generates negative externalities on the people and the planet.

Reference

Singh, K. and Clark, J.S. (2016). Voices from Religions on Sustainable Development, German Federal Ministry for Economic Cooperation and Development (BMZ), Division 111: Churches; political foundations; social structural programmes; religion and development, Bonn, Germany.

INDEX

Note: Page numbers in *italics* indicate a figure and page numbers in bold indicate a table on the corresponding page.

3Ps (people, planet and profitability) 329, 332; people 328, 333–335; planet 328, 335; profitability 328, 335–337; ROA 336–337; salary disparities 333; value creation 335–336; women in different industries 334–335
5Ps (people, planet, prosperity, peace and partnership) 9–10, 342
2030 Agenda for Sustainable Development 1, 10

aamla (*Phyllanthus emblica*) 99
Aarong 298
Abd al-Jabbar, Q. 115
Abdullah, M. 121–123, 126–127
Abdul M. M. 126
Abdul Razak, D. 300
Abrahamic religions 69–70; Christianity and sustainability 73–74; Islam and sustainability 74–78; Judaism and sustainability 70–73; *see also specific religions*
Academic Journal Guide 142
Acaravci, A. 191
Accenture *46*
accountability 148–149
Acemoglu, D. 221, 232
Achrol, R. S. 21
Adams, C. A. 140, 141, 149
Adams, R. B. 329
'*adl* (good governance and justice) 311
Adrian, T. 13
Afkhami, M. 132
Afshar Cultural Foundations 282
Agarwal, A. 102
age **271**
agricultural-based commodities 24
agricultural sector 8
Ahimsa 99
Ahmad, A. U. F. 308
Ahmad, K. 126
Ahsan, A. 126, 127
AIA 149
Airbnb 330
air pollutants 7
air pollution 4, 6–7
ajjhattam 83
Akcomak, I. S. 229
Alatas, F. 75–77
al-Baji, A.-W. 114
Albert, J. 132
Alborz Cultural Foundation 283, 285
al-Bukhari 128, 129
Al Dimishiqi, A.-F. J. 114
Alexander, C. 5
Algan, Y. 229
Al-Ghazali, A. H. 114, 116, 308
Al-Hakimi, M. R. 281
Alizade, z. 283
Al-Jayyousi 311
al-Jaziri, A. a.-Q. b. M. 115
Allah (SWT) 110, 112–115
Allen, T. 123
Al-Madani, A. A. 183n1
Al Maida 111
Al-Mulali, U. 190–191, 203
Al-Muqaddimah (Ibn Khaldun) 309, 318, 320, 322
al-Muslim 129
al-Qaradawi, Y. 126, 127

Al-Sadr, M. B. 75
altruism 276, 284; defined 277; and development 277–279; forgiveness 278; Islam and sustainable development 281; self-sacrifice 278–279; sustainable development and intrinsic motivation 278–281; Waqf 282–284
aluminum–molybdenum-based plating 25
Alvaredo, F. 220
Amanatullah, E. T. 333
Anderson, D. 26
Anheier, H. 288
animal feed 245
Apostolo, B. 142
Arana, J. E. 278
Arcadis 330
arhām (social capital) 311
Aristippus 254
Aristotle 254
ariyo aṭṭhṅgiko maggo 86
Arndt, J. 21
Arora, S. 61
Arouri, M. 196
Arthington, A. H. 27
ASEAN Economic Community (AEC) 318
Asghari, M. 191, 197
Ashoka 289
ASIAN-5 economies 192
Asia-Pacific Economic Cooperation (APEC) 318
Asif, M. 192
Askari, H. 122, 281
Askary, S. 140
Association of Business School (ABS) 142
Asutay, M. 75–77
Aswirna, P. 292, 296
Atharava Veda 97–98
attānam upamam katvā 84
Auditing for Islamic Financial Institution (AAOIFI) 144
Aufderheide, P. 191–192
Auqaf 282
Auto Regression Model Distributed Lag (ARDL) model 193
avidyā (ignorance) 100
Avdukic, A. 69
awakening (*bodhipakkhiyādhammā*) 88
Awqaf 77
Aydin, C. 190
Ayres, R. U. 238–239
Azid, T. 1, 105, 111, 342
Baas, P. 23
Badrinath, S. G. 62
Bahn, O. 248
Bakhtiari, S. 282
Ball, S. J. 281
Banarjee, A. V. 229
Banerjee, S. B. 21
Bangladesh Rural Advancement Committee (BRAC) 288–294, 297–299, 302–303; artificial insemination 298; BRAC Chicken 298; BRAC Cold Storage 298; BRAC Dairy 298; BRAC Fisheries 298; BRAC Nursery 298; BRAC Printing Pack 299; BRAC Silk 299; BRAC's Recycled Handmade Paper 299; BRAC's Salt 299; BRAC's Sanitary Napkin and Delivery Kit 299; BRAC's Seeds and Agro 299; organogram *293*; social enterprises 297
Bano, M. 9, 122, 124
Barber, B. M. 330
Barboza, D. 24
Barnabas 73
Barone, G. 228
Barry, N. 279
Barth, E. 226, 234n6
Basu, K. 278
Batini, N. 7–8
Baumol, W. J. 254
Baycan, T. 41
Baynes, T. M. 238
Beard, T. R. 56
Bebbington, J. 141
Becker, G. S. 55–56, 57, 63
Becker's optimal penalty 58
Becker's theory of rational crime 55–56
Beckmann, D. 330
behavioural moderation 128
Bekhet, H. A. 190
Belk, R. W. 108
Bellamy, C. 22
Belt and Road Initiative (BRI) countries 193
Benabou, R. 279
Benavides-Velasco, C. A. 329
Benito, G. R. G. 336
Benson, H. 89
benzene 26
Berger, Peter 319
Bergh, A. 228
Bernasek, A. 330
Beutel, A. M. 330

Bhagavadgītā 97, 100
Bhat, P. I. 96
Bhatt, G. 3, 4
Bhopal tragedy 60, 64n2
Bibi, S. 193
Bielawski, M. 26
Big Issue 289
Bilimoria, D. 330
Binder, M. 257
bio-degradable waste, reuse *47*
biodiversity, threat to 23–24; cultural services 23; provisional services 23; regulatory services 23; supporting services 23
bio fertilizer 45, 49
biomass 240, 246; DE/capita for Canada 243–245; food system 248; metabolism 248
bio-waste, reuse 45
Bishnoi faith 103n5
Bishnoi movement 99
Bjørnskov, C. 228, 229
Blankenberg, A. 257
Bloach 193
blue economy 5–6, 14n6
Bode, R. 279
Bodhi, B. 86, 88
Bodhicaryāvatara 83
Boettke, P. 106
Bolster, P. J. 62
Boltzen, W. J. W. 24
Bond, N. R. 27
Borgatti, S. P. 22
Borhan, H. B. 205
Botsman, R. 231
Botticini, M. 72
Boulding, K. E. 35
Boyden's human ecological model 238
BRAC *see* Bangladesh Rural Advancement Committee (BRAC)
Bradshaw, P. 330
Brady, D. 23
Brahman (absolute reality) 101
Brehm, J. 56
Brekke, K. A. 35, 62–63
Brewer, J. 89
Brewitt, S. 330
Brierley, J. A. 142
Brihadaaranyaka Upanishad 101
Briñol, P. 89
Broad, R. 254
Brundtland, G. 9, 22, 25, 311
Brundtland Commission 309
Brundtland Report 102
Bruneau, J. 254
bubble-technology 45
Buddha 82, 87
Buddhism 81–82, 343; achievements in life 88; boundless openness 84; disciple 87; and the Fourth Industrial Revolution 82; interdependency and sustainable development 82–85; law of interdependency 82; mindfulness for sustainability 87–90; noble friendliness 84; non-substantiality (*anatta*) 83; truths for sustainable living 85–87
Buddhist Approach to Global Educations in Ethics 82
Buddhist Approach to Harmonious Families Healthcare and Sustainable Societies 82
Buddhist Approach to Mindful Leadership for Sustainable Peace 82
Buddhist Approach to Responsible Consumption and Sustainable Development 82
Burke, S. 329
Burke, T. R. 109
Burki, U. 1, 105, 237, 328, 342
Burritt, R. L. 141
Butchart, S. H. M. 27
buyer–seller relationships 21

cadmium 25
Cahuc, P. 229
Cajee, Z. A. 309
Calmfors, L. 227
Canada, socio-economic metabolism of 237; DE to DEC ratio 242; direct energy input (DEI) 242; domestic energy consumption (DEC) 242, 245; domestic extraction (DE) 241–242; energetic metabolism 239–240; energy flow analysis (EFA) 239–240; energy flows, indicators 241–243; imports and exports 242; low carbon economy 247–248; material flow analysis (MFA) 239–240; metabolism 243–246; physical trade balance (PTB) 242; renewable energy 243; Sankey representation 243, *244*; social metabolism 238–239; sustainability transition 246–249; sustainable agriculture 248–249; system boundary 240–241

capitalism 142, 289
carbon-based pricing 3–4
carbon bubble: climate risk 9; unburn able carbon 9
carbon dioxide 37
carbon dioxide (CO_2) emissions 3–5, 189–190, 194, 220, 256–257, **271**; high-income countries 189; intensity of 192–193; low-income countries 189; middle-income countries 189; reduction 6, 45, 233n1
carbon foot prints 9
carbon monoxide (CO) 7
carbon negative effect 48
carbon-neutral sustainable world 1
carbon taxes 4
cardiovascular mortality 23
Carli, L. L. 330–331
Carney, M. 4
Carpenter, G. S. 21
Carrington, W. 140, 149
Carson, R. 256
Carson, S. 89
Carter, M. R. 277
Carvalho, J.-P. 76
Cason, T. N. 61
Castanas, E. 6–7
Castellani, V. 190
Castillo, M. 277
Catholicism 73
Chalmers, K. 141
Chami, R. 6, 278
Chapman, D. 203
Chapra, M. U. 76, 78, 126, 127, 313
characteristic-based trust 29
Charak Samhita 99
Charfeddine, L. 195
Charity Organization 282
Chaudhry, M. O. 105
Chenet, H. 8–9
Cherry, K. 277
child mortality 28
China-ASEAN Free Trade Area (CAFTA) 318
Choudary, S. P. 43
Christian Association of Nigeria 74
Christianity and sustainability 73–74
Christie, I. 73
chronic heavy drinking 116n2
Church, J. A. 23
churches 10
circular business models 43–49, *46*; Accenture *46*; circular supply-chain models 44–45; product as service 45; product life-extension models 45; recycling models recycle waste 45; resource recovery 45; sharing platforms 45; sustainable value characteristics 44; typologies 45; value-creation dimension 43
circular economy 4–5, 35–36, *40*; circular business models 43–49; complex system changes 39–42; consumer preferences 42–43; defined 35, 41–42; economy 37–39, 43; lifestyle behaviour 42–43; policies for sustainability transition 49–50; sustainability transition 43; theoretical foundation 36–43; transition 41; *see also* circular business models
Clark, A. E. 262
Clark, J. S. 9, 10–11, 97–102, 343
Clarke, F. 140
Clarke, M. 9, 121, 123
Clemens, M. 310
climate change 1, 229, 342; agri-food sector 8; biodiversity, threats to 23–24; consequences of 24; defined 22; freshwater, decline in quantity and quality of 22–23; health risks 23; higher temperatures and increased risk 22; and human health 6–7; sea level rising 23
climate-friendly biogas 45
Climate health 8
climate-related volatility 24
closed-loop recycling cycle 5
Closs, D. 21
coal-fired power plants 2
Coase, R. H. 61
Coase theorem 61
cognitive functioning and creativity 89
Cohen, M. A. 56, 62
Colbert, B. A. 329
Collier, D. 232
Collins, K. M. 329
Collins, R. 72
command-and-control (CAC) regulation 53–54, 63, 64n1
Commission on Sustainable Development (CSD) 312
Common Good within Catholicism 73
competitive market 114
Comte, A. 277
concentration 86

conditionality (*idappaccayatā*) 82
condominial-based sewage systems 28
Connelly, B. 22
consciousness 93n4
Consoli, D. 50
consumption–production–environment link 7
contentment 85
conventional truth 93n3
Cook, P. J. 109
Cooper, T. 5
corporate social responsibility (CSR) 63
corporate sustainability 149
Corrigall, E. 330
corruption 343–344
corruption perception index (CPI) 319
Cosmic Common Good 73
cost-plus financing 114
Costanza, R. 4
COVID-19 pandemic 12–13, 105, 116, 344; free market and 109–110; lockdowns 13
Cowton, C. J. 142
Crang, M. 4, 5
Cribb, R. 61
Critical Perspectives on Accounting 141
Cropper, M.L. 64n1
crowding-out effect 280
Cultural Foundation of Education 284
Cummins, R. A. 256
Curran, L. M. 27

Daan (voluntary giving) 100, 102
Dacholfany, M. I. 292, 296
Dahlstrom, R. 1, 21, 29, 342
Dalai Lama 343
Daly, H. E. 256
Dant, R. P. 21
Dar, J.A. 192
Dasgupta, S. 62
Davidson, R. J. 89
DC Design 289
decarbonisation of transport 224
Deci, E. L. 279
deforestation 7–8
Dehbashi, V. 193
Delmas, M. A. 329
delusion 87
Deneulin, S. 9, 121, 122, 124
Denmark: labor productivity 223; wind energy in 224–225
De Ribeiro Fiuza, A. F. 256–257, 262
Desai, R. M. 105, 106
Deshpandé, R. 29
Despeisse, M. 4
Destek, M. A. 189, 194
DeTemple, J. 74
development and religion 121–132
De Villiers, C. 141
Dharma (absolute reality) 96–97, 100–102, 343
Dharma Drum Mountain 10
dharmic sustainability 101
Dharti Mata (Earth as mother) 97–98
DHL 328
diarrhea 28
Diekmann, A. 254
Dien, M. 127
Dieselgate *see* Volkswagen emissions scandal
dina de-malkhuta dina (Henkin) 71
di Rattalma, M. F. 59
direct energy input (DEI) 242
Divine Revelation 77
domestic credit to private sector (DCP) 195, *202*, 214; by banks (DCB) 195, *202*, 214; provided by financial sector (DCF) 195, *202*, 214
domestic energy consumption (DEC) 242, 245
domestic extraction (DE) 241–242
Dorminey, J. W. 142
Downing, P. B. 55
Driscoll–Kraay Standard Errors approach 264
driving force-state-response (DSR) 312
Duflo, E. 229
Dukkhanirodha 86
Dukkhanirodhagāminī Patipadā 86
dukkh-apatikkūlā 88
Dukkhasamudaya 86
Dunlap, R. 254
DuPont 57, 64
Duroy, M. Q. 262
Dwyer, F. R. 21

Eagly, A. H. 329, 330–331
Easterlin, R. A. 255–257, 262
EAT-Lancet Commission Report 7
Echevarria, C. 254
Eckel, C. C. 330
Eckstein, Z. 72
ecological degradation 189

ecological footprints (EFP), financial development and 189–194, *200*; construction of variables 195–197; data 194; descriptive statistics 197–202; domestic credit to private sector *200*; domestic credit to private sector by banks *201*; domestic credit to private sector by financial sector *201*; econometric specification and data description 194–195; methodology 197; results of fixed effects 205–208; results of pooled OLS 203–205; results of random effects 208; results of system GMM 208–214; trends *201*
ecological quality 203
ecology scarcity of land resources 5
econometric model 194
economic activities under Kopotren **301**
economic growth 203
economic growth-centred sustainability 81
economy: equilibrium stage in 37; green growth 36; markets of *37–38*
EcoWatch 60
Edriyanti, R. 308
Educational Complex 284
education as commodity 280
Effiong, E. 205
egoism 277
El-Ansary, A. I. 23
electric vehicles 224
El-Ghazali 75
El-Halaby, S. I. A.-R. 140
Elkington, J. 22, 110, 116, 328
Ellen MacArthur Foundation 5, 39, 42
Ellis, S. 121, 124
Elster, J. 278
Ely, R. J. 329
Emanuel, K. 232
Emergency Planning and Community Right to Know Act (EPCRA) 60
emission tax 54, 58
employment condition of youth 11
empty nature of reality (*anatta*) 88
enacted legislation (*takkanot ha-kahal*) 71
"end-of-life" model 35
energetic metabolism 239–241; *see also* metabolism
energy consumption (EC) 28, 191, 196, 203
energy-efficient technology 192
energy flow analysis (EFA) 239–241; DE to DEC ratio 242; direct energy input (DEI) 242; domestic energy consumption (DEC) 242; domestic extraction (DE) 241–242; imports and exports 242; physical trade balance (PTB) 242; renewable energy 243
energy flows, indicators 241–243
Energy Transition Act 9
Engelen, B. 279, 280
Enlightenment Movement 77
environmental degradation 189, 191, 194
environmental Kuznets curve *219*
environmental orientation 21
environmental pollution 193
Environmental Protection Agency (EPA) 60
environmental quality 62, 191, 196, 254; in Iran 193; in Pakistan 193
environmental regulation 53; economic theory of rational crime 55–56; enforcement 54–55; instruments 53–54; investments to evade enforcement 57–58; noncompliance with 56–60; violations 55–56, 62; *see also* informal regulation
environmental sustainability 42, 64, 232
environmental tax 59
environment and happiness 254–257; correlation matrix **259**; cross-sectional data of developed countries **272–273**; cross-sectional data of developing countries **274–275**; descriptive statistics **258**; Driscoll–Kraay standard errors regression results **267**; EE regression results **266**; empirical analysis and results 260–264; FE regression results **265**; LIML regression results **263**; methodology 257–260; pooled OLS regression results **261**; regional happiness *260*; regression results of system GMM **268**
environment Kuznets curve (EKC) 191
EPA's 33/ 50 program 61
equality: and prosperity 225–226; and spirituality 74; *see also* inequality and sustainability
equilibrium stage in economy 37
Erosy, P. 237
Erixon, L. 226
Escribá-Esteve, A. 329
Eshkevari, S. M. 282
Esteban, J. 70
Esty, D. C. 24

etcetera 77
Ettema, J. 23
Ethical Trading Initiative (IEH) 332, 335
Eurocentric theory 76
European Environment Agency 4, 7
extrinsic motivation 279–280

Faccio, M. 330
Fagerberg, J. 39, 41, 50
Fairbrother, M. 254
faith (*din*) 308
faith-based organizations (FBO) 10, 344
Fannani, Kyai Zainuddin 291, 296
Fasa, M. I. 291
Fatemi, F. 283
fasād (corruption) 115, 311
Ferrer-i-Carbonell, A. 257
Ficke, A. A. 23
finance market *37–38*
financial development and ecological footprints 189–195; construction of variables 195–197; data 194; descriptive statistics 197–202, **198–199**; econometric specification and data description 194–195; methodology 197; results of fixed effects 205–208; results of pooled OLS 203–205; results of random effects 208; results of system GMM 208–214
financial development and environmental degradation 192
financial institutions 8, 192, 214, 345; sustainability approach 9; sustainability of Islamic 139, 144, 149
financial market liberalisation and deregulation 72
Financing Sustainable Growth 9
Finkelstein, S. 329
Fischer, J. H. 278
Fischer-Kowalski, M. 238–239, 240, 246
fixed effects: for high-income countries **207**; for low-income countries **209**
Food and Agriculture Organization 27
food consumption habbit 7–8
food transformation 7–8
Fore, Henrietta H. 89
foreign direct investment (FDI) 189, 191, 196, 205
forgiveness 278
formations 93n4
fossil fuels 3, 38; burning 6; consumption 229; divestment 9; mining and extraction 25; use, taxes on 220
Foster, K. 278
Four Noble Truths 85–87, 91; *Dukkha* 86; *Dukkhanirodha* 86; *Dukkhanirodhagāminī Patipadā* 86; *Dukkhasamudaya* 86
Francis, Pope 73
Frankfurt School's social ecology framework 238
Franzen, A. 254
free education 232
free market 107–110
Frenette, E. 248
freshwater availability, decline in 22–23
Frey, B. S. 279–280
Friedman, M. 337
Frosch, R. 5
fuel taxes 220

Gallopoulos, N. 5
game theory 279
Ganda, F. 193
Gandhi, M. 102
Gangopadhyay, S. 61
Garas, S. 149
Gardner, J. 256
GDP per capita **271**
Gebhardt, G. F. 21
Geissler, S. 240
gender, top management and 329–330; gender approaches in Scandinavia/Norway 331–332; psychological attributes of women 330–331; salary disparity 333
gender equality 132
generalized method of moments (GMM) 193
Georgescu-Roegen, N. 5
Ger, G. 108
Gertz, G. 105
Ghafory-Ashtiany, M. 71
Ghisellini, P. 4
Ghittori, S. 26
Ghoshray, S. 27
Ghrara (uncertainty) 77
Gierlinger, S. 243, 245
Gillani, S. 196
Gillingham, K. 3
Gingrich, S. 239

Gini ratio (Gini coefficient) 317
Glick, P. 331
Global Employment Trends for Youth 2020 11
Global Footprint Network 194
global happiness *259*
global warming 3
God-conscious individual 130
Godelier's society-natural model 238
Goldeng, E. 331, 336
Goleman, D. 89
Golnaz, G. 132
Gómez-Baggethun, E. 280
Gomez-Mejia, L. R. 333
González, C. L. 140
Goodhart, D. 232
Goodin, R. E. 280
Goodland, R. 309
Goto, N. 239
Gowdy, J. M. 257
Graham, J. 79, 96
Grameen Danone 289
Gray, J. 107, 108–109
Gray, R. 109, 141
great whale conveyor belt 6
greed 87
green bonds 9
Green credit guidelines 9
green gross domestic product (GGDP) 310
green growth economy 36
greenhouse concentration 192
greenhouse gases (GHG) emission 2, 246, **271**; in Canada 247; control 24; increase in 3; social cost 3
Greenstone, M. 60
green transition 233
Gregon, N. 4, 5
Grewal, D. 21
gross calorific value (GCV) 240
gross domestic product (GDP) 310
Grossman, G. M. 191
Grossman, P. J. 330
Grüner, E. 239
Grünfeld, L. A. 336
Gudeman, S. 109
Gundlach, G. T. 21
Gunthen, S. 126

Haar, G. 121, 124
Haas, A. L. 248
Haberl, H. 238–241, 245–246
habitat for freshwater fish 23
Habs 281
Hadith 126, 128, 136n15, 145
Hambrick, D. C. 329
Hamdan, R. 192
Hamid, S. 122, 126
Hamilton, J. T. 56, 62
Hamilton, K. 310
Hamprecht, J. 28
Handbook of Mindfulness: Theory, Research, and Practice 89
Hanna, R. 60
Hansen, L. 23
Hansen test 214
happiness 85, 254, 281; defined **271**; *see also* environment and happiness
haram (prohibitive products and services) 77
Harford, J. D. 55
Hargreaves-Heap, S. 279
Harrington, W. 56
Harrington Paradox 56
Harris, M. 310
Harvey, D. 109
Hasan, R. 122
Hasan, Z. 141
Hashim, R. 78
Haslam, S. A. 330
Hassan, A. 309
Hastings, O. P. 228, 232
hatred 87
Hayek, F. A. 106–108, 116n1
Haynes, J. 121, 124
Haynes, K. 141
health, defined 88
heavy metals 7
Hedblom, D. 63
Heide, J. B. 21
Hekkert, M. 35, 41–42
Henkin, R. 71
Herbert, W. 89
Herrington, R. 51n1
Hertwich, E. G. 28
Hesterly, W. S. 22
Heyes, A. G. 54, 56, 58–59, 63
high-income inequalities 228–229
high-level pre-COP21 policy 9
hikmah (wisdom) 311
Hill, R. J. 191
Hinduism 96–97; *Artha* (wealth) 96, 100; collectiveness, focus on 98; *Daan* (voluntary giving) 100, 102; defined

96; *Dharma* (absolute reality) 96, 100; Earth as mother (*Dharti Mata*) 97–98; goals of life 96; *Kama* (pleasure) 96, 100; *Moksha* (freedom) 96, 100; peace and nature 98; people 100–102; planet 97–100; prayers 98; protection of environment 98–100; religion-ethical framework 97; religious pillars and welfare 100–101; sacred or secular 101–102
Hirsch, F. 255
Hitam, M. B. 205
Hjort, I. 59, 232
Ho, D. 61
Hoegh-Guldberg, O. 22
Holmberg, S. 228
Honkasalo, A. 39
Hood, E. 25
Hoogenboom, G. 22
Hosseini, H. 114
Huang, J. 330
Huff, D. L. 28
Hult, G. T. M. 22, 25
human actions (*akusala-kamma-patha*) 87
human-centred sustainable development 76
humankind 314
human-produced substances 26
Human Scale Development (HSD) 85
human self (*ātman*) 101
human society 319
human sustainable development index (HSDI) 310
human underdevelopment 12
Huse, M. 329, 330
Hussein, I. N. A. 303
hybrid-electric trucks 247

Ibn Iskandar 114
Ibn Iyas, M. b. A. 113
Ibn Khaldun 113–114, 313–315, 320, 322; model 313; on poverty 317; sustainable development 313–316
Ibn Qudamah 114
Ibn Taimiyah 113
Ibn Tulun, M. b. A. 113
ignorance 93n4
ihsān (beauty and sustainable development) 129, 311
IJIMEFM 149
ijtihād (independent effort or reasoning) 311
Ilaiah, K. 101
Imam Reza (AS) 282
impermanence (*anicca*) 83, 88
inclusiveness 11–12
income distribution 233
Indonesia and sustainable development 316; earthquakes 321–322; economic aspects 316–319; economic inequality 317; environmental aspects 321–322; poverty 317; social aspects 319–321
industrial interdependence 4
industrial system 42
inequality and sustainability 220–221; climate change challenge 229; low-income inequality and good economic performance 226–228; Nordic model 221–226; trust and risk-sharing 229–232
infāq 314
infectious diseases 23
informal regulation 60; community pressure 61–62; consumers' influence on firms' environmental performance 61; morally motivated workers 62–63; public disclosure programs 60; stock market reactions 62
Inglehart, R. 254, 262
Inglehart's post-materialism hypothesis 254
institutional-based trust 29
institutional environment 21
intellect (*'aql*), 308
interdependent dynamic process 83
inter-faith cooperation 344
interfirm governance 21
Intergovernmental Panel on Climate Change (IPCC) 229
International Financial Reporting Standard (IFRS) 149
International Institute of Financing and Accounting (IIFA) 145
International Monetary Fund (IMF) 3
international trade 191
intrinsic motivation 279–280
Iqbal, Z. 125
Iran 277; Alborz Cultural Foundation 284–285; financial development and trade 193; Pasteur Institute of Iran 284–285; Waqf and development in 282; Waqf in education and science in 283–284; Waqf in health development in 282–283; Waqf institution's 277
Irwin, D. 3
Isha Upanishad 98

Islahi, A. A. 107, 113–114, 115
Islam, S. 123
Islam and sustainable development 74–78, 281, 308; *see also specific entries*
Islamic accounting (*hisab*) 139–140; before AAOIFI **145**; during AAOIFI-IFRS period **150–183**; after AAOIFI **146–148**; horizontal accountability 140; mapping analysis of 144–149; supporting studies and mapping method 141–144; and sustainability 140–141; vertical accountability 140
Islamic belief system 126–127
Islamic boarding school 296–297
Islamic civilisation 77
Islamic developmentalism 76; clusters of themes *131*; defined 123; family planning 121; female leadership 121; gender equality 121; human behaviour 128; religion aversion 123–124; self-dependence in socio-economic terms 129
Islamic Development Bank (IDB) 148
Islamic economics 74
Islamic finance products and services 139
Islamic financial architecture 183n1
Islamic Financial Institution (IFI) 140
Islamic Financial Services Board (IFSB) 149
Islamic financial system 288
Islamic journals 142–143
Islamic market behavior 105–107; free market 107–110; Islamic injunctions and the "Triple Bottom Line" 115–116; Islamic moral market economics 110–115
Islamic moral market economics 110–111; monopolies 115; negating exploitation 114; price mechanism 113–114; *Quranic* injunction 111–113
Islamic Shari'ah 282
Islamic social finance 288
Islamic society, cultural advancement of 283
Ismail, S. F. A. 288
Iyer, E. S. 21
Iyer, R. 102
Iyer, S. 76

Jalil, A. 304
Jamali, D. 81
Jamaludin, K. S. 291
James, R. 124, 125
Jawad, S. 132
Jegen, R. 280
Jernelov, A. 93n1
JIABR 149
Jianakoplos, N. A. 330
Jiang, B. 21
Johannesen-Schmidt, M. C. 329
Johnson, B. 330
Johnson, J. E. V. 330
Johor Islamic Religious Council (JIRC) 291
Jones, B. 124, 125
Jones, C. 22
Jørgensen, S. 43, 45
Journal of Accounting Education 142
Journal of Accounting Literature 141
Journal of Business Ethics 142
Journal of Islamic Accounting and Business Research 142
Judaism: monotheism 70; and sustainability 70–73

Kabat-Zinn, J. 89
Kadambe, S. 58
Kaffarah 281
Kahana, E. 279
Kahf, M. 77, 126, 127
Kama (pleasure) 96, 100
Kamahara, H. 239
Kamali, H. M. 122, 125–126, 127
Kambhu, J. 56, 58
Kampa, M. 6–7
Kandhakas of the *Vinaya Pitaka* 90
Kangujam, L. 2
Kappelle, M. 23
karma 101
Karbalaei, A. 282
Karma's theory 96
Kashyap, R. K. 21
Kasri, N. S. 288, 294–295, 300, 305
Kassarjian, H. H. 22
Kates, R. 123
Katircioglu, S. T. 189, 190, 195
Katz, J. P. 333
Katzenstein, P. J. 227
Kauffman, E. 9
kehillah 71
Kellert, S. 255
Kelley, D. C. 84
Kemp, R. 41
Kenneth, P. 123

Kenter, J. O. 73
Ketchen, D. 22
Keyl, P. M. 279
Khaldun, I. 114, 320
Khaleel, F. 69, 96
khalifah (trustee or vicegerent) of Allah 291, 314
Khan, W. A. 330
Kharas, H. 105
Khlif, H. 141
Kiaee, H. 276
Killawi, R. L. 141
Kimmel, M. S. 331
al-Kinani, Y. b. U. 113
Kincaid, D. C. 28
King, B. 61
Kinsley, D. 9
Kirchherr, J. 35, 41–42
Kirchmaier, T. 329
Kirzner, I. 106–108
Kisgen, D. J. 330
Kiyai 295–296
Klenow, P. 3
Klipper, M. J. 89
Klugman, J. 331
Kneese, A. V. 238
Kogler, D. F. 41
Konar, S. 62
Konrad, A. M. 330
Kopf, D. 13
Korhonen, J. 39
Krausmann, F. 239–241, 243, 245–246, 248
Krueger, A. B. 191
Kumar, S. 329
Kumbaroglu, G. 192
Kuruppu, C. 81
Kuskovaa, P. 239
Kusumadewi, E. W. 304
Kuznets curve: environmental *219*; N-shaped *219*
Kyoto Protocol 102

labour market *37–38*
labour movement 226
Lacy, P. 44
Lahrash, O. M. A. A. 139
Lake, P. S. 27
Lakshmi (wealth) 96, 102
Langer, E. J. 89
Langrill, R. 106, 108–109
La Porta, R. 230
Larkin Sentral Property Berhad 288, 299–300, 303–304; Waqf asset management *295*
Lawson, T. 126
Leal, S. 22, 28
Le Bruyn, E. S. 328, 330
Ledec, G. 309
Lee, D. R. 58
Lee's model of pollution control 58
Lefebvre, H. 109
Leiserowitz, A. 123
Lele, C. 256–257, 262
Lenzen, M. 256
León, C. J. 278
Levine, A. 71, 72
Lewis, M. K. 140
Liberation War in Bangladesh 290
Lieb, P. 330
life-cycle analysis 5
limited information maximum likelihood (LIML) estimator 262
Limits to Growth 102
Lin, Y. 191, 196
Linder, S. H. 56
linear business models 43; loss of capacities 44; loss of life cycles 44; loss of resources 44; loss of values 44
linear economic model 4, 35, *40*
Lippold, M. A. 89
livestocks 8
living beings 97
Losey, J. E. 24
Lotfalipour, M. R. 193, 203
low carbon economy 247–248
low carbon freight transportation 247
low carbon innovation 3
low-carbon stock indices 9
low-income inequality 223, 226; and good economic performance 224–228
Luni, T. 191, 196
Lunn, J. 121, 124
Lusch, R. F. 43
Lusk, J. L. 278
Luttrell, A. 89

MacIntyre, A. 109
Madrueño, R. 123, 124
Magnani, E. 191
Mahomed, Z. 288
Mair, J. 291
MAJ 149

Majeed, M. T. 189, 190, 191, 196, 203, 254, 255
Maji, I. K. 190
majjhimāpatipadā 85
malnourishment 12
malnutrition 23, 321
Manikarachchim, I. 14n7
Mankiew, N. G. 310
maqāsid al-Sharī'ah 308
Marchica, M.-T. 330
Marcum, J. P. 279
Marini, M. M. 330
Markard, J. 246
market: based regulation 53–54, 64n1; based sustainability 22; dynamism 21; of economy *37*; failure 37–38; orientation 21
Marx, K. 109, 238, 317
maṣlahah (public interest) 311
Maslow, A. H. 254
Maslow's hierarchy of needs theory 254
Mason, P. A. 329
Masruchin 296, 302
material and energy flow accounting (MEFA) indicators 243
material development 128
material flow analysis (MFA) 237, 239–240; human population 239; infrastructure built by humans 239; livestock 239
materialism 102
materiality 93n4
Matthews, E. 239
Matti, C. 50
Maududi, S. A. A. 75
Max-Neef, M. A. 85, 87
Mayoral, L. 70
Mazhar, M. 190
Mazzucato, M. 39
McArthur, J. W. 105, 249
McBride, M. E. 56
McCloskey, D. 107, 108
McDonnell, M. H. 61
McKinsey 5
McMichael, A. J. 255
Meacham, N. 21
Melo, J. C. 28
Mendleson, N. 21
Menkhoff, L. 330
mental and physical experience (*yathā bhūta ñanadassna*) 88
mentality 93n4
Méon, P.-G. 229
Mergaliyev, A. 76
Mertig, A. 254
Mesagan, E. P. 193
meta-analytic method 141
metabolism 238, 240, 243–246
Michel, P. 309
Millennium Development Goals (MDGs) 123, 276, 312
mindfulness 88–91
mindfulness-based childbirth 89
Mirakhor, A. 122, 125, 126, 279
Mocetti, S. 228
Moene, K. 226–228, 233n3
Moghadam, H. E. 193, 203
Mohammad, M. T. 320–321
Mohammed, A. S. M. 192, 203
Moksha (freedom) 96, 100
monoculture agriculture 8
monotheism 127
Mooney, A. C. 329
Moore, M. J. 109
Moorman, C. 29
moral foundations theory 79, 96
moral hazards 111
morality and religion 9–11
morally motivated workers 62–63
moral virtues 86
Morris, M. W. 333
Mostaghel, R. 42, 44
motivations 279
Mrabet, Z. 195
Mueller, J. 108
Mukhlisin, M. 139, 142
Müller, D. B. 238
Mumtaz, S. 190
Mura, R. 330
Murad, M. H. 316
Music, G. 279
Mustafida, R. 139
Muzarie, M. 296
Myrick, C. A. 23

Nadhr 281
Nahlik, M. E. 247
Namazi Hospital 282
nano-technology 247
Naranjo-Gil, D. 329, 330
Narayanan, Y. 10–11, 101, 102, 149
Natalucci, F. 13
National Register of Company Accounts (NRCA) 332

Neem 102
Nelson, R. R. 41
net calorific value (NCV) 240
net development indicator 310
net investment 310
Neuteleers, S. 279, 280
Ng, A. 279
Nicholls, R. J. 23
Niedderer, K. 89
Nielsen, S. 329, 330
Nijkamp, P. 41
Nill, J. 41
Nilsson, T. 278
Nishioka, Y. 240
nitrogen oxides (NO_x) 7
Nnandi, C. 105
"no animal products for breakfast or lunch" rule 8
non-food agro 7
non-self (*anatta*) 83
Nordic countries: climate change challenge 229; creating and sharing wealth 221–224; digital competitiveness 223; digital transformation 221; economic and social performance **222**; electric vehicles in Norway 224; employee autonomy 230; environmentally sustainable solutions 224; equality and prosperity 225–226; equality–efficiency-driven economic strategy 225; examples 224–225; free education 232; labour movement 226; low-income inequality 223; low-income inequality and good economic performance 224–228; organizational change and new technology *225*; risk-sharing and wealth-sharing 232; small wage differentials 226; social trust 228; technological modernisation 226–227; trust, importance of 229–231; unemployment benefits 232; welfare states 232; welfare state support risk-taking and restructuring 227–228; wind turbines in Denmark 224
North, D. C. 331
Norwegian Environmental Protection Agency 56
Norwegian Pollution Control Act 56
not-for-profit organisations 81
Novak, M. 107
Noy, D. 96
N-shaped Kuznets curve *219*
Nwachukwu, M. I. 193
Nyborg, K. 55, 56, 62–63
Nygaard, A. 29

Oates, W. E. 64n1, 254
Odean, T. 330
Oestenstad, G. T. 59
Ogbonnaya, J. 74
Oghazi, P. 42, 44
Oh, S. 21
Oh, Y. 58
oikonomia 72
Oliva, P. 57, 60
Omer Ibn Khattab 113
Omni-present Creator 128
One God/ One Faith duality 70
opportunity cost 130
Oras, K. 239
Organisation for Economic Co-operation and Development (OECD) 35
Østenstad, G. T. 53
Ostrom, E. 39
Ostrom's social ecological system (SES) 238
Oswald, A. J. 256, 262
Ottoman Empire 114
Ouchi, W. G. 29
oxygen formation 6
oxygen solubility 23
ozone (O_3) 7
Ozturk, I. 191, 203

Padma Purana 99
Palmatier, R. W. 21
Palvia, A. 330
Panayotou, T. 191
panchamahabhutas 97
Pargal, S. 60–61
Parida, V. 43
Paris Agreement, 2015 1–2, 9, 35, 106, 342
Parker, D. V. 26
Parker, G. G. 43
Parris, T. 123
Parry, I. 4
Parsons, T. 72
Pasteur Institute of Iran 285
Patagonia 328
Patz, J. A. 23
Payne, K. 228
peepal 99, 102
Pekovic, S. 329
Pemananda, U. 81

people, planet and profitability (3Ps) 329, 332; people 328, 333–335; planet 328, 335; profitability 328, 335–337; ROA 336–337; salary disparities 333; value creation 335–336; women in different industries 334–335
Perelman, Debra 330
period, ordinary least squares (OLS) 193
Peters, G. P. 28
Petersen, M. 124, 125
Petkeviciute, N. 309
Petty, R. E. 89
Pfeffer, J. 22
physical trade balance (PTB) 242
phytoplankton 6
Pickett, K. 228, 232
Piketty, T. 220
Pirages, D. C. 309
Plachy, J. 26
pneumonia 28
Polanyi, K. 107, 108–109
pollution 53
Pollution Inventory (PI) 60
pollution tax 55–56, 59
Polonsky, M. J. 21
Pond, E. 248
Pondok Modern Darussalam Gontor 291–292, 295–297, 300–302, 304; governance structure of *297*
pooled ordinary least squares (OLS): for high-income countries **204**, 205; for low-income countries **206**
Post, J. E. 328
Postmes, T. 330
Potvin, C. B. 247
Powell, P. L. 330
Preston, L. E. 328
price-dependent analysis 280
price fixation 114
principal component analysis (PCA) 256
private market 60
production–consumption equation 5
product market *37–38*
progeny (*nasl*) 308
Program for Pollution Control, Evaluation and Rating (PROPER) 60
property (*māl*) 308
Prophet Muhammad (PBUH) 106, 113, 117n7–8, 126, 136n12, 136n14, 136n17, 148, 282
proteins of plants 8
psychological happiness 254
public/common goods market *37–38*
purusharthas 101

Qajar dynasty 283, 285n3
Qalamchi Cultural Foundation 284–285
Qard al-Hasan 281
Qi, S. 192
Quintana-García, C. 329
Qur'an 106, 110, 112, 135n1–136n11, 136n13, 136n16, 343–344; Islamic accounting (*hisab*) 139–140; *see also Sharī'ah*
Qutub, S. 107

Rabbinic Judaism 72
radical business models 43
Ragins, B. R. 331
Rahman, S. 308
Rakhsha Bandan 99, 103n3
Rakodi, C. 9, 121, 124
Raksha Sukra Movement 99
Rāmāyana 99
random effects: for high-income countries **210**; for low-income countries **211**
Rasmussen, K. 105, 249
Ratnapala, S. 106
Raupova, O. 239
Rautela, R. 96–99
Raven, R. 246
Raza, S. A. 193
Razavi, A. Q. 282
recycling 4
Reda, A. 113–114
regional happiness *260*
Reiersen, J. 220, 230
Reike, D. 35, 41–42
Reim, W. 43
Reklima 45; binding CO_2 47–48; circular economy model *47*; greenhouse 45–47, *47*; local food production 48; renewable energy sector 48; restoring food soil 49
Relaxation Response, The (Benson and Klipper) 89
religion and sustainable development 9–11, 343
religious-discipline 134
religious harmony 344
religious teaching and sustainable development 70
renewable energy 38, 243
Reno, J. 5
resource scarcity 238

respirable particulate matter 7
respiratory illnesses 23
return on assets (ROA) 336–337
Reve, T. 21
Revlon 330
Reynaert, M. 56–57
Riba (interest) 77
Rich, B. 191–192
righteous livelihood (*sammāājiva*) 90
Rigolini, A. 330
Rigveda 97
Rio + 20 Conference goals 276
risk-sharing and wealth-sharing 232
Ritchie, J. E., Jr. 330
Ritter, B. A. 331
Robèrt, K.-H. 21, 22, 25, 29
Robinson, J. 220–221
Rodrik, D. 227, 232
Rogers, P. 22, 28, 309
Roman, J. 6
Rossidy, I. 78
Rothbard, M.N. 106–108
Rothstein, B. 228
Rubenstein, D. B. 141
Rubin, J. 76
Rudman, L. A. 331
Ruiz-Pérez, M. 280
Rumah Wakaf 302
Rutqvist, J. 44
Ryan, J. D. 89
Ryan, M. K. 330
Ryan, R. M. 279

Sachs, J. 12–13, 123
Sachs, S. 328
Sacks, J. 107–109
ṣadaqah (charity) 111, 281, 288, 314
Sadeq, A. 122, 289
Sadr, K. 282
Saeed, A. 126
Saez, E. 220
Safavid dynasty 282, 285n1
safe freshwater 27
Sahal, K. A. 291, 294
Sala, S. 190
Salancik, G. 22
Salim, Emil 311
Sallee, J. M. 56–57
salvation 96
sam'sāra 101
Samveda 97
Samyutta Nikaya 83
Sanatan Dharma 96
Sandberg, N. H. 248
Sandel, M. J. 280
Sankey representation 243, *244*
Sant Tulsidas 100
Sāriputta 87
Sarkodie, S. A. 189, 194
Sati Pasala 90
Satipatthana Sutta 88
Satrams 10
Schaffartzik, A. 238–239
Schaltegger, S. 141, 149
Schandl, H. 238–239
Scheid, D. 73
Schmidheiny, S. 192
Schmidt-Traub, G. 105
Schoitsch, E. 247
Schot, J. 36, 39, 41–42, 49, 50
Schultz, P. P. 89
Schulz, N. 238–239
Schumpeter, J. A. 41
Schurr, P. H. 21
Schwab, K. 221
Schwartz, C. E. 279
Scitovsky, T. 255
Scott, R. C. 89
se'ah be-se'ah prohibition 72
sea levels, rising 23
Secchi, D. 277
Seelos, C. 291
Seetanah, B. 192
Segerson, K. 58
Sehrawat, M. 193
Seierstad, C. 330
self (*nafs*) 308
self-indulgence (*kamasukallikānuyoga*) 85
self-mortification (*attakilamātanuyoga*) 85
self-regulation 89
self-sacrifice 278
Selinger, L. 123
Sen, A. 121
Senbel, M. 190
Seppälä, J. 39
Sepulveda, L. 289
Sfeir-Younis, A. 11
Shah, N. 193
Shaiva (devotees of the god *Shiva*) 96
Shakeel, M. 191
Shakta (devotees of the goddess) 96
Shāntideva 83–84
Shapira, R. 56
Shavell, S. 56

Sharīʻah 77, 107, 125–129, 133–135, 144, 149, 314; belief system and individual discipline 134; on body exposure 127–128; on marriage and family life 127; non-compliant financial activities 128; physical efforts 134; social responsibility 134
Sherry, J. F., Jr. 21
Shetty, S. 329
Shoba, K. 96
Shravana (Shravan Poornima) 103n3
Shukri, M. H. 294–295, 300, 305
Siahaan, D. 300, 311
Siano, A. 59
Siddiqi, M. N. 313
Siddique, H. M. A. 191, 203
Simonis, U. E. 239
Singh, K. 9–11, 97–102, 343
Singh, S. J. 238–239, 245
Sjödin, D. 43
Slater, S. 22
small wage differentials 226–227
Smarta 96
Smith, A. 318
social economy 289
social enterprise and Waqf 289–290; BRAC 290–294, 297–299, 302–303; establishment 290; governance and transparency 292; Larkin Sentral Property Berhad 299–300, 303–304; Pondok Modern Darussalam Gontor 291–292, 295–297, 300–302, 304; research methodology 290; sustainable business model 297
social finance 288
social integration 89
social metabolism 238–239
social sustainability 232
social system 239
social trusts 221, 228, 233n4; importance of 229–231; risk-sharing and wealth-sharing 232
society 319
socio-ecological system 238
socio-economic development, Islamic approach to 121–132
socioeconomic inequalities 12, 72
socio-economic metabolism 239
socio-economic metabolism of Canada 237; DE to DEC ratio 242; direct energy input (DEI) 242; domestic energy consumption (DEC) 242; domestic extraction (DE) 241–242; energetic metabolism 239–240; energy flow analysis (EFA) 239–240; energy flows, indicators 241–243; imports and exports 242; low carbon economy 247–248; material flow analysis (MFA) 239–240; metabolism 243–246; physical trade balance (PTB) 242; renewable energy 243; Sankey representation 243; social metabolism 238–239; sustainability transition 246–249; sustainable agriculture 248–249; system boundary 240–241
socio-economic status (SES) 72
socio-economic systems 229
socio-technical systems 36, 41
soil erosion 191–192
solar and wind energy 225
Solarin, S. A. 197, 205
Solberg, A. G. 330
Soleimani, M. 276
Sonfield, M. 329
Speier, C. 21
Spengler, J. D. 240
spiritual consolation and sloace 128
spiritual orientation 134
St Augustine 73
Stavins, R. N. 24
Steinmueller, W. E. 36, 39, 41–42, 49, 50
Stern, D. I. 191, 196, 254
Stern, L. W. 21
STIRPAT model 192
Stockholm declaration 308
Stokey, N. L. 196
Storr, V. H. 106, 108–109
Stough, R. 41
Stranlund, J. 54, 55
Strezov, V. 189
suffering (*dukkha*) 83–84, 86, 91
Sughandy, A. 309, 310
sukha-kāmā 88
Sulemana, I. 254
sulphur dioxide (SO_2) 7
Sultana, N. 139
Sundstrom, E. 331
Sunley, P. 41
Sunnah 106, 110–112
supply chain 21–22; biodiversity and productivity 26–27; environmental issues 22–24; human needs meeting 27–28; human-produced substances 26; mining and extraction of fossil fuels

25–26; political-economy approaches 21; research implication 28–29; sustainably oriented principles 25–28
Suraiya, J. 101, 102
Suri, V. 203
Surrah Al-Baqarah 113
Surrah Al Furqan 111
sustainability 70, 238; based principles 21–29; Buddhist perspective on 81–90; carbon-based pricing strategy 3–4; Christianity and 73–74; circular economy 4–5; climate change and human health 6–7; COVID-19 pandemic 12–13; defined 308; *dharmic* 101; economic growth-centred 81; education 319; financial sector and sustainable development 8–9; food transformation 7–8; greenhouse gases emission 2–3; green to blue economy, shifting from 5–6; inclusiveness 11–12; Islam and 74–78; Islamic accounting 139–141; Judaism and 70–73; mindfulness for 87–90; morality and religion 9–11; transition 50, 246–249; UN's perspective on 81; *see also* sustainable development; Sustainable Development Goals (SDGs)
sustainability transition challenges (SDGs) 49
sustainable agriculture 248–249
sustainable business model 297
sustainable consumption 72
sustainable development 5, 39, 84–85, 309–311; concept of 311–312; defined 276, 309; environment 315, 321; humankind 314; Ibn Khaldun and 313–314, 316–322; justice 315; modern interpretation compared to Ibn Khaldun's era 315–316; principle of 93n1; Sharī'ah 314; wealth 315
Sustainable Development Goals (SDGs) 1, 11–13, 13n1, 35, 70, 81, 85, 99, 105, 123, 276, 312; Decent Work and Economic Growth (SDG 8) 13; Gender Equality (SDG 5) 13; Good Health and Well-Being (SDG 3) 1, 11–13; Multilateralism (SDG 17) 13; No Poverty (SDG 1) 13; Peace, Justice and Strong Institutions (SDG 17) 16; Reduced Inequalities (SDG 10) 13; Zero Hunger (SDG 2) 13
Sustainable Development Summit, 2015 73
Sutta Pitaka 90
Svendsen, G. T. 228
Svirskaite, I. 309
system boundary 240–241
system GMM: for high-income countries **212**; for low-income countries **213**

Tabarsi, A. 281
Tadesse, S. 192
Tahir, S. 122
Taimiyah, Ibn 113
take–make–dispose model 4
"take-make-waste" approach 43
takkanot ha-kahal 71
Tamazian, A. 192
Tan, P. 86
Taşpinar, N. 189
technological modernisation 226–227
Tee, K. 149
Teece, D.J. 38, 43
Teigen, M. 331
Telle, K. 55–56
ter Weel, B. 229
Tessema, A. M. 149
The Natural Step (TNS) 25
theory of annihilationism (*uccheda-diṭṭhi*) 84
theory of eternalism (*sassata-diṭṭhi*) 84
theory of interdependency (*paticcasamuppāda*) 82–84, 90
Thomas, A. 123
Thomas, C. D. 23
Thunberg, G. 2, 13n2
Tilak, B.G. 96, 103n1
tilakkhaṇa 90
time value of money and efficiency 130
Tirole, J. 279
Tittensor, D. 121
Tiwari, A. K. 255, 256, 257, 262
Todd, W. L. T. 84
Tomalin, E. 10, 125
top management and gender 329–330; empirical evidence with the 3Ps 332–337; gender approaches in Scandinavia/ Norway 331–332; psychological attributes of women 330–331
Toseef, A. 237, 247
Tosi, H. L. 333
Toxics Release Inventory (TRI) 60

trade union density 233n2
Tranfield, D. 183
Transparency International (TI) 319
Trichopoulou, A. 7
triple bottom line (TBL) approach 328
Trostle, R. 24
Truffer, B. 246
trust 111; importance of 229–231; *see also* social trusts
Tukker, A. 255
tulsi (*Ocimum tenuiflorum*) 99, 102
Tulsidas 100
Turton, R. 26
Tyndale, W. 121
Tzedakah 10

Ulrich, R. 254, 256
ultimate truth 93n3
unemployment **271**; benefits 232
UNEP Inquiry platform 9
Uninhabitable Earth: A Story of the Future, The (Wallace-Wells) 229
United Nations (UN) 81
United Nations Environment Program (UNEP) 106
universal capitalist theory 76
unnatural sex orientation, rights of those having an 132
unsatisfactoriness (*dukkha*) 83, 88
UN's Day of Vesak (UNDV) 82
Upaniṣad 101
urbanization 191, 196
urban population **271**
usher 111, 117n9
Uslaner, E. M. 228
usury (*riba*) 145
Uthman Ibn Affan 289
Uyarra, E. 50

Vähämaa, E. 330
Vähämaa, S. 330
Vaillancourt, K. 248
Vaishnava (devotees of the god *Vishnu*) 96
value-based economy 107
value-chain logistics 43
value creation 335–336
value-free developmental programmes 124
value-free secularism 132
Van Alstyne, M. W. 43
van Den Bergh, J. C. J. M. 24
van der Vegt, G. S. 331
van Dorn, A. 13
Van Staden, C. 141
Van Vuuren, M. M. I. 23
Varah Purana 99
Vargo, S. L. 43
Vastu shastra (science of architecture) 98
Vasudhaiva Kutumbakam 99
Vaughan, M. 24
Vázquez, S. 123, 124
Vedas 96
Veenhoven, R. 256
Veeramani, A. 248
vegetation zones 23
Venerable Sāriputta 87
Vieito, J. P. 330
Vienna social ecology 238
Vitousek, P. M. 22
volatile organic compounds (VOCs) 7
Volkswagen emissions scandal 57, 64
Vörösmarty, C. J. 22

Wackernagel, M. 190, 194
wage bargaining 226–227
wage differentials 226–227
Wallace, L. 26
Wallace-Wells, D. 229, 232
Wallerstein, M. 226–227, 233n3
Wang, Q 196
Waqaf An-Nur Corporation Berhad 290
Waqf 10, 76, 281, 288; in education and science in Iran 283–284; in health development in Iran 282–283; Islamic Republic of Iran, development in 282; Land Management System 302; *see also* social enterprise and Waqf
Waqf Administration 282
Warner, K. D. 74
Warsono, S. 139
Wassiah 281
waste generation 42
wastewater recycling 28
water deficiencies 28
water pollution 205
Watson, S. R. 3, 4
Watson Jr, W. D. 55
Weber, M. 72, 108
Weisz, H. 238–239, 242, 245
welfare states 227–228, 232
well-being 89
Welsch, H. 256
Werner, S. 333
whale pump 6
whales, carbon capture potential 6

Wheeler, D. 61
Wheeler, J. V. 330
White, M. P. 262
Whittington, G. 140
Wicks, D. 330
Wilkinson, R. 228, 232
Willett, W. 7
Williams, C. C. 281
Williamson, O. E. 22, 337
Wilson, E. O. 254–255, 264
wind turbines in Denmark 224
Winston, A. W. 24
Winter, S. G. 41
wisdom 86
women, top management and 329–330; gender approaches in Scandinavia/Norway 331–332; psychological attributes of women 330–331; salary disparity 333; share in different industries **334**, 334–335, **335**
women rights 132
World Commission on Environment and Development (WCED) 311
World digital competitiveness ranking *224*
World Economic Forum 36
World Health Organization (WHO) 23, 28, 105, 117n4, 255

Xiong, L. 192

Yajur Veda 97–98, 102
Yamagishi, T. 230–231
Yanagisawa, Y. 240
Yardley-Jones, A. 26
yatza ha-sha'ar mechanism 72
Yayasan Pemeliharaan dan Perluasan Wakaf Pondok Modern (YPPWPM) 300
Yellow Vests movement 220
yesh lo mechanism 72
Yoder, J. D. 331
Yousef, T. M. 139

zakāh 76–77, 315, 320
Zakaria, M. 193
zakat 111, 288, 343
Zaltman, G. 29
Zaman, A. 75–77
Zarkasyi, K. I. 291, 294
Zarsky, L. 191, 197
Zelechowski, D. D. 330
zero waste 43
Zhang, C. 191, 196
Zhang, S. 189
Zhang, Y. J. 189, 203
Zingales, L. 56–57
Zorraquin, F. J. 192
Zucker, L. G. 28–29
Zwally, H. J. 23

Printed in the United States
by Baker & Taylor Publisher Services